The Politics of Unfree Labour i

How, and why, did human trafficking out of Russia escalate at the beginning of the twenty-first century? Why did some labour migrants from Uzbekistan, Tajikistan and Kyrgyzstan find happy work situations in Russia whereas others became trapped in forced labour? This book focusses on human trafficking out of the Russian Federation since the collapse of the Soviet state and on labour migration into it from Central Asia, and on some internal movement. It looks at the socio-economic reasons behind labour flows and examines key social, political, legislative and policy responses. Discussion includes how the Russian press covers these topics and what politicians, experts and the public think about them. Based on interviews, polls and focus groups in Russia, this book is rich in original research which highlights different Russian perspectives on exploitation in unfree labour. It gives examples of entrapment in prostitution, in construction work, on farms and in begging rings.

Mary Buckley is a Fellow of Hughes Hall at the University of Cambridge. She has published extensively in the field of Soviet and post-Soviet politics, society, history and foreign policy. Her books include *Mobilizing Soviet Peasants: Heroines and Heroes of Stalin's Fields* (2006), *Redefining Russian Society and Polity* (1993) and *Women and Ideology in the Soviet Union* (1989).

The Politics of Unfree Labour in Russia

Human Trafficking and Labour Migration

Mary Buckley

Hughes Hall, University of Cambridge

CAMBRIDGE
UNIVERSITY PRESS

CAMBRIDGE
UNIVERSITY PRESS

University Printing House, Cambridge CB2 8BS, United Kingdom

One Liberty Plaza, 20th Floor, New York, NY 10006, USA

477 Williamstown Road, Port Melbourne, VIC 3207, Australia

314–321, 3rd Floor, Plot 3, Splendor Forum, Jasola District Centre,
New Delhi – 110025, India

79 Anson Road, #06-04/06, Singapore 079906

Cambridge University Press is part of the University of Cambridge.

It furthers the University's mission by disseminating knowledge in the pursuit of
education, learning, and research at the highest international levels of excellence.

www.cambridge.org
Information on this title: www.cambridge.org/9781108419963
DOI: 10.1017/9781108325639

First published 2018

Printed in the United Kingdom by Clays, St Ives plc

A catalogue record for this publication is available from the British Library.

Library of Congress Cataloging-in-Publication Data
Names: Buckley, Mary (Mary E. A.), author.
Title: The politics of unfree labour in Russia : human trafficking and labour
   migration / Mary Buckley, Hughes Hall, University of Cambridge.
Description: Cambridge, United Kingdom ; New York, NY : Cambridge
   University Press, 2017. | 9781108412704 (paperback) | Includes
   bibliographical references and index.
Identifiers: LCCN 2017035941 | ISBN 9781108419963 (hardback)
Subjects: LCSH: Human trafficking—Russia (Federation) | Human
   smuggling—Russia (Federation) | Forced labor—Russia (Federation) |
   Illegal aliens—Russia (Federation) | Russia (Federation)—Emigration
   and immigration.
Classification: LCC HQ281 .B783 2017 | DDC 364.15/51—dc23 LC record
   available at https://lccn.loc.gov/2017035941

ISBN 978-1-108-41996-3 Hardback

ISBN 978-1-108-41270-4 Paperback

To all who kindly let me interview them

Contents

Tables

Map

Map 1 Map of the Russian Federation Situated Within the Commonwealth of Independent States and with Surrounding States and Borders. Drawn by David Cox.

Acknowledgements

My debts are many and I am delighted to acknowledge them all.

This project sprouted in the Easter term of 2004 when I was a Visiting Fellow at the Centre for Research in the Arts, Social Sciences and Humanities (CRASSH) at the University of Cambridge on a one-term placement under a 'Migration' theme. It was followed by research in Moscow and St Petersburg in September 2004 funded by the Cultural Exchange agreement between the British Academy and the Russian Academy of Sciences, a programme now regrettably no longer in existence, to the detriment of research. The Russian Academy of Sciences, the Institute of Socio-Economic Problems of the Population in Moscow, and the Criminology Section of the Institute of Sociology in St Petersburg merit gratitude for their support and welcome. A small grant from the Elisabeth Barker Fund at the British Academy gave further backing in 2004 and 2005, followed by another research visit through the Cultural Exchange in April 2007.

Crucial funding for a nationwide public opinion poll in the Russian Federation and the running of two focus groups in June 2007 on attitudes towards various aspects of human trafficking was also awarded by the British Academy. An Emeritus Fellowship from the Leverhulme Trust made possible a second nationwide poll in September 2014 to gather longitudinal data and to run two further focus groups. The second survey widened the scope of the project to incorporate issues of labour migration into Russia. Gratitude is owed to these funding bodies for covering research expenses. Warm acknowledgment is owed to the Levada Analytic Center for organising the polls and focus groups in both years. For their help I should like to thank Alexei Grazhdankin, Alexey Levinson, Svetlana Koroleva and Rita Stepina.

I finally began writing this book in October 2014 and am especially grateful to the Rockefeller Foundation for awarding me a writing residency in May 2016 at the Villa Serbelloni in Bellagio on Lake Como to concentrate on research into the Russian language, history and law tests for incoming migrant workers. This rare-life opportunity to work intensively in this wonderfully tranquil setting a second time, twenty-six years after my first residency, was an honour and a privilege. For making my stay so pleasant, I warmly thank Pilar Palacia, Elena Ongania and all my fellow residents who contributed to a highly stimulating time.

Earlier papers from which this book has picked up threads were delivered at CRASSH, University of Cambridge, in May 2004; St Antony's College, Oxford, in March 2005; the Fakultät für Geschichtswissenschaft, Lehrstuhl für osteuropäische Geschichte, Ruhr-Universität Bochum, May 2005; Koç University, Istanbul, Turkey, in June 2006; the School of Public Policy, University College, London, November 2007; Hughes Hall, Cambridge, in 2007 and 2015; Birkbeck College, London, June 2015; annual conferences of BASEES, Fitzwilliam College, Cambridge, in 2005, 2008, 2013 and 2017; the VII and VIII World Congresses of ICCEES in Berlin in 2005 and Stockholm in 2010; and annual conventions of ASEEES in Boston, Philadelphia and Washington, DC, in 2013, 2015 and 2016. Thanks are due to those present who gave feedback and raised questions, particularly to Steven Barnes and Lauren McCarthy.

Numerous people in Russia have willingly helped in this project. I have enjoyed interviews, discussions and talks with a range of experts and specialists, and it gives me great pleasure to name those who permit me so to do. Since 2004 Natalia Khodyreva has been a regular source of helpful information and update. In 2004 and 2007, Elena Tiuriukanova, now sadly deceased, shared her recollections and reflections on the politics of pressing for anti-trafficking legislation. In this first phase of the project I also enjoyed revealing conversations in Moscow with Alberto Andriani, Robert Aronson, Juliette Engel, Svetlana Iakimenko, Tat'iana Kholshchevnikova, Maria Mokhovo, Anna Rubtsova and Mariana Solomotova. In St Petersburg, the Russian Academy of Sciences kindly organised my first conversation with Khodyreva and illuminating meetings with Dmitrii Kiriukhin at the Department of Criminal Investigation of the Ministry of Internal Affairs, with a judge in Dzherzhinkii district, and talks with Yakov Gilinsky and Yakov Kostyukovsky.

After the project widened to include labour migrants going into Russia, I benefited in 2013 from conversing with Kirill Boychenko and in 2014 from meetings with Sergei Boldyrev, Sergey Brestovitsky, Nikolai Kurdiumov, Julia Melnichouk, Juliana Pavlovskaya, Dmitry Poletaev, Vyacheslav Postavnin, Roman Rybakov, Olga Rybakova and Natalia Vlasova as well as discussions via Skype with Svetlana Gannushkina and Elena Timofeeva. They generously explained some of the complexities in changing migration policy and what was contentious. Warm thanks are due to them all for the time they devoted to me in their busy lives and especially to Kirill Boychenko for painstakingly arranging these meetings. I am hugely grateful to everyone who spoke to me for their time and kindness. This book is dedicated to them all.

For indispensable feedback and comments on early drafts of the history chapter, which took me back into centuries which I do not normally explore in detail, nor of which I dare to claim research expertise beyond secondary sources, I owe special thanks to Simon Dixon, Diane Koenker, William Rosenberg and Maria Zezina. I am also grateful to Andrew Cohn for his feedback on the Introduction and Conclusion. For suggestions on how best to translate some phrases in colloquial Russian, I owe a debt to Maria Zezina and Nikolay Kozhanov. For drawing to my attention a Memorandum that circulated in the Duma, I thank Iurii Zhukov. Gratitude is also due to two anonymous reviewers arranged by Cambridge University Press for their reflections. The arguments, interpretations and conclusions expressed in this book, however, are mine alone. Those named above may, or may not, agree with me and cannot be held responsible for my assessments, omissions and errors.

My editor, John Haslam, deserves thanks for his backing, as do Julie Hrischeva for her efforts and Karen Anderson for her thorough copyediting. It would be remiss not to thank Lynda Stratford at Cambridge University's Computing Service for cleansing my laptop of uninvited guests.

Finally, for sharing summer dacha life, travels in Russia, concerts and plays across the decades, I am grateful to Maria and Kolia for all the good times. For many a happy meal, I am also indebted to them both and to Iurii, Rimma, Natalia, Leonid, Anna, Polina, Miasachnik, Tania and Luda. They have all enriched my understanding of life in Russia which somehow became a part of my mental world.

Note on Transliteration, Websites and Permissions

A word is in order about style. I have followed the Library of Congress transliteration system with the exception of names and words whose more customary English forms are now widely adopted. Thus, I use Yel'tsin rather than El'tsin, Dostoyevsky, not Dostoevskii, and Yaroslavl, not Iaroslavl. Words will include *aia* and *iu* rather than *aya* and *yu*. Some Russians in their publications in English or on their business cards also offer options different from conventional transliteration systems. In keeping with their preferences, where relevant I refer to Juliana rather than Iuliana and Julia rather than Iuliia. Variations in spellings across names will also be found for the same reason, so Sergei, Sergey, Aleksei, Alexey, Natalia, Natal'ia, Dmitrii and Dmitry can all be found. When a person's surname has been presented in more than one way in English, I standardise it to the Library of Congress system, so I refer to Tiuriukanova rather than Tyuryukanova. Where professional preference is for an *aya* ending on a surname, I adhere to that, so refer to Pavlovskaya and not Pavlovskaia, although most endings will be *aia*. As is customary, I have dropped soft signs from the end of some words in the text, so *oblast'* is referred to as oblast. In the footnotes, however, all soft signs are present for accuracy in Russian. Articles whose final word ends with a soft sign and which happens to sit inside a quotation within a quotation will consequently have four closing apostrophes.

All websites cited here were checked again throughout February 2017 to confirm their continued availability on-line. The majority were still obtainable and so have no 'accessed' date after the citation and can be safely read as having been available on 1 February. The minority that have been removed and that cannot be traced elsewhere include a date when they were last accessed.

Permission has been granted by Taylor and Francis for reprinting selected data from my earlier article 'Public opinion in Russia on the politics of human trafficking', *Europe-Asia Studies*, Vol. 61, No. 2, March 2009, pp. 213–248, which can also be accessed via www.tandfonline.com. I should also like to acknowledge minimal crossover and fragments taken from this book for my 'Recent Russian press coverage of unfree labour', in Melanie Ilic, ed., *The Palgrave Handbook of Women and Gender in Twentieth-Century Russia and the Soviet Union* (London: Palgrave, 2018).

Introduction

Russia is a vast and beguiling country which captivates, holds and repeatedly lures back those who study it. This land is often stereotypically seen in the West as one of snow, glistening golden onion domes, icons, repressive troubles, dramatic upheavals, Orthodox priests with long beards, informers, secret police, suffering, communalism rather than individualism, country dachas and vodka. Whilst there is something suggestive in each of these images, realities are always more complex.

Like many states in the world today, the Russian Federation has been experiencing patterns of migration which have made important socio-economic and political impacts on the country itself, on its 'near abroad' and globally. Although many do find employment that suits them and which is quite legal and non-exploitative, thousands of Russian citizens have been trafficked out of their homeland into different forms of unfree labour across the world, whether into prostitution, construction or begging. Some foreign citizens have also been trafficked into Russia, and others may arrive legally and freely from other states but subsequently find themselves in work situations in which they lack a legal contract and are underpaid, unpaid or trapped in jobs that are semi-legal, underground or which involve forced labour in debt-bondage, much like those who are trafficked. Some Russians have also been trafficked within Russia's borders or have merely migrated within their own country looking for work in another region but then found themselves deceived and unexpectedly ended up in forced labour.

Brief stories to be discussed in later chapters highlight these three migration trends in different directions. Elena's tale is that of someone trafficked out of Russia. She was unemployed and living with her grandmother in a rural area of Kursk oblast which a journalist described as a place of 'mud' and 'no work'. An acquaintance said 'go to Guseinov, he will help you'. She did so and Guseinov promised her a good salary as a waitress abroad. His wife Tamara accompanied Elena to the United Arab Emirates (UAE) where they spent a happy first evening in a hotel. So far, Elena did not suspect that anything was amiss. The next day Tamara took her to an apartment and introduced her to its owner. Elena was handed over and found several other 'girls' already there.[1] They were forced to work in prostitution, eventually servicing ten to fifteen men a night. They were constantly locked up and, if they broke a rule, were beaten.

Siarkhon Tabarov's story is one of trafficking into Russia from Central Asia. He saw a television advertisement from a local job agency in Tajikistan offering a good job in Russia. Siarkhon signed a document and travelled with other Tajiks to Rostov. The employer took their passports, drove them into the mountains and then made them walk to a remoter area. These migrants were then told they would be quarrying by hard labour. Siarkhon and the others immediately refused but were bullied and told they would be deported if they did not comply. The men worked for eighty-five days with no pay. They lived in an abandoned refrigerator truck sleeping on filthy mattresses. Any protest was met with a denial of food.

Sergei's ordeal is one of slavery and forced labour within Russia. At forty-three years old, he travelled in 1996 from Murmansk to Makhachkala in Dagestan looking for work. When he got off the bus, a stranger approached and offered to set him up in a job in a brickworks. Subsequently Sergei was kept against his will as a forced labourer for an astonishing eighteen years. His documents were taken away, and he was given only old clothes and some food. He tried to escape, was caught and was then put to work herding cattle. Sergei was finally freed by the organisation Al'ternativa, which has set itself the goal of discovering and releasing slaves.

Many different adults and minors tell stories of enduring entrapment in a variety of predicaments. What each has experienced in common is deception, degrees of illegality and invariably threats and coercion, which often result in a form of unfreedom. Whilst many may attempt to resist and take action to get out of their situation, others have reported a lack of agency or felt limited capacity for initiative due to control or possession by another or by others. Outcomes can vary, depending upon several factors far more complex than the restrictive 'either/or' duality around which discussions of 'agency' versus 'victim' often pivot. Then again, many arrivals who are not trafficked are well treated and enjoy the success that they sought. It matters very much who employs them, just as it mattered who a serf's landholder was in the eighteenth and nineteenth centuries or who a slave's owner was in medieval Russia. Much also depends upon how individuals handle themselves, what decisions

---

[1] I use the terms 'girl' or 'woman' as cited in the original source.

they make, how they attempt to execute them, which relationships they have built or lack, and how they negotiate their realities. Migration processes and unfree labour predicaments are complex, and understandings of them should be nuanced. I use the term 'unfree labour' as an umbrella concept under which 'forced labour', 'bonded labour', 'slavery' and 'serfdom' are subsumed. These terms are unpacked below and will be found throughout the book. What is evident is that those in unfree labour situations are unable to enjoy citizenship rights, even when in their own countries. They do not possess what I call 'enabled citizenship'. Reference will also be made to work situations where there is some form of exploitation, such as non-payment or underpayment of wages, but which may not merit the label 'unfreedom'.

Objectives and Guiding Questions

This is a book about the politics, policies, social impacts and perceptions of migration flows out of, into and within the largest country in the world that end up either in some form of unfree labour or in exploitation along a continuum which at its worst end may merit the label 'slavery'. It sets out to provide an interdisciplinary case study about the politics in Russia surrounding issues of human trafficking, migration and labour exploitation, as well as their associated narratives, expert assessments and public appraisals. It offers a macro-picture of the dynamics of particular migration flows, the nature of press coverage about them and their impact on society, politics and policy. Scrutiny of the outflows does not discuss departures from Russia to study or to live and work elsewhere that do not involve the process of human trafficking. The outmigration of professionals into their specialist fields or of students falls outside this book's scope. Examination of inflows concentrates on migrants from Central Asia, particularly from Uzbekistan, Tajikistan and Kyrgyzstan, whilst acknowledging that others have also arrived from Azerbaijan, Armenia, Georgia, Ukraine, Eastern Europe, the People's Republic of China (PRC), Vietnam and the Democratic People's Republic of Korea (DPRK). The latter cluster will be mentioned only in passing as space requires more detailed focus on those from one region.

Discussion is concerned with how the historical, socio-economic and political context of Russia has shaped these migration flows since the protracted collapse of the USSR. It looks at why and how patterns of human trafficking developed and examines which social and political actors attempted to forge 'human trafficking', or 'torgovlia liud'mi' in Russian (literally, 'trade in people'), into a recognised social issue requiring attention on legal and political agendas. It asks how they went about it, with what success and who opposed them. The media are central to the construction of news, so analysis asks how the Russian press covered these initiatives and explores the types of stories that newspapers relayed to readers about the trafficked and their traffickers. Other central themes include how experts in non-governmental organisations (NGOs) and women's groups assessed developments in society and explained their own aims in trying to bring about change. A key question is how experts' views diverged from those of the public concerning the significance of both human trafficking and labour migration for their country and for its citizens. Crucially, discussion looks at how economic needs and social attitudes have affected Russia's policies on incoming labour migrants. It again asks about the role of the press and how it has portrayed the lives of labour migrants from Central Asia and exposed the problems, hazards and exploitation they may face. Opinions, beliefs and narratives are powerful elements within social fabrics globally and particularly on questions of migration. Analysis therefore scrutinises what the Russian public thinks about labour migrants from elsewhere on Russian territory and looks at the more specialist reflections of experts upon the recent history of migration policies and their implications for migrants. The study asks about the impacts that the processes of human trafficking and labour migration have made on the Russian Federation and how they have shaped the narratives circulating in the media, in politics, in NGOs and in wider society.

Migrating out for Work, But Trafficked

The first migration flows to be examined are those in which individuals left Russia for work in other states. The trafficked were promised good remuneration by those who recruited them and arranged their passage. Instead, however, upon arrival in a foreign destination, the workers found themselves trapped in a situation of forced labour, generally in a job not of their choosing. This is an example of human trafficking, not smuggling. In the early 2000s, thousands of Russians, like Elena, found themselves trafficked into brothels far-flung across the world. There were flows into Eastern Europe, particularly to Hungary, the Czech Republic, Croatia and Bosnia-Herzegovina. Routes to Western Europe took them to Germany, the Netherlands, Greece, Cyprus, Italy, Spain, the UK and Ireland. Another route went into Scandinavia. From the Russian Far East streams flowed to the PRC, Japan and Thailand. Through Azerbaijan and Armenia, the flows went to Turkey and to the UAE. Others reached Israel, the United States of America and Canada. Other East European women, particularly those from Moldova and Ukraine, found themselves in similar situations.

The reasons for the growth in trafficking out of Russia were several. The 'push' factors of factory closures, sell-offs and job losses in the 1990s in a context of 'wild capitalism' (*dikii kapitalizm*) caused workers to seek employment elsewhere. In a labour force segmented in some sectors by gender, those women who had not already lost their jobs were likely to be concentrated in low-paid work. They, like unemployed men, had an impetus to leave with the aim of earning more.[2] Travel abroad was not restricted as it had been in the USSR and so, with borders much easier to cross, opportunities for migration appeared greater, horizons widened and hopes and expectations grew. Moreover, the 'pull' factors which promised well-paid jobs and the lure of the West tempted workers into solving their problems by leaving Russia, if only for a short time. The emotional factor of the desire to escape narrow social worlds also contributed to the flow from small towns and rural areas, spurred by the hope of exciting adventures in new places and, for some, of finding a Western husband, with the rosy expectation of a more comfortable life. Indeed, since the Gorbachev era, television programmes, soap operas and films had been popularising notions of better lives elsewhere. Underpinning all these factors were the survival needs of earning money to support oneself and possibly one's offspring or parents back home. Together, however, these all required migration, not trafficking. During this period, there were vast opportunities for organised crime to establish transnational networks in human trafficking or for entrepreneurial individuals to make occasional opportunistic deals for their own benefit, such as selling an acquaintance. Facilitating factors for crime outweighed inhibitors.

To many Russians looking for work, foreign countries looked promising. The US government in 2004, however, estimated that 600,000 to 800,000 men, women and children were trafficked across borders every year, of whom 80 per cent were women and girls and as many as 50 per cent minors.[3] Figures from the International Labour Organization (ILO) in the mid 2000s estimated that there were 12.3 million people in the world trapped in 'forced labour, bonded labour, forced child labour, and sexual servitude at any given time', and other estimates gave a range of

---

[2] Some argued that women suffered worse unemployment than men, and others contested this. See Sarah Ashwin and Elain Bowers, 'Do Russian women want to work?', in Mary Buckley, ed., *Post-Soviet Women: From the Baltic to Central Asia* (Cambridge: Cambridge University Press, 1997), pp. 21–37; and Sue Bridger, Rebecca Kay and Kathryn Pinnick, *No More Heroines? Russia, Women and the Market* (London: Routledge, 1996).

[3] Cited in US State Department, TIP Report 2006, www.state.gov/j/tip/rls/tiprpt/2006/index.htm.

from 4 million to 27 million.[4] In 2012 the ILO gave an increased global figure of 20.9 million in forced labour, an estimated 3 out of every 1,000 persons worldwide, of whom 11.4 million (55 per cent) were women and girls and 9.5 million men and boys (45 per cent).[5] By 2014, however, all global estimates had increased. The Global Slavery Index issued by the Australian Walk Free Foundation put the global estimate at 35.8 million, which in 2016 it increased to 45.8 million in 167 countries.[6] Inevitably there have been criticisms and queries about the methodologies of data collection and the estimates reached, but no international organisation has disputed the gravity of the problem. It was one from which, structurally, the new Russian Federation could not be immune and into which some of its citizens would be drawn.

Migrating in for Work, Freely or Trafficked

The second process to be discussed concerns patterns of arrival from Central Asian states which may, or may not, result in labour exploitation with varying degrees of deception. At its worst, this process can result in unwelcome forced labour in Russia, as endured by Siarkhon Tabarov, thus sharing similar experiences of entrapment and exploitation with those trafficked out. Often those who end up in forced labour arrive legally and independently, seeking work. If they do not fully understand the law or if existing regulations make it hard for workers to behave entirely legally regarding registration or the length of their stay, then they risk getting sucked into illegal forms of help which will take advantage of them. Labour migrants may turn to people offering quick solutions to their plight, sometimes members of their diaspora already in Russia who may trick them and ask for payment for services that could have been obtained much more cheaply and officially, if only the migrant had known how. Labour migrants are especially vulnerable to unfree labour situations in periods when in Russia there are labour shortages in given sectors or locations and when in nearby states there are prevailing hardships, unemployment or lower wages. Sometimes 'intermediaries' or 'middlemen', known as *posredniki*, channel migrants into forced labour situations for their own reward. Even migrants with legal documents may find their 'legality' queried

---

[4] US State Department, TIP Report 2006.

[5] ILO, 'New ILO global estimate of forced labour: 20.9 million victims', ilo.org/global/topics/forced-labour/news/WCMS_182109/lang--en/index.htm. The ILO volunteered that the methodology had been 'revised and improved', giving 'a more robust figure'.

[6] The Walk Free Foundation's Global Slavery Indexes for 2013, 2014 and 2016 are at www.walkfreefoundation.org/resources.

and challenged by those in authority in a confusing 'grey' area between 'legal' and 'illegal', in which they may be required to pay a bribe anyway. Russian experts and specialists on migration have put forward various recommendations for ending labour abuse, and policies have changed over recent years in different ways. Some hate crimes against migrant workers with darker skins have also been evident in society, as across Europe and in North America, so xenophobia is one factor affecting policies.

Migrating Within, But Trapped in Forced Labour

A third process is that of Russian citizens, like Sergei, who become trapped in forced labour, or *prinuditel'nyi trud*, in their own land. This often comes about not because, like foreign incoming *gastarbaitery*, as Russians like to call the guest workers, they need to acquire permission to work for a specified time period, but merely because they need a job, are tricked in the recruitment process and subsequently find themselves in unfree labour. They may be duped, sold or even drugged and kidnapped. Of course, Russia is not alone in having problems of forced labour. Most states of the world, to varying degrees, have forms and patterns of unfree labour within their borders. The sheer size of Russia, however, and the remoteness of much of the land mass, makes it especially ripe for unfree work situations to develop, drawing in those living in poorer parts and willing to travel to other regions for employment. There are tempting economic opportunities for those wishing to exploit the vulnerable, the marginalised or the unsuspecting living within the state's own borders as well as those arriving from poorer countries in the 'near abroad' or further away.

Geographic expanse and the changing nature of border regimes are just two of many relevant factors in fluid pictures of migration and exploitation. It is worth underlining that today's Russian Federation, as shown on the map, has a massive territory of 6.59 million square miles, roughly one-ninth of the world's land. It spans more than 6,200 miles from the European continent in the west to the Pacific Far East and stretches over eleven time zones. Russia extends to the Arctic in the north, possesses nine major mountain ranges and is about 10 per cent swamp. Its land mass is almost twice the size of the USA. Given Russia's expanse, it was most unlikely that the country would have escaped contemporary problems of unfree labour in this globalised world. Russia shares land borders with fourteen states, the highest world figure, which makes it unsurprising that leaders and peoples have always had a deep sense of being surrounded and of being geo-politically vulnerable.[7] Given its numerous borders, it was also unlikely that the dynamics of migration, whether in or out, would be unaffected by changes and continuities in adjacent states and those beyond them.

Before 1991, Russia was formally known as the Russian Soviet Federated Socialist Republic, or RSFSR, and was one of fifteen republics that made up the Union of Soviet Socialist Republics, or USSR. This Soviet Union was a massive state of 8.6 million square miles, one-sixth of the world's habitable land. It was situated both in Europe and in Asia, as is Russia today, and its republics shared borders with Finland, Norway, Poland, Hungary, Czechoslovakia, Romania, Turkey, Iran, the PRC, the Mongolian People's Republic, the DPRK and Afghanistan. According to the last Soviet census of 1989, it had 286.7 million people. Just over half of these, namely 147.4 million, were in the RSFSR, which was the largest republic.[8] The USSR finally collapsed after a protracted process of social and political change under Mikhail Gorbachev.[9] By 2013 the population of the Russian Federation had dropped to 143.3 million and had increased a little by 2016 to 146.5 million.[10] With such a diversity of neighbours in the 'near abroad' of former Soviet republics and beyond, routes out of Russia for traffickers are multiple and varied, providing several opportunities for exit routes which can be switched when necessary. The border with the PRC alone runs for just over 2,600 miles.

Although the USSR as a political system collapsed more than twenty-five years ago, different linkages have persisted over this territorial space despite new state borders. Not only are there relatives, friends and remembered colleagues elsewhere, there are also more general 'connections' of shared histories, memories of holidays and of favourite Soviet movies, songs, actors and singers. There is a haunting sense of shared cultural threads and of Moscow as a magnet, whether for a special visit

---

[7] This figure includes the Russian enclave of Kaliningrad and its borders with Poland and Lithuania.

[8] Goskomstat SSSR, *Naselenie SSSR 1988: Statisticheskii Ezhegodnik* (Moscow: Finansy i Statistiki, 1989), p. 8. In 1959 the population of the USSR was 208.8 million and in 1979 it reached 262.4 million. The corresponding figures for the RSFSR were 117.5 million and 137.4 million.

[9] See Archie Brown, *The Gorbachev Factor* (Oxford: Oxford University Press, 1997); Stephen White, *Gorbachev and After*, 3rd edn (Cambridge: Cambridge University Press, 1992); Richard Sakwa, *Russian Politics and Society*, 4th edn (London: Routledge, 2008), chs. 1–2; Mary Buckley, *Redefining Russian Society and Polity* (Boulder, CO: Westview Press, 1993); and Mary Buckley, 'The disintegration of the USSR: a complex protracted process', *Journal of Irish and Scottish Studies*, Vol. 1, No. 2, 2008, pp. 251–264.

[10] Federal'naia Sluzhba Gosudarstvennoi Statistiki (Rosstat), *Demograficheskii Ezhegodnik Rossii: Statisticheskii Sbornik* (Moscow: Rosstat, 2013), p. 21. Rosstat's updates are at www.gks.ru/wps/wcm/connect/rosstat_main/rosstat/en/figures/population.

from afar, for study in a prestigious institution or as a cultural centre. Memories span borders, such as recollections of every New Year's Eve when El'dar Riazanov's 1975 comedy film *Irony of Fate* (*Ironiia Sudby, ili s legkim parom*) would be screened and delight millions. Although perceptions of what the USSR was now vary across its former constituent parts and peoples, there are nonetheless lingering senses of familiarity and commonalities, stronger in some states than in others. This particularly applies to attitudes within Central Asian states regarding the appropriateness of their labour flows into Russia, which pre-date current borders. For Russia's part, having to cope in 1989 with the loss of empire in Eastern Europe and then in 1991 with the USSR's own final implosion, the image that its leaders liked to project on the world stage of their country as a '*velikaia derzhava*', or great power, was seriously undermined. Moreover, these events generated an identity crisis for leaders and citizens and spawned reflection and soul-searching as to what remained of the Russian national idea. The hasty formation of the Commonwealth of Independent States (Sodruzhestvo Nezavisimikh Gosudarstv), or CIS, on 8 December 1991 in a meeting between Boris Yel'tsin and the leaders of Ukraine and Belarus, was an attempt initially to hold the Slavic republics together by some loose inter-state links and to deal with issues emerging from the disintegration of the USSR. It quickly widened on 21 December through the Alma Ata Protocol to include Armenia, Azerbaijan, Kazakhstan, Kyrgyzstan, Moldova, Tajikistan, Turkmenistan and Uzbekistan, but achievements were limited.[11] The setting up of the Eurasian Economic Union (EEU) of the most committed states of Russia, Belarus and Kazakhstan came into force on 1 January 2015. There had been a prior history from the mid 1990s of attempts at effective customs union, but declarations outweighed successes.[12] Armenia's membership of the EEU quickly followed on 2 January and that of Kyrgyzstan in August 2015. Both the CIS and EEU are relevant to the topics of human trafficking and labour migration not only because citizens across them experience these processes but because agreements have resulted in shared plans for anti-trafficking initiatives and have also defined the requirements of labour migrants entering Russia.

---

[11] Moldavia (as Moldova was formerly known) was an associate member up to 1994. Georgia joined in 1993, then left in 2008. Turkmenistan and Ukraine did not ratify the agreement. See Mark Webber, *CIS Integration Trends: Russia and the Former Soviet South* (London: Royal Institute of International Affairs, 1997).

[12] Rilka Dragneva and Kataryna Wolczuk, 'Russia, the Eurasian Customs Union and the EU: cooperation, stagnation or rivalry?', Chatham House briefing paper, August 2012.

Conceptualisations and Definitions

'Human trafficking' is not synonymous with 'slavery', and these two concepts should not be conflated. Rather, human trafficking is a process which is highly likely to end in some form of labour exploitation which in its severest form may constitute what many academics and experts do define as 'slavery', although both terms for some scholars are either unsatisfactory, controversial or both. Political leaders, lawyers, those in NGOs and many academics in their research, however, do use these concepts and apply them. In so doing, they generally follow the definition of human trafficking adopted in one of the three Palermo Protocols, the 'Protocol to Prevent, Suppress and Punish Trafficking in Persons, Especially Women and Children' (the anti-trafficking Protocol), which supplemented the United Nations (UN) Convention Against Transnational Organised Crime, or Palermo Convention, which the General Assembly approved in 2000 and which came into force in 2003. In this Protocol, human trafficking is portrayed as a process that involves 'the recruitment, transportation, transfer, harbouring or receipt of persons' which is 'by means of the threat or use of force or other forms of coercion, of abduction, of fraud, of deception, or the abuse of power or of a position of vulnerability'. Integral to this definition is 'control' over another person 'for the purpose of exploitation'.[13] Trafficking from Russia has generally involved recruitment through deception about paid employment to be provided later and elsewhere and does not usually involve payment in advance by workers for the costs of their transit. In covering travel costs, the trafficker later claims an inflated debt for these upon the worker's arrival elsewhere, which leaves the trafficked person in a predicament of debt-bondage. As a consequence, the process of human trafficking is most likely to result in the undermining of personal security, human rights, dignity and the self-esteem of the target workers, unless they manage to escape. Regional organisations such as the Organization for Security and Co-operation in Europe (OSCE), the Council of Europe (CoE) and the European Union (EU) have followed UN definitions and adopted policies, recommendations, directives and

---

[13] The text of the 'Protocol to Prevent, Suppress and Punish Trafficking in Persons, Especially Women and Children' can be found at www.ohchr.org/EN/ProfessionalInterest/Pages/ProtocolTraffickingInPersons.aspx. In 1949, the UN General Assembly approved the Convention for the Suppression of Traffic in Persons and of the Exploitation of the Prostitution of Others. It described trafficking as an 'evil', endangering the welfare of the individual, family and community, and stated that the consent of the trafficked person was irrelevant to the prosecution of the exploiter. The 1949 Convention created no monitoring body and was not widely ratified. See www.ohchr.org/EN/ProfessionalInterest/Pages/TrafficInPersons.aspx.

strategies on the prevention of human trafficking, the rehabilitation of those affected by it and the prosecution of the traffickers.[14]

In legal terms, human trafficking is conceptually distinct from smuggling. The latter occurs when an individual pays a person in advance to transport him or her to a particular destination, generally arriving in another state illegally and without the promise of a job from the smuggler. The initial agreement in legal terms involves consent, although it may indeed be a coerced form of consent if the migrant is trying to flee a war zone or repressive state or get out of a dire economic situation. The UN Protocol 'Against the Smuggling of Migrants by Land, Sea and Air' defines smuggling as 'the procurement, in order to obtain, directly or indirectly, a financial or other material benefit, of the illegal entry of a person into a State Party of which the person is not a national or a permanent resident'.[15] The informal agreement between client and smuggler, however, may also involve deception and share some of the characteristics of trafficking. Sociologists have contested the sharp distinction between them, cautioning that the lines in reality may be blurred. Smuggling may not always involve a straightforward deal, and smugglers may let down their clients in transit or otherwise place them at risk. This became starkly evident in cases of migrants smuggled across the Mediterranean sea from Libya to Italy and of Afghans, Iraqis and Syrians smuggled from Turkey to Greek islands.[16] News reporters often confuse these legal concepts and talk about 'traffickers' when they mean 'smugglers'.

Other than 'human trafficking', key terms referred to in this book are 'forced labour', 'bonded labour', 'slavery' and 'serfdom'. These four categories of labour, which in some ways overlap, are all different forms of 'unfree labour'. In 1930 the ILO's Convention on Forced Labour defined that term in Article 2.1 as 'work or service which is exacted from any person under the menace of any penalty' and for which the person had

---

[14] For details, see OSCE, 'Combating trafficking in human beings', www.osce.org/secretariat/trafficking; Council of Europe's Group of Experts on Action against Trafficking in Human Beings (GRETA) annual report, www.humanrightseurope.org/2015/04/anti-human-trafficking-unit-publishes-annual-report/; the EU Directive of 2011 on preventing and combating trafficking in human beings, ec.europa.eu/anti-trafficking/legislation-and-case-law-eu-legislation-criminal-law/directive-201136eu-e; and 'EU Strategy towards the Eradication of Trafficking in Human Beings (2012–2016)', ec.europa.eu/anti-trafficking/eu-policy/new-european-strategy-2012-2016.en.

[15] See www.unodc.org/unodc/en/human-trafficking/smuggling-of-migrants.html.

[16] Tom Kington, 'Children among 400 lost as migrants sail to Europe', *The Times*, 15 April 2015. Smugglers on more than one occasion tossed their passengers overboard.

not offered themselves 'voluntarily'.[17] This Convention depicted 'forced labour' as synonymous with 'compulsory labour'. The term gained more widespread coinage after the ILO set out to gather statistics on validated reports of its existence. A more recent unpacking of the concept from the ILO in 2014 led to a more nuanced definition: 'forced labour refers to situations in which persons are coerced to work through the use of violence or intimidation, or by more subtle means such as accumulated debt, retention of identity papers or threats of denunciation to immigration authorities'.[18]

'Bonded labour' and 'debt-bondage' are terms which refer to a mechanism through which forced labour can be economically compelled and today are frequently used in connection with instances of human trafficking. For example, in much of the human trafficking out of the Russian Federation in the 1990s and early 2000s, women and girls may have responded to newspaper advertisements offering highly paid work in another country as a waitress, nanny or dancer, been unable to pay for their fare there or to provide appropriate documents and so become indebted to the recruiter who offered to cover the costs of their travel and arrange the necessary paperwork. Trafficked persons committed themselves later to pay back the money out of future wages. Invariably, however, they found themselves trapped in prostitution against their will instead of working in waitressing. Not only were they deceived, but now they were stuck in situations of 'bonded labour' in which they were already in debt, or in 'debt-bondage'. Work in debt-bondage thus became an insecure and unfree form of security for money owed, a debt which could be unfairly inflated or increased through an imposed system of fines for minor transgressions or for breaking arbitrary rules set by the captor. What the ILO refers to as 'subtle' means of coercion such as 'accumulated debt' may also be accompanied by violence, threats and debasement. Many analysts would deem the predicament of forced labour and debt-bondage to be tantamount to 'slavery', even though the workers are not legally 'owned' in a more classical sense of slavery.

There is a huge scholarly literature on what constitutes 'slavery' with discussions revolving around questions of the role of the master, the powerlessness of the slave, property rights, relations of production, the nature of the society, outsider status, kinship ties and physical

---

[17] The ILO's 'Forced Labour Convention, 1930 (No. 29)' is available at www.ilo.org/dyn/normlex/en/f?p=NORMLEXPUB:12100:0::NO::P12100_ILO_CODE:C029. For the ILO's 'Abolition of Forced Labour Convention, 1957 (No. 105)', see www.ilo.org/dyn/normlex/en/f?p=1000:12100:0::P12100_ILO_CODE:C105.

[18] ILO, 'The meanings of forced labour', www.ilo.org/global/topics/forced-labour/news/WCMS_237569/lang-en/index.htm.

movement.[19] The nature of the relationship between master and slave can vary across slave systems and within them. In the past, different forms of slavery were legal, such as in ancient Rome, the southern states of the USA or medieval Russia before serfdom. 'Slavery' today, however, or what some feel more comfortable describing as 'unfree labour' or 'forced labour', is illegal and refers to the control and coercion of a person by violence, or threats of violence, and their economic exploitation to the advantage of the coercer. The slave may receive no wages or just subsistence. Slaves usually lack the freedom to walk away from their predicament or may be deterred from doing so out of fear of the consequences.

At the international level, there have been various treaties, conventions and general recommendations specific to slavery and forced labour aimed at prevention. Multilateral treaties included the 1904 International Agreement for the Suppression of the White Slave Traffic, the 1910 International Convention for the Suppression of the White Slave Traffic, the 1921 International Convention for the Suppression of the Traffic in Women and Children and, under the League of Nations, the 1933 International Convention for the Suppression of the Traffic in Women of Full Age. In 1926, also under the League of Nations, a Convention to Suppress the Slave Trade and Slavery was signed in Geneva, and in 1930 the ILO adopted a Convention Concerning Forced or Compulsory Labour.

How, then, has the concept of 'slavery' been defined? Article 1 of the Convention of 1926 saw slavery as 'the status or condition of a person over whom any or all of the powers attaching to the right of ownership are exercised'. According to Article 2, 'the slave trade includes all acts involved in the capture, acquisition or disposal of a person with intent to reduce him to slavery; all acts involved in the acquisition of a slave with a view to selling or exchanging him; all acts of disposal by sale or exchange of a slave acquired with a view to being sold or exchanged, and, in general, every act of trade or transport in slaves'.[20] A Protocol of 1955 amended the League of Nations Convention and also in 1956 refined the definition of slavery. This Supplementary Convention referred more broadly to 'slavery, the slave trade, and institutions and practices similar to slavery', regretting that they had not been eliminated. It called for their 'complete abolition' whether or not they were covered by the 1926 definition of slavery. Article 1 now included 'debt bondage', 'serfdom' and 'any institution or practice' in which a woman 'without the right to

---

[19] Relevant references are in footnotes 1 to 3 in the next chapter.
[20] See 'Slavery Convention' at www.ohchr.org/EN/ProfessionalInterest/Pages/SlaveryConvention.aspx.

refuse' was given in marriage, transferred by her husband to another person or liable upon the death of her husband to be inherited by another person.[21]

Other international documents are pertinent too. The Universal Declaration on Human Rights adopted in 1948 by the UN General Assembly championed 'freedom from fear and want' as well as the 'dignity and worth of the human person' and 'the security of the person'. Article 4 held that 'No one shall be held in slavery or servitude' and that 'slavery and the slave trade shall be prohibited in all their forms'. Article 5 specified that 'No one shall be subjected to torture or to cruel, inhuman or degrading treatment or punishment', and Article 16 maintained that marriage could be entered into only with free and full consent of those of 'full age'.[22] The International Covenant on Civil and Political Rights echoed in Article 8 the ban on slavery and added that, 'No one shall be required to perform forced or compulsory labour.'[23] With different emphases, the International Covenant on Economic, Social and Cultural Rights referred in Article 1 to 'the right to self-determination' and in Article 7 to 'the right of everyone to the enjoyment of just and favourable conditions of work'. This included remuneration, fair wages, a decent living and safe and healthy working conditions, equal opportunities in promotion and periodic holidays, rest, leisure and reasonable working hours.[24] Both Covenants were adopted by the General Assembly in 1966 and came into force in 1976. More detailed consideration is given to minors in the UN Convention on the Rights of the Child, in force since September 1990. Its Preamble, citing the earlier Declarations of the Rights of the Child of 1924 and 1959, holds that children require 'special safeguards and care' because of 'physical and mental immaturity'. Article 35 requires states to 'take all appropriate national, bilateral and multilateral measures to prevent the abduction of, the sale of or traffic in children for any purpose or in any form', and Article 36 calls for protection against 'forms of exploitation prejudicial to any aspects of the child's welfare'.[25]

Kevin Bales has persuasively argued for the need to view slavery not just legally but with recognition of its complexities and evolving nature.

---

[21] See 'Supplementary Convention on the Abolition of Slavery, the Slave Trade, and Institutions and Practices Similar to Slavery' at www.ohchr.org/EN/ProfessionalInterest/Pages/SupplementaryConventionAbolitionofSlavery.aspx.

[22] UN, 'Universal Declaration of Human Rights', www.un.org/en/universal-declaration-human-rights/index.html.

[23] Available at www.ohchr.org/EN/ProfessionalInterest/Pages/ccpr.aspx.

[24] Available at www.ohchr.org/EN/ProfessionalInterest/Pages/CESCR.aspx.

[25] The text of 'The Convention on the Rights of the Child' is at www.ohchr.org/EN/ProfessionalInterest/pages/crc.aspx.

He contends that today a 'new slavery' exists in which the people are merely 'disposable', set in a situation distinct from the legally owned slaves of the past.[26] Any traditional responsibilities of an owner to a slave are lacking in this post-modern context in which illegal control is maintained through coercion and violence. Bales views 'slavery' sociologically as a patterned relationship between humans, one that can take 'various forms' and 'achieve certain outcomes'. The different forms are themselves set in cultural, religious, social, political, ethnic, commercial and psychological contexts. He portrays the core attribute across forms as 'a state of control' which is 'based on violence or its threat' and a 'lack of payment beyond subsistence'. Integral to the core in Bales's analysis is 'the theft of labor or other qualities of the slave for economic gain'.[27] More recently Jean Allain and Kevin Bales have argued that 'exercise of control' over a person is tantamount to possession and that 'possession is the *sine qua non* of slavery'.[28] Here they are keen to stress that the situation is *de facto* one of 'ownership' and 'property', even if not formal legal ownership of the person.

Serfdom is another form of labour considered 'unfree' and banned by international law. Legally it is distinct from 'slavery', although some historians perceive it as similar in some respects. It was common across feudal Western Europe and constituted a form of legal bondage in which the peasant worked for a lord, was permitted subsistence farming on certain fields and in return received protection. Serfdom was thus a legal, economic and social relationship. Serfdom developed later across Central and Eastern Europe, including parts of Russia but excluding Siberia. Unfree labour in nineteenth-century Russia, however, was not only about work on landed estates. There was also *katorga*, or penal servitude, a form of forced labour integral to Peter the Great's modernising project. Subsequently in the USSR a system of labour camps, or Gulag, was established in which prisoners laboured on projects for the construction of Soviet socialism.[29] Prisoners of war (POWs) constituted another category of unfree labour, common across states. Some historians have also cast the collectivisation of agriculture in the USSR in the same light.

---

[26] Kevin Bales, *Disposable People: New Slavery in a Global Age* (Berkeley: University of California Press, 2004).

[27] Kevin Bales, *Understanding Global Slavery: A Reader* (Berkeley: University of California Press, 2005), pp. 8–9.

[28] Jean Allain and Kevin Bales, 'Slavery and its definition', Law Research Paper No. 12-06, Queen's University, Belfast.

[29] The word 'Gulag' is a shortened form of its formal title of 'Glavnoe upravlenie ispravitel'no-trudovykh lagerei i kolonii', which can be translated as 'Main administration of corrective labour camps and colonies'.

Theoretical Approaches

There are several ways in which scholars have approached the study of the topics of human trafficking, forced labour and slavery. Historians have produced a literature on developments in different parts of the world with chronologies, descriptions and analyses of patterns of slavery, its consequences and campaigns to end it. Historians also make clear different types of slavery in the past, as in the work of Richard Hellie on Russia which identifies eight categories of slave.[30] More recently, John Picarelli has underscored the importance of recognising the differences between chattel slavery, indentured servitude, peonage and today's 'unfree labour', which he hesitates to call slavery.[31]

Social scientists have adopted various frameworks to studying human trafficking with emphases on different bundles of independent variables. Some embed human trafficking within studies of migration and focus primarily on the dynamics of the 'push' and 'pull' factors involved in the wider process of the 're-forging' of states and societies. Socio-economic factors and historical context are crucial to making sense of these.[32] Others offer what they call 'a global perspective' in multi-disciplinary anthologies discussing trafficking across continents.[33] Some come at it very much from the prism of 'slavery', an old form of labour exploitation in contemporary contexts. Bales, cited above, prefers to refer to a 'new slavery' of more easily disposable people. Approaches overlap and converge on many points. Those who scrutinise human trafficking from a human rights perspective, such as Human Rights Watch (HRW), Amnesty International and the American Bar Association (ABA), begin conceptually from 'violations of human rights'. Nonetheless, human trafficking can result in a 'contemporary form of slavery', and so a human rights perspective can echo aspects of the previous approaches. Moreover, most approaches incorporate some discussion of human rights violations in the trafficking process. Jennifer Suchland, however, has questioned the utility of focussing on violations of human rights, arguing that this

---

[30] Richard Hellie, *Slavery in Russia 1450–1725* (Chicago: University of Chicago Press, 1982).

[31] Chattel slavery refers to legal ownership. Indentured servitude applies when a person agrees to work for a specified length of time. Peonage connotes debt-bondage or working off a debt. Whereas chattel slavery has largely ended, unfree labour has not. See John T. Picarelli, 'Historical approaches to the trade in human beings', in Maggy Lee, ed., *Human Trafficking* (Cullompton, UK: Willan Publishing, 2007), pp. 26–48.

[32] Stephen Castles, Hein De Hass and Mark J. Miller, *The Age of Migration: International Population Movements in the Modern World*, 5th edn (London: Palgrave Macmillan, 2013).

[33] Kimberly A. McCabe and Sabita Manian, eds., *Sex Trafficking: A Global Perspective* (Plymouth: Lexington Books, 2010).

discourse does not address how human trafficking 'is intertwined in the constitutive operations of economic systems'.[34]

Members of some governments initially perceived human trafficking as a crime and as a potential threat to public order and national security. Their starting frame was one of 'law and order'. Criminologists adopt a similar starting point of 'law breaking'. In particular, they focus on the role of transnational crime, organised crime and forms of corruption. Quick off the mark in studying human trafficking from Russia from this perspective were Louise Shelley and Sally Stoecker. They explored the relevance of the 'political–criminal nexus' as a legacy of the USSR and its 'raider mentality' towards resources, including persons, for quick profits within an 'illicit global economy'.[35] Such trade in humans amounted to a 'commodification of persons' at the hands of criminal organisations with 'their own form of authoritarianism'.[36] Like many others, they stress 'the complexity of the trafficking phenomenon'.[37] Also, using transnational organised crime as a central focus, Phil Williams has taken a broad market perspective by looking at the context of commodity markets and at the 'opportunities, cost–benefit calculations and risk considerations' of the 'modern slave traders'. He argues that the structure of markets and market dynamics are relevant as they generate facilitators of trafficking and inhibitors, with the former being stronger.[38] This fits into a broad perspective which calls for examination of the structural and proximate factors which shape human trafficking. The former refer to social, economic and political context and the latter to policy and governance issues.[39] A related but distinct

---

[34] Jennifer Suchland, *Economies of Violence: Transnational Feminism, Pansocialism, and the Politics of Sex Trafficking* (Durham, NC: Duke University Press, 2015), p. 1. For a summary of her argument, see pp. 1–21.

[35] Louise I. Shelley, 'The changing position of women: trafficking, crime and corruption', in David Lane, ed., *The Legacy of State Socialism and the Future of Transformation* (Lanham, MD: Rowman & Littlefield, 2002), pp. 207–222.

[36] Sally Stoecker, 'The rise of human trafficking and the role of organized crime', *Demokratizatsiia*, Vol. 8, No. 1 (Winter 2000), pp. 129–144; Sally Stoecker, 'Human trafficking: a new challenge for Russia and the United States', in Sally Stoecker and Louise Shelley, eds., *Human Traffic and Transnational Crime* (Lanham, MD: Rowman & Littlefield, 2005), pp. 13–28.

[37] Stoecker and Shelley, 'Introduction', in Stoecker and Shelley, eds., *Human Traffic*, pp. 1–12. See also Louise I. Shelley and Robert W. Orttung, 'Russia's efforts to combat human trafficking: efficient crime groups versus irresolute societies and uncoordinated states', in William Alex Pridemore, ed., *Ruling Russia: Law, Crime and Justice in a Changing Society* (Lanham, MD: Rowman & Littlefield, 2005), pp. 167–182.

[38] Phil Williams, 'Trafficking in women: the role of transnational organized crime', in Sally Cameron and Edward Newman, eds., *Trafficking in Humans: Social, Cultural and Political Dimensions* (New York: United Nations University, 2008), pp. 126–157; see, too, Phil Williams, ed., *Russian Organized Crime: The New Threat?* (London: Frank Cass, 1997).

[39] Edward Newman and Sally Cameron, 'Introduction: understanding human trafficking', in Cameron and Newman, eds., *Trafficking in Humans*, pp. 1–17.

approach regarding crime and law enforcement by Lauren McCarthy examines how the functioning of the Russian criminal justice system and its incentives and disincentives provide structural reasons which make it difficult to prosecute under anti-trafficking clauses.[40] Some politicians in states losing large numbers of women and girls to prostitution abroad have also remarked upon the threat to the country's gene pool and birth rate, seeing the issue through a demographic prism.

Scholars who pay special attention to the variable of gender emphasise the importance of a sexualised world, the international political economy of sex, the objectification of women and entrenched discriminatory and patriarchal attitudes towards women as sex objects.[41] Regarding the trafficking of women and girls, Sheila L. Croucher sums up the situation as 'the transnational marketing, export, exchange and exploitation of women'.[42] Kat Banyard argues that the sex trade 'manufactures consent', resulting in 'commercial sexual exploitation on an industrial scale'. She analyses how myths circulating in 'pimp states' are 'used to create a culture and set of laws that encourage and facilitate men's paid sexual access to women's bodies'.[43] Women are thereby rendered de-humanised targets, enduring a violation of their boundaries, and receive no empathy.[44] From these perspectives, human trafficking and the nature of unfree labour cannot fully be grasped without an appreciation of gender politics and the roles of misogyny and violence. Putting it differently, Tat'iana Svad'bina, Ol'ga Nemova and Tat'iana Pakina highlight the combined influences of a 'mass propaganda of luxury' and the 'psychological, management and marketing' techniques adopted by traffickers and set in a context in which women's status in Russia has been lowered. They argue that a 'crisis in the family' and 'a deformation of moral norms' have denied girls their potentials.[45] Looking at UN peacekeeping missions, Jasmine-Kim Westendorf and Louise Searle have discussed how abuses of differential

[40] Lauren A. McCarthy, 'Beyond corruption: an assessment of Russian law enforcement's fight against human trafficking', *Demokratizatsiia*, Vol. 18, No. 1 (Winter 2010), pp. 1–17; and her *Trafficking Justice: How Russian Police Enforce New Laws, from Crime to Courtroom* (Ithaca, NY: Cornell University Press, 2015).

[41] Jan Jindy Pettman, *Worlding Women: A Feminist International Politics* (London: Routledge, 1996), pp. 157–207; Chris Corrin, 'Transitional road for traffic: analysing trafficking in women from and through Central and Eastern Europe', *Europe-Asia Studies*, Vol. 57, No. 4, June 2005, pp. 543–560.

[42] Sheila L. Croucher, *Globalization and Belonging: The Politics of Identity in a Changing World* (Lanham, MD: Rowman & Littlefield, 2004), p. 166.

[43] Kat Banyard, *Pimp State: Sex, Money and the Future of Equality* (London: Faber, 2016), pp. 6–10.

[44] Banyard, *Pimp State*, pp. 28–51.

[45] Tat'iana Svad'bina, Ol'ga Nemova and Tat'iana Pakina, 'Sovremennyi trafik rabotorgovli: prichiny, posledstviia, profilaktika', *Sotsiologicheskie issledovaniia*, No. 2, 2014, pp. 43–48.

power and trust by peacekeepers can sexually exploit the vulnerabilities of those they were sent there to protect.[46]

A wide approach which focusses on sustainable livelihoods is integral to development studies and political ecology. It concerns the capabilities, assets and activities needed for means of living. Robert Chambers and Gordon R. Conway argue that 'a livelihood is sustainable which can cope with and recover from stress and shocks'.[47] Those trapped in debt-bondage have no sustainable livelihood or, at best, a highly compromised one which itself is characterised by stress. In fact, debt-bondage is a predicament from which escape is required and a new start necessary before livelihoods begin to be sustainable. The lives of some labour migrants from Central Asia may also fall into this category. Even if not in debt-bondage, many migrants find that their attempts at sustainable living may be challenged by reduced pay, the complexities and costs of obtaining documents for registration and work, and pressures to pay bribes, as well as prohibitive housing costs which may result in having to rent 'mattress space' in cramped accommodation with others, known as *rezinovye kvartiry*, or 'rubber flats'. Study of sustainable livelihoods developed in the 1990s as an attempt to go beyond existing ways of looking at poverty and to broaden analysis to include questions of vulnerability, social exclusion and command over resources and social networks.[48] Anthropologists in their ethnographic case studies of the livelihoods of labour migrants and family members left behind shed detailed light on personal dimensions, perceptions and understandings of migration processes and outcomes which aggregate statistical data do not offer.[49] Thus the literature on different forms of vulnerable and unfree labour operates at several 'levels of analysis' with varying perspectives which pose both distinct and overlapping questions.

My own approach here is an interdisciplinary one. The story of human trafficking out of Russia, into it and within it needs to be explained

---

[46] Jasmine-Kim Westendorf and Louise Searle, 'Sexual exploitation and abuse in peace operations: trends, policy responses and future directions', *International Affairs*, Vol. 93, No. 2, March 2017, pp. 365–387.

[47] Robert Chambers and Gordon R. Conway, 'Sustainable rural livelihoods: practical concepts for the twenty-first century', IDS Discussion Paper, 1 December 1992.

[48] The notion of 'sustainable livelihood' was put forward by the Brundtland Commission on Environment and Development and further considered in 1992 at a UN Conference on 'Environment and development'.

[49] Eleonora Fayzullaeva, 'Labor migration in Central Asia: gender challenges', in Linda Racioppi and Katherine O'Sullivan See, eds., *Gender Politics in Post-Communist Eurasia* (East Lansing: Michigan State University Press, 2009), pp. 237–265; Madeleine Reeves, 'Clean fake: authenticating documents and persons in migrant Moscow', *American Ethnologist*, Vol. 40, No. 3, 2013, pp. 508–524.

by looking at historical, socio-economic, legislative, political, law enforcement, demographic, gender and attitudinal factors, all of which are essential to an understanding of the changing nature of livelihoods, their fluidities and complexities, and the responses within state and society. Part of this requires listening to how Russians themselves perceive the social and political settings in which developments have unfolded. For this reason, I have interviewed as many experts and activists in the field of anti-trafficking and labour migration as I have had the research time and funding to do, and also designed opinion polls and focus groups to tap into what the public thinks. Underpinning this discussion is the methodological conviction that attention to how individuals express and present their arguments, beliefs and fears, be they experts, the public or migrants, illustrates how they approach, perceive and comprehend the realities and issues around them. I have not for this book conducted face-to-face interviews with the trafficked. I consider there to be ethical questions about doing this and also that it is more appropriate for Russian psychologists to do so than a foreigner from a part of the world in which they may have endured forced labour. There are, moreover, sufficient reports available to know the contours of what trafficked women and men, as well as labour migrants, have been through. This book instead looks at wider historical, political, social and attitudinal contexts and dynamics in which the trafficked and labour migrants are situated. Nor have I interviewed traffickers or 'employers' of those in debt-bondage.

Chapter Breakdown: The Russian Case Study

What merits a Russian case study if human trafficking into unfree labour is a global trend? Case studies of different countries and regions provide documentation and analysis of local patterns and configurations which may show distinctiveness. Russia does have certain characteristics not shared by all states, which include the size of its landmass, its geography of being encircled, the length and variety of its borders and its categorisation of being part of a collapsed empire and a former superpower. Such case studies by specialists of different countries can subsequently feed into wider comparative understandings of similarities and differences across the world. Investigation into the actions of concerned women's groups, NGOs and some politicians in pushing for change illustrates what can be achieved in an authoritarian system and suggests what the limits to success might be and the brakes on it, especially in a system marred by some corrupt practices. The nature of articles in the press and the social attitudes of citizens about a particular problem may vary across the world, linked to the nature of local histories, economic pressures and cultural patterns across states. Experts on migration policy in Russia may hold views similar to or different from those in other states, and the best way to discover these is to meet and question them and to read the literature that they produce. Thus, from an interdisciplinary perspective, the structure of this book traverses historical, legal, political, sociological and attitudinal dimensions of the issues of human trafficking and labour migration in a particular part of the world and in the largest state.

Precisely because of the existence of different forms of unfree labour in Russia's history, Chapter 1 offers a brief overview of their nature. It introduces – for those social scientists who may be unfamiliar with aspects of Russia's distant historical examples – illustrations of different types or categories of *kholopstvo* (slavery), not prevalent today, in order to underline how varied its forms have been. Serfdom was legally and conceptually distinct from slavery, although some historians view it as 'virtually slavery', whilst others disagree with that interpretation. This historical chapter discusses the ways in which labour was restricted, controlled and debased, indicating variations in patterns and complexities in developments. It also describes the forced labour in Russian prisons under the tsars, the hard labour regimes of the Soviet Gulag, the work extracted from POWs and the impact of the forced nature of the collectivisation of agriculture on the peasantry.

Against this historical backdrop, Chapter 2 moves directly into the case study of the contemporary Russian Federation and focusses on the years after the collapse of the Soviet state up to early 2017. It traces the political dimensions inside the country of naming the problem of human trafficking and getting it recognised in the State Duma, the lower house of the Federal Assembly, as an urgent issue needing attention, debate and policies. Domestic NGOs, women's groups, international actors, some enlightened officers in the Ministry of Internal Affairs (MVD) and a handful of people's deputies in the State Duma fought to make human trafficking a crime. They did not get the specific law on human trafficking that they had been battling for, but President Vladimir Putin did finally in 2003 call upon the Duma to approve amendments to the Criminal Code to include anti-trafficking articles. The chapter explores the difficulties and hurdles of forging human trafficking into a political issue and traces the protracted attempts to get politicians to take it seriously. It captures some of the assessments and feelings expressed by those who battled in anti-trafficking work.

The Russian press has played an important role in the process of educating its readers about the thousands who were trafficked out of the country. Chapter 3 offers a survey of how national newspapers covered stories of human trafficking, exploring the sorts of messages that they delivered about it and the images of the trafficked and traffickers that they constructed. What Russian citizens learnt about human trafficking came from the press, television and films unless they had personal knowledge of it from their own localities and acquaintances. As in all countries, reporting varies across newspapers. Whereas some provided calm and informative reporting, others told considerably more sensational stories, and one in particular asked the age-old Russian question, embedded deep in its political culture, of '*kto vinovat?*' or 'who is to blame?'

What, then, did the public think about human trafficking? Many, it seemed, blamed the women and girls themselves for ending up in prostitution. Three of the ways in which social scientists can find out about the views in society are by conducting opinion polls, running focus groups and doing face-to-face interviews. Working from the assumption that it matters for our understanding of foreign societies that we examine how its citizens perceive issues and evaluate them, I undertook research using all three of these techniques. Chapter 4 presents the results of responses to questions about human trafficking in nationwide public opinion polls conducted in 2007 and 2014 across the Russian landmass, thereby enabling comparisons of views held over time through longitudinal data. It also shows how men and women held similar attitudes on most issues connected with human trafficking with the exceptions of how strongly they blamed trafficked women and girls and of how welcoming they would be towards trafficked returnees. On questions concerning the reasons behind trafficking, on state capacity to tackle it and on recommended policies for returnees, there were no significant differences in responses according to gender.

Moving from the quantitative data gathered in the population surveys, Chapter 5 takes a deeper look at the reactions, views, thought processes, arguments and ideas expressed in focus groups held in 2007 and 2014. Discussion here provides qualitative 'thick descriptions' generated by the interactions of Russian citizens confronting various aspects of human trafficking and unfree labour.[50] Illuminating pictures emerged of what was known and not known about human trafficking and of how participants characterised it. There was evidence of both highly informed contributions and also misconceptions. Each group shaped debate with varying emphases as participants worked through the questions posed and reacted to what others said, thereby developing their own group dynamic, which included some momentum and lively disagreements. The passage of seven years between the first two focus groups and

---

[50] For the classic text on 'thick description', refer to Clifford Geertz, *The Interpretation of Cultures: Selected Essays* (New York: Basic Books, 1973).

the second two shed light on variations over time in the points made, the degree of shock and level of indifference.

How likely were experts in NGOs and in research settings to agree with what members of the public said? Chapter 6 examines the conclusions and recommendations expressed in interviews and in follow-up e-mails between 2004 and 2016 from those most knowledgeable about human trafficking. These specialists were keen for the problem to be tackled and for those who suffered from it to receive adequate assistance and rehabilitation. Whilst they shared these goals, the points that they chose to emphasise or the way that they assessed some aspects of human trafficking varied, such as regarding the scale of outflows or the significance of given policies. Across the world, in all policy areas, specialists highlight different aspects of issues. These discussions underscored the hazards of assuming just one 'Russian view' or of more short-sightedly assuming a 'Russian mindset', as outsiders sometimes do.

From expert opinions on human trafficking, the book moves on to complete its macro-picture by looking at labour migration into and within Russia. Chapter 7 sketches a brief history of recent in-migration from Central Asia for work, noting a prior trend in the Soviet era. It discusses representative press reports on the problems, changing hurdles and challenges that migrants face, and it also draws on information given in press releases from the Russian police. In particular, it considers the significance of different angles that journalists take in their reporting and the nature of the questions they pose. The chapter considers the significance of how the press covers stories and the categorisations of unfree labour that it suggests. Discussion includes how Russians themselves may unwittingly get drawn into unfree labour situations in their own country, be it on farms, in brickworks, in prostitution, in metal work, in begging rings or in forced theft.

Russian legislation on labour migrants at first sight looks complex, largely due to many changes in these laws over recent years and flurries of amendments followed by more amendments to those amendments. Chapter 8 sets out to summarise key legislation and its changes. Without going into too many technicalities, it highlights developments in government policies to provide the necessary context for subsequent discussions. It also includes material on pressures on the state from a public concerned about competition in the labour market. Anti-migrant attitudes and xenophobia are also relevant factors, and the chapter presents selected examples of hostile views and actions, including hate crimes.

Experts in migration play a crucial role in responding to policy and in making recommendations for change. Chapter 9 examines their thoughts expressed in face-to-face interviews and in specialist journals concerning policies on registration, quotas and *patenty* (licences to work) and on tests in Russian language, history and law which now apply to some *gastarbaitery*. As well as discussing assessments of policy direction, this chapter surveys specialist views on illegal migrants, middlemen, management mechanisms, corruption and anxieties about migrants in the Russian population. Evidence shows a committed community of professionals who are keen to improve the lot of migrants arriving in Russia and a readiness to advocate policies for the incomers' smoother integration into localities.

What the public thinks about labour migrants has been especially relevant to changes in government policy due to sometimes negative, even aggressive and violent, reactions to incoming workers, often fuelled by nationalists in different groups and spurred on by some politicians. Russia is indeed not alone in living through years of hostility to foreign migrants. In the second decade of the twenty-first century, the United Kingdom witnessed the anti-immigrant policies of the United Kingdom Independence Party (UKIP), then led by Nigel Farage, which fed into the pro-Brexit vote of 2016 to leave the EU. An increase in reported hate-speech and hate crimes followed it. Across the years, the more extreme British National Party (BNP) has been visible in street marches. Other right-wing parties in Europe share anti-migrant views, such as the Front National in France, the Dutch Party for Freedom, the Freedom Party of Austria, Jobbik in Hungary, the Danish People's Party and the grassroots movement in Germany of 'Patriotic Europeans Against the Islamicisation of the West', known as Pegida, which in January 2015 saw 25,000 demonstrate in Dresden after the attack on the offices of the newspaper Charlie Hebdo in Paris. The growth of Islamic State of Iraq and Syria (ISIS) and associated terrorist attacks elsewhere in the world, such as in Paris in 2014, Tunisia in 2015 and also on board a Russian airliner over Egypt's Sinai desert, in Brussels and Nice in 2016, and London, St Petersburg, Tanta, Alexandria and Paris again in the first four months of 2017, quickly followed by Manchester in May and London once more in June, have added fuel to negative sentiments, as have allegations about the maltreatment of women in Germany by some migrants. Anti-migrant hostility in 2016 was also integral to Donald Trump's campaign to become the Republican candidate for the US presidential race and persisted into his final campaign and into his presidency. Through populist slogans he advocated building a wall between the USA and Mexico and called for an end to Muslims entering the country. Russian citizens are not global outliers when they criticise labour migrants, but their attitudes do constitute one factor that feeds into their politicians' considerations when they formulate and speak about migration policies.

Examination of Russian public opinion on foreign labour migrants in Chapter 10 scrutinises the results of two questions posed in my updated nationwide survey of 2014 which illustrate strong backing for jobs in Russia to be given to Russians only and a tepid welcome for incomers, but with a recognition that arrivals need money and are driven to leave their own countries due to a lack of jobs there. This was the very predicament that Russians themselves faced ten to twenty years earlier when they sought work in other states as a solution to economic problems at home. These results are compared with those of earlier surveys done by others. The chapter also discusses data from two focus groups held in 2014 which provide more vivid 'thick description' of the beliefs and arguments held about migrant labourers and what they mean for Russia and for the migrants themselves away from home. These data reveal more concern about what Russians might lose than for how migrants might suffer, in sharp contrast to the views of specialists on migration. The chapter closes by exploring some critical and positive opinions expressed by migrants themselves cited in other sources.

The concluding chapter takes a wider look at global estimates of unfree labour in some of the worst offending states in the world and raises pressing questions of security, citizenship, rights and ethics.

Unfree Labour in the Russian Past

The three examples of forced labour endured by Elena, Siarkhon and Sergei are contemporary versions of old forms of unfree labour that date back centuries. In the past, despite the existence of far-flung trade routes, the patterns were not as speedily interlinked as they are in the twenty-first century's globalised world with its fast-paced technologies and electronic connections. Although today's forced labour is hardly a new phenomenon, it is located in different socio-economic and international contexts from those of the distant past. It is also set in distinct regional patterns, often with varying local configurations.

Over the centuries, this immense Russian landmass of steppe, mountains, volcanoes, tundra and bog, much of it inhospitable due to climatic factors and northerly position, inevitably saw invasions, migrations and exiles. Massive movements and upheavals have taken place on its soil and these, to varying degrees, have remained deep in historical memory. In 1237 the Mongols crossed the river Volga and dominated the disunited Russian principalities, having already conquered much of Asia. Known as Tatars to Russians, they subjugated the peoples there for more than 200 years. After Muscovy rose to become the dominant principality, there followed wars in different directions. To the west, the state was vulnerable to invasion from Poland-Lithuania and from Sweden, and to the south from Tatar raids. Much later came Napoleon in 1812, the Ottoman empire in 1853 and the Nazis in 1941. To the east, Russia's quest for a warm-water port led to a short and unsuccessful war with Japan from 1904 to 1905. An understanding of Russian politics and society requires that we grasp a geographical imperative of Russian history or of what Tibor Szamuely aptly dubbed 'the threefold tasks of defence, re-conquest and colonization'.[51] Russia has a geopolitical vulnerability that the USA, with its two long sea coasts, a friendly Canada to the north and weaker Latin American states to the south, does not share. So before focussing on the politics of the contemporary migration trends to be discussed, the next chapter provides a short survey of how conquest and colonisation in the Russian past contributed to the shaping of its history of unfree labour patterns.

---

[51] Tibor Szamuely, *The Russian Tradition* (London: Fontana, 1988), p. 36.

1   Unfree Labour in Russian History

Various forms of human bondage, ill-treatment and debasement have prevailed for millennia, whether legal, illegal or 'part-legal', whether in pre-capitalist economic formations or under capitalism, state socialism or military dictatorship and whether in shadow or black economies. Forced labour can be integral to imperialism, war and pillage and can be perpetuated by the state in its use of captives and prisoners. In today's world, illegal patterns of unfree labour may also occur in some states with the collusion of law enforcement organs which should be there to protect citizens and ensure national security. Pictures can be complex and vary according to century, region, country, location, political structures, economic system, type of society, population density, labour scarcity and local issues. Unfree labour and forms of labour exploitation can thus be situated in a variety of political and socio-economic contexts and settings.

What the literature describes as 'slavery' has a global history. Although publications in the West have focussed disproportionately on ancient Greece, the Roman empire and the southern USA, unfree labour has not been restricted to these examples.[1] William D. Phillips has underscored that slavery has 'appeared in nearly every part of the world', has been traced back to 'the earliest civilizations of Mesopotamia and Egypt' and has also been found in 'more recent societies at various levels of development'.[2] There is general agreement that slavery existed in medieval Europe, in Scandinavia, the Caribbean, Latin America, Africa, Asia,

---

[1] David Brion Davis, *The Problem of Slavery in the Age of Emancipation* (New York: Vintage Books, 2015); Paul E. Lovejoy, *Transformation of Slavery: A History of Slavery in Africa*, 3rd edn (Cambridge: Cambridge University Press, 2012); Keith Bradley, *Slavery and Society in Rome* (Cambridge: Cambridge University Press, 1994); Eugene D. Genovese, *Roll Jordan Roll: The World Slaves Made* (New York: Vintage Books, 1974); Eugene D. Genovese, *The Political Economy of Slavery: Studies in the Economy and Society of the Slave South* (New York: Vintage, 1967); and William Lee Miller, *Arguing About Slavery: The Great Battle in the United States Congress* (New York: Alfred A. Knopf, 1996).

[2] William D. Phillips, Jr., *Slavery from Roman Times to the Early Transatlantic Trade* (Manchester: Manchester University Press, 1985), p. 3.

China and Russia, in both rural and urban settings.[3] Slavery has also been evident in Christian and Muslim societies. Slavery can take root in various contexts with different dimensions but which share a common core of 'un-freedom' or 'non-freedom'. Likewise, situations that technically by definition are not 'slavery' but which involve maltreatment, debasement and abuse of dignity across a spectrum may occur too, but fall short of full confinement.

Given that the main focus of this book is on the contemporary Russian Federation, why include one chapter that presents different forms of unfree labour patterns earlier? The purpose is to illustrate how varied in Russian history categories of unfree labour have been. This is because a key task of social science is to generate classifications and typologies and to discuss norms, patterns and values. Historians have been known to rebuke social and political scientists for their a-historicity, for not taking more nuanced approaches to unfree labour and for being unaware of its past complexities. This overview introduces different categories of unfreedom from the Russian past to illustrate its various forms and contours and to show how deep the roots of unfreedom went. The objective is to sketch a wider introductory portrait of Russia given its past and the scale of unfreedom endured. As such, it sets out to highlight the tapestry of coerced labour over time.

This book does not contend, however, that there was an inevitable linear development from slavery and serfdom to unfree labour today, or that forced labour for Russia is 'a way of life' best explained by the existence of a servile culture of subordinates. Neither slavery nor serfdom was a necessary prerequisite for the development of current forms of labour exploitation or for the growth of modern forms of slavery as some scholars would define them. Rather, they were prior categories of unfreedom in a land from which many Russians have since travelled to other lands and found themselves restricted, confined or even enslaved there. They are also antecedents of patterns of exploitation in which both Russians and non-Russians might find themselves on Russian territory, but not their direct causes. Just because Russians 'enslaved' their own in the past, it does not automatically follow that this is a determining independent variable making it inevitable in the present. This book does not

---

[3] Léonie J. Archer, ed., *Slavery and Other Forms of Unfree Labour* (London: Routledge, 1988); Robert Edgar Conrad, *World of Sorrow: The African Slave Trade to Brazil* (Baton Rouge: Louisiana State University Press, 1986); Herbert S. Klein, *African Slavery in Latin America and the Caribbean* (Oxford: Oxford University Press, 1986); Anthony Reid, ed., *Slavery, Bondage and Dependency in South East Asia* (St Lucia: University of Queensland Press, 1983); Eduardo Galeano, *Open Veins of Latin America: Five Centuries of the Pillage of a Continent* (London: Profile Books, 2009).

suggest such grand causality, especially given the global nature of forms of unfree labour and labour exploitation. At most, it acknowledges that Russia and many other countries have endured forced labour in the past too, often harsh.

Russian history, however, has certain distinguishing features. Richard Hellie has underscored that slavery was one of its oldest social institutions and that the number of laws about it was 'staggering'. Russia, moreover, was the only country ever to have had a government department 'devoted solely to the issue'.[4] The state and its laws defined different categories of unfreedom. In all centuries, unfreedom in some shape was one of Russian society's norms, whether in slavery or later serfdom, or in forced labour during penal servitude in *katorga*, or in the forced labour of the Soviet Gulag. Carceral forms of labour, however, are analytically quite distinct from Hellie's eight categories of slavery. Hard labour performed by prisoners is not unique to Russia and is found in other penal systems and during wartime when demanded of POWs. The ways in which prison labour is organised and treated may, however, vary across the political systems in which it is located and depend upon how those in charge in specific locations treat their prisoners. The forced collectivisation of agriculture in the 1930s can also be construed as a form of unfreedom for those who did not want it.

This chapter looks briefly at the 'what' and 'how' of these different categories and unpacks their characteristics, relationships and mechanisms of subordination. It contends that the geographic vastness of the Russian landmass in certain historical contexts has lent itself to the use of unfree labour. Periods in which there were keen attempts to produce more, whether in agriculture or in industry, to develop the economy and to 'modernise', as leaders variously understood that term, have been conducive to the utilisation of unfree labour. This was particularly the case in the drive to push frontiers further and to colonise more land, especially in areas of low population density. Similarly, the need to build an army and a fleet, develop transport links and form distribution networks created demands for labour. A common factor is labour shortage at a time of increased demand for it. In all centuries, it is pertinent to ask what factors and mechanisms facilitate, encourage and perpetuate unfree labour. Another question pertaining to Russia is whether cultural attitudes towards 'the individual' in society played a part.

---

[4] Richard Hellie, 'The peasantry', in Maureen Perrie, ed., *The Cambridge History of Russia: From Early Rus' to 1689*, Vol. I (Cambridge: Cambridge University Press, 2006), pp. 286–297.

Distinguishing Features

A case can be made that the history of unfreedom in Russia is distinctive in key ways. Firstly, eight different categories of 'slave' have been identified, rendering the picture complex and variegated. Secondly, among these categories, and rare in slave systems, was the possibility of 'self-sale' into 'voluntary' slavery for protection and avoidance of tax. Thirdly, distinct from the Western tradition, upper classes could find themselves in a form of unfreedom through the system of *pomest'e*, or conditional service land-holding. Under this, in the words of Tibor Szamuely, the aristocracy was 'not merely subdued or tamed' but was without privileges or a full right to land ownership and 'left unreservedly at the mercy of the state that had placed it in bondage'. The introduction of the *pomest'e* system meant a 'degradation' of these once 'free serving-men' into the 'Sovereign's slaves' and compulsory military service for the *pomeshchiki*, or landhold-ers, was unavoidable up to 1762 when it was no longer obligatory. In holding land 'by grace', the nobleman was 'tied to the state by bonds of compulsion'.[5] This, however, involved a very different kind of bond from the labour extracted from slaves and serfs or from the harsh demands of *katorga* and forced labour in the Gulag's notorious camps of Kolyma, Vorkuta, Noril'sk and Karaganda, where a sentence often meant death.

Landholding was not about full private ownership at all. In Geroid T. Robinson's terms, the noble landlord was simultaneously 'an hereditary State-servant' and 'an hereditary serf-master'.[6] With these lands came the peasants on them who were thereby enserfed. Thus, fourthly, over the years, a system of serfdom emerged as part of a process 'in the making' due to an 'expanding system of overlordships', what Robinson charac-terises as 'a progressive encroachment upon the economic and personal status of the peasant' and a 'triumph of the servile system'. Even though the tsars were increasing their power over the landlords, the grip of the latter over the peasants was 'even more conspicuous'.[7] As time passed, according to Peter Kolchin, divisions and differentiations amongst peas-ants 'became meaningless and gradually evaporated' as 'slaves slowly merged with serfs'.[8] Moreover, as highlighted by Jerome Blum, the one explicit restriction imposed by tsars on the power of landlords over serfs

---

[5] Szamuely, *The Russian Tradition*, pp. 52–53. Military service was long. In 1793, it was reduced from life to twenty-five years and subsequently in 1834 to twenty years with five in reserve, down in 1855 to twelve years with three in reserve.

[6] Geroid T. Robinson, *Rural Russia Under the Old Regime: A History of the Landlord–Peasant World and a Prologue to the Peasant Revolution of 1917* (New York: Macmillan, 1957), p. 26.

[7] Robinson, *Rural Russia*, pp. 12–25.

[8] Peter Kolchin, *Unfree Labor: American Slavery and Russian Serfdom* (Cambridge, MA: Belknap Press of Harvard University Press, 1987), p. 37.

was that the peasants 'must not suffer ruin'. In short, depending upon the behaviour of the *pomeshchik* and the way in which his or her steward treated serfs in the owner's long absences, as well as the nature of the obligations demanded from serfs, the lives of serfs in Blum's assessment 'varied widely'. Nonetheless, they shared an unfreedom which increased in magnitude over time, but which fell harder on some types of obligations than others.[9] Other factors that affected the *pomeshchik's* behaviour and the serf's response included population density on the land, whether the harvest was good or bad, if there was famine, the wider economic situation and if it was a time of peasant rebellion.[10]

A different category of unfreedom is that of convict labour and of forced labour in exile. Peter the Great introduced *katorga* to facilitate his reforms. He used convict labour to build the new city of St Petersburg and the port of Rogervik on the Baltic coast. Alan Wood has observed that it was 'the collective muscle-power of conscript or convict oarsmen' that propelled the wooden galleys of Peter's new Russian navy.[11] War was a driver, and industrialisation and 'modernisation' depended upon the labour of prisoners or what Andrew Gentes dubs the 'malleable workforce' which could accomplish feats due to its vast numbers at a time when technology was lacking. After Peter, the locus of *katorga* shifted to Siberia, and exile there was the tsarist penal code's harshest form of punishment and could amount to perpetual exile in Siberia (*ssylka na katorgu v Sibir'*).[12] In remote places with harsh climates and low population density, criminals were removed from the society of European Russia as a 'release valve' and deposited on its margins to perform manual labour and work in factories whilst labouring in shackles in what Gentes sees as 'commodifying the human body' and serving as a 'colonizing tool'.[13] Such forced labour enabled economic development even if it did so inefficiently and at huge human cost. It also helped the process of colonisation of a landmass where free settlers were sparse. Those who survived

[9] Jerome Blum, *Lord and Peasant in Russia from the Ninth to the Nineteenth Century* (Princeton, NJ: Princeton University Press, 1961), chs. 6 and 7.

[10] For an economic argument on serfdom involving a high land/labour ratio, see Evsey D. Domar, 'The causes of slavery or serfdom: a hypothesis', *Journal of Economic History*, Vol. 39, No. 1, March 1970, pp. 18–32.

[11] Alan Wood, 'Introduction: Siberia's role in Russian history', in Alan Wood, ed., *The History of Siberia: From Russian Conquest to Revolution* (London: Routledge, 1991), pp. 6–7. He notes that *katergon* is a medieval Greek work for 'galley'. It entered Russian in a nautical sense and moved from meaning galley slave to hard labour in penal servitude.

[12] Alan Wood, 'Russia's "Wild East": exile, vagrancy and crime in nineteenth-century Siberia', in Wood, ed., *History of Siberia*, pp. 117–137; and Andrew A. Gentes, *Exile to Siberia, 1590–1822* (London: Palgrave Macmillan, 2008).

[13] Gentes, *Exile to Siberia*, pp. 4, 16.

and who stayed also populated the land. Petty criminals who were exiled could also be required to build fortifications such as on the Kola peninsula, in Orenburg and in Astrakhan, and to perform manual labour, even if they were not categorised as *katorga*.

The Soviet state, too, harnessed forced labour, which became integral to its grand socialist modernisation plans in construction projects, mining, road works and factories. The vast Gulag with its different categories of camps and settlements used the labour power of its inmates, often to their breaking point, in order to serve the Soviet economy and ideologically in order to redeem them through work, where redemption was deemed possible. Steven Barnes contends that prisoners were ordered hierarchically from the most to the least redeemable through a 'complex matrix of identities'.[14] Political prisoners incarcerated for being 'enemies of the people' under Article 58 of the Criminal Code were in a minority and were considered less reformable than the 'socially friendly common criminal'.[15] Under Stalin around 18 million spent time in the Gulag's camps and prisons. The figures peaked in 1953 when 5.2 million were in camps, colonies and internal exile and, of these, more than 2.4 million were in corrective labour camps and colonies.[16] The harshest were viewed by Alexander Solzhenitsyn as protracted murder camps. On the fate of a prisoner, he commented: 'it wasn't only his body. His soul was crushed too.'[17] Soviet policy to collectivise agriculture ushered in for historians another category of unfree labour, reminiscent in some respects of serfdom before it.

Unpacking the Historical Categories

Slave Holding

What, briefly, are the key characteristics and contours of these identified categories of unfreedom? In the years before Kievan Rus, Norse raiders in the Viking era took Slavic, German and Baltic slaves. Trade routes ran from the Baltic sea to Novgorod and Kiev and then to Constantinople in the Byzantine empire. The raiders also travelled via the river Volga to the Middle East. Slaves were thus an important part of trade.

---

[14] Steven A. Barnes, *Death and Redemption: The Gulag and the Shaping of Soviet Society* (Princeton, NJ: Princeton University Press, 2011), p. 5.

[15] Barnes, *Death and Redemption*, p. 87.

[16] Barnes, *Death and Redemption*, p. 202.

[17] Alexander Solzhenitsyn, *The Gulag Archipelago, 1918–1956*, trans. Thomas P. Whitney (London: Book Club Associates, 1974), p. 504.

Historians agree that most peasants were 'free' when Kievan Rus was formed at the end of the ninth century, but that it was nonetheless a 'slave-holding society' and that 'slaves seem to have been the staple of its foreign commerce'.[18] As Blum has put it, from the Kievan era peasants 'had the right to come and go' as suited them but only so long as they had not indentured themselves. This was the case right into the fifteenth century.[19] Soviet historiography of the ninth to fifteenth centuries, however, according to Aleksandr Zimin, had largely neglected the study of slavery, which remained 'manifestly inadequately illuminated' due to a concentration by academics on the collapse of clans and a focus on the Marxist concept of the construction of feudalism.[20] As Sergei Bakhrushin put it, in the ninth and tenth centuries, 'slave' simply meant 'an object of trade'.[21] Janet Martin has described how slaves were 'consistently exported' along with pelts, wax and honey from Kievan Rus to Byzantium in return for silks, satins, jewellery and glass.[22] Ibn Fadlan has been quoted by Zimin and by Andrei Kovalevskii for his observations that 'special value' was accorded to female slaves, or 'beautiful girls [devushki-krasavitsy] for the merchants'.[23] Zimin added, 'girls for Russia represented a particular importance as a commodity'.[24] George Vernadsky described how certain tribal and clan leaders 'rose above the clan community and formed the foundation of an aristocratic upper class'. This class 'depended on slave labour'. War was the 'primary source' since those 'prisoners who could not redeem themselves were turned into slaves'.[25] In addition, 'the Russes used periodically to collect tribute' and this came 'partly in money, but mostly in kind – slaves, food products and furs'.[26] When slaves were traded in exchange for silk fabrics, spices, wines and fruits, they were conducted 'in their chains'

---

[18] Szamuely, *The Russian Tradition*, p. 17.

[19] Blum, *Lord and Peasant*, p. 106.

[20] Aleksandr A. Zimin, *Kholopy na Rusi: S Drevneishikh Vremen do Kontsa XVv* (Moscow: Nauka, 1973), pp. 5–6. Zimin documents the changing vocabulary. Church literature used the word *cheliad* for slave. Other terms were *semia, ognishche, dom, otrok* and *parobok*. The word *roba* applied initially to women who ploughed, from the verb *robit'*, an ancient term for the later *pakhat'*. *Roba* came to mean female slave.

[21] Zimin, *Kholopy na Rusi*, p. 22; Sergei V. Bakhrushin, 'Nekotorye voprosy istorii Kievskoi Rusi', *Istorik-Marksist'*, No. 3, 1937, p. 171.

[22] Janet Martin, *Medieval Russia, 980–1584* (Cambridge: Cambridge University Press, 1995), p. 63.

[23] Quoted in Zimin, *Kholopy na Rusi*, pp. 22–23, from Andrei P. Kovalevskii, *Kniga Akhmeda Ibn Fadlana o ego Puteshestvii na Volgu v 921–922 gg.* (Khar'kov, 1956), p. 142.

[24] Zimin, *Kholopy na Rusi*, p. 23.

[25] George Vernadsky, *The Origins of Russia* (Oxford: Clarendon Press, 1959). He points out that 'slaves were known, collectively, as *čeliad*', coming from the root of *čel* meaning 'clan', pp. 103–104.

[26] Vernadsky, *The Origins*, p. 192.

along the banks of the river Dnepr.[27] The territory of Rus, however, endured periodic raids from nomads such as the Pechenegs from the southern steppe. They came, as Geoffrey Hosking notes, for 'grain, luxury goods and slaves'.[28] Indeed, Rus was put under huge pressure from the nomadic world, and an advancing 'Mongol onslaught', as Szamuely dubbed it, ravaged Russia 'with a destructive fury', thereby 'erasing' the 'flourishing Kiev civilization'.[29] The power centre of Rus shifted to the north-east. In 1223, the Mongols crossed the Volga and subjugated a vast landmass for more than 200 years, which according to one interpretation thereby cut it off from Europe.[30] Rus amounted to a huge territory of warring principalities.

Tatar and Turkic nomads on the steppe between the Volga and the Dnepr attacked parts of Russia. Their 'devastating raids', according to Szamuely, 'had one object: slaves'. As a result, Russian slaves were transported into the Crimean Khanate.[31] The Mongol empire was bound by the Silk Road, stretching from China to Eastern Europe.[32] The merchant caravans exchanged slaves, fur, fish and caviar from Russia for silks, spices and ceramics. There were, however, regional variations. Charles Halperin has argued that the rich agricultural and urban region of Vladimir-Suzdalian Rus 'suffered much harm' from the Mongols' 'periodic depredations' to curb its power, that there was 'a certain amount of incidental destruction' and that 'slave-raiding forays along the borders were not uncommon'.[33] As well as collecting slaves, the Mongols extracted an annual tribute. On occasion the people would vent their anger at Mongol domination and taxation, as in 1262. Hosking holds that 'townspeople objected particularly to the practice of taking away for slavery or conscription householders who could not or would not pay their dues'.[34]

Quite how much Russia suffered economically is subject to debate. By the end of the fifteenth century, the Golden Horde was no longer united but had fractured into different khanates. Halperin underlines that, even after the Golden Horde had gone, 'the international trade it had nourished continued' and Vladimir-Suzdalian Rus 'enjoyed the greatest

[27] Vernadsky, *The Origins*, p. 286.

[28] Geoffrey Hosking, *Russia and the Russians: A History* (Cambridge, MA: Harvard University Press, 2001), p. 34.

[29] Szamuely, *The Russian Tradition*, p. 32.

[30] For the argument that Russia was not entirely cut off, see Paul Dukes, *A History of Russia 882–1996*, 3rd edn (London: Macmillan, 1998).

[31] Szamuely, *The Russian Tradition*, p. 32.

[32] Martin, *Medieval Russia*, p. 142. See also Reinhard Wittram, *Russia and Europe* (Norwich: Jarrold and Sons Ltd, 1973).

[33] Charles J. Halperin, *Russia and the Golden Horde* (London: I. B. Tauris, 1987), pp. 76–77.

[34] Hosking, *Russia and the Russians*, p. 55.

access to the lucrative oriental market', despite all its prior sufferings.[35] Finally, under Ivan III and Ivan IV (Ivan the Terrible), the dominance of Moscow was finally established and not without its prior co-operation with the Mongol Horde which included collecting its tributes.

Richard Hellie's highly detailed and comprehensive analysis presents a typology of eight kinds of slavery, or *kholopstvo*, in Muscovy: hereditary (*starinnoe*) slavery which referred to those whose parents had been slaves and so they were too; full (*polnoe*) slavery which had three origins of either self-sale, marriage to a slave or upon becoming a steward or housekeeper without the employer stipulating that free status could be kept; registered (*dokladnoe*) slavery which referred to elite slaves, most notably estate managers; debt (*dolgovoe*) slavery for 'defaulters and criminals unable to pay fines'; indentured (*zhiloe*) slavery, a status into which people would sell themselves for a specified term of years and would subsequently be freed; voluntary (*dobrovol'noe*) slavery which occurred when a person had worked for another for three to six months and could then be converted at the employer's request; 'limited service contract slavery' (*kabal'noe*) which could mean a process of self-pawning for one year, then to be converted into self-sale and full slavery 'upon default of repayment' and then 'self-sale for the life of the purchaser'; and finally military captivity.[36] Hellie argues that it is impossible to give accurate percentages within each category at any given time, but that the most important types were hereditary, full and limited contract slavery.

Commenting on early modern Russia, Erika Monahan has underscored that 'slavery was a normal part of Siberian life – an unquestioned fate for some, a survival strategy for destitute others, and an enduring threat for natives and Russians in the borderlands'. The Kalmyk economy, for example, was fed by 'slave raiding' which attacked Russian and Tatar settlements, capturing 'all ranks'.[37] Slaves could be sold to markets in the Ottoman empire or sold back into the Russian empire through ransom.

---

[35] Halperin, *Russia and the Golden Horde*, p. 85. Halperin points out the complexity of the impact made by the Mongols and that some areas escaped much damage 'through political dealings or geography'. Even in areas like Vladimir-Suzdalian Rus, different principalities could do well or be harmed at different times.

[36] For the fullest account, consult Hellie, *Slavery in Russia*, pp. 33–71. See, too, his 'Recent Soviet historiography on medieval and early modern Russian slavery', *Russian Review*, Vol. 35, No. 1, January 1976, pp. 1–32.

[37] Erika Monahan, *The Merchants of Siberia: Trade in Early Modern Eurasia* (Ithaca, NY: Cornell University Press, 2016), p. 154.

From Slavery to Serfdom

In Russian history, slavery and serfdom were technically distinct and described by different words. Slaves were '*kholopy*' and serfs were called '*krepostnye*'. Slaves did not pay taxes and did not have the obligations of a serf, who was tied to his or her owner's land. Many historians, following Hellie, hold that serfdom had its roots in slavery and was still a form of bondage. Hellie dates serfdom back to the 1450s and holds that from 1462 to 1613 the majority of the population 'were peasants who were becoming serfs, perhaps 85 per cent'. The others, 'perhaps 5 to 15 per cent', were slaves.[38] Moreover, enserfment over time 'descended into slave-like conditions', and by the end of the sixteenth century the obligations of peasants had been hugely increased. In Hellie's estimation, the prior norm of enslaving one's own helped to make this possible. This picture contrasts starkly with the process of enslavement in the USA, which was totally reliant on the transportation of black Africans.[39]

A relevant skeletal periodisation here for an overview of slavery and serfdom can be broken down into distinct, if overlapping, periods. There are the years before the ninth century which merit no more comment than given above. Then the ninth to fifteenth centuries were the years from Kievan Rus through Mongol invasion in 1223 to the warring principalities and the emergence of Muscovy as dominant, in which slaves might be captured, traded and used in households. During the years from 1462 to 1613, following Hellie, peasants were 'becoming' serfs, enabled by the huge territorial expansion of Muscovy, serious labour shortages, political centralisation and the growing power of the tsars. Kolchin depicts enserfment as a 'drawn-out process' in stages which spanned 'some three hundred years'.[40] Key laws and decrees over time shaped, restricted and debased the lives of peasants.

If peasants ran away, and hundreds of thousands did, their flight caused consternation among the gentry, especially where population density was low and land plentiful. As the Russian state expanded in size through colonisation and annexation, its extending frontier meant the potential advance of landholding and with it the geographical advance of serfdom.[41] Where the state did not give land to nobles, as in Siberia, serfdom did not

---

[38] Hellie, 'The peasantry', p. 294.

[39] For a comparative history, see Kolchin, *Unfree Labor*.

[40] Kolchin, *Unfree Labor*, p. 2. For variations across the land, see Valerie Kivelson, *Cartographies of Tsardom: The Land and Its Meanings in Seventeenth-Century Russia* (Ithaca, NY: Cornell University Press, 2006).

[41] Once it had become the dominant principality, Muscovy expanded hugely. It grew roughly sevenfold in size from 1462 to 1533, then doubled again before the end of that century. See Kolchin, *Unfree Labor*, p. 4; and Richard Pipes, *Russia Under the Old Regime* (Harmondsworth: Penguin Books, 1982), pp. 79–84.

materialise, and the peasants here were called state peasants and were not 'owned'. These included the 'black ploughers', or *chernososhnye*, who worked on land in the north that was not sought after due to its poor quality, and the single-homesteaders, or *odnodvortsy*, whose ancestors had been servicemen who settled on frontiers in the south and east.[42] Peasants who wished to escape the clutches of serfdom might also try to set themselves up beyond the frontier or become Cossacks. By the mid eighteenth century, more than half of the peasantry were serfs.

Over time, the peasants' prior freedom to move was increasingly curbed. This is often dated by historians as beginning in 1497 when the law code, or *Sudebnik*, permitted them to move away only in the two-week period around St George's Day on 26 November after the harvest, and only if they had given notice and paid an exit charge. In fact, this followed a practice already in place in the expanding monasteries which had become 'thriving economic enterprises' in the countryside. Hellie argues that records indicate that the 'initiation of serfdom' resulted from government grants to the monasteries, which were effectively 'pay-offs for civil-war support' to help limit peasant mobility after the harvest.[43] The *Sudebnik* applied this generally to all serfs. Thereafter from 1581 came forbidden years for movement and the repeal of the right of peasants to move on St George's Day on selected lands, which in 1592 was extended to all peasants.[44] Of significance in this history, Blum argues, was an increase in borrowing and indebtedness from the 1450s and during the sixteenth century, as this was crucial 'in bringing about the ultimate enserfment of the mass of Russia's rural population'.[45]

Coming at questions of slavery from a different angle, Michael Florinsky holds that in the first half of the seventeenth century 'evasion of obligations towards the state was facilitated by the remarkable development' of the 'ancient institution of "voluntary" slavery'. As either temporary (as *zakladnichestvo*) or for life through a contract (as *kabal'noe kholopstvo*), it was notionally based on a loan. Its advantage for the slave was that it meant exemption from taxation and other obligations to the state and brought some protection. Moreover, although it was what Florinsky

---

[42] On state peasants, consult Blum, *Lord and Peasant*, pp. 475–493; Pipes, *Russia Under the Old Regime*, pp. 144–150; and Kolchin, *Unfree Labor*, pp. 26, 39.

[43] Richard Hellie, *Enserfment and Military Change in Muscovy* (Chicago: University of Chicago Press, 1971), pp. 77–92. For full details of the complexities and of disagreements among historians about how mobile the peasants were, consult Blum, *Lord and Peasant*, pp. 109–113.

[44] For details, see Hellie, 'The peasantry', p. 296. Pipes dates the suspension of movement as permanent at 1603. There were 'no more periods left' when the peasant had a right to leave. The state began to keep records of debts owed by peasants to landlords.

[45] Blum, *Lord and Peasant*, p. 116.

sees as a 'drastic method of escape from their difficulties', it attracted 'people from every stratum of society', including the *dvoriane*, or gentry, and 'especially the burghers'. Two consequences were 'a mass desertion of taxpayers' and a depletion of fodder for the army.[46] Various attempts to stop this failed until a law of 1642 prohibited it and required slaves to resume their former status. This was confirmed in a Code, or *Ulozhenie*, of 1649. Florinsky underscores that 'strange as it may appear' this was 'resented'. Many voluntary slaves 'denounced the tsar and his legislation in no uncertain terms'. This was because the status of freeman brought 'inescapable and crushing burdens' whereas dependence upon a lord 'might or might not be unbearable'.[47]

Of huge relevance to peasants' lives were several laws enacted by Peter the Great at the 'climax' of what Robinson depicts as 'a process of regimentation' because it was then that the nobles' service to the state became 'obligatory'. Thereafter, the peasant was 'more than ever a serf' from whom more was extracted in either money or labour or both.[48] In 1700 Peter required all male slaves and serfs whose owners had freed them to report to the army. Those not drafted 'had to return to bondage, though they could choose their master'.[49] Vital, too, was the poll tax of 1724, or soul tax, which meant that male subjects henceforth had to pay tax as individuals, which was more lucrative for the state than when they paid as part of a household. Peasants who were not in the military were to be categorised as either serfs or state peasants. Those who owned the serfs were responsible for collecting tax from them, while officials took it from the state peasants.[50] In 1724 Peter the Great, 'by fiat', also converted all household slaves into household serfs, who now were required to pay taxes too. The formal institution of slavery and its freedom from tax obligations were thereby abolished.[51] As a consequence, the possibility of entering slavery as an institution of 'relief' and some protection was terminated. Peter needed tax revenues for his wars and, by abolishing *kholopstvo*, he acquired tax payers. Simon Dixon holds that slavery 'was not so much abolished as allowed to wither away'. The *kholopy* at that time were 'perhaps 10 per cent of the Muscovite population' and they

[46] Michael T. Florinsky, *Russia: A History and an Interpretation*, Vol. I (New York: Macmillan, 1967), p. 276.
[47] Florinsky, *Russia*, p. 280. See, too, the arguments from R. E. F. Smith in his introduction with R. H. Hilton in *The Enserfment of the Russian Peasantry* (Cambridge: Cambridge University Press, 1968), p. 26.
[48] Robinson, *Rural Russia*, pp. 25–26.
[49] Blum, *Lord and Peasant*, p. 415.
[50] Blum, *Lord and Peasant*, pp. 463–464.
[51] Hellie, 'The peasantry', p. 295.

'disappeared' as landowners managed to satisfy their 'need for labour and prestige' from the growing number of serfs.[52] It was crucial firstly to obtain labour and secondly to manage to hold it.

Subsequently, as Hellie sums up, 'Peter's heirs by the end of the eighteenth century converted the serfs into near-slaves, the property of their lords (owners).'[53] Serfs had to pay for the use of land, and they could make payments called *obrok* in cash and/or in kind, which might include grain, butter or meat. Otherwise they were required to perform labour obligations, known as *barshchina*, which meant working on the lord's land as well as on their own allotment. Paul I set the eventual supposed norm for *barshchina* at three days' work for the noble and three for their own allotment, with Sunday and 'fourteen specified church holidays' free.[54] In fact, harsher *pomeshchiki* demanded additional days from their serfs, so it mattered very much to serfs who the noble was that owned them and what was demanded of them. Those serfs on *obrok*, however, could enjoy more freedom from interference and could leave an estate temporarily, if given permission to do so, in order to trade, work in a factory or take casual jobs. By the 1850s, 28.5 per cent of serfs paid *obrok* and 71.5 per cent were on *barshchina*.[55] Noblemen preferred the latter as the former granted the peasant more freedom. Owners might punish a serf 'who had incurred disfavour by shifting them from *obrok* to *barshchina*'.[56] Landlords could also require other services from their peasants, such as carting duty which was spent transporting goods, often in winter. This could take days or weeks. Blum characterises it as 'one of the most detested' of all payments.[57] In short, the obligations of a serf could be 'a formidable burden'. Moreover, the gentry enjoyed various mechanisms by which they could control serfs.[58]

The gentry also possessed serfs who worked in the household, or *dvor*, and were called *dvorovye liudi*, or household people. Generally, they had once worked on the lord's land but had been converted in status. This meant that they had lost their allotments. Blum observes that they were used 'for every imaginable kind of service' in the house and

---

[52] Dixon qualifies this with the observation that 'native Siberian slaves continued to be traded through the eighteenth century'. See Simon Dixon, *The Modernisation of Russia, 1676–1825* (Cambridge: Cambridge University Press, 1999), pp. 81–82.

[53] Hellie, 'The peasantry', p. 297.

[54] Blum, *Lord and Peasant*, p. 446.

[55] For variations and complexities in patterns of obligation, refer to Kolchin, *Unfree Labour*, p. 65; and to I. D. Koval'chenko, *Russkoe Krepostnoe Krest'ianstvo v Pervoi Polovine XIXv* (Moscow: Izdatel'stvo Moskovskogo Universiteta, 1967).

[56] Blum, *Lord and Peasant*, p. 449.

[57] Blum, *Lord and Peasant*, pp. 453–454.

[58] Blum, *Lord and Peasant*, p. 455.

garden and even as performers for amusement. Their lives have been described as 'often the harshest and most demoralizing' due to 'constant contact' with their owner 'who had complete control over them', and they were more liable than serfs on the land to 'frequent – and sometimes frightful – punishments from captious lords and mistresses'. Blum adds that females were 'often misused by lecherous masters'.[59] Aleksandr Radishchev in his reflections of the countryside also made a similar observation. In describing 'a good and charitable master', Radishchev regretted that 'neither the wives nor the daughters of his peasants were safe from him. Every night his emissaries brought him his chosen victim for that day's sacrifice to dishonour. It was known in the village that he had dishonoured sixty maidens, robbing them of their purity.'[60] Serfdom was not only about *obrok* and *barshchina*, but also included elements of gender politics.

Thus key points for this discussion of servility concern the nature of the relationship between tsars and landlords, on the one hand, and the resultant relationship between lords and peasants, on the other. Under the system of *pomest'e*, conditional service began at the age of fifteen, was lifelong and could end only if there was disability and in old age, depending upon the period. Richard Pipes describes the gentry as 'servitors', not as Szamuely does as the 'Sovereign's slaves'. Most served in the cavalry, reporting in the spring. Norms for the military servitors were ultimately based on the number of households on their land.[61] Robert Crummey notes that being a cavalryman was 'a lifelong and virtually full-time occupation'. Furthermore, he had to provide his own horses, weapons and some food. By the mid sixteenth century, rulers expected all men who owned an estate, whatever its form of tenure, to serve them, and this was usually in the army. Furthermore, they were required to bring along 'other warriors corresponding to the size of their estates', and among the ranks of their armed retinues were slaves. One estimate suggests that as much as one-third of the Muscovite army was composed of slaves.[62]

Of relevance to our contemporary topic of human trafficking is another argument. Richard Pipes notes that richer landlords who needed more people to work on their land might acquire them by taking on from another landlord peasants who were in debt and unable to pay it off. The landlord would settle the debt on their behalf and then install the

[59] Blum, *Lord and Peasant*, p. 457.
[60] Aleksandr N. Radishchev, *A Journey from St Petersburg to Moscow*, trans. Leo Wiener (Cambridge, MA: Harvard University Press, 1958), p. 134.
[61] Pipes, *Russia Under the Old Regime*, p. 96.
[62] See Robert O. Crummey, *The Formation of Muscovy* (London: Longman, 1987), p. 10–11.

peasants on his own land. Pipes points out that 'many peasants were shifted about in this fashion'. The dilemma for the peasants, however, was that they soon became indebted to their new landlord so, although relieved of the first debt, actually they 'gained little'. Pipes observes that 'the redemption of debtors resembled more traffic in human beings than the exercise of the right of free movement'.[63]

As for the daily lives of serfs, there was a lack of legal protection. Robinson comments that, according to the Code of 1649, 'the peasant's interests remained undefined and unprotected' and that the Code 'contributed greatly to the degradation of peasants'.[64] It, moreover, did not permit serfs to denounce the *pomeshchik* except if they were making an accusation of treason. This denial of appeal to the tsar, however, was ignored by many peasants, who did send communal peasant petitions complaining about various maltreatments. In response to their petitions, the peasants were frequently punished with prison, a whipping or even banishment.[65] Historians differ on whether it is apt to call the serf a 'slave'. Some, such as Szamuely, view the 1649 *Ulozhenie* as signifying the 'final legalisation' of a serfdom 'in most respects indistinguishable from classical slavery'. It was a 'servile bondage' or, put differently, the serf was a 'bond slave'. It signified a 'threefold bondage': firstly, to the landlord and his or her descendants; secondly, to the soil; and, thirdly, to the tax-paying estate.[66] Hellie, however, warns against confusing the two concepts. He posits that they were 'different and separate' institutions but that 'serfdom was moulded by the institution of slavery'.[67] Pipes, too, distinguishes serfdom from slavery, although he insists that this is not tantamount to the exoneration of serfdom. He views the worst feature of serfdom as not 'the abuse of authority' but rather 'its inherent arbitrariness'.[68] Nonetheless, others, including Florinsky, contend that serfdom 'differed little from slavery'.[69] This is why I prefer the term 'unfree labour' to capture them both.

---

[63] Pipes, *Russia Under the Old Regime*, p. 103. V. O. Kliuchevskii argued that Russian peasants from the thirteenth to fifteenth centuries regularly migrated, moving on when land became exhausted. See Kliuchevskii, *A History of Russia* (London: J. M. Dent, 1911–1913), Vol. I, p. 217. Blum, however, argues that Kliuchevskii 'exaggerates the mobility of the population'. See Blum, *Lord and Peasant*, p. 112.

[64] Robinson, *Rural Russia Under the Old Regime*, p. 20.

[65] Blum observes how Catherine II responded to peasant petitions with a decree that punished them and the composers of the appeal with the knout and banishment to hard labour in Siberia. See Blum, *Lord and Peasant*, p. 28.

[66] Szamuely, *The Russian Tradition*, pp. 55–68.

[67] Hellie, *Slavery in Russia*, p. xvii.

[68] Pipes, *Russia Under the Old Regime*, p. 154.

[69] Florinsky, *Russia: A History*, p. 280.

Because a slave could be bought and sold and 'had no meaningful rights', John Westwood casts the serf as 'property' and as 'virtually a slave'. Nonetheless, the gentry might rarely, for moral or economic reasons, release serfs to freedom.[70] Yet one disincentive for doing this was that a noble's standing, as John Gooding has put it, was 'judged not by the area of land he owned' but rather 'by the number of souls', and that 'one hundred or more male serfs was the sign of someone substantial'. At the other extreme, the punishments that a landowner could inflict included 'beating, chaining, making the guilty stand barefoot in the snow', enrolment in the army, banishment to another estate and, in extreme cases, to Siberia.[71] Pipes, however, warns against generalising from the worst cases of punishment or from examples of the very worst behaviour from landholders to the entire picture.[72]

Punishments, however, could backfire. Steven Hoch has illuminated how some punishments were indeed counter-productive if they stopped a serf from working. These included confinement or making those guilty of a crime wear an iron collar called the *sheinaia rogatka*, which was finally banned as torture. The job of a bailiff was to maintain social order as well as ensuring that the peasants worked and that the estate ran. In his analysis of the village of Petrovskoe, Hoch found that whipping with a *rozga*, or birch, was the most common form of punishment in more than 90 per cent of cases. More serious ones, around 10 per cent, brought a flogging, the shaving of half of a man's head and beard and demand for a fine. Shaved heads were a mark of shame. Fines were not liked as the entire household was collectively responsible for paying and sometimes livestock were required as well. Theft brought severe punishments too, and it was often easy for peasants to steal from the estate. They also stole from each other. Hoch depicts a life with 'an appalling level of tension, conflict, violence, and punishment' and in which discord in households was common and wife-beating 'usual'.[73] Despite core commonalities, however, there were variations in experiences.

[70] John N. Westwood, *Endurance and Endeavour: Russian History 1812–1986*, 3rd edn (Oxford: Oxford University Press, 1990), p. 13.

[71] John Gooding, *Rulers and Subjects: Government and People in Russia, 1801–1991* (London: Arnold, 1996), pp. 12–13. Most lords had fewer than one hundred and 'about one-third had no more than ten'. The grand noble families who possessed the most serfs and land were the Sheremetevs, Iusupovs, Kurakins, Vorontsovs and Gagarins. Steven L. Hoch estimates that 'no more than 4 percent of all the serf owners possessed 54 percent of serfs'. See his *Serfdom and Social Control: Petrovskoe, a Village in Tambov* (Chicago: University of Chicago Press, 1986), p. 3.

[72] Pipes, *Russia Under the Old Regime*, p. 151. He quotes a British visitor to Russia who concluded the life of the peasant in Russia seemed better than in Ireland.

[73] Hoch, *Serfdom and Social Control*, pp. 160–161.

Another contribution from Hoch is the argument that, despite the legal nature of the relationship between lords and peasants, the state actually played only a 'minor role' in maintaining the institution of serfdom. This was because rural Russia as late as the first half of the nineteenth century was 'not merely undergoverned' but it was 'largely ungoverned'. Hoch's analysis of controls on the behaviour of serfs at 'a microcosmic level', based on study of records of the Gagarin estate in Petrovskoe, led him to conclude that 'microecologies' and 'varying seigneurial policies' managed to create 'noticeable differences even among neighboring settlements'. Furthermore, the relationship between bailiffs and serfs was best characterised by 'conflict and compromise, not supremacy'. As in many peasant societies, and indeed on collective farms of the Soviet 1930s, and also in negative responses to rural Stakhanovism, there were patterns of resistance through 'noncooperation, apathy, mischief making, and negligence'.[74] Some would interpret these behaviours as exhibiting agency against debasement. James C. Scott would dub them 'weapons of the weak'.[75]

At their most rebellious, peasants revolted with agency writ large but were doomed to be defeated. Paul Avrich's classic analysis of uprisings in the seventeenth and eighteenth centuries triggered by Ivan Bolotnikov, Stepan (Stenka) Razin, Kondrati Bulavin and Emelian Pugachev highlights their disparate patterns and the nature of their mass movements and of Cossack leadership. Avrich quotes Alexander Pushkin describing them as 'senseless and merciless'.[76] Their historical details are not directly relevant to this book other than to note the social scientific point that, under certain economic circumstances such as poor harvest and hunger and, in particular, conditions of high tension, daily struggles with particular flash points might generate rebellion.

Some tsars were considerably more repressive than others. Szamuely has referred to 'mass murder as an act of state policy' made most graphic in 1570 when Tsar Ivan IV arrived in Novgorod and had thousands put to death, perpetuating 'grisly savageries'. These included: 'impaling, flaying alive, boiling, roasting on spits, frying in gigantic skillets, evisceration and,

[74] Hoch, Serfdom and Social Control, pp. 1–2, 10. Hoch describes how the bailiffs had to regulate male behaviour without undermining their 'patriarchal authority' and how the 'serf functionaries' as drivers and overseers of the serfs were often themselves caught between the bailiffs and the serfs. If they overlooked a peasant infraction they could be punished. The bailiff wanted 'work obligations' performed, and the serfs were not always enthusiastic to do so, leaving the overseer 'in a wretched position' between them. See Hoch, Serfdom and Social Control, p. 174.

[75] James C. Scott, Weapons of the Weak: Everyday Forms of Peasant Resistance (New Haven, CT: Yale University Press, 1985); and his Domination and the Arts of Resistance: Hidden Transcripts (New Haven, CT: Yale University Press, 1990).

[76] Paul Avrich, Russian Rebels: 1600–1800 (New York: W. W. Norton, 1976).

most mercifully, drowning'.[77] This was not slavery, however, but condemnation to torture and death, or 'state torture'. Isabel de Madariaga has also discussed the 'capriciousness and cruelty' of Ivan's rule, the despotism of his *Oprichnina* and the 'sadism' unleashed on the governing elite which spread 'in widening circles throughout the country in an orgy of debauchery'.[78] Medieval Western Europe suffered brutalities too, and Russia was not alone in meting out cruelties.[79] The tsarist system of autocratic rule, however, readily enabled such abuses should a tsar wish to commit them.

Serfdom was finally ended after four long centuries by the reforming Tsar Alexander II with the 1861 Emancipation Edict. By then there were sufficiently widespread reservations about the institution, and the percentage of serfs had, in any case, declined to 37.7 per cent of the population. Defeat in the Crimean War in 1856 prompted more critical scrutiny of serfdom and its appropriateness for Russia. According to the Edict, the serfs became 'legal' persons and were permitted to own property and to choose whom to marry without needing permission. For two more years, however, the current arrangement would remain in place. Former obligations to the lord continued in a transition period, and only in the future would the lord lose authority. If a lord agreed to sell land, the peasants were responsible over forty-nine years for redemption payments for their allocated plot at an estimated 80 per cent of its assessed value. In fact, the landholders kept the best pasture and woodland for themselves. There also remained some restrictions on the movement of peasants. Angered at having to pay for what they considered 'their' land by right, and struggling anyway to meet the payments on top of taxes, the former serfs remained in many ways disadvantaged. Mechanisms which subordinated them persisted in new shapes. The peasants blamed the landholders for a bad deal and believed that the outcome was not the one the tsar had advocated. In the countryside, rumours abounded and peasants expressed their outrage in the agency of disturbances. One argument holds that they were worse off after emancipation.[80]

---

[77] Szamuely, *The Russian Tradition*, p. 44. Virginia Cowles gives the example of Ivan the Terrible nailing the French ambassador's hat to his head because he had annoyed him. See Virginia Cowles, *The Romanovs* (Harmondsworth: Penguin, 1974).

[78] Isabel de Madariaga, *Ivan the Terrible: First Tsar of Russia* (New Haven, CT: Yale University Press, 2005).

[79] See Warren C. Brown, *Violence in Medieval Europe* (Harlow: Longman, 2011); Richard W. Kaeuper, ed., *Violence in Medieval Society* (Woodbridge: Boydell Press, 2000).

[80] For details, consult Pipes, *Russia Under the Old Regime*, pp. 162–170; Gooding, *Rulers and Subjects*, pp. 3–64; Boris Mironov, 'The Russian peasant commune after the reforms of the 1860s', in Ben Eklof and Stephen P. Frank, eds., *The World of the Russian Peasant: Post-Emancipation Culture and Society* (Boston: Unwin Hyman, 1990), pp. 7–43. Also relevant was the fact that the land did not go to the peasant as an individual but to the commune, whose existence persisted.

Penal Servitude

The third category here for discussion is that of penal servitude in imperial Russia and then in the USSR. In 1696 Peter the Great required prisoners on the Don to help to construct Russia's fleet for his Azov campaign against the Ottomans, thereby introducing *katorga*. Convict workers, known as *katorzhnye* or *katorzhane*, worked in European Russia in Petersburg, along the Baltic and in Orenburg and Astrakhan. Not until after 1767 were they sent to toil in Siberia and the Far East, a vast expanse of land that became associated with forced labour in exile.[81] Convict labour sent to Siberia, the North and the Far East mined gold, silver and lead, and worked in ironworks, distilleries and linen mills and in the Okhotsk and Irkutsk salt works. One estimate suggests that, between 1823 and 1860, 44,904 men and 7,467 women were in *katorga* in Siberian exile.[82] Gentes has remarked upon the relationship between increased output and labour demand. Looking at the Nerchinsk mining district, he observed that as 'production increased rapidly' this 'in turn stimulated the demand for large numbers of penal labourers'.[83] As the mines became less productive, however, and as the numbers of convicts swelled after the Polish insurrection, many prisoners were relocated to the Kara valley and to Sakhalin island. Conditions were extremely harsh. On a visit there in 1890, Anton Chekhov witnessed the exhaustion suffered by prisoners in their journey to Sakhalin. He described how they laboured in irons with their chains clinking as they dragged a load. Chekhov also wrote of the epidemics, traumatic injuries, frostbite, apoplexy, scurvy, typhoid, tuberculosis, pneumonia, conjunctivitis, syphilis and mental illness that the prisoners suffered. Dramatically, he also reported that 'many were drowned, frozen to death, crushed by trees; one was torn to bits by a bear'.[84]

When, in 1885, the American George Kennan travelled into Siberia, he encountered a marching party of 360 men, women and children setting out from a forwarding prison in Tiumen. He observed 'a faint jingle of chains as some of the men, tired of standing, changed their positions or threw themselves to the ground'. He commented upon the 'hard, unsympathetic face' of the officer in charge and the way in which

---

[81] For fuller details, consult Andrew Gentes, '*Katorga*: penal labour and tsarist Siberia', *Australian Slavonic and East European Studies*, Vol. 18, Nos. 1–2, 2004, pp. 41–61.

[82] Sergei Maksimov, *Sibir' i Katorga*, Vol. II (St Petersburg: Transhelia, 1871), p. 320.

[83] Gentes, '*Katorga*', p. 45.

[84] Anton Chekhov, *The Island: A Journey to Sakhalin*, trans. Luba Terpak and Michael Terpak (New York: Washington Square Press, 1967). Chekhov observed 'a complete lack of medical inspection' and reflected that people 'age and grow senile very early in life' (p. 365).

the exiles 'crossed themselves devoutly'. He described the convict barges that took them to Tomsk, sometimes crowded 'to the point of suffocation' and sometimes just half loaded.[85] On his visits to prisons, he encountered 'inconceivably foul air', 'sickening odors and 'more pitiable human misery'.[86]

Gentes has argued that the Romanovs in particular were 'wedded to a penology of banishment'. Moreover, although political prisoners were among the numbers of *katorzhnye*, up to 1905 they constituted no more than 2 per cent and were 'generally' treated 'much better than other exiles'.[87] A key point, however, is that these areas had minerals to be extracted and a need for factories, but population density was low and so there was insufficient labour power. At times of labour deficit in a context of a drive for industrial development when there is high demand for workers, those punished by incarceration may be mobilised by the state for forced labour. And integral to *katorga* was debasement and abuse. Convicts could suffer corporal punishment with the knout and later the *plet'* (lash) and also have their nostrils slit (even after slitting had been banned, as prohibitions could be ignored). Convicts could have their forehead and cheeks branded with the letters B-O-P in Cyrillic for V-O-R in Latin script meaning 'thief', with 'K' for *katorga* or with 'Б' (B) for *brodiaga*, meaning vagabond. These were mechanisms of brutality which demeaned and effectively tortured in violent patterns of subordination. Fyodor Dostoyevsky vividly described the hours before sleep as a time of 'noise, uproar, laughter, swearing, the clank of chains, smoke and grime, shaven heads, branded faces, ragged clothes, everything defiled and degraded'. Thirty men slept side by side in overcrowded conditions on a wooden platform. He remarked, 'I don't understand now how I lived through ten years in it.'[88]

There were other categories of convict sent into exile which were not deemed the same as *katorga*. 'Exile to labour' (*ssylka na rabotu*), for example, was in fact *katorga* in practice by a different name. Also 'exile to permanent settlement' (*ssylka na vechnoe poselenie*), which might be deemed to be a pardon from *katorga*, still required labour in a mine or factory. Common to all three categories was a loss of rights and any property.

---

[85] George Kennan, *Siberia and the Exile System*, Vol. I (London: James R. Osgood, McIlvaine and Co., 1891), pp. 107–118. He also observed that a priest went into the cages of prisoners on the barge and held a prayer service. He noted 'the deep-voiced chanting of the priest mingling with the high-pitched rattle of chains'.

[86] Kennan, *Siberia*, Vol. I, pp. 302–321.

[87] Gentes, 'Katorga', p. 44.

[88] Fyodor Dostoevsky, *The House of the Dead*, trans. Constance Garnett (Ware: Wordsworth, 2010), p. 10.

None was permitted to return home without permission. Mikhail Speransky attempted to reform the system but only managed in 1822 to reduce *katorga* from life to twenty years.[89] Reform did not yet mean that the state would end its mobilisation of forced labour.

In 1943 the Soviet state again used the term *katorga*, even though it had initially dismissed it as yet one more reactionary practice of unjust tsarism. As before, the *katorga* divisions that were formed within corrective labour camps of the Gulag were made up of the most dangerous criminals, who were put to heavy work in harsh settings. This practice was then further extended into new 'special camps'. Barnes has shown how unpleasant and dehumanising practices were integral to *katorga* and to the special camps. These included putting a number on a convict's clothing, using handcuffs, locking the barracks and isolating political prisoners from criminals. In these camps death rates were higher. There were also corrective labour camps, 'the most direct descendant' of the secret police camp system of the 1920s and early 1930s for those with sentences over three years and corrective colonies for shorter sentences.[90]

Historians such as Hosking have categorised work in the Gulag camps as 'indeed slave labour' and as a form of 'state slavery'. Inmates laboured in logging, in mining, in road and railway construction and in factories. Often the locations were remote out in the Far East. Others were in Siberia, the Urals and Kazakhstan.[91] Towns and cities in harsh locations were born out of the arrival of Gulag inmates. Their labour extracted the natural resources upon which the existence of these areas depended. Vorkuta, for example, grew up in the Arctic and was based on coal. Other settlements developed along the river Ob and owed their origins to oil and gas.

A crucial part in convict labour was played by Dal'stroi, or the Far Eastern Construction Trust, which was set up in 1931. More than 90 per cent of its workers were prisoners, although the figure dropped to 80 per cent at the end of 1930s and 70 per cent in the 1940s. In 1932, the Administration of North East Corrective Labour Camps (USVITL) was set up under Dal'stroi and was known as Sevvostlag. In 1932 Dal'stroi was allocated 16,000 prisoners, yet only 9,928 arrived alive. Prisoners who were sent the long distances out to Kolyma 'travelled like livestock'

---

[89] For fuller discussion of *katorga* and of Speransky's work in Siberia, refer to Gentes, *Exile to Siberia*, pp. 95–193.
[90] Barnes, *Death and Redemption*, pp. 20–21.
[91] Hosking, *Russia and the Russians*, p. 468.

in what they dubbed 'Stolypin cars'.[92] John Stephan describes how they were then 'herded' into transit camps outside Khabarovsk and Vladivostok which were plagued by typhoid, and subsequently packed into the holds of ships in order to sail the 1,700 miles to Nagayevo at the tip of a remote peninsula. He cites the example in 1933 of the *Dzhurma* which became lodged in ice. More than 1,000 prisoners froze to death, and the guards survived by eating them.[93] Thereafter the number of arrivals steadily increased: '27,390 in 1933, 32,304 in 1934, 44,601 in 1935, 62,703 in 1936 and 80,258 in 1937'.[94] They were generally greeted upon disembarking by a form of Soviet triumphalism – supposedly welcoming music from a band. Dal'stroi's headquarters was inland at Magadan. In 1932 it was just a cluster of huts, but by 1936 had grown into a town of 15,000.[95] Forced labour spawned towns and the brutal exploitation of those who worked in them.[96]

By the time of the German invasion of the USSR in June 1941, the prison camps in Siberia, the Far North and Central Asia were, as Harold Willets put it, 'choked with slave labourers'.[97] The Terror of 1937–1938 had produced millions for forced labour. During wartime its victims were 'extensively used' to extract non-ferrous ores in the harsh climates of Kolyma-Indigira, Noril'sk in the Arctic and Karaganda in Central Asia.[98] War also brought new forced labourers in the form of POWs, in what Stephan has called the 'internationalisation' of Kolyma, as Poles, Finns, Estonians, Latvians, Lithuanians, Romanians, Hungarians, Germans, Austrians and Czechs were taken as the Red Army annexed or occupied new territories. Of the 10,000 Poles who came, only 600 survived. They were followed by Japanese POWs. More than 600,000 Japanese

---

[92] Railway carriages for transporting prisoners were called *zak* cars (an abbreviation of *zak-liuchennye*, meaning prisoners). Solzhenitsyn notes that prisoners called them Stolypin cars. Five of the nine compartments were for prisoners and had no external windows. Solzhenitsyn describes slow journeys of more than eight days in crowded conditions where sometimes 'they started to die off': Solzhenitsyn, *Gulag Archipelago*, pp. 491–493.

[93] John J. Stephan, *The Russian Far East: A History* (Stanford: Stanford University Press, 1994), ch. 22.

[94] Stephan, *The Russian Far East*, p. 226.

[95] Stephan, *The Russian Far East*, ch. 22.

[96] Although Dal'stroi had begun its existence under the Labour and Defence Council, in March 1938 it was moved to the People's Commissariat of Internal Affairs, or NKVD. Stephan observes that this enabled the NKVD 'to strengthen its involvement' in the economy of the Far East and its gold, platinum, coal, logging, road and railway construction and fisheries. See Stephan, *The Russian Far East*, p. 228.

[97] Harold T. Willets, 'The USSR at war (1941–1945)', in Archie Brown, Michael Kaser and Gerald S. Smith, eds., *The Cambridge Encyclopedia of Russia and the Former Soviet Union* (Cambridge: Cambridge University Press, 1994), p. 112.

[98] Michael Kaser, 'Planning in wartime and in reconstruction', in Brown et al., eds., *The Cambridge Encyclopedia*, p. 394.

in areas that were occupied by the Red Army and Pacific Fleet were interned inside the USSR, along with 200,000 of the Japanese and Korean inhabitants of south Sakhalin and the Kuriles. About 60 per cent of these were in brigades in the Far East around Khabarovsk, Magadan, Nakhodka and elsewhere. Roughly 50,000 Japanese POWs worked on the building of the Baikal–Amur Mainline (BAM) railway; others mined coal, worked on construction projects or were sent between the Far East and the Black Sea. Between 1947 and 1949, most POWs were repatriated but, between 1945 and 1956, more than 62,000 Japanese POWs met their death in the labour camps.[99]

Personal stories about the impact of forced labour were more likely to be written by imprisoned intellectuals with a flair for prose than by ordinary criminals. Those stories also took time to emerge due to the necessary political silences and personal psychological pain. When they finally appeared, the works of Solzhenitsyn, Evgenia Ginzburg and others revealed the horrific dimensions of debasement which numbed the soul and challenged the body.[100] Changing political context can alter the role of legal forced labour in the economy and modify its shape and contours. Nikita Khrushchev's de-Stalinisation freed many, even though corrective labour as a policy did not cease. In 1957, however, Dal'stroi was 'quietly abolished'.[101] But the policy of using prison labour in harmful conditions deemed dangerous to health did not cease. Such a prisoner was dubbed 'khimik' from the word 'chemistry'. Although the prison term might be reduced because of the nature of the work, health could suffer. This befell those sent to clear up after the leak at the Chernobyl nuclear reactor in 1986.[102]

Collectivisation

A fourth category of unfree labour can be found in the collectivised peasant. The Soviet state championed the forced industrialisation of industry and the collectivisation of agriculture as heroic advances to usher in 'socialism-in-one-country' on the march towards communism.[103]

[99] For fuller details, see Stephan, *The Russian Far East*, pp. 225–255.

[100] Solitary confinement was part of the treatment of political prisoners. See Evgenia Ginzburg, *Into the Whirlwind*, trans. Paul Stevenson and Maiya Harari (London: Harvill Press, 1999).

[101] Stephan, *The Russian Far East*, p. 256. Before closing, Dal'stroi 'lingered on as a ward' of the Ministry of Non-ferrous Metals.

[102] David R. Marples, *The Social Impact of the Chernobyl Disaster* (London: Macmillan, 1988).

[103] For an official interpretation, refer to I. Laptev, *Sovetskoi Krest'ianstvo* (Moscow: Gosudarstvennoe Izdatel'stvo Kolkhoznoi i Sovkhoznoi Literatury, 1939).

Historian Mikhail Vyltsan has commented that 'all-out' collectivisation (*sploshnaia kollektivizatsiia*), which began at the end of 1929, was portrayed as a 'critical moment' (*perelomnyi moment*) in Soviet history, but that the literature was characterised by dogmatism.[104] Nonetheless, some Soviet historians did begin to explore 'serious errors and perversions' as well as 'groundless accusations' that took place.[105] In fact, many critics have viewed collectivisation as analogous to a 'second serfdom' or 'a new serfdom', or as 'genocide', due to the coercion integral to it and its consequences. Sergei Zhuravlev has drawn attention to words written in 1930 on a fence in the village of Shevedevsk in Riazan, which read: 'we fought for freedom, shedding our blood, and now they herd us into real contract slavery' (*kabala*).[106] Zhuravlev remarked that these words of heavy fate and lost freedom were not from the times of the Tatar–Mongol yoke, nor from the songs of the supporters of Stenka Razin, but from the height of mass collectivisation. The sentiment in those Russian words, however, echoed unfreedoms of the past.

Many debates have taken place about the nature and significance of collectivisation, just as they have about aspects of serfdom under the tsars. Selecting here just what is relevant to the topic of unfree labour, the following points can be made. Firstly, collectivisation was a forced process (*nasil'stvennaia kollektivizatsiia*). Although many *bedniaki*, or poor peasants, supported it, large numbers of unwilling peasants were indeed threatened, coerced and 'persuaded' to pool their land and animals and would not necessarily have freely chosen to do so. Jerry Hough and Merle Fainsod cast it as a transformation to destroy the petty bourgeois peasant revolution achieved in 1917.[107] Secondly, integral to collectivisation was a process of de-kulakisation (*raskulachevanie*) effectively a 'key weapon' in a strategy to dispossess the rich peasants known as kulaks by confiscating their land, homes, animals and even clothing, and by expelling large numbers to the north and east crammed on 'death trains', where many

---

[104] Mikhail A. Vyltsan, *Zavershchaiushchii Etap Sozdaniia Kolkhoznogo Stroia* (Moscow: Nauka, 1978), p. 5. See also Mikhail A. Vyltsan, *Sovetskaia Derevnia Nakanune Velikoi Otechestvennoi Voiny* (Moscow: Politizdat, 1970).

[105] Mikhail A. Vyltsan, Viktor P. Danilov, Vladimir V. Kabanov and Iurii A. Moshkov, *Kollektivizatsiia Sel'skogo Khoziaistva v SSSR. Puti, Formy, Dostizheniia: Kratkii Ocherk Istorii* (Moscow: Kolos, 1982), pp. 219–220.

[106] Sergei V. Zhuravlev, 'Dokumental'naia istoriia "chetvertoi Rossiiskoi revoliutsii"', in Lynne Viola, Tracey Macdonald, Sergei Zhuravlev and Andrei Mel'nik, *Riazanskaia Derevnia v 1929–1930gg. Khronika Golovokruzheniia: Dokumenty i Materialy* (Moscow and Toronto: Rosspen, 1998), p. vi. The Russian is: 'My borolis' za svobodu, Prolivaia krov' svoiu, A teper nas zagoniaiut, V nastoiashchu kabalu.'

[107] Jerry Hough and Merle Fainsod, *How the Soviet Union Is Governed* (Cambridge, MA: Harvard University Press, 1982), p. 148.

'died of cold, hunger and disease'.[108] Moshe Lewin depicts a harrowing 'total war' on the kulaks which in places was 'chaotic, brutal and cruel', although treatment varied across districts and regions.[109] The Russian historian Nikolai Ivnitskii was eight years old in 1930 when he witnessed collectivisation. He characterised it as 'the cruel and inhuman policy' to liquidate the kulaks as a class, designed to help solve the grain crisis. He documents 'force and coercion with intimidation and repressions'. In just three and a half months at the beginning of 1930, 140,724 were arrested, followed by a further 283,717 later that year. Many went before the dreaded *troika* to be sentenced.[110] In this early wave, 18,966 were shot, 99,319 imprisoned and 47,084 exiled.[111] Although the goal was to wipe out the kulaks, in fact categorisations varied, peasants could be wrongly classified and there were tensions anyway in the countryside due to the huge poverty of the *bedniaki*, which could stir situations. In the republics of the Caucasus, Central Asia and Buriat Mongolia, the governments were ready to take decisive measures to prevent peasants driving their cattle across state borders and emigrating.[112] In sum, forced movement onto farms or into exile was a key element of collectivisation. The human cost was high, and famine was one of the results. Nikolai Ivnitskii argues that as labour became forced (*prinuditel'nyi*), its productivity was low. Moreover, circumstances were not propitious as peasants slaughtered animals rather than pooling them, had insufficient food to eat as grain was taken from them and developed low morale to the point of suicide. In the famine of 1932–1933 an estimated 7 million died.[113]

Thirdly, a law of 1932 denied collective farmers internal passports. Even though these could be used as a mechanism for controlling urban workers, it meant a total lack of mobility for the peasantry and a lack of equality with urban dwellers.[114] Fourthly, there were analogies with serfdom, and Sheila Fitzpatrick argues that 'serfdom lived on in peasant

---

[108] Moshe Lewin, *Russian Peasants and Soviet Power* (London: George Allen and Unwin, 1968), p. 506.

[109] Lewin, *Russian Peasants and Soviet Power*, pp. 486–487.

[110] The *troika* of three was made up of the local communist party secretary, a special police and a state procurator.

[111] Nikolai A. Ivnitskii, *Sud'ba Raskulachennykh v SSSR* (Moscow: Sobranie, 2004), p. 11.

[112] Nikolai A. Ivnitskii, *Repressivnaia Politika Sovetskoi Vlasti v Derevne, 1928–1933g* (Moscow: Institut Rossiiskoi Istorii RAN, 2000), p. 125.

[113] Nikolai A. Ivnitskii, *Golod 1932–1933 Godov v SSSR* (Moscow: Sobranie, 2009), pp. 241–243.

[114] From 1974, it was possible for those in the countryside to apply for a passport. Previously, under Khrushchev, some who had permission to work or study in towns could also acquire one, as could army conscripts. Despite these opportunities, the mass of rural dwellers stayed attached to the land.

memory'.[115] The state, for example, imposed taxes and procurements and set very low prices for the produce, milk and meat that it bought. Obligations to the state were imposed both on the *kolkhoz* as a unit and on households from their private plots of land. Since regulations specified quotas, and these anyway were not necessarily easy to meet, there were indeed parallels with having to deliver to the serf-owning gentry of earlier centuries. The labour required was therefore reminiscent of the serf's labour obligations of *barshchina* but now with miserly payment. The result was that peasants were kept poor if they had not already starved to death. Fitzpatrick holds that the peasantry 'displayed many of the characteristics of unfree labor' in their approach to their predicament.[116]

A huge literature has discussed issues of resistance to collectivisation and of the 'weapons of the weak' used in daily life on the *kolkhoz*, such as foot-dragging. It has also explored patterns of accommodation, even Stakhanovism, and the wide diversity of responses according to year, place, economy, changing policies and the significance for gender.[117] Variation in local circumstances applied to collectivisation just as it had to serfdom. The central point here is that the *kolkhoz* required a pattern of labour into which peasants had been coerced, generally with threat and some violence, and which was a fate hard to evade. Lynne Viola depicts it as 'one of the greatest tragedies of the twentieth century' resulting in 'inexpressible suffering and repression'.[118]

Submissiveness Before Authority?

Given the roles of slavery, serfdom and *katorga* in Russian history, it would be remiss not to refer to a perspective adopted by Daniel Rancour-Laferriere. He sees in Russia a psychological attitude of 'submissiveness before authority' which has been instilled for centuries and

[115] Sheila Fitzpatrick, *Stalin's Peasants: Resistance and Survival in the Russian Village After Collectivization* (Oxford: Oxford University Press, 1994).

[116] Fitzpatrick, *Stalin's Peasants*, p. 129.

[117] A small selection includes: Stephen G. Wheatcroft and Robert W. Davies, 'Agriculture', in Robert W. Davies, Mark Harrison and Stephen G. Wheatcroft, *The Economic Transformation of the Soviet Union, 1913–1945* (Cambridge: Cambridge University Press, 1994), pp. 106–130; Vyltsan, *Zavershchaiushchii Etap*; Vyltsan, *Sovetskaia Derevnia*; Lynne Viola, *Peasant Rebels Under Stalin: Collectivization and the Culture of Peasant Resistance* (New York: Oxford University Press, 1987); David Moon, *The Russian Peasantry 1600–1930: The World Peasants Made* (London: Longman, 1999); Mark B. Tauger, 'Soviet peasants and collectivization, 1930–1939: resistance and adaptation', *Journal of Peasant Studies*, Vol. 31, Nos. 3–4, April–July 2004, pp. 427–456: Mary Buckley, *Mobilizing Soviet Peasants: Heroines and Heroes of Stalin's Fields* (Lanham, MD: Rowman & Littlefield, 2006).

[118] Lynne Viola, 'Predislovie redaktora', in Ivnitskii, *Repressivnaia Politika*, p. 3.

has perpetuated.[119] He notes that the Mongols 'extracted obeisance' and the Orthodox Church held that believers were 'slaves of God' (*rab bozhii*). Folklore also enshrined submissiveness, as in 'keep your head bowed and your heart submissive'.[120] Proverbs, too, contain a masochism of self-destructive proportions, as in 'he offers up the rod to be used against himself'.[121] Rancour-Laferriere argues that suffering was elevated to a superior moral good, which at its most extreme was found in the mass suicides by fire of the Old Believers. He stresses that Russians did not merely suffer but 'have concocted for themselves a veritable cult of suffering'.[122] Amongst the Slavophiles he depicts a servility to foreign peoples and an innate striving to community. The *mir*, or village commune, is above all a collective, and it is the submissiveness of the individual that holds the collective together. This, according to Rancour-Laferriere, carries consequences for psychology and behaviour and is aptly summed up in the much-quoted description of Russians by themselves as a 'long-suffering people' (*terpelivy narod*). He traces how Russian literature is infused with the consequences of suffering and self-denial, as in Pushkin's characterisation of Tat'iana in *Evgenii Onegin*, in Lev Tolstoy's asceticism and in characters created by Fyodor Dostoyevsky and Vasilii Grossman. Rancour-Laferriere cites Dostoyevsky's phrase 'the need to suffer' (*potrebnost' stradaniia*) as encapsulating his point. Similarly, Herzen describes how 'anguish eats away at us' and Vladimir Lenin talked of a 'great servility' (*velikoe rabolepstvo*) before priests, tsars, landowners and capitalists. Rancour-Laferriere also cites Evgenii Evtushenko's references to 'slavish blood' and 'servile patience' (*priterpelost'*) as illustrative of his argument.[123]

How valid is Rancour-Laferriere's case that Russian habits of obedience 'have been the cause, not the result, of political autocracy'? Can one really conclude that peasants were complicit in their own exploitation? It is an uncomfortable conclusion that a cultural submissiveness as a product or result is also a determining independent variable. This book prefers to see it as largely determined and, even if evident in many cultural threads and at worst partially 'shaping', it is not necessarily the dominant driver itself. It might be an element within interactive processes, but not an absolute unable to be modified. To the reader's relief, Rancour-Laferriere acknowledges that not all Russians have this 'servile psychology

---

[119] Daniel Rancour-Laferriere, *The Slave Soul of Russia: Moral Masochism and the Cult of Suffering* (New York: New York University Press, 1995), pp. 5–17.

[120] 'Derzhi golovu uklonnu, a serdtse pokorno.'

[121] 'On sam na sebia palku podaet.'

[122] Rancour-Laferriere, *The Slave Soul of Russia*, p. 5.

[123] Rancour-Laferriere, *The Slave Soul of Russia*, pp. 2, 42, 58, 62.

of subordinates'. It merits mention that Marshall Poe's investigation into the veracity of foreigners' accounts of the tsar as tyrant concludes that the notion of 'natural slavery' was wanting, as 'Muscovites were certainly capable of protestation.' Poe argues that the 'language of mastery and servitude was a habitual part of everyday Muscovite political expression, a means of polite interaction', which foreign observers misunderstood and on it 'imposed an idealised concept of slavery'.[124] Some Russian journalists today, however, evidently see the role of submissiveness as a timely question. In some recent reporting of forced labour inside Russia, the very question of 'why are they submissive?' has occasionally been posed about those trapped in it.

Conclusion

This brief overview of the key characteristics of unfreedoms in Russia's past leaves out many complexities. Some historical debates have been knowingly glossed over or simply given a passing nod. The priority was to highlight different categories of unfree labour which are generally wider than those discussed today in the social science literature. A handle on historical variety is crucial for an understanding of the possible shapes, contours and dimensions of unfree labour. Categories of unfreedom are shaped by complex historical, socio-economic, political, geographic, cultural and personal variables, whose combinations and interactions contribute to what unfree labour looks like. These factors set the parameters for manoeuvre, negotiation and defiance.

For most of the time peasants complied, resisted or redefined their roles as best they could within the prevailing structures of authority which were largely determining. Similarly, those sentenced to *katorga* and to hard labour in the Gulag had demands placed upon them that shaped the boundaries of their existence. Quite what latitude they had for self-definition hung on the precise nature of the work expected, prison rules, how guards treated them in their setting and inter-relations between inmates. The same would apply to POWs worldwide. Collective farmers may have enjoyed more space for self-expression within family units and with close friends, but their lives too were circumscribed by lack of passports, lack of freedom to move, and a precarious existence.

---

[124] Marshall T. Poe, '*A People Born to Slavery': Russia in Early Modern European Ethnography, 1476–1748* (Ithaca, NY: Cornell University Press, 2000), pp. 225–226. Poe reflects that, when the term *kholop* was originally adopted, '"slave" may have connoted, paradoxically, both fealty and dignity rather than simple submission': Poe, '*A People Born to Slavery*', p. 208.

Persuasion and coercion onto farms and de-kulakisation variously took their toll. Nonetheless, mechanisms of adaptation developed.

The nature of the daily exploitation of people today in forced labour, like that of slaves, serfs, prisoners and *kolkhozniki* before them, is shaped by several factors. One crucial variable is how their traffickers, 'owners' and bosses treat them in personal interaction and how they themselves respond. This, in turn, is shaped by whether they are locked up, are fed, or endure threats, violence or rape or if they live elsewhere off-site from their work but perhaps with fake documents but nonetheless earning something, negotiating their realities and sending remittances back home. Demand for their labour is a common factor and often, too, a lack of local labour for that job, particularly in manual labour or in commercialised sex.

2   The Politics of Getting Human Trafficking onto Agendas

Unlike serfdom, which was legal in tsarist Russia, the process of human trafficking in contemporary Russia is a crime. Likewise, holding someone in servitude in unfree labour flouts international law and breaks Russian law, as it did not in pre-Petrine Russia. Taking slaves as booty in war and Mongol raids for plunder took on more lawless characters, abhorrent to the Slavic principalities, and were perhaps closest in style to today's kidnappings. Now, centuries after Kievan Rus, Mongol domination, the rise of Muscovy and tsarist Russia, international conventions ban slavery, human rights declarations champion dignity and security, and the UN protocol on human trafficking sets out to prevent it internationally and to encourage punishment of the traffickers across states. Successes, however, have been limited given the huge scale of the trade in people, although there have indeed been convictions of traffickers, just fewer than ideal. Russia's own anti-trafficking efforts have not prevented human trafficking, and neither have those of other states. Indeed, even adopting anti-trafficking legislation in Russia proved to be a political struggle for its advocates. The object here is to reconstruct the context and dynamics of that struggle from origins to outcomes, highlighting key political steps. This chapter traces the history of what transpired and incorporates how activists themselves assessed what happened.

Waves of Trade in People and Estimates

During the 1990s and early 2000s, the flow of people trafficking out of Russia and the CIS escalated. It predominantly affected women and girls, although men and boys were also among the outflows. In a global context, post-Soviet women became what Donna Hughes dubbed the 'fourth wave' of trafficked women after the first wave of Thais and Filipinos, the second of Dominicans and Colombians and the third of

56

Ghanaians and Nigerians.[1] In the global sex market, Slavic women were especially valued.

Initial estimates of the numbers trafficked out varied hugely and were both unreliable and unverifiable given the 'hidden' nature of the crime. The OSCE conjectured that, in the decade after the USSR imploded, more than half a million came from just the former Soviet Union, with most from Russia. Subsequently, in the early to mid 2000s, the figure of 50,000 trafficked per year from the territory of the CIS was widely cited, with some NGOs estimating that number from Russia alone.[2] Elena Tiuriukanova, then one of Russia's leading academic analysts of labour migration, estimated in 2006 that between 'roughly 35,000 to 57,750' annually came out of Russia.[3] Official statistics from the Prosecutor General's Office of the Russian Federation identified more than 30,000 crimes committed in Russia in the sphere of human trafficking from 2004 to 2009 but, as Russian lawyer Kirill Boychenko observed, these were just 'the tip of the iceberg'.[4]

Much trafficking happened through a process of deception which began in several ways. Most commonly in the 1990s and early 2000s a job seeker might respond to a newspaper advertisement offering highly paid work abroad as a waitress, au pair, dancer, nurse, office worker or labourer, or in escort services. The citizen then contacted a false employment agency where seemingly professional people described wonderful opportunities elsewhere and offered to help pay travel costs, later to be taken out of wages. Sometimes a 'friend' or an acquaintance promised to set a worker up through contacts, instead deceiving them and profiting themselves. As the years passed, workers were increasingly recruited on the Internet.

---

[1] Donna M. Hughes, 'The "Natasha" trade – the transnational shadow market of trafficking in women', *Journal of International Affairs*, Vol. 53, No. 2, Spring 2000, pp. 455–481. Also by her: 'The "Natasha" trade: transnational sex trafficking', *National Institute of Justice Journal*, No. 246, January 2001, pp. 8–15; and 'Trafficking for sexual exploitation: the case of the Russian Federation', Migration Series No. 7 (Geneva: IOM, 2002).

[2] For various estimates, see Aleksandr Danilkin, 'Zhenu otdai diade . . .', *Trud*, 21 March 2006; Andrei Sharov, 'Rabotorgovtsy XXI veka: v Moskve obsudili problemy iuridicheskoi pomoshchi zhertvam torgovli liud'mi,' *Rossiiskaia gazeta*, 29 October 2010; and Oksana Yablokova, 'A step towards fighting sex slavery', *Moscow Times*, 28 January 2004. Yablokova cites one source claiming that 50,000 were trafficked from the CIS 'to the USA alone'.

[3] Elena Tiuriukanova, *Human Trafficking in the Russian Federation: Inventory and Analysis of the Current Situation and Responses* (Moscow: UNICEF, ILO, SIDA, 2006), p. 5.

[4] Kirill Boychenko, 'Prevention of human trafficking in the Russian Federation', paper delivered in 2012 at the Carr Centre for Human Rights, Harvard University, www .youtube.com/watch?v=heo8KIJ_tx8.

The pattern that followed was one of debt-bondage. From the start the trafficked person is saddled with a debt for inflated travel costs, accommodation and food, all of which are difficult to pay back on low wages. The activity is underground, which makes it hard to detect. Many of the trafficked left Russia legally on tourist visas but upon arrival elsewhere had their passport confiscated and found themselves controlled by others, unwillingly enslaved in prostitution, domestic labour or factory or construction work. Others travelled on forged documents provided by traffickers. Generally, not knowing the language of the country in which they found themselves, the trafficked either could not or would not speak out, often fearing law enforcement officials due to low levels of trust in them in their state of origin. Many were reluctant to run to the police for help and may anyway have found themselves locked up by their captors. Women and girls were initially sold into brothels for sums ranging from $5,000 to more than $12,000. If they resisted, they were raped and beaten into submission. Some were sold on to new owners.[5]

The kidnapping and sale of children also occurred. Reports revealed that they were lured from the street, taken from orphanages, refugee camps or their own homes, and even sold by officials in children's homes or by parents. Speaking in 2004, Leonid Chekalin, who was head of Children Are Russia's Future, pointed out that there were 650,000 in children's homes and 'at least 500,000 living on the country's streets'. This meant that minors were ready pickings for predators. He reported that 190 child-trafficking networks had been detected in the early 2000s.[6] Those captured could end up as child prostitutes, be sold to paedophile groups or become incorporated into begging rings. Some analysts commented that more money could be made by trafficking women and minors into prostitution than by dealing in drugs, arguing that the risks were lower. Moreover, drugs and guns were generally sold once, whereas women and girls could be repeatedly traded.

---

[5] See Elena Tiuriukanova, Vera Anishina, Dmitrii Poletaev and Stanislav Shamkov, *Prinuditel'nyi Trud v Sovremennoi Rossii* (Moscow: IOM, 2004); Elena Tiuriukanova and Liudmila Erokhina, eds., *Torgovlia Liud'mi* (Moscow: Izdatel'stvo Academia, 2002); Ol'ga A. Orlova, ed., *Protivodeistvie Torgovle Liud'mi: Trenerskii Portfel'* (Moscow: Sestry, 2004); Liudmila Erokhina and Mariia Buriak, *Torgovlia Zhenshchinami i Det'mi v Tseliakh Seksual'noi Ekspluatatsii v Sotsial'noi i Kriminologicheskoi Perspektive* (Moscow: Profobrazovanie, 2003); Shelley, 'The changing position of women'; Stoecker and Shelley, eds., *Human Traffic*.

[6] No named author, 'Aid group alleges massive child-trafficking in Russia', www.stopvaw .org/26oct2004; and Mary Buckley, 'Children's rights: young and vulnerable', *World Today*, August/September 2008, pp. 16–18.

Political Dimensions

Arguably the issue of human trafficking from the mid 1990s has several political dimensions. Firstly, there is the political activity of domestic pressure groups and NGOs which, before 2003, named the problem, set out to publicise it and attempted to persuade the Russian government to pass anti-trafficking legislation. Secondly, there is the ongoing international dimension of the US government waging a global war against human trafficking and pressing governments in all countries to fight against it. Thirdly, other international and regional actors such as the OSCE, International Organization for Migration (IOM), ILO, United Nations International Children's Emergency Fund (UNICEF), Swedish International Development Agency (SIDA) and HRW regularly publish reports and call for policy development. Fourthly, foreign embassies in Russia fund seminars and research and encourage prevention. Fifthly, there are political developments in the State Duma. These include support for the drafting of an anti-trafficking bill, followed by the Duma's subsequent failure to pass it into law, and finally the amendment of the Criminal Code at the end of 2003, which introduced anti-trafficking articles. Sixthly, there is the politics of the mafia gangs and traffickers in their relations with the trafficked, whom they trick into working for them and exert control over by physical and/or psychological abuse in conditions of unfree labour. This is not strictly a gender politics of male trafficker subjugating female job seeker as both sexes are known to be traffickers. Whilst forced female subordination is part of the picture, those exploiting her may include her own sex. Men, too, are victims of male and female traffickers. For those who contend that the personal is always political, the relationship between trafficker and trafficked is inevitably a political one of influence, control and coercion of an 'other'.[7] Seventhly, the same criterion of personal politics can be applied to the relationship between the client paying for sex and the trafficked woman who does not wish to be placed in this situation, which raises the further question of the political nature of the global sex markets and the culpability of clients. Only in instances when the sex worker willingly concurs would this argument not apply.[8]

Challenging Denials

For a long time, the problem of human trafficking was denied by the Russian government, political parties and many law enforcement officials.

---

[7] For the classic explanation of why the personal is political, see Kate Millet, *Sexual Politics* (London: Granada Publishing, 1969).

[8] Some psychologists question quite how 'willing' this work is likely to be, depending upon wider circumstances and personal history.

Despite the efforts of the Duma's Security Committee in 1997 to discuss all kinds of trafficking, which its members viewed as internationally a 'symbol of Russia's weakness', the issue did not grip the Duma beyond in 1998 amending the Criminal Code to ban sex trafficking in minors by criminal groups.[9] This was enshrined in Article 152. For many politicians, human trafficking otherwise remained what political scientists dub a 'non-issue'. In sharp contrast, worried women's groups, NGOs, academics and a handful of politicians insisted that it was a pressing 'problem' and not to be dismissed as fictive. To publicise it, they put out reports and handbooks describing what human trafficking was and what unfree labour situations entailed.[10] In Geneva, as early as 1994, the IOM had held an important seminar on the 'International response to trafficking in migrants and the safeguarding of migrant rights', which generated materials to be tapped.[11] Similarly, the OSCE in 1999 ran a review conference on 'Trafficking in human beings: implications for the OSCE'.[12] Natalia Khodyreva, a psychologist and organiser of the Institute of Non-Discriminatory Gender Relations in Petersburg, revealed that it was in 1995 when her crisis centre received information about 'the first cases of trafficking in Russian women', followed by information a year later from German women's organisations about trafficked Russians working in German brothels.[13] Despite growing evidence, patterns of official denial in Russia persisted. Some politicians and officials still lacked knowledge about it and others argued that the Criminal Code as it stood was adequate for convicting traffickers, using Article 240 on recruitment into prostitution and Article 241 on the organisation of prostitution.

---

[9] See Shelley and Orttung, 'Russia's efforts', p. 174; and Louise I. Shelley, 'Focus: trafficking in human beings,' *Organized Crime Watch – Russia*, Vol. 1, No. 2, February 1999, p. 2. Shelley refers to 'the sense of alarm' conveyed at a Duma roundtable in October 1997 by the chair of the Duma's Security Committee about 'the seriousness and scope' of trafficking in women and children at a time of 6.5 million unemployed women and 2.5 million minors 'roaming the streets'.

[10] Vsemirnyi Al'ians Protiv Torgovli Zhenshchinami i Tsentr Protiv Nasiliia i Torgovli Liud'mi, *Standartnye Pravozashchitnye Printsipy Obrashcheniia s Litsami, Postradavshimi ot Torgovli Liud'mi* (Perm, 2002); Tsentr Protiv Nasiliia i Torgovli Liud'mi, *Prava Cheloveka i Torgovlia Liud'mi: Spravochnik* (Perm, 2002); Tsentr Protiv Nasiliia i Torgovli Liud'mi, *Predotvrashchenie Torgovli Liud'mi: Opyt Nepravitel'stvennykh Organizatsii* (Perm, 2002): Erokhina and Buriak, *Torgovlia Zhenshchinami i Det'mi*; Krizisnyi Tsentr dlia Zhenshchin, *Protivodeistvie Torgovle Liud'mi: Zakonodatel'stvo i Praktika Sotsial'noi Pomoshchi* (St Petersburg, 2003).

[11] Eleventh IOM Seminar on Migration, 26–28 October 1994.

[12] OSCE, 'Trafficking in human beings: implications for the OSCE', Background Paper, 1999, www.osce.org/odihr/16709.

[13] Natalia Khodyreva, 'Gender violence and cost of socio-psychological rehabilitation and legal assistance: Russian Federation', paper presented at the First World Conference of Women's Shelters, 8–11 September 2008, Edmonton, Canada.

Still others were concerned about the budgetary implications of doing anything at all.

That politicians might deny the existence of a problem is not novel and occurs globally across political systems and issues. 'Problems' need to be politicised before they win the status of 'issues' for the political arena to process them. Sometimes a phenomenon is 'known', such as the slave trade in the 1800s, but not deemed by a sufficient number of politicians to be problematic or to require challenge. During the Gorbachev era, the policy of *glasnost*, meaning 'publicity' or 'openness', facilitated the recognition of official 'non-problems' of the past which Soviet ideology had declared to be the blight of capitalist states only. Slowly, pressing social questions concerning prostitution, drug taking, abortion, infant mortality rates, maternal mortality, bullying in the army, health care and housing problems were named and discussed.[14] In the post-Soviet space, however, some in NGOs made a case that high levels of corruption and the involvement of some officials in domestic prostitution did not facilitate the quick acknowledgment of its existence or the 'labelling' of the problem. The reality that the problem of human trafficking went '*tam*', or 'there', crossing borders out of Russia, led some politicians to declare that it was not a domestic problem but rather a 'foreign' one and therefore for other states to tackle, and not Russia's responsibility.

Interviews conducted in Russia reveal different dimensions of this early picture. Tiuriukanova insisted that 'people denied it', referring to '*chinovniki*' or officials. At a time when international organisations and NGOs were naming it, Tiuriukanova witnessed many politicians saying 'what problem?'[15] Khodyreva considered that 'many politicians in the Duma believed that the women were stupid' and felt 'why should we support them?'[16] This was the misogynistic 'stupid woman' reflex reaction. Putting it differently, Tat'iana Kholshchevnikova, administrator of the Duma Legislation Committee, viewed the deputies' coolness about the issue as a simple lack of understanding, or '*neponimanie*'.[17] She named Vladimir Zhirinovskii and Aleksei Mitrofanov of the Liberal Democratic Party (LDPR) as among those not grasping its significance. Most strongly in favour of the legislation, in her view, were Elena Mizulina, Pavel Krasheninnikov, Anatolii Kulikov and Ekaterina Lakhova. A different perception again was held by Dr Juliette Engel, an American doctor who in 1999 set up the MiraMed Institute in Russia, initially to work

---

[14] For elaboration, see Buckley, *Redefining*, pp. 17–139.
[15] Interview with Elena Tiuriukanova in Moscow, September 2004.
[16] Interview with Natalia Khodyreva in St Petersburg, September 2004.
[17] Telephone interview with Tat'iana Kholshchevnikova, March 2005.

with orphans, but she then broadened its focus to include trafficking victims. She revealed her 'amazement at the total ignorance of trafficking in Russia' and reiterated that 'no one believed' that it was taking place, nor grasped 'how significant it was'. Engel added that 'nothing is easy in Russia'.[18] In 2002 MiraMed spawned the Angel Coalition, which it claimed brought together forty-three women's groups and NGOs across the CIS, growing to sixty-one by 2007. Next, in June 2003, MiraMed set up a Moscow Trafficking Victim Assistance Centre which devoted itself to rescue and repatriation, aided in its work by a toll-free hotline.[19]

A related key issue, according to Tiuriukanova, was that for a long time there was insufficient collaboration between the active NGOs and state structures. The NGOs were giving psychological, legal and social help to those who had been trafficked, but state structures were not conversant with the problems, working instead according to the principle that 'there are no statistics – there is no problem'. She believed that they also viewed women's predicaments as less important and as 'private', being more concerned to maintain 'their power and hypocrisy' about sexual exploitation. In Tiuriukanova's opinion, the critics had a disdainful attitude towards social organisations and she believed that some opponents of fresh legislation profited from the sex industry themselves. Bureaucratism, in any case, hindered collaborative projects.[20] Matters were not helped, according to Maria Mokhova of the Moscow crisis centre Sestry (Sisters), by differences in perspectives and opinions across NGOs, particularly over the issue of whether or not prostitution should be legalised or whether it was an 'evil' to be prevented.[21] In addition, although many NGOs were willing to work together, their relationships were also complicated by the fact that they were competitors for Western funding.[22]

---

[18] Interview with Juliette Engel in Moscow, September 2004. Engel's initial goal in Russia was to help children, but once there she saw the gravity of human trafficking and took that on too.

[19] Angel Coalition, 'The Angel Coalition: research, education, training and public information programs for the prevention of sexual trafficking of girls and young women from Russia and the CIS', Moscow.

[20] Interviews with Tiuriukanova in Moscow, April 2004, September 2004 and June 2007; Elena Tiuriukanova, 'Zhenskaia trudovaia migratsiia i torgovlia liud'mi iz Rossii v kontekste mirovogo migratsionnogo rezhima', in Tiuriukanova and Erokhina, eds., *Torgovlia Liud'mi*, p. 163.

[21] Interview with Maria Mokhova in Moscow, September 2004.

[22] Tensions can prevail within NGO communities in any country if views differ. Here different perspectives on sex work, competition for grants, and personal assessments of others were all relevant. One interviewee said: 'everyone has their priorities'. For wider discussion of issues affecting how women's groups operate, see Valerie Sperling, *Organizing Women in Contemporary Russia: Engendering Transition* (Cambridge: Cambridge University Press, 1999), pp. 182–219.

Those in NGOs flagged up resilient prejudices in the social fabric. Deeply embedded social attitudes about the worth of women who went into prostitution deterred many from prioritising the problem. Opinions included: women deserved what happened to them since they must have known prostitution would be required; if they did not know in advance, they were incredibly naïve and foolish and so deserved what they got; they were 'bad' rather than 'good' women, so not deserving of rehabilitation and protection; they were now 'dirty', to be shunned socially by families and communities due to the shame that they brought; they had lowered themselves, so now this was all they were good for anyway. Those who voiced these arguments viewed anti-trafficking work as a low priority.

As Tiuriukanova looked back at these years, she reflected that, 'it all began in 1997 with the Global Survival Network conference in Russia' when 'lots of people were invited to come from the scientific community and other institutions'. What occurred was a 'confrontation'. There were 'the NGOs who had known about human trafficking for a long time and worked with it' and 'officials who said it did not exist'.[23] The US Global Survival Network and the International League for Human Rights had gone to Moscow with the documentary film entitled *Bought and Sold*, which exposed human trafficking out of Russia into prostitution. One aim was to demonstrate that the problem existed and needed action.[24] Engel's MiraMed organised one hundred showings of this film as part of an energetic campaign to educate the public about human trafficking, which included events in orphanages, schools and colleges, targeting at-risk girls and young women.

In the mid to late 1990s social scientists and activists also became aware of the scale of domestic violence inside Russia.[25] Their findings were shared at galvanising conferences. Marina Pisklakova of the Russian Academy of Sciences was someone who recognised that this was a serious 'problem', too long ignored. She was picked by the US Embassy to

---

[23] Interview with Tiuriukanova, September 2004. See Global Survival Network, 'The trafficking of NIS women abroad', International Conference in Moscow, 3–5 November 1997, www.friends-partners.org/partners/stop-traffic/1998/0029.html.

[24] See Gillian Caldwell, Stephen Galster and Nadia Steinzor, *Crime and Servitude: An Exposé of the Traffic in Women for Prostitution from the Newly Independent States* (Washington, DC: Global Survival Network, 1997).

[25] In the late 1990s, the MVD estimated that every day around 36,000 women in Russia were beaten by their husbands or partners. See United Nations Population Fund, 'A house divided: domestic violence in the Russian Federation', 28 November 2007, www.unfpa.org/news/house-divided-domestic-violence-russian-federation. Official and non-official statistics appear to agree that between at least 12,000 and 15,000 women are murdered per year. Consult Janet Elise Johnson, *Gender Violence in Russia* (Bloomington: Indiana University Press, 2009), p. 32; and Natalia Rimashevskaia, ed., *Razorvat' Krug Molchaniia: O Nasilii v Otnoshenii Zhenshchin* (Moscow: URSS, 2005).

attend a conference in 1997 of a Vital Voices Democracy Initiative in Vienna. In 1997 Pisklakova set up a domestic violence hotline in Russia which became Center ANNA, a national centre for the prevention of violence. Pisklakova then launched a national campaign entitled 'There is no excuse for domestic violence'.[26] Mokhova at Sestry also operated a hotline for calls about domestic violence from 1998 and before her, from 1990, Director Natalia Gaidarenko had run a part-time helpline.[27] Mokhova told me that she began to receive calls about human trafficking even though 'our concern is sexual violence. We don't ask specifically about human trafficking. Human trafficking is complex. We don't take on that question, but everyone is our problem and we take on the individual.'[28] Evidently, those operating hotlines, just like Khodyreva's centre in Petersburg, could not avoid coming across the consequences of human trafficking. Mokhova gave me one example of a grandmother who had telephoned because she suspected that her granddaughter had been trafficked. In such cases, Mokhova saw her role as that of co-ordinator with other organisations.

In May 2002 MiraMed and the Angel Coalition launched their first anti-trafficking public education media campaign with press conferences held in six Russian cities, which then gained newspaper and television coverage. The Angel Coalition had strong members in St Petersburg, Nizhnii Novgorod, Yaroslavl, Petrozavodsk, Cheliabinsk and Irkutsk. A network of its safe houses opened first in Kazan, Petrozavodsk, Murmansk and St Petersburg with more planned for 2004 in Irkursk, Cheliabinsk, Yaroslavl and Nizhnii Novgorod.[29] The Angel Coalition also held meetings and training sessions with law enforcement officers. In other education campaigns, an NGO called the Kesher Project, which

---

[26] Alyse Nelson, ed., *Vital Voices: The Power of Women Leading Change Around the World* (San Francisco: John Wiley and Sons, 2012), pp. 17–20. For more on domestic violence, see Lynne Attwood, '"She was asking for it": rape and domestic violence against women', in Buckley, ed., *Post-Soviet Women*, pp. 99–118; and Johnson, *Gender Violence in Russia*.

[27] See Mariia Mokhova, 'Pomoshch' i reabilitatsiia zhertv torgovli liud'mi, nezavisimyi blagotvoritel'nyi tsentr pomoshchi perezhivshim seksual'noe nasilie "Sestry", Rossiia, Moskva', in Orlova, ed., *Protivodeistvie*, pp. 241–244; for information about the work of Natalia Gaidarenko, see Attwood, '"She was asking for it"', pp. 108–111.

[28] Interview with Mokhova, 2004.

[29] The Angel Coalition's website at www.angelcoalition.org/aboutcoalition.html was taken down after its demise. Its annual reports and bulletins, as well as those of the Moscow MiraMed Institute, remain in paper copy, such as *MiraMed Institute*, Winter 2002, pp. 1–4. The Angel Coalition also drew up guidelines for a safe house in Moscow as a 'model' for the entire country, described in Angel Coalition, '"Angel House": a safe house for victims of trafficking in the city of Moscow', 3 April 2004. In 2000 the Angel Coalition wrote an appeal to Putin ('Obrashchenie k Putinu') calling for legislative action. This was confirmed to me by Natalia Khodyreva in St Petersburg in September 2004 and by another source in 2014 off the record.

had initially focussed on domestic violence in the Jewish community, inevitably got drawn into issues surrounding human trafficking too. Its director Svetlana Iakimenko described how they agonised about whether to show another film about trafficking entitled *Lilia Is Forever* to fourteen- to sixteen-year-olds, and eventually did so with the permission of their parents, who viewed it first.[30] During these years some activists received personal threats and negative publicity for their anti-AIDS and anti-trafficking work, a topic about which they are reluctant to talk in much detail. One told me that she had endured two years of unpleasantness which was 'a very hard period' and 'from this I understood the double standard'.[31]

This context of accumulating solid evidence and growing awareness about both domestic violence and human trafficking made it hard for researchers, activists and ultimately politicians to dismiss findings. Repeated exposés in the press also began to question some of the myths circulating about trafficked women and girls. Research data made stark people's vulnerability to traffickers and challenged the opinion that they all wanted to be prostitutes or that they were necessarily 'at fault' themselves. In 1999 Khodyreva and Maria Tsvetkova interviewed 1,200 women and girls between the ages of sixteen and thirty who wished to go to another country either to work or to find a husband. The sample was drawn from St Petersburg, the small town of Vyborg near the Finnish border and also the village of Sosnovo.[32] Among those interviewed, Khodyreva and Tsvetkova found little to differentiate urban and rural women. Most were dazzled by the promises of dollar figures. Among them, 35 per cent hoped to work abroad according to their future specialism (ranging from psychologist, manager in tourism, teacher, social worker to computer programmer), and 17.7 per cent saw themselves in highly paid work as factory directors, financiers or bankers. In this latter grouping, however, there was no correspondence between rather unreal aims and their educational level and current employment. A small proportion, 4.5 per cent were ready to perform unqualified work in the service sector, and 0.4 per cent named religious pursuits. Just 2.2 per cent were 'prepared for anything', which included prostitution, and a lower 1.6 per cent were ready to work in entertainment. Just over 8 per cent were what Khodyreva and Tsvetkova

---

[30] Interview with Svetlana Iakimenko in Moscow, April 2007.
[31] Confidential source, Russia. There was a period when some in the Russian Orthodox Church were also highly critical of anti-AIDS campaigns.
[32] Natalia Khodyreva and Mariia Tsvetkova, 'Rossiianki i iavlenie treffika', *Sotsiologicheskie issledovaniia*, No. 11, 2000, pp. 141–144. The authors emphasise, however, that their findings are based upon those who came willingly to the crisis centre, and therefore the sample is 'self-selected', making the methodology 'limited'.

saw as a group prepared to take risks by working 'around sex services' as dancers and in massage parlours.[33] They found that the sample did not have a fully realistic grasp of the difficulties they could encounter in a foreign country, with 39 per cent foreseeing psychological and language problems but under 1 per cent fearing sexual violence. The education levels of this sample were as follows: 26.3 per cent enjoyed higher or incomplete higher education, 43.7 per cent had specialist secondary education and 30 per cent incomplete secondary education. Most of them – a high 79 per cent – lived with their parents, 7.4 per cent named the income per head as equivalent to more than $125 per month and 57 per cent as less than $35.[34]

Khodyreva and Tsvetkova concluded that the driving motive behind these women's desires for migration was their search for better material well-being and not for work in the sex industry. Alongside an unrealistically rosy picture of working abroad was also the hope of getting married there. One-third of the women interviewed wanted to find a husband and, although they were all looking for work outside Russia, 93 per cent believed that a man should provide for a woman and her children.[35] Another smaller survey of 165 females from different regions of Russia who were planning in 2000 to leave for work elsewhere showed that 84 per cent ruled out working in the sex industry and 7 per cent dismissed it as 'undesirable'. Just 2 per cent replied 'it depends how much it pays'. When asked a different question about what work they would like, 90 per cent opted for 'where the pay is less but sexual services are excluded'. Five per cent were happy with 'where the pay is higher but sexual services are not excluded', and 5 per cent did not say.[36]

Alongside the growing awareness of human trafficking among activists and academics came praise for US initiatives. In one sense this was ironic given that many in Russia criticised the USA for its intervention in Kosovo in 1999 and for its invasion of Iraq in 2003, but, on the topic of trafficking, female activists commended it highly.[37] Khodyreva believed that 'without

---

[33] Khodyreva and Tsvetkova, 'Rossiianki i iavlenie treffika'. See, too, Natalia Khodyreva, 'Sexuality for whom? Paid sex and patriarchy in Russia', in Aleksandar Stulhoger and Theo Sandfort, eds., *Sexuality and Gender in Postcommunist Eastern Europe and Russia* (New York: Haworth Press, 2004), pp. 243–259; and Natalia Khodyreva, *Sovremennye Debaty o Prostitutsii* (St Petersburg: Aleteiia, 2006).

[34] Khodyreva and Tsvetkova, 'Rossiianki i iavlenie treffika', p. 141.

[35] Khodyreva and Tsvetkova, 'Rossiianki i iavlenie treffika', p. 143.

[36] Elena Tiuriukanova, 'Female migration trends and policy recommendations', in Stoecker and Shelley, eds., *Human Traffic and Transnational Crime*, p. 101.

[37] For Russian responses to Kosovo, see Mary Buckley, 'Russian perceptions', in Mary Buckley and Sally Cummings, eds., *Kosovo: Perceptions of War and Its Aftermath* (London: Continuum, 2001), pp. 156–175.

Western influence nothing would have happened'.[38] Kholshchevnikova underscored the fact that 'all international humanitarian organisations helped, such as the IOM, the Association of American Lawyers and UNICEF'. In her words, 'they were important because they had international experience and they were needed since it is a cross-border issue. We could not do it without them.' She praised the US Embassy for helping with seminars and for inviting international experts. In her view, 'they played a positive role and this continues'.[39] Tiuriukanova singled out US prosecutor Thomas Firestone for his helpful suggestions on how to formulate a bill, and also Nancy Petit from the US Embassy for her support. Tiuriukanova added that money from US Agency for International Development (USAID) and International Research and Exchanges Board (IREX) had been most welcome. When John Miller from the State Department came to Russia, she reported that he kept asking, 'when will there be a law?'[40] Pressure from the US government can often backfire, as Russian politicians do not like being what they perceive as 'lectured at' by another state and not treated as an 'equal', particularly by the USA, which at times can be heavy-handed, but in this particular instance many activists welcomed the legal guidance and financial support. Activists lauded global US financial backing as crucial. Germany's Gerhard Schröder also came in for praise as did the Swedish, Swiss and British Embassies for small grants. Reportedly, USAID spent more than $10 million in anti-trafficking work in over thirty countries in 2002.[41]

Reflecting back, Tiuriukanova was convinced that 'the Ministry of Internal Affairs was the best mechanism or motor for change'. This was because 'they knew they needed a law'.[42] In fact, in April 2002, the MVD had created a working group in order to make recommendations about legislation. In a briefing in August, an MVD department head, Evgenii Sadkov, indicated what exactly needed to be clarified in law. He pointed out that 'today there is no definition of human trafficking. There

---

[38] Interview with Natalia Khodyreva in St Petersburg, September 2004.

[39] Telephone interview with Tat'iana Kholshchevnikova, March 2005. For details of the legislative process, see Kholshchevnikova's four articles: 'Sravnitel'naia tablitsa popravok k proektu federal'nogo zakona No 304898-3 "O vnesenii izmenenii i dopolnenii v Ugolovnyi kodeks RF"', in Orlova, ed., *Protivodeistvie*, pp. 176–188; 'Proekt Federal'nogo zakona "O zashchite zhertv torgovli liud'mi: 30 oktiabria 2003 goda"', in Orlova, ed., *Protivodeistvie*, pp. 189–195; 'Proekt Federal'nogo zakona "O protivodeistvii torgovle liud'mi: 18 marta 2003 goda', in Orlova, ed., *Protivodeistvie*, pp. 196–213; and 'Formirovanie zakonodatel'stva Rossiiskoi Federatsii o protivodeistvie torgovle liud'mi', in Orlova, ed., *Protivodeistvie*, pp. 214–220.

[40] Interviews with Tiuriukanova, September 2004 and April 2007.

[41] US State Department, TIP Report 2003, www.state.gov/documents/21555.pdf.

[42] Interview with Elena Tiuriukanova in Moscow, April 2007.

is no distinction between who is the law-breaker and who is the victim.' He called for increased scrutiny of businesses which could be concealing human trafficking, such as travel agencies, firms offering work abroad and marriage bureaux. Sadkov advocated the need to specify norms 'for protecting those who become an object of trade'.[43] His colleague, Viktor Plekhanov, a deputy head in a Directorate concerned with organised crime, illustrated the inadequacy of legislation. He observed that, in the past year, just 24 criminal cases had been opened under Article 152 of the Criminal Code on traffic in minors, 52 under Article 240 and 191 under Article 241. He deduced that since Moscow alone had more than 70,000 prostitutes, the number of legal cases had to be a 'drop in the ocean'. His preference was to legalise prostitution, reasoning that the positive consequences outweighed negative ones, maintaining that it would reduce human trafficking. As further justification, he alleged that 'in the majority of civilised countries this business operates quite legally'.[44] The priority for Mizulina and many others, however, was to criminalise human trafficking. Even those activists who did not necessarily oppose the legalisation of prostitution at some future date viewed fighting now for anti-trafficking legislation as a much higher priority.

Of importance in this context was the impact of legislation in the USA on the process of pushing for change inside Russia. In 2000 the US Congress passed the Victims of Trafficking and Violence Protection Act, which required the State Department to produce annual Trafficking in Persons (TIP) reports on the situation in all states of the world and to document what was being done to combat it.[45] In 2001 and 2002 Russia was categorised as failing to meet minimum standards as it had 'done little' to fight against it. So Russia was put in the lowest category, Tier 3.[46] Following these developments, Mizulina set up a working group in order to produce a draft law on human trafficking. By February 2003, after much hard work which drew on the expertise of a small number of deputies in favour of the legislation and with representation from the Ministries of the Interior, Labour and Justice, the Prosecutor General's Office and NGOs, a draft bill on human trafficking was approved by

---

[43] Roman Ukolov, 'Stanet li drevneishaia professiia legal'noi', *Nezavisimaia gazeta*, 28 August 2002.

[44] Ukolov, 'Stanet li drevneishaia professiia legal'noi'. Critics of this argument in the West, such as Donna Hughes, held that legalised prostitution both encouraged and hid human trafficking.

[45] This was followed by updated Trafficking Victims Protection Reauthorization Acts in 2003, 2005, 2008 and 2013. For details, see www.state.gov/j/tip/laws/.

[46] US State Department, TIP Report 2001, www.state.gov/j/tip/rls/tiprpt/2001/3930.htm; and TIP Report 2002, www.state.gov/j/tip/rls/tiprpt/2002/10682.htm.

the Duma's Legislation Committee. As deputy head of the committee, Mizulina commented that 'it was time that something be done'.[47] Committee members had received legal advice from US officials in this process. It was, however, rumoured that a factor behind the bill's existence was concern that being placed in the lowest tier of the US TIP Report would result in the loss of a large amount of aid. This was not, however, the motive behind the NGOs involved, even if it was one of the pressures on Mizulina.

Despite these efforts and continuing pressures on politicians from the USA, NGOs, women's groups and researchers, the bill did not pass. In fact, at its first reading, only a handful of deputies bothered to attend. Reception in the Duma was extremely poor. The fact that three Duma committees were central to trafficking as a problem – the Legislation Committee, Security Committee and Committee for Family and Children – was not sufficient to guarantee a high profile for the issue. Kholshchevnikova confirmed that 'not more than ten deputies turned up for the first reading of the bill'. She added that 'but this does not mean very much since it is all on internal television and deputies watch it whilst they are busy in their offices'.[48] Reluctant to criticise the Duma, she was nonetheless unable to convince that Duma interest was high and admitted that many deputies criticised the need for a bill to be considered at all.

A key reason why the Duma did not pass it into law was that it was broad in scope, almost an ideal bill, and so it prompted huge budgetary reservations. Quite simply, the cost of implementing it was massive. Witness protection alone, which was part of the initial draft, was expensive, as were preventative measures and rehabilitation. The necessary expenditure required commitments from ministries that they were reluctant to give. There was also the thorny political question of who would co-ordinate all the elements of the bill across institutions. According to Tiuriukanova, the first draft bill had insufficient time anyway in the Duma to make much headway. She recognised in retrospect that to have passed the whole package would have been most unlikely since too much was demanded. The pragmatic advantage of tabling the draft was that it put the topic on the political agenda and enabled others, in her words, 'to prepare the climate' for later legislation. Tiuriukanova depicted this as a necessary 'first step'.[49]

---

[47] Nabi Abdullaev, 'Bill makes human trafficking a crime', *Moscow News*, 19 February 2003.
[48] Telephone interview with Tat'iana Kholshchevnikova, March 2005.
[49] Interview with Tiuriukanova in Moscow, September 2004.

On the one hand, a case can be made that the bill was overambitious. It wanted too much all at once from a cool and unreceptive Duma, where it was politically unwelcome and so highly unlikely to be taken seriously. Politically unviable bills get tossed out. Moreover, at this stage, the president and his administration were not indicating their support for it. Yet on the other hand, in asking for a broad and well-thought-out anti-trafficking package, the bill paved the way for a slimmed-down version later that was more politically acceptable. Despite negative reactions to the bill in the Duma, the State Department's TIP Report in 2003 moved Russia up into Tier 2 on the grounds that, although it did not 'fully comply' with minimum standards for eliminating trafficking, it was 'making significant efforts to do so'. Whether as encouragement of the direction of activities in Russia, or as good diplomacy, or as a genuine reflection of US official hopes only to be thwarted later in the year, it commended that 'central government officials showed a strong increase in political will to recognize and confront their trafficking problem'.[50]

The Russian press in 2003 printed occasional articles on how the anti-trafficking bill was received in the Duma, although it was far from headline news. In *Rossiiskaia gazeta*, Oleg Tatarchenkov reported in August that, so far, the bill had failed to pass into law and scrutiny would be postponed into the autumn. He warned that the past two summer months had shown that those who traded in people (*rabotorgovtsy*) 'did not go away on vacation' and continued to work out new ways of evading law enforcement. He commented that initially some in law enforcement had viewed the anti-trafficking law 'sceptically' since there were already articles in the Criminal Code on kidnapping and on trade in minors. Why add more complicated articles, they reasoned, that were more difficult to enforce when they could work with the ones they already had? The key for its supporters, Tatarchenkov pointed out, was to bring Russian law into line with international law and to avoid being in the US State Department's Tier 3 alongside Afghanistan and Iraq. He then posed the question of whether the law's aim 'was not to protect Russia from people-traders, but from economic sanctions?' Whilst this was indeed one narrative in circulation, Tatarchenkov went on to make a case for the dire need for prison terms for those who enslaved others, citing cases of slavery in the Caucasus and of captives in Chechnia. His message was that the concept of *rabotorgovlia* was needed in the Criminal Code.[51]

[50] US State Department, TIP Report 2003, www.state.gov/j/tip/rls/tiprpt/2003/21277.htm.

[51] Oleg Tatarchenkov, 'Novyi zakonoproekt dolzhen zastavit' ikh govorit", *Rossiiskaia gazeta*, 6 August 2003, p. 6.

Official Attitudes Alter

Slowly, official attitudes in Russia altered. Although the initial reception in the Duma was very poor, as the months passed there was a large change in the view at the apex of the political system. In Kholshchevnikova's words, 'Putin played a most important role. He was in the know. He was predisposed to act.'[52] Off-the-record sources told me that they believed that, by the end of 2003, Putin had become convinced that trafficking was indeed a horrible crime. Moreover, the loud message from Washington to the world was that this was a top priority. In his speech to the UN General Assembly in September 2003, President George W. Bush made special mention of Iraq, Afghanistan, Iran and human trafficking, emphasising that trafficking was a 'special evil'.[53] One source believed that Russian leaders 'did not wish to be seen to be doing nothing about the problem' and to be perceived globally as not promoting anti-trafficking legislation. Putin was apparently concerned about Russia's image in the world. As this source put it: 'we saw a considerable change in the Russian view'.[54] Louise Shelley and Robert Orttung have added that Mizulina, behind the scenes, cannily tried to influence Putin through working closely with Georgii Poltavchenko, who was one of Putin's close friends with a background in the KGB (Komitet Gosudarstvennoi Bezopasnosti, or secret service) and in the Federal Tax Police. He had earlier worked with Putin in St Petersburg and was now the president's personal representative to the Central Federal Okrug. Yaroslavl is situated within this okrug and is the city from which Mizulina was elected, so he was a ready contact for her.[55]

It was only after more than a year of intense pressure and political manoeuvring that Putin was finally moved to support amendments to the Criminal Code which would introduce anti-trafficking articles. Given that the Duma would more or less automatically follow Putin's lead, there was a readiness now to vote in the amendments. This was not the massive legislative package that had come out of the Duma's Legislation Committee ten months earlier, but it did change the law. It certainly did not give the active NGOs and women's groups everything that they had hoped for, but it did make human trafficking a crime. On 27 October 2003, after introducing his favoured amendments to the Duma, Putin gave a speech

---

[52] Telephone interview with Tatiana Kholshchevnikova, March 2005.
[53] See 'Statement by His Excellency Mr George W. Bush, President of the United States of America, address to the United Nations General Assembly, September 23, 2003', www.un.org/webcast/ga/58/statements/usaeng030923.htm. For approval of Bush's anti-trafficking record, see 'Dzhordzh Bush protiv bordelei', *Izvestiia*, 22 May 2006.
[54] Off-the-record source, Russia, September 2004.
[55] Shelley and Orttung, 'Russia's efforts', p. 176.

in the Kremlin to members of the government. He told them that the amendments set 'norms that will entail strict liability' for human traffickers and those who use slave labour. He characterised trafficking as 'part of international organised crime' and 'one of the most serious and pressing problems we face today'. Moreover, it was 'unfortunately a particularly urgent issue for us here in Russia'. He recognised that 'a growing number of Russian citizens, above all women and children, are falling victim to these cynical crimes'. He couched trafficking as 'a form of modern slavery that entails the most brutal and cruel violations of human rights'.[56] A serious gap in the law would finally be filled. On 21 November, these amendments as part of a wide bundle of other amendments were passed in the Duma, the lower House of the Federal Assembly, and on 26 November were approved in the Federation Council, the Upper House. All the amendments were published in full in the press.[57]

A new Article 127.1 declared that *torgovlia liud'mi*, or trafficking in persons, was punishable by a term of up to five years. The same act with regard to two or more persons, or to a minor, committed through false documents, through the use or threat of force, or for the purpose of removing organs or tissues from the victim was punishable by a term of three to ten years. If committed by an organised group, or a threat to lives and health, punishment of eight to fifteen years was possible. The article defined human trafficking in persons as 'the buying–selling of a person or other actions committed for the purpose of such person's exploitation in the form of recruitment, transportation, transfer, harbouring, or receipt of such person'.[58] Article 127.2 on the use of slave labour (*ispol'zovanie rabskogo truda*) referred to 'the use of the labour of any person over whom power similar to the right of ownership is exercised, if such person, for reasons beyond his control, is unable to refuse to perform such labour or services'. This too was punishable by imprisonment up to five years. The term increased from three to ten years if committed with regard to two or more persons, with a minor, by an official, through blackmail, force or threat of force, or through the use of false documents or destruction

---

[56] Embassy of the United States, Moscow, 'Russian president Vladimir Putin: excerpt from the speech at a meeting with members of the Russian government (Moscow, Kremlin, October 27, 2003)', moscow.usembassy.gov/tip-transcript20.html.

[57] Federal'nyi zakon Rossiiskoi Federatsii ot 8 dekabria 2003g N162-F3 'O vnesenii izmenenii i dopolnenii v Ugolovnyi kodeks Rossiiskoi Federatsii. Priniat Gosudartsvennoi Dumoi 21 noiabria 2003. Odobren Sovetom Federatsii 26 noiabria 2003', *Rossiiskaia gazeta*, 16 December 2003, p. 10. The list included the two relevant articles of 'Stat'ia 127.1: Torgovlia liud'mi' and 'Stat'ia 127.2: Ispol'zovania rabskogo truda'.

[58] Federal'nyi zakon Rossiiskoi Federatsii ot 8 dekabria 2003g N 162-F3 'O vnesenii izmenenii i dopolnenii v Ugolovnyi kodeks Rossiiskoi Federatsii' can be accessed in English at www.legislationonline.org/documents/action/popup/id/4188/.

of the victim's documents. If the acts specified in 127.2 resulted in death through negligence or severe damage to health, then imprisonment could range from eight to fifteen years.

Official papers that circulated inside the Duma illustrated just how keen the top of the political system then was to pass legislation. Before the Criminal Code was amended, an 'Explanatory Memorandum' was circulated in the Duma outlining the 'necessity' of amending the Code. The Memorandum informed deputies that trafficking in persons was a 'many-sided and developing phenomenon' which was 'growing and changing' in a setting of 'economic globalisation, labour mobility, technological progress and poverty'. Moreover, 'political corruption' was part of the picture. The Memorandum focussed on the personal humiliation and threat to dignity that resulted from trafficking and argued that it amounted to a denial of constitutional rights. It stressed that there were 'very many examples' of the sale of both sexes for different work which involved deception and often the use of narcotics. It informed deputies that there was a thriving 'market' that was like a 'conveyor' operating throughout Russia's regions. The Memorandum observed that the 'huge market in prostitution is very well known and many firms work in it'. A woman trapped in it 'loses all human rights', and 'many have died'. Moreover, unemployed men inside Russia could be promised work in other regions such as Abkhazia, Chechnia, Georgia and the 'near abroad' and end up sold into slavery. 'Many criminal groups' were forming, specialising in the sale of workers.[59]

Of note was the fact that the document also explicitly linked trafficking to terrorism and to Chechnia.[60] It highlighted the disappearance of 'around a thousand' people involved in counter-terrorism in Chechnia who were held in captivity and then sold into slavery in other countries 'as an ordinary good'. Among them were those sold on for the sale of organs. The message to the Duma was that the lack of anti-trafficking legislation needed to be addressed since it resulted in 'the fast expansion of this type of criminal business'.[61] The joining up of the political issues of terrorism, Chechnia and human trafficking in this way made

[59] 'Poiasnitel'naia zapiska k proektu federal'nogo zakona "O dopolnenii stat'ei 126-1 Ugolovnogo kodeksa Rossiiskoi Federatsii"', circulating memorandum, 2003.

[60] Chechnia is a republic within the Russian Federation.

[61] 'Poiasnitel'naia zapiska k proektu federal'nogo zakona'. During the formulation process, there were many official responses to suggestions from the regions. The Assembly in Krasnoiarsk krai, for example, objected to what it saw as a duplication of Article 152 on trade in minors and recommended that the article be removed. The government responded to this and other details raised in *Ofitsial'nyi Otzyv Pravitel'stva RF*, No. 2.12–17/1166, 12 September 2003.

a stronger case to politicians for vital legislation than mention of trafficking alone would have done, giving it added punch. In short, terrorism and Chechnia added a political legitimacy to the narrative of the urgency of legislation (although this was not a priority linkage made by Russian women's groups, which viewed the issue as meriting action in its own right). The Memorandum also insisted that a lack of legislation contravened international law and the Constitution of the Russian Federation. Finally, it informed deputies that 'many civilized states', such as the USA, Holland, Germany, Poland, Ukraine and Belarus, had anti-trafficking legislation, and therefore Russia should adopt it too.[62] By naming these particular states, there was a subtext which implicitly suggested that Russia should not lag behind Western states in progressive anti-trafficking legislation and should stand alongside its close friends, Belarus and Ukraine. The argument that we must do what 'civilised' or 'normal' states do was often used during the Gorbachev era as a policy legitimator, and has been since. Passing legislation, however, is not synonymous with its implementation and enforcement.

Tiuriukanova took a very pragmatic view of the process. Although Russia still lacked the full-blown anti-trafficking law that its advocates had wanted, it did finally have anti-trafficking articles in the Criminal Code, and these were absolutely 'key' for her. As she viewed it, 'we needed to amend the Criminal Code for something to happen'.[63] Similarly, a district judge whom I interviewed in St Petersburg looked back at 2003 as 'a huge step'. The 'gravity' (*tiazhest'*) of human trafficking, however, in his view was not harsh enough for such a 'terrible crime'. He explained that some investigative techniques, such as phone tapping, could not be used at the degree of *tiazhest'* accorded it. He predicted that human trafficking would be made a graver crime, which indeed it was in 2008. He also expected clarification of the phrase 'for the purpose of exploitation', whose meaning was unclear to law enforcement officers, thereby rendering Article 127.1 tricky to use.[64] That phrase ended up being removed.

International and Domestic Pressures for Implementation and More Legislation

After the Criminal Code had been amended, the process of exerting international pressure on Russia did not stop. In fact, the USA insisted on the need for more Russian legislation. On 27 January, in the building of the

---

[62] 'Poiasnitel'naia zapiska k proektu federal'nogo zakona'.
[63] Interview with Tiuriukanova, September 2004.
[64] Interview with a district judge in Dzerzhinskii raion, St Petersburg, April 2007.

presidential administration in Moscow, the First All-Russian Assembly of Non-Governmental Organisations convened under the aegis of the Commission for Women, the Family and Youth under the President's Plenitentiary Representative to the Central Federal Okrug, Poltavchenko. Plans for this initiative had been announced in the autumn of 2003 and were receiving support from the US Embassy in Moscow. Mizulina was the chair of the organising committee and the declared aim of the January gathering was 'to work out a general strategy for preventive measures against human trafficking and creation of a co-ordinating centre for bringing together the work of NGOs and the organs of state power'.[65] Those invited, as listed by Kholshchevnikova, were members of NGOs, Russian and foreign academics, experts, social figures, politicians in the Duma and Federation Council, representatives of state power in the regions, members of the presidential administration and the government. In short, a broad range of interested parties was on the guest list. The organising committee called for replies and details of presentations by 1 November 2003. There was strong commitment from the Americans and NGOs who wanted to keep up the momentum of anti-trafficking initiatives. The IOM afterwards reported that representatives from more than eighty NGOs who had been working in anti-trafficking over the previous ten years attended from across Russia's regions.[66] It was a big affair.

Poltavchenko began by reading a statement from Putin which expressed confidence in the productiveness of their work and the hope that the gathering 'will unite the efforts of government bodies and non-governmental organisations and will help solve this problem', which he characterised as 'one of the most dangerous threats to civilisation'.[67] Secretary of State Colin Powell of the USA also addressed the Assembly and spoke of the 'strong emotion' he felt about the victims of trafficking in prostitution and slave labour and as child soldiers. Powell said, 'you wanted to cry and reach out and grab these young people who have been so badly exploited by these evil, evil men and women'. He argued that 'the pimp and the client both exploit the victim, and so both must be held accountable'. Furthermore, 'corruption is the knob that opens the

---

[65] Tat'iana Kholshchevnikova, 'Pervaia VseRossiiskaia Assembleia nepravitel'stvennykh organizatsii po problem protivodeistviia torgovle liud'mi', information sheet, 24 October 2003.

[66] IOM, 'Prevention of human trafficking in the Russian Federation', www.no2slavery.ru/eng/facts_and_documents/

[67] Aleksandra Samarina, 'Pauell i Poltavchenko pokonchat s rabotorgovlei', *Nezavisimaia gazeta*, 28 January 2004; Oksana Yablokova, 'A step toward fighting sex slavery', *Moscow Times*, 28 January 2004; and her 'New Russian law is one of country's first steps against human slavery', *St Petersburg Times*, 3 February 2004.

door to trafficking', and 'governments and organizations of civil society must fight corruption' and also ponder problems of 'forced labor' which hitherto had received less attention than deserved. He emphasised that new norms resulted from enforcement and that 'good intention is not enough'. The message to Russia from the US government was clear – enforce the law and bring the traffickers to justice.[68]

Powell used this opportunity to call for more legislation: 'your agenda is clear. You must make this national assembly work to coordinate the activity of NGOs and government. You are taking a genuinely revolutionary step today.' He suggested that, if successful, Russia would provide a model for other countries. What was required next was legislation on witness protection and a national referral system. Powell underscored that the USA 'is with you in spirit, but also in practical terms, working together to stop the trafficking' and 'sharing ideas about legislation' and 'about mobilizing civil society'. Powell pitched all this as 'a new war' to defeat traffickers and 'to rescue, save and rehabilitate the victims'. It was, moreover, comparable to the war against international terrorism in combating an international trade that was depicted as immoral and intolerable. He praised the role that the US Embassy in Moscow had been playing 'in supporting Russia's anti-trafficking efforts', thereby making public for the international community what was already known but without going into the extent of that involvement.[69]

Mizulina expressed her view that official circles had been neglecting the question of rehabilitation because Poltavchenko's office had been excluded from earlier discussions. She talked of the Duma's lack of kindness (*dobro*) in 2003 by failing to pass all of the Legislation Committee's recommendations and put this down to the 'elementary' and 'traditional' problem that interested parties 'could not choose' which institution 'would take on co-ordination of general efforts and control the others'. She went on to recommend that today they should create a new commission under the presidential administration.[70] In her press report on the Assembly, Aleksandra Samarina suggested that not all the departments involved with anti-trafficking were interested in its realisation. She also quoted Senator Liudmila Narusova's exasperation with some in law

[68] US Department of State, 'Remarks at Russian Trafficking in Persons Conference, Secretary Colin L. Powell, January 27, 2004', 2001-2009.state.gov/secretary/former/powell/remarks/28520.htm. I have discussed it in 'Menschenhandel als Politikum: Gesetzgebung und Problembewusstsein in Russland', *Osteuropa*, special edition on 'Mythos Europa – Prostitution, Migration, Frauenhandel', Vol. 56, No. 6, 2006, pp. 195–212.
[69] Cited in Buckley, 'Menschenhandel als Politikum'.
[70] Samarina, 'Pauell i Poltavchenko pokonchat s rabotorgovlei'.

enforcement. Narusova charged that 'any militia man can open a newspaper and read the advertisements with telephone numbers for "leisure" and "services"'. Samarina remarked upon how 'decisive and even optimistic' the representatives of the NGOs were, in contrast with some from law enforcement. She felt that, 'by hook or by crook, they are pushing forward the basic law in its different directions'.[71] Boris Gavrilov, Deputy Head Investigator in the MVD, admitted that police efforts to date in fighting trafficking had been 'far from sufficient'.[72]

Another press report on the Assembly by Oksana Yablokova included an observation made by legal expert Aleksandra Kareva, who worked with the Stop Violence Association which united crisis centres across Russia. Kareva told everyone that, in the past six months, centres had offered counselling to around 200 victims of human trafficking and their relatives. She also shared a story about a young Russian woman who had signed up to study languages in Europe but had instead been taken to Poland to work in forced labour on a farm where she was not paid. She was later discovered by the authorities and deported.[73] The graphic message emerging during the Assembly was that help with rehabilitation was essential and pressing. Many of the earlier challenges persisted as NGOs attempted to underscore the gravity of the reality on the ground.

Efforts around the topic of human trafficking continued after this First Assembly, and in March 2004 a Russian parliamentary delegation, led by Anatolii Kulikov and including Elena Mizulina, went to Washington, DC, accompanied by Nancy Petit and Tom Firestone from the US Embassy. This had been organised by the Law Enforcement Section of the US Embassy and the US Department of Justice. US officials imparted the advantages of an inter-agency approach to human trafficking, including the crucial role of NGOs.[74] While in the USA, the delegation met an Uzbek who had served time for trafficking girls from Petersburg to the USA. *Izvestiia* reported how the Uzbek described the reality of the business and pointed out how hard it was to prosecute. He revealed that his 'roof' (*krysha*), or protection, had been high-placed Uzbek officials. Mizulina's response was that, since the main witness to trafficking was 'the victim herself', it was therefore necessary that 'the witness speak'.[75] Legislation on witness protection was thus vital.

[71] Samarina, 'Pauell i Poltavchenko pokonchat s rabotorgovlei'.
[72] Yablokova, 'New Russian law'.
[73] Yablokova, 'New Russian law'.
[74] Reported in Vital Voices Global Partnership, *Trafficking Alert*, International Edition, April 2004, p. 2.
[75] Reported in Anzhelika Salik, 'Ratifitsirovana konventsiia protiv torgovli liud'mi', *Izvestiia*, 15 April 2004.

Kulikov supported the idea of a witness protection programme, as advocated by the US administration, and he warned that members of victims' families were being threatened and 'were afraid to come out because they are being blackmailed'.[76] Mizulina also made the point that 'this is a very safe business for criminals because the witnesses are so scared to testify and the victim is frightened . . . and sometimes told that her family or children [are] not safe'. She noted that official statistics suggested that 48 per cent of the women who were reported to have been sent abroad were minors.[77] By April 2004 the message from Russia's Interior Ministry was also that 'human trafficking poses a threat to Russia's national security'. The key parts of the world exploiting Russian women and girls were freshly named to be the UAE, Thailand, Turkey, Europe and the USA. Boris Gavrilov reported that data from criminal cases suggested that girls could earn from $300 to $700 a day, and he went on to claim that part of the money earned from sexual services 'is used to finance international terrorism'.[78]

Parts of the package that had been integral to the rejected bill on human trafficking were subsequently adopted in piecemeal fashion. In 2004 a general law on witness protection was finally passed in the Duma on 31 July, approved in the Federation Council on 8 August and signed into law by Putin on 20 August. It provided government protection for crime victims, witnesses and others involved in criminal judicial proceedings, but this was not specifically 'trafficking victim protection legislation'. The US State Department's 2004 Trafficking in Persons Report criticised that 'trafficking victims had no specially defined status under Russian law, nor specific mechanisms to assist or protect them'.[79] However, to show increased commitment to tackling human trafficking in April 2004, the Federation Council ratified the United Nations Protocol to Prevent, Suppress and Punish Trafficking in Persons, Especially Women and Children that it had signed in 2000. This meant that the Russian Federation was now formally bound to adhere to the Protocol.[80]

In 2004 the US State Department split Tier 2 of the annual TIP Report into two categories. There was now a regular Tier 2 and also a new Tier 2 Watch List. This new Watch List included states where the number

---

[76] UN Wire, 'Russian lawmakers propose witness protection to curb sex trade', 16 April 2004. The Wire also noted that Russia had lacked a witness protection programme since the 1970s, when the USSR repealed it.

[77] UN Wire, 'Russian lawmakers'. See, too, Elena B. Mizulina, *Torgovlia Liud'mi i Rabstvo v Rossii: Mezhdunarodno-Pravovoi Aspekt* (Moscow: Iurist', 2006).

[78] Buckley, 'Menschenhandel als Politikum'.

[79] US State Department, TIP Report 2004, www.state.gov/j/tip/rls/tiprpt/2004/33192.htm.

[80] Salik, 'Ratifitsirovana konventsiia protiv torgovli liud'mi'.

of victims was significant or increasing, those which failed to show an increase in their efforts and those which had made commitments to future efforts which needed monitoring. Russia was moved down onto the Watch List 'for lack of progress on victim protection measures'. The Report also commented that 'trafficking-related complicity among Russian officials' was a 'continuing concern'.[81] Russia remained on the Tier 2 Watch List until 2013.

Criticisms, Hopes and Developments After Articles 127.1 and 127.2

Khodyreva's assessment, then, of progress on the ground was somewhat bleak. In interview in 2004, she feared that, even if money were allocated to state structures to help rehabilitate women who returned from being trafficked, the *chinovniki* would not let the structures have the funding. She argued that special cadres were needed to work with the women, but that this 'will not happen'. Khodyreva feared that the prevalence of *otkat*, or corruption, would stop it. She observed that 'other laws do not work, so why should this one?' Whilst it was good to have a change to the Criminal Code, the question was, 'how to realise it?' She feared that there might be just one legal case arising out of sixty instances. The problem was a general one of implementation of the law, and she characterised the legal system as 'feudal'. Moreover, it was hard to prove that all the elements of trafficking were present. She maintained that 'they all hide each other'. The main problem was that 'they do not believe her [the woman] and it is hard to prove'. Khodyreva also felt that 'when there is recognition that she is the victim, then there will be progress'.[82] Above all, effective legislation on witness protection specifically for trafficking victims was needed.

Khodyreva also considered that tackling terrorism was the real priority. As she put it, 'there is here the idea that we all suffer because of terrorism, so why protect her?' In addition, she feared that fighting terrorism might lead to draconian measures and result in it costing women more money to leave for work in other states. A further problem for Khodyreva was how the MVD would proceed. In its search for information, its police might put pressure on the returned women to talk, blame them, then threaten them if they do not give information. Next they put pressure on the crisis centres to give a list of names, which they cannot due to a code of client confidentiality. The militia, she explained, sometimes come and say, 'you are covering up prostitution'. Khodyreva condemns these methods as 'not

[81] US State Department, TIP Report 2004, www.state.gov/j/tip/rls/tiprpt/2004/33192.htm.
[82] Interview with Khodyreva, September 2004.

normal, not civilised', adding that 'they do not know how to work' and 'we are not generally protected'.[83] One senior investigator in the MVD in an interview admitted to me that there were problems of co-ordination and regretted that often 'we only know about it [human trafficking] when they return. Research follows on then.' He underscored that a huge problem for law enforcement was that 'girls are afraid to speak about it'. Moreover, if there were 25,000 applications for visas and 60 per cent of these were for women under forty, 'we cannot vet all of these'.[84]

Some, such as Mizulina, still hoped for a fuller anti-trafficking law at a later date. In November 2004 at a hearing in the Duma on fighting forced labour, she blamed the presidential administration for dragging its feet. She informed the Duma that so far nine human trafficking cases had been opened under Article 127.1, but 'not one' on slave labour under Article 127.2.[85] She noted that data from the ILO indicated that there were a million slaves inside Russia. She proceeded to describe how a criminal group had transported underage girls from Voronezh oblast to Moscow, where they were sold into a brothel. Each girl earned the owners up to 80,000 roubles a month. When the brothel was raided, twenty-two workers were found between the ages of just fifteen and seventeen. The change in the law had enabled the brothel organisers to be threatened with up to fifteen years in jail. She gave other up-to-date examples of human trafficking out of Russia to Malta, China and Belgium and condemned the job agencies involved.[86]

Following on from such evidence, Mizulina argued that 'one article in the Criminal Code for fighting human trafficking is insufficient'. She referred back to the full-blown law that had been formulated in the Legislation Committee which 'everyone supported' but then it 'got stuck' (*zastrial*) in the presidential administration, 'where it has already been lying for a year and a half'. She blamed this on the reluctance to set up a commission to co-ordinate the work of the militia with the NGOs which helped victims.[87] A fuller human trafficking law, however, did not materialise after the introduction of witness protection. Budgetary responsibility and co-ordination across ministries remained sticking points. Mizulina now recommended a clause to punish those using the services of prostitutes which would include imprisonment. She viewed the problem 'not in those who offer sexual services but in those who call for them'.[88] She was against criminalising

[83] Interview with Khodyreva, September 2004.
[84] Interview at Criminal Investigation of the MVD, St Petersburg, April 2007.
[85] Aleksandr Kolesnichenko, 'Klient vsegda vinovat', *Novye izvestiia*, 30 November 2004.
[86] Kolesnichenko, 'Klient vsegda vinovat'.
[87] Kolesnichenko, 'Klient vsegda vinovat'.
[88] Kolesnichenko, 'Klient vsegda vinovat'.

prostitution itself as this would make trafficking victims afraid to go to the militia, and also it was very hard to establish 'whether a girl fell into a brothel willingly or not'.[89] This question of whether or not to legalise prostitution still simmered in sections of wider Russian society, and within the NGO community there were supporters and opponents.[90] Many in society, however, opposed the Swedish model of making the client liable.

In March 2006, a Second All-Russian Assembly of Non-Governmental Organisations took place in Moscow. Representatives from sixty-three NGOs attended, a reduced number from those present at the First Assembly two years earlier.[91] In his press coverage of the gathering, Aleksandr Danilkin adopted the headline: 'Russia has become a leader in human trafficking'. The Assembly declared that the scale of human trafficking within Russia and 'for export' was a threat to state security and the national gene pool. Danilkin reported that Mizulina deplored the fact that, despite anti-trafficking legislation in 2003, followed by the law on witness protection and the ratification of the Convention on Transnational Crime, 'the situation remains alarming, as before'. Mizulina argued that human trafficking had still not been recognised 'as no lesser an evil than terrorism'. Danilkin conveyed a key message from the Assembly to be that until recently the 'shameful word "slavery" was not spoken'.[92]

The wider political context, however, was beginning to see moves to regulate the NGO sector. In 2006, a new law was passed that required NGOs to register and go through various time-consuming procedures. Simultaneously Western sources of funding were criticised. The attempts to exert controls over the NGO community, however, did not mean that anti-trafficking activities ceased, although some organisations suffered from reduced funding and bemoaned time spent on increased paperwork. Space here limits coverage of all relevant collaborations and conferences that took place, but suffice to say that work went on in different ways. Alumnae from Vital Voices pursued anti-trafficking work in the Russian Far East, as did others.[93] The Angel Coalition ran regional training sessions in Petrozavodsk, St Petersburg, Murmansk, Kazan and Yaroslavl, bringing together law enforcement and government representatives.[94]

---

[89] Kolesnichenko, 'Klient vsegda vinovat'.
[90] Juliette Engel, for example, strongly opposed legalisation but Elena Tiuriukanova sympathised that sometimes women had a financial need to turn to prostitution.
[91] IOM, 'Prevention of human trafficking in the Russian Federation'.
[92] Danilkin, 'Zhenu otdai diade . . .'.
[93] Vital Voices, 'Vital Voices alumnae leading anti-trafficking efforts in Russian Far East', Information Bulletin on Vladivostok, 2006.
[94] Angel Coalition, 'Training and legislative lobbying', in 'About the Coalition', www .angelcoalition.org/drupal/en/content/about-coalition, accessed in 2006 and since removed.

The Angel Coalition also worked with Moscow city's Duma on information campaigns in airports and on the metro.[95] It regularly convened conferences, drawing NGOs and researchers together from across the Russian Federation and also from Ukraine, Tajikistan and Sweden, as well as representatives from Russia's Federal Migration Service (FMS), the Office of the Ombudsman, the MVD, Russian press and HRW. Key issues that were discussed included the MVD's work in combating trafficking, ways of identifying victims, co-operation between NGOs and law enforcement, projects across Russia, medical and psychological rehabilitation programmes, hotlines, the safety of shelter staff, a safe house project in Tajikistan, work in children's homes, co-operation with government structures and recommendations for improving anti-trafficking and rehabilitation work.[96]

In February 2008, another important international conference convened in Moscow with more than eighty participants. It looked at the interim results of a project entitled 'Prevention of human trafficking in the Russian Federation', jointly organised by the IOM, the National Anti-Criminal and Anti-Terrorist Foundation and the OSCE. Experts delivered reports on counter-trafficking measures in three pilot regions. The purpose was to come up with advice for policy, prevention, capacity building and the rehabilitation and reintegration of the victims.[97] Aiming to raise more awareness, the IOM selected the popular Russian singer Valeriia to work as a partner in counter-trafficking initiatives.[98] Tiuriukanova and other academics and organisations continued to publish research findings in Russian and English which expanded the literature on unfree labour and exploitation.[99] Importantly, NGOs and social scientists kept on calling for government commitment to shelters for the trafficked who managed to return and for victim support and rehabilitation. It remained the case that

---

[95] MiraMed Institute, 'Annual program report', 1 December 2006.

[96] Angel Coalition, 'International conference: developing a multifaceted approach to repatriation and reintegration of human trafficking victims', 27 February–1 March 2007, Moscow.

[97] IOM Moscow Times, Issue 10, March 2008, p. 10. For a brief overview of the IOM's project from March 2006 to December 2009, see Moscow.iom.int/old/activities_countertrafficking-preventioninRF.html.

[98] In February 2008, Valeriia attended a Forum in Vienna organised by the UN Global Initiative to Fight Human Trafficking (UNGIFT), reported in IOM Moscow Times, Issue 10, March 2008, p. 12.

[99] Tiuriukanova produced a huge number of publications and papers up to her untimely death. These include: 'Gendernye aspekty migratsionnoi statistiki', in Marina E. Baskakova, ed., Gendernoe Neravenstvo v Sovremennoi Rossii Skvoz' Prizmu Statistiki (Moscow: Izdatel'stvo Nauchnoi i Uchebnoi Literatury, 2004), pp. 252–278; Human Trafficking in the Russian Federation: Inventory and Analysis; Prevention of Human Trafficking in the Russian Federation (Moscow: IOM, 2007); see, too, Yakov Gilinsky, 'Problems of human trafficking in Russia', paper delivered at an international conference on 'Problems of human security in the era of globalization', Kyoto, 10–11 December 2004.

it was members of NGOs with international funding who continued to take on these commitments, not the Russian state.

Tensions further increased between the political leadership and civil society after Putin's re-election as president in 2012. Accusations of electoral fraud resulted in demonstrations in Moscow's Bolotnaia ploshchad. Subsequently, amendments to the law of 2006 on NGOs sped through the Duma, passing on 20 July 2012.[100] NGOs that received foreign financial support were required to register as 'foreign agents', allegedly for engaging in political activity. The NGOs generally refused to register as agents and stood together. Although little happened immediately, the state did somewhat arbitrarily start to crack down in the following year.[101]

Convictions, Policing and Tier 3

As the years passed after the Criminal Code had been amended, conviction rates under Article 127.1 were not especially high given the huge scale of the problem. In 2006, however, the US State Department praised Russia for improving its law enforcement measures. The Annual TIP Report observed that 'police significantly increased the number of trafficking investigations from 26 in 2004 to 80 in 2005'. Apparently sixty of these cases involved sexual exploitation and twenty were concerned with forced labour. Criminal prosecutions were also up fivefold. There were eleven prosecutions in 2004 and fifty-three in 2005. There were 'at least' nine convictions of traffickers, and six were sentenced to prison terms of between three and a half and eight years. US officials complained, however, that no official Russian statistics were released, so data had to be culled from press and other sources. The Report called for development of a system to 'track convictions and sentences'.[102]

Lauren McCarthy has argued that, as well as the complexities of human trafficking cases, the very nature of Russian law enforcement and its investigative processes made prosecution under Article 127.1 difficult due to the separation of investigative and prosecutorial functions, which had made 'ownership' of human trafficking cases hard. Specified time

---

[100] Federal'nyi zakon Rossiiskoi Federatsii ot 20 iiulia 2012g N. 121-F3, 'O vnesenii izmenenii v otdel'nye zakonodatel'nye aktye Rossiiskoi Federatsii v chasti regulirovaniia deiatel'nosti nekommercheskikh organizatsii, vypolniaiushchikh funktsii inostrannogo agenta, priniat Gosudarstvennoi Dumoi 13 iiulia 2012, odobren Sovetom Federatsii 18 iiulia 2012', *Rossiiskaia gazeta*, 23 July 2012.

[101] For fuller details, see Mary McAuley, *Human Rights in Russia* (London: I. B. Tauris, 2015), pp. 297–307.

[102] US State Department, TIP Report 2006, www.state.gov/j/tip/rls/tiprpt/2006/65990 .htm.

limits on investigations also affected the process.[103] These were precisely the points described to me by the district judge in St Petersburg quoted above.[104] In addition, criteria for promotion in the police and the time limits put on investigations provided disincentives to exploring complex and time-consuming cases, which those of human trafficking definitely were. Many members of NGOs also confirmed that it was easier for the police to win convictions under Article 240 on recruitment into prostitution and Article 241 on organising prostitution than it was under Article 127.1, due to its many parts.[105] A further complication in gathering evidence for 127.1 was the puzzling wording of the phrase 'for the purpose of their exploitation'. The district judge in 2007 had described the dilemma: if the trafficker who recruited, transported and transferred the trafficked person did not personally exploit them because they had sold them on, and it was the purchaser who subsequently did this in a literal sense, then was the evidence sufficient to convict the recruiter under 127.1?[106] McCarthy held that the text of 127.1 'paralyzed law enforcement' and prompted 'cautious' behaviour, which showed they were 'afraid to use a law they do not fully understand because they fear reprimand from above and adverse effects on their performance statistics'. It was the phrase 'proof of intent to exploit', as well as the complexity of cases, that held back convictions. Finally, to minimise confusion, an amendment was introduced in 2008 which made clear that transactions involving individuals were indeed a crime, whether or not there was intent to exploit. Importantly too, this amendment of 2008 set the minimum sentence now at six years, no longer five, which in Russian law meant a 'grave crime'. This qualitatively different categorisation and *tiazhost'* gave law enforcement more investigative tools, as the district judge had explained.[107]

Conviction rates under Article 127.1 nonetheless remained relatively low. In 2011, the US State Department's TIP Report noted that in 2009 there had been ninety-nine prosecutions and seventy-six convictions for human trafficking in Russia. In 2010, however, the corresponding figures were sixty-two and just forty-two. Sentences ranged from several months up to twelve years in prison.[108] Although the TIP Reports were correct that there were few convictions under Article 127.1, law enforcement did

[103] McCarthy, 'Beyond corruption', pp. 1–12.
[104] Interview with a district judge, Dzerzhinskii raion, St Petersburg, April 2007.
[105] Most interviewees made this point, as do many articles.
[106] Interview with a district judge, 2007.
[107] For fuller discussion of relevant aspects of the criminal justice system, see McCarthy, 'Beyond corruption'.
[108] US State Department, TIP Report 2011, www.state.gov/j/tip/rls/tiprpt/2011/164233 .htm.

nonetheless secure prison sentences for traffickers using those articles of the Criminal Code which were less time-consuming to prove. Therefore, the US figures did not offer a full picture of convictions. US officials again complained about difficulties in gaining access to statistics and still having to rely on the Russian press and on connections for information. Although before the adoption of Article 127.1 into law, efforts to prosecute had proceeded under Articles 240 and 241, there had been technical problems regarding their applicability. These articles, however, were reformulated and thereby rendered more useful due to a widening of their remit and inclusion of more aggravating factors such as transport across borders, the illegal holding of someone abroad and violence or threat of violence. McCarthy observed that, 'whether inadvertently or purposely', the improvements to these clauses 'made it even less likely' for officers to attempt to use Article 127.1. This was because in cases of prostitution law enforcement now enjoyed 'the ability to cover a wider number of situations under a law they already knew how to use'.[109] The police record would therefore look more favourable if convictions under Articles 240 and 241 were added to those of 127.1.

When the police assess that it will be tricky to secure sufficient evidence for convictions under Articles 127.1 and 127.2, or if they know that internal institutional deadlines will not provide them with enough time to gather the necessary information, then they may productively use Articles 240 and 241 instead, which are easier to work with, although they may mean lighter punishments. Drawing on Russian data, McCarthy has been able to show that there was, in fact, an increase in the use by law enforcement of Articles 240 and 241 even after the incorporation of anti-trafficking articles in the Criminal Code. There was a 187 per cent jump in usage of Article 240 and a 174 per cent increase in Article 241. By 2008, there was a peak of 655 cases pursued under Article 240 and 1,831 under Article 241. Although these data do not indicate if the cases could have been charged under Article 127.1, nonetheless using these alternative articles, McCarthy concludes, 'seems to be an effective strategy for prosecuting traffickers without having to confront the disincentives created by the trafficking law'. Her own interviews with law enforcement revealed that in some regions, such as Nizhnii Novgorod, the practice was to open trafficking cases under Article 240 to be 'on the safe side'. These particular interviewees admitted that they had no experience of using Article 127.1.[110]

---

[109] McCarthy, *Trafficking Justice*. This offers a different methodology on collecting data on sentencing from that adopted in the TIP Reports.
[110] McCarthy, *Trafficking Justice*, pp. 182–184.

In 2013, the US State Department took a firmer stand. Its annual TIP Report downgraded Russia from its Tier 2 Watch List, where it had sat for nine years since 2004, back to its lowest classification of Tier 3 where it had also been placed in 2001 and 2002.[111] This meant that, in the eyes of the State Department, Russia was not sufficiently meeting anti-trafficking standards. In fact, over the years, Russia had been diplomatically praised for making some efforts, but regularly criticised for not setting up shelters or adequate psychological counselling services for returnees, for not making enough convictions and for not having a comprehensive strategy in place or formal national procedures. The 2013 TIP Report, however, talked of Russia's 'minimal progress in efforts to protect and assist trafficking victims', its 'limited efforts to prevent trafficking' and its lack of effort to 'reduce the demand for commercial sex acts'.[112] In criticising Russia, US leaders and officials tread on sensitive ground as, historically, Russian leaders have not liked being told how to run their domestic system by outsiders and deem it to be 'interference' in internal affairs.

In 2013 Konstantin Dolgov, the Russian Foreign Ministry's Plenipotentiary for Human Rights, reacted strongly. Dolgov accused the TIP Report of using an 'unacceptable ideological approach that divides nations into rating groups depending on the US State Department's political sympathies or antipathies'. He added that this matched the logic of other 'democratizing tools', such as the Magnitsky Act,[113] used in the light of 'the alleged deterioration of the human rights situation' in Russia. Dolgov concluded that a 'politicizing of human trafficking' hampered international co-operation and that Russia would not fulfil 'demands that look almost like an ultimatum'.[114] The official Russian reaction was loud and strong. There had been criticisms before of the TIP Reports from the Foreign Ministry for being 'politicised' and 'not objective', as in 2009, but never this angry.[115] More calmly, the Russian press simply reported the results of the TIP Report. *Rossiiskaia gazeta* observed that the United States may apply sanctions to states which 'poorly fight against people

---

[111] This was called an 'auto downgrade' introduced to apply from 2011 to those countries which had sat on the Tier 2 Watch List for more than two years.

[112] US State Department, TIP Report 2013, www.state.gov/j/rls/tiprpt/2013.

[113] Sergei Magnitsky was a lawyer who accused Russian tax officials of fraud. He was imprisoned and died. In 2012 the United States introduced a bill to prohibit entry into the United States of those Russians deemed responsible for his death. In response Russia passed the Dima Yakovlev law which prevented US citizens from adopting Russian children on the grounds that abuse of adoptees had occurred.

[114] 'Moscow attacks US human trafficking report as politicized and arrogant', RT, 20 June 2013, rt.com/politics/trafficking-arrogant-politicized-report-992/.

[115] See 'MID RF schel doklad Gosdepa SShA ne ob"ektivnym', *Nezavisimaia gazeta*, 19 June 2009.

trafficking'. It noted that Russia lacked 'minimal standards' in this regard and so found itself categorised alongside Algeria, China, the Democratic Republic of Congo, Cuba, Equatorial Guinea, Eritrea, Iran, Kuwait, Libya, Mauritania, North Korea, Papua New Guinea, Saudi Arabia, Sudan, Syria, Uzbekistan, Yemen and Zimbabwe.[116] The paper did not comment further. *Nezavisimaia gazeta* also gave a crisp nine-line coverage which revealed that the Civic Chamber had dubbed the TIP Report a 'diversion' and had claimed that Russia was 'not the main territory' of people trafficking, which was surely Kosovo and the Balkans. More oddly, the Civic Chamber put the categorisation down to 'political games around the Syrian question'. The paper reported these quotations, also without comment, and ended with the bland statement that the TIP Report had categorised Russia for not meeting the necessary standards.[117]

A large number in Russia must have known that what the report had said was indeed the case. Two views on the 2013 TIP Report were expressed to me by Russians working in anti-trafficking. One held that it was accurate, fair and justified, saying 'I agree with Tier 3. Now the situation is even worse if we compare it with the years 2003–2009. There are no NGO networks like the Angel Coalition thanks to the state fighting against NGOs.'[118] The second observed that, in compiling the report, the Americans are not always sensitive to information that is passed to them confidentially from Russians and that printing it without prior permission can cause problems for their sources, which may not help the NGO community.[119]

No one in NGOs, however, contested the apt criticism of a serious lack of adequate support for men and women returning from unfree labour, whether by escape, release or rescue. They continually stressed the serious need for immediate psychological support, medical checks, legal help and somewhere to live. Indeed, the provision of essential shelters has been both rare and short-lived. The productive work of MiraMed, for example, had come to an end. The Angel Coalition's nine shelters had to close for financial reasons.[120] The shelter used by Natalia Khodyreva's Crisis Centre for Women in St Petersburg closed in December 2007.[121]

---

[116] Viktor Feshchenko, no title, *Rossiiskaia gazeta*, 20 June 2013.
[117] No named author, 'Doklad SShA o rabotorgovle v Rossii v Obshchestvennoi Palate nazvali diversiei', *Nezavisimaia gazeta*, 20 June 2013.
[118] E-mail interview with an activist in the Russian NGO sector, September 2013. Reference is made here to the Russian law of 2012 on NGOs.
[119] Confidential interview in Russia.
[120] Natalia Khodyreva, 'Gender violence and cost of socio-psychological rehabilitation and legal assistance: Russian Federation', paper presented at the First World Conference of Women's Shelters, 8–11 September 2008, Edmonton, Canada.
[121] Khodyreva, 'Gender violence'.

And the shelter set up in March 2006 in Moscow by the IOM also shut down since the then mayor, Iurii Luzhkov, refused in November 2009 to take it over as had been the hope of those at the IOM, who could only fund it for a short time. Apparently, the mayor said that the filth of trafficking did not exist in his city and that sustaining the shelter would blacken Moscow's image.[122]

Without doubt, the IOM's shelter was highly professional and merited emulation. During its three-year existence, it helped 423 people who formerly had been confined in unfree labour, 59 per cent of whom co-operated with law enforcement agencies and some of whom had been referred to the shelter by the police. Specialist approaches were used with the victim: police, a social worker and a psychologist were all in one room at the same time. Sixty-three per cent of the victims who came for help were women between eighteen and twenty-eight years of age, and 37 per cent were male. The forms of forced labour they had been in broke down into 53 per cent sexual, 44 per cent labour and 3 per cent begging.[123] According to Alberto Andriani, then Co-ordinator of the Project on the Prevention of Human Trafficking at the IOM in Moscow, the aim had been to 'establish a model facility for rehabilitation and referral'. The shelter had offered a package of airport reception, temporary accommodation, qualified medical, psychological and social assistance, legal advice and the development of individual reintegration plans.[124] Anna Rubtsova, Project Assistant and Co-Director, emphasised the importance of 'developing sustainable inter-agency mechanisms for the referral of trafficking victims'.[125]

Another shelter had opened in 2008–2009 in Vladivostok as a result of collaboration between the local administration and the IOM, which provided six months of funding. Thereafter it was locally supported.[126] By 2013 this shelter had places for just six women, still funded locally.[127] In 2015, however, lack of funds meant that it was no longer able to function. A centre funded by the International Committee of the Red Cross in St Petersburg also had to suspend many of its operations,

[122] Confidential interview in Russia.
[123] IOM, *Predotvrashchenie Torgovli Liud'mi v Rossiiskoi Federatsii* (Moscow: IOM, 2008). For an overview of the work of the IOM in Moscow, listen to Kirill Boychenko on 'Prevention of human trafficking in the Russian Federation', www.youtube.com/watch?v=MZKOToe33N8.
[124] Interview with Alberto Andriani in Moscow, April 2007.
[125] Interview with Anna Rubtsova in Moscow, April 2007.
[126] E-mail correspondence from Juliana Pavlovskaya, Olga Rybakova and Julia Melnichouk, 26 July 2016.
[127] Interview with the lawyer Kirill Boychenko in Moscow, August 2013. He had previously worked at the IOM shelter.

in particular regarding accommodation for trafficking victims.[128] Priorities were now on short-term accommodation for refugees, particularly from Ukraine and Syria. Its hotline was maintained but much assistance to victims and potential victims was taken up by the IOM. In addition, the IOM continued its support for a state facility which provided shelter to the vulnerable, including victims of trafficking. Notably, it co-operated with a state-run Centre for Social Adaptation in Moscow, known as the 'Liublino' Centre which offered safe accommodation, meals, health checks and assistance with renewing documents. This centre was ready to help all vulnerable men and women, including migrants, the stateless, the disabled and crime victims. It comes under the capital's Department for Social Protection. Those at the IOM in Moscow find 'Liublino' a 'reliable partner'.[129] In addition, shelters do exist in Russia for victims of domestic violence, but these do not address the complexities of human trafficking cases. Officials often comment that those who have been trafficked should seek help in local hospitals. These, however, lack the specialised package of treatment needed that the IOM shelter had painstakingly provided.

Staff at the Moscow office of the IOM have in recent years praised aspects of the work of the Russian Orthodox Church. They imparted how after 2013 some local priests became concerned about the fate of the homeless and migrant labourers, and this extended to women and girls. This was a pleasant surprise, given some reluctance on the part of the Church at the beginning of the century to provide assistance to women and girls returning from trafficked situations.[130] The Church's press secretary, Vasilii Rulinskii, explained in 2016 that the Church now ran twenty-eight crisis centres which provided shelters for pregnant women and women with children.[131] On a visit to London, Vladimir Legoida, Chair of the Moscow Patriarchate Department for External Church Relations with Society and Mass Media, indicated that the Church offered pregnant women a place in a shelter if they chose to have their child.[132] One of the Church's shelters that it briefly ran collaboratively with the IOM, however, had to close for financial reasons.[133] Nonetheless, it retained a

---

[128] Interview with Boychenko, Moscow, August 2013.
[129] E-mail correspondence from Juliana Pavlovskaya, Olga Rybakova and Julia Melnichouk from the Moscow office of the IOM, 10 May 2016.
[130] Interview at the Moscow office of the IOM, September 2014.
[131] E-mail communication from Vasilii Rulinskii, 2 March 2016. Further data can be found at www.diaconia.ru/statistic.
[132] Chatham House, London, 9 February 2016. When asked what would happen if a woman felt unable to keep her child, he replied 'we are working on that'.
[133] US State Department, TIP Report 2016, www.state.gov/j/tip/rls/tiprpt/countries/2016/258848.htm.

shelter in Pervomaiskii and a small one in Rostov-on-Don for victims of domestic violence.[134]

As well as deploring Russia's poor track record in victim assistance and the provision of shelters, TIP Reports continued to lament low conviction rates. The 2014 Report noted that in 2013 law enforcement agencies had registered 66 human trafficking crimes, of which 63 concerned sexual exploitation. The Report also stated that media coverage had revealed that the government in 2013 had investigated 'at least 15 potential sex trafficking suspects under Article 127.1' and not fewer than 5 of labour trafficking under 127.2. The figures, it criticised, were lower than those of 2012 when 70 sex trafficking cases and 17 of labour trafficking were investigated. Prosecutions and convictions were also down. In addition, sources indicated that, in 2013, 23 traffickers were imprisoned and 9 given suspended sentences and that, in 2012, 26 were sent to prison and 7 given suspended sentences. The 2014 TIP Report commented that, 'in some regions of Russia, experts report that authorities ignore or fail to pursue cases of human trafficking'. It did not, however, identify exactly where. By implication there were serious political inadequacies in regional law enforcement and criminal justice systems.[135] This Report castigated Russia for its 'low political will to address human trafficking'.[136] Similarly, the 2015 Report described the Russian government's 'limited efforts to prevent trafficking' in another harsh assessment.[137]

Looking back at 2015, the 2016 TIP Report echoed previous ones. It imparted that the Investigative Committee had reported just fourteen investigations under Article 127.1 and four under 127.2, but gave no information about initiated prosecutions. The Supreme Court's statistics indicated that that there had been forty-eight convictions under 127.1 and ten under 127.2, with forty-seven of these resulting in prison sentences. Information was scanty, however, on the use of Articles 240 and 241.[138] A repeated charge was that Russia's government 'demonstrated unwillingness to design and implement a comprehensive response to human trafficking', and still lacked a national action plan and a lead agency to co-ordinate anti-trafficking measures. Moreover, the

[134] E-mail correspondence from Juliana Pavlovskaya, Olga Rybakova and Julia Melnichouk, 26 July 2016.

[135] US State Department, TIP Report 2014, www.state.gov/j/tip/rls/tiprpt/countries/2014/226804.htm.

[136] US State Department, TIP Report 2014, www.state.gov/j/tip/rls/tiprpt/countries/2014/226804.htm.

[137] US State Department, TIP Report 2015, www.state.gov/j/tiprpt/rls/tiprpt/countries/2015/243519.htm.

[138] US State Department, TIP Report 2016, www.state.gov/j/tip/rls/tiprpt/countries/2016/258848.htm.

government 'generally did not undertake efforts to protect human trafficking victims'. The report claimed that legislation to implement such a framework 'has been stalled at the highest political levels'.[139] Russia's categorisation was kept at Tier 3 in 2014, 2015 and 2016.[140]

Prominent figures in Russia did, however, continue to draw attention to human trafficking and to call for active co-operation across states. In 2012, Vladimir Kolokol'tsev in his capacity as head of the MVD of Russia, spoke out at a meeting of the heads of law enforcement from more than 100 countries at the 81st Session of the General Assembly of Interpol. Presenting a paper on 'Human trafficking and the contraband of a "living good"', Kolokol'tsev maintained that slavery in Russia was viewed as 'one of the main global threats of modern life'. He revealed that, 'in the past five years, law enforcement in Russia had exposed 17,000 crimes connected with different kinds of human trafficking, namely the use of slave labour, kidnapping, recruitment into prostitution and the organisation of prostitution'. He declared his general satisfaction with the results of law enforcement but felt that the potential of international police co-operation 'is not yet exhausted'. Kolokol'tsev acknowledged some good results in tackling illegal migration and revealed that the activities of forty international criminal groups had been exposed. Their members included citizens of Russia, Belarus, Moldova, Uzbekistan and Tajikistan.[141]

Two years later, Kolokol'tsev expressed more critical views of Russia. He admitted that, 'Russia needs to develop a set of preventive measures against crimes related to the sexual exploitation of people', noting that it was a crime with 'a high degree of latency'. Kolokol'tsev felt that 'detecting primary data' should be 'a priority task' for law enforcement agencies and that 'a set of inter-departmental preventive measures' that were also educational was needed. Effectively in agreement with the US TIP Reports, but not explicitly declaring so, he called for 'attention' to be paid 'to the provision of aid to the victim of human trafficking'. He admitted that this was 'a serious problem', as Russia 'virtually lacks appropriate specialized state rehabilitation centres'. He reported that in 2013 there had indeed been sixty-six registered instances of human trafficking, of which sixty-three were for sexual exploitation. He did not declare that this was just the tip of the iceberg but he did elaborate that there were

---

[139] US State Department, TIP Report 2016, www.state.gov/j/tip/rls/tiprpt/countries/2016/258848.htm.

[140] All US State Department TIP Reports can also be accessed via www.state.gov/j/tip/rls/tiprpt.

[141] No named author, 'Kolokol'tsev prizval Interpol aktivnee borot'sia s rabotorgovlei', *Argumenty i fakty*, 5 November 2012; Mikhail Falaleev, 'MVD ukrepliaet sotrudnichestvo s Interpolom', *Rossiiskaia gazeta*, 5 November 2012.

also 'nearly 3,500 related crimes' such as 'organising and convincing individuals to engage in prostitution, illegal manufacturing and distribution of pornographic material, including indecent images of children'.[142] Kolokol'tsev stands out amongst Russian ministers in calling for doing more about human trafficking inside Russia and for recognising the huge lack of rehabilitation centres for the trafficked. As well as emphasising the 'physical and psychological harm to an individual', he underscored the wider impact on society which amounted to 'the distortion of social and moral values'.[143] By contrast, Sergei Lavrov in his statement to the 20th Meeting of the OSCE Ministerial Council in December 2013 announced that Russia 'was in favour of greater attention being paid by the OSCE to the shameful phenomenon of trafficking in human beings', adding that child trafficking was 'particularly perturbing'. As foreign minister, his brief was external, advocating 'a comprehensive approach to this problem, including the trade in human organs and tissues'.[144] He did not, unlike Kolokol'tsev, express the need for more anti-trafficking action inside Russia but rather called upon the OSCE to pursue it.

Conclusion

The political dimensions of forging human trafficking into a recognised issue on Russia's governmental agendas were complex and protracted, involving international and domestic pressures on the Russian political system. Although in the late 1990s and early 2000s, researchers and those in NGOs increasingly spoke out about human trafficking out of Russia, particularly into prostitution, this naming of the problem did not make it instantly into a recognised political issue. There were hurdles to be overcome, views to be challenged and politicians to be persuaded. There was foot-dragging in the Duma, despite an active Legislation Committee and notwithstanding growing international evidence of what was happening to those who were trafficked into unfree labour. Part of the necessary action included the organisation of educational campaigns and conferences to inform, share and sway opinion. A broad mobilisation of pressure on the state developed momentum. The selected quotations from those involved in the process show a vivid mix of exasperation,

---

[142] Voice of Russia, Interfax, 'Set of measures needed to prevent human sex trafficking in Russia – Interior Minister', 28 March 2014, sputniknews.com/voiceofrussia/news/2014_03_28/set-of-measures-needed-to-prevent-human-trafficking-in-Russia.

[143] Voice of Russia, 'Set of measures'.

[144] OSCE, 'Statement by Mr Sergey Lavrov, Minister for Foreign Affairs of the Russian Federation, at the Twentieth Meeting of the OSCE Ministerial Council, Kyiv, 5 December 2013', www.osce.org/mc/109306?download=true.

determination, drive, optimism, pessimism, scepticism, pragmatism, resignation and perseverance. They viewed legislation as a first necessary step, yet simultaneously were concerned about whether it would be sufficiently implemented and did not anyway see it as going far enough.

Although only a tiny handful of Duma deputies in 2002 and 2003 took human trafficking seriously, it finally required Putin's presidential leadership to call upon the Duma to support the introduction of Articles 127.1 and 127.2 into the Criminal Code. Being a largely compliant institution, the Duma at last concurred. Arguably, given the nature of the Russian political system and the attitudes in it held about human trafficking at that time, Putin's advocacy from the very apex of the system was absolutely crucial. Had he not backed legal change, one wonders how long it might otherwise have taken. A director of a regional centre believed that in the end 'the human trafficking project was from the top, not from below'. She stressed that not only was Mizulina very active but, very importantly, 'the ministries were involved – Education, Health, Social Protection and the MVD. They moved carefully.'[145] Yet although 'the top' had ultimately been decisive, 'below' had done a great deal of the preparatory groundwork.

[145] Off-the-record interview in Russia.

3   Press Reporting on Human Trafficking out of Russia

Integral to the history of the naming of human trafficking as a problem were exposés in the press, and there was a flurry of articles at the beginning of the 2000s across a wide range of newspapers. Most visible to the public were the individual stories covered by journalists and the statistical estimates that they reported. Newspapers also quoted experts, politicians, law enforcement officers and those in international organisations about the impacts of human trafficking and unfree labour on society. The public and some specialists, however, considered that by 2014 there was a new silence about human trafficking out of the country, and they also believed that outflows had reduced. It had become a topic which was apparently less 'seen'. One prevailing view was that articles had disappeared. In fact, trawls of the press showed that there was still some coverage in the public domain, albeit reduced. News about migrant labour coming into Russia tended to drown out awareness that trafficking both out of the country and within it was ongoing. Moreover, migrants were visible on Russia's streets whereas those who were sold into forced labour elsewhere simply disappeared, a loss known only to those close to them. A disparity between perceptions of trends and their realities developed. If the 'threat' of incoming *gastarbaitery* was overplayed in people's minds, continuing patterns of human trafficking into unfree labour elsewhere were underplayed.

The aim of this chapter is to introduce the main narratives about human trafficking that came out of the Russian press. It scrutinises the information that journalists presented, the messages they delivered or implied, the images of the trafficked and traffickers that they constructed and the arguments, if any, that they made. Although different newspapers reported similar statistical estimates and told like tales of debt-bondage and abuse, their chosen details, interpretations, questions, angles, suggestions and styles often varied. Selected here for discussion are a small number of articles which are representative examples of the large number read.[1] The stories are tracked historically to highlight thematic developments over time. These often reflect background context, such as instability in Kosovo and Bosnia, pressure for anti-trafficking legislation, developments in society, increased use of social media, statistical updates and changing concerns and questions.

Sources

The examples cited have been culled from a trawl of eight national newspapers: *Izvestiia, Rossiiskaia gazeta, Nezavisimaia gazeta, Argumenty i fakty, Komsomol'skaia pravda, Moskovskii komsomolets, Pravda* and *Trud*. These represent different types of readership (serious, popular, youth and labour). I conducted manual library-based trawls of stored newspapers and also web-based searches for articles using the terms '*torgovlia liud'mi*', '*treffiking*', '*seks-rabstvo*', '*prostitutsiia*', '*rabstvo*' and '*rabotorgovlia*'. Thus, what I have read is linked to the nature of the newspapers' own headings, categorisations and search engines. Although discussion is based on articles written after 2000, one can find occasional articles published in the 1990s. A trawl of selected newspapers back into the 1980s revealed mainly silences.

From scrutiny across the press, three distinct types of approach inductively emerge. Firstly, there is crisp, informative and constructive reporting which avoids myths, plays down sensationalism and attempts a reasonably objective analysis. Articles in *Izvestiia, Nezavisimaia gazeta* and *Rossiiskaia gazeta* generally fit this mould. Secondly, there are articles which go for attention-grabbing headlines, sensational reporting and sometimes titillating coverage. *Komsomol'skaia pravda* and *Moskovskii komsomolets* are frequently styled in this manner. Thirdly, there are stories which dwell on 'who is to blame'. Articles in *Pravda* frequently fit the pattern of exposing a crime and then highlighting a central target to name and shame. Some papers may also present more than one approach, such as *Argumenty i fakty*, which can offer excellent reporting but frequently with a sensational edge to it. Indeed, the topic of sex trafficking by its nature can sound unpleasant or horrific in the blandest of reporting, making it sometimes hard to avoid shades of sensationalism.

---

[1] For an analysis by categories, see Mary Buckley, 'Press images of human trafficking from Russia: myths and interpretations', in Rebecca Kay, ed., *Gender, Equality and Difference During and After State Socialism* (London: Palgrave, 2007), pp. 211–229.

The First Flurry of Stories: 2000–2005

One of the earliest revelations about human trafficking was made in 2000 in *Argumenty i fakty*. It reported the story of Vera from Astrakhan, who was travelling by bus with a friend to work in Turkey. When the bus stopped for a break at a café in Bucharest, the driver made a telephone call, and soon some men arrived, paid him and took the girls 'by the hair' and jostled them into a car. Many articles talked of 'girls' (*devushki* or *devchonki*) as well as 'women' (*zhenshchiny*). The men, in addition, had captured three Bulgarians and one Moldovan. Initially the girls were locked up in Belgrade and then taken to Kosovo. They ended up in Uroshevats where they were forced into prostitution, beaten and fined 'for the smallest fault'. They had to service the boss's friends and also soldiers of different nationalities. The girls were afraid that, when the clients tired of them, they would demand replacements and then their captors would kill them and sell their organs. This is indeed what happened to Vera's friend. Vera witnessed her murder and was herself lucky to escape and tell this story.[2] This was a case of handover after kidnapping from public transport in a deal done by the driver with unfree labour as the result.

The article commented that Interpol and the UN now saw Kosovo and Albania as 'the criminal centre of Europe'. The ease of crossing borders here meant that narcotics, arms sales, human trafficking and the sale of organs 'are thriving'. Groups of different nationalities, including Russians, Albanians, Bulgarians, Romanians, Serbs and Macedonians were active. The reporter was permitted to accompany the police for two days to see the nature of their work. On the outskirts of Prishtina, Kosovo's capital, they went into a building where girls were being held. Torches shone on a 'terrible picture'. In inhuman conditions, they detected two girls to a bed, filthy bedding and tiny dilapidated rooms separated by curtains. Entrapped were girls who had 'already long ago ceased to look like girls'. They had become unwashed drinkers and smokers 'with empty eyes, fearing everything'. Now that the police had arrived, they realised that at last they would be freed. Using the tool of reported speech, the paper quoted the powerful words of one girl: 'And for what? Where can I now go like this? It will only be worse. It's best to die here.' The author observed 'the voice in which she spoke this was already dead'.[3] The story was a huge eye-opener for readers unaware of developments in global trouble spots. Another article covered the involvement of UN peacekeepers and NATO servicemen in brothels in Bosnia into which East European women had

---

[2] No named author, 'Na Kosovskom dne', *Argumenty i fakty*, 24 May 2000.
[3] 'Na Kosovskom dne'.

been trafficked. The grim conclusion was that 'they are there on a mission to help normalise the situation and in effect broke the law'.[4]

Story after story revealed developing patterns of human trafficking. In 2001 journalist Mikhail Lamtsov discussed what had happened to fifteen-year-old Iana and her friend Maria. Apparently Iana's father's last words to her before she travelled to Karlovy Vary in the Czech Republic were: 'I hope you don't like it there and soon come home.' They had been promised $100 a day for work as waitresses. A man called Oleg had set them up and provided false passports into which he glued their photographs. *En route* by car, they were told to be quiet at the Ukrainian border with Slovakia. Their photographs, however, did not really match the data in the passports. Oleg managed, it seemed with practice and an informal understanding, to settle matters at the border. At their final destination, the owner of a chain of nightclubs, Marek, met them. Lamstov reported Iana's words that '*muzhlany*[5] looked at us like dolls in a cheap shop'. Then 'Marek touched her hair, stroked her thigh, it seemed like an x-ray, everything was visible.' Marek paid the courier 5,000 German Marks for four girls. They were then taken to different nightclubs. A client paid 180 Marks for a session, and Marek took 130 of these which were supposedly for protection, food and accommodation. Some of the men were 'rude', some wanted to pay less and one dissatisfied client seized hold of Iana's throat. It took three of the bouncers to get him off. Thereafter she felt panic at the sight of men's hands and began to drink for courage. She admitted later that 'I lived in constant fear.' She tried to feign hysterics but Marek responded with 'I will kill you slowly. First, I will break a leg, then an arm.' One Christmas when the boss was drunk, quite spontaneously Iana decided to run. She hitchhiked to Prague and had enough money to buy a train ticket to Zakapathia. At the border, she announced, 'they sold me into slavery'. Lamstov told readers that data from the UN indicated that in 2001 there were 10,000 underage girls in brothels in Europe, and 'most of them' had come from 'unfortunate families in countries of the former Soviet Union'.[6] His report presented several images of the trafficked girls. They were aspiring to improve their lot in life and ready to travel but in the process had become victims and had been treated as forced sex objects. Iana nonetheless took the initiative to escape, a risk in itself, but succeeded. This was not one-dimensional journalism stressing victimhood alone.

---

[4] No named author, 'OON i NATO torguiut "zhivym tovarom"', *Nezavisimaia gazeta*, 4 August 2001.

[5] *Muzhlany* connotes rude and coarse men.

[6] Mikhail Lamstov, 'Seks-rabyni v Karlovykh Varakh', *Argumenty i fakty*, 14 August 2001.

In the early 2000s, alongside such stories, articles gave readers statistical estimates of global slavery and of numbers thought to be trafficked out of Russia. In 2002 journalist Vasilina Vasil'eva in *Nezavisimaia gazeta* cited the US State Department's figure of 'around 700,000' trapped in forced labour worldwide, 'mainly women and children'. Competing higher estimates, she informed, put global slavery at 4 million people. Vasil'eva also told readers that, according to the OSCE, 'after the disintegration of the Soviet Union roughly 10 million inhabitants of the Commonwealth of Independent States were sold into the brothels of Europe for a song'. Vasil'eva then publicised a message heard in the media many times since: 'it is staggering that trade in a living good is profitable in all countries of the world and brings the next biggest income after narcotics and weapons'.[7]

Her article was packed with information, typical of reporting in more highbrow papers. Vasil'eva explained how Russian citizens were being unsuspectingly duped. Guilty operators included tour companies, marriage bureaux and entrepreneurial individuals. With implicit disapproval, she added that newspapers 'quite calmly' advertised for 'young women from 18 to 24' to work abroad and earn what looked like large dollar sums. Painting a graphically horrible picture, she revealed how women could endure transit across the border in the boot of a car, then end up in a filthy brothel and be forced into violent sex, pick up different illnesses, be beaten and go hungry. She grimly stressed that in recent years traffic into the sex industry 'had deeply rooted itself in Russia and CIS countries'. So they had become 'providers of prostitutes for Western Europe, North America and the Middle East'. It was the USA, however, asserted Vasil'eva, not CIS countries, which was ahead in battling against human trafficking.[8]

Vasil'eva regretted that, although the problem was evident, in 2002 Russia had no anti-trafficking legislation. She attacked officials' apparent indifference to the problem with: 'Isn't it strange how many officials allege that this problem falls outside their competence or that women leave their motherland willingly for economic reasons and that force against them takes place outside the country?' Data from the UN, she underlined, indicated that women were forced into prostitution and striptease and did not generally embark upon these jobs willingly.[9] The clear message to the Russian public was that action in Russia was overdue and that there was no place for complacency.

---

[7] Vasilina Vasil'eva, 'Schet seks-rabyn' iz stran SNG idet na milliony: rost torgovli zhivym tovarom stimuliruetsia otsutstviem dolzhnykh zakonov', *Nezavisimaia gazeta*, 18 February 2002.

[8] Vasil'eva, 'Schet seks-rabyn' iz stran SNG'.

[9] Vasil'eva, 'Schet seks-rabyn' iz stran SNG'.

Six months later in the same paper, journalist Andrei Viktorov reported the arrest in New York of three former citizens of the USSR who had trafficked 'girls from Russia and forced them into striptease'. Apparently, this criminal group began working at the end of 1999 and 'at least 30 women from Russia' had been tricked. They knew that they were going to work as dancers 'but not naked'. Their documents had been taken from them, and their captors threatened to harm their families back home if they refused to comply. Viktorov used this tale to contrast US and Russian legislation. The criminals in the USA were likely to get up to twenty years in jail, but in Russia there was no legislation to deter them. He quoted Viktor Plekhanov, a deputy head in the MVD, to the effect that 'we don't have criminal punishment for trade of a "living good"', even though in recent years it had increased six times.[10] All Russian law enforcement could do about illegal trafficking out of Russia was to use Articles 240 and 241 in the Criminal Code concerning prostitution and its organisation, even though in Viktorov's view the permitted punishments for these crimes were 'laughable' compared with those meted out in the USA. So, the MVD was working seriously on fresh articles on human trafficking for the Criminal Code, and drafts were being looked at in the Ministries of Justice, Labour, Education and Culture. Like Vasil'eva, Viktorov made a case for legislation and showed approval of US law. Some journalists were attempting, as opinion shapers, to contribute to the political struggles for anti-trafficking legislation and exert pressure.

Another early article revealed that a Russian immigrant, one Aleksei Mishulovich, was arrested in Chicago in 1998 along with three of his associates. *Nezavisimaia gazeta* described him as 'one of the main international Mafiosi' and he was sentenced to nine years and four months. Apparently, this criminal business had been flourishing since 1996. They promised women, particularly Latvians, work in 'respectable nightclubs' and salaries of $60,000 a year. Weapons, ammunition, women's documents and photographs of their future victims were discovered. Mishulevich had told the women that, if they wanted to return home, they would first have to pay him $60,000. Since none of them could, they were trapped. The newspaper observed that therefore the women were in 'indefinite debt-slavery' (*bessrochnaia kabala*).[11]

In a similar style of reporting, Natal'ia Kozlova in *Rossiiskaia gazeta* covered the arrest in Los Angeles of five former Russian citizens. They

---

[10] Andrei Viktorov, 'Bruklinskaia filosofiia russkogo striptiza; v Soedinennykh Shtatakh arestovany torgovtsy tantsovshchitsami iz Rossii', *Nezavisimaia gazeta*, 29 August 2002.
[11] No named author, 'Seks-biznesmen iz Rossii budet sidet' v Amerike', *Nezavisimaia gazeta*, 16 February 2002.

were guilty of trafficking at least fifty women from Russia and Ukraine into the sex industry.[12] She also noted how another case had opened in Sweden because a thirteen-year-old Russian girl had been locked up for two years in a van and sold for sex by a man as he travelled the streets of Europe. The girl had previously run away from alcoholic parents at ten years old and subsequently been kidnapped. Three men were involved, and they were also holding a minor from the Middle East. As this news broke, it was announced that workers in children's homes in the north of Russia might be taking children to Scandinavia for work in prostitution, and investigation into this was underway.[13] Kozlova went on to reflect that 'a market in sex slaves has always existed in the world. But in the last ten years the situation in this market has sharply changed' and that according to the UN 'hundreds of thousands' of women and girls from Eastern Europe and the countries of the former Soviet Union had been sold to European, Asian and American markets. In addition, the Germans had revealed that 87 per cent of the prostitutes in their state were from Eastern Europe.[14] Kozlova's message concerned how varied the origins and outcomes of sexual exploitation in unfree conditions could be.

Similarly informative articles which drew on the results of academic research were published in *Izvestiia*. In 2004 journalists Anastasiia Naryshkina and Ilona Vinogradova reported that Elena Tiuriukanova, Elena Mikhailova and Maia Rusakova had interviewed thirteen returning 'sex slaves' aged between sixteen and twenty-eight. Their findings showed that the women's parents tended to have average or low social status and that many of them were alcoholics. The women had secondary or secondary specialist education and had been trained as a cashier, sales assistant, cook, seamstress, dressmaker and teacher of choreography. Some had previously worked according to their training, while others had sold goods in markets, and a few had been prostitutes. All were single or divorced, and some had children. Without exception, they were destitute, so it would not have been difficult for them to be tempted by the chance of an allegedly attractive and better life elsewhere. Poverty was the driver. The minority who had suspected that prostitution might be required had not imagined the degree of exploitation that it would entail.[15] One of the women interviewed was Maria, who had taught dance choreography in Vladivostok.

---

[12] Natal'ia Kozlova, 'Otrublennaia golova pod krasnym fonarem', *Rossiiskaia gazeta*, 31 January 2003.

[13] Kozlova, 'Otrublennaia golova'.

[14] Kozlova, 'Otrublennaia golova'. For examination of an outflow to Germany, see Fedor Luk'ianov, '"Zhivoi tovar" – potok s Vostoka', *Rossiiskaia gazeta*, 3 November 2000.

[15] Anastasiia Naryshkina and Ilona Vinogradova, 'Kazhdaia Rossiiskaia "devochka" prinosit khoziaevam pritonov po $200', *Izvestiia*, 16 April 2004.

She then moved with her mother and son to St Petersburg but could not find a job. When Maria saw an advertisement for dancers in a *corps de ballet* in the USA it looked like an inviting opportunity which offered thousands of dollars. So she signed a contract, the agency arranged her air ticket and documents and she travelled quite legally on a tourist visa. Upon arrival, the contact took her passport and she was thrown into a brothel.[16] Although *Izvestiia* did not present a full academic analysis, enough details were included for readers to grasp the seriousness of the trend and some of its 'push' and 'pull' factors.

By giving examples of how human trafficking happened, the press enlightened the public about what the many newspaper advertisements offering 'good work' abroad might really mean. The press included warnings that often the recruiters could be visited in their offices where jobs were arranged face to face and it all looked legitimate and above-board, but this was not always so. Naryshkina and Vinogradova told readers that there had been a roundtable in Moscow on the sexual exploitation of Russians at which representatives of the MVD, UN, ILO and others were present. Data suggested that a trafficked woman in 2004 could earn her 'boss' $200,000 a year.[17] The message was that the issue was being discussed at the highest levels and that exploiters were doing very well financially out of this crime.

Another type of story highlighted the awful psychological consequences. Journalist Ekaterina Karacheva in *Argumenty i fakty* described the shocking story of fourteen-year-old Ilsa who came from a happy family but her father had died in a mining accident. Her mother could not cope and took an overdose, and so Ilsa went to live with her grandparents, who were pensioners. When their neighbour suggested work abroad, it seemed a good solution. Upon arrival in Tel Aviv, however, this underage girl was sold into a brothel for $8,000. There she was raped, beaten and given little to eat, managing to sleep for only three or four hours a night. After five years of this ordeal, 'Ilsa went out of her mind.' Her boss actually bought her a plane ticket and sent her back to Moscow. There she was met by members of the Angel Coalition who helped her to get back home to Saratov oblast. Her relatives, however, 'for a long time' did not want to know her. Moreover, whenever she saw a man, 'hysterics began', and so she needed to spend time in a psychiatric hospital. Karacheva's concise reporting sharply conveyed the brutality of the experience

---

[16] Naryshkina and Vinogradova, 'Kazhdaia Rossiiskaia "devochka"'. This story is also told in greater detail and more sensationally in Natal'ia Panasenko, 'Piat' devochek kupil – i ty millioner', *Moskovskii komsomolets*, 24 April 2004.

[17] Naryshkina and Vinogradova, 'Kazhdaia Rossiiskaia "devochka"'.

and the terrible consequence of a psychologically wrecked young life. There was no discussion of the value of counselling, however, or of whether time might heal. Readers were left to draw their own conclusions.[18]

Another article in the same paper set out to educate readers in terminology. Artem Kostiukovskii pointed out that the term 'human trafficking', or '*torgovlia liud'mi*', for many readers probably connoted the American slave trade or even Russian serfdom, but in fact it was alive today. He also instructed that criminologists often used the term '*treffiking*' instead. He went on to describe one way in which the process had occurred for a college graduate. Alina had completed her studies and was looking for a job. She happened to meet a well-dressed and confident woman, Zhanna, who impressed her as 'a real businesswoman', and Alina felt that she was someone to emulate. Zhanna had sat on a stool next to Alina in a bar. They chatted and agreed to meet again. In the next conversation, Alina revealed that her mother was doing three jobs to try to make ends meet and that she herself needed a job. Zhanna explained that she could arrange one, and within three weeks of their 'friendship' Alina had signed a contract to work as a cleaner in Germany earning $800 a month. Zhanna said she would pay for the air ticket, and Alina could pay her back later.[19]

Upon arrival in Munich, some men met Alina and took her to a flat. They confiscated her passport, beat her and in turn raped her. Alina found herself in a brothel, expected to service up to twelve men a day. Her captors deterred her from going to the police by telling her that it would be worse for her. They alleged that the police were connected to them, that without documents no one would listen to her anyway and that, according to local law, she would be given 'not a short sentence' in prison. Kostiukovskii made a convincing case that traffickers were worldly people who knew how to win a woman's trust and hook her. Then, in a foreign country where the victim does not know the language, the girl becomes dependent upon her controller. Kostiukovskii underscored that the trafficking syndicates were 'very well organised'.[20] After three months, police raided the brothel. Fearing prison, Alina was allegedly met with the words 'poor thing, why did you come here? Didn't you guess what work this would be?' After that she was helped by a psychologist through interpreters in a crisis centre and three months later deported to Russia. Kostiukovskii remarked that Alina was one of the lucky ones. Those stuck

---

[18] Ekaterina Karacheva, 'Krasavitsy-rabyni', *Argumenty i fakty*, 5 January 2004. See also Aleksandr Kliuchnikov, 'Arabskie kanikuly', *Argumenty i fakty*, 5 May 2004.

[19] Artem Kostiukovskii, 'Treffik bez granits', *Argumenty i fakty*, 28 April 2004, www.aif.ru/online/spb/558/07. In fact, '*treffiking*' has been spelled in more than one way in Cyrillic, including '*trafik*' and '*trefiking*'.

[20] Kostiukovskii, 'Treffik bez granits'.

in prostitution abroad for many years were 'less fortunate', and those trafficked not for prostitution but for organs 'not lucky at all'.[21]

Like other papers, *Pravda* was quick to publish cases of trafficking, cite statistics and discuss what was happening to changing Russian society. In 2003 Gennadii Efimov reported on an international conference held in Murmansk co-organised by the Angel Coalition in Moscow, the women's crisis centre 'Iris' in Sweden and the Congress of Women of Kola Peninsula. Participants included representatives from Swedish, Norwegian and Murmansk social organisations, the Swedish criminal police, the Swedish Ministry of Industry, Employment and Communications and the Murmansk police. *Pravda* declared that it was 'not accidental' that the conference was in Murmansk as 'in the past several years' the number of women leaving the Kola peninsula for Finland, Sweden and Norway had 'sharply increased'. Women and girls had been tempted by advertisements for 'cheap tourist trips' and 'work abroad'. They then found themselves sexually exploited in private homes and on camp sites and subsequently sold into slavery to 'rich foreigners'. The Swedish police knew that in 2002 at least seventy women from Murmansk oblast were working as prostitutes in Sweden. Those at Iris maintained that the numbers were several times higher than the official statistics stated.[22]

After imparting this information, *Pravda* delivered several messages to readers. Firstly, more than 80 per cent of trafficked women believed that they were going into legal work that was not prostitution and that they were forced into it against their will. This again challenged the popular notion in circulation that 'they are just prostitutes anyway'. Secondly, evidence already showed that they were being trafficked to Israel, Turkey, Greece, Spain, Italy, the Netherlands, Sweden, Switzerland 'and also' to the USA, Japan, Egypt and other countries. Russia was only just beginning to realise that human trafficking 'was a serious and huge problem'. Thirdly, NGOs such as the Angel Coalition had hopes for the draft federal law against human trafficking introduced into the Duma. Fourthly, necessary prevention entailed giving out information about the hazards of trafficking, particularly to the unemployed and students. *Pravda* advised that, if women planned to travel, they should make copies of their passport and obtain job contracts. The latter should be checked and then copies of both documents left with parents and friends. Fifthly, *Pravda* reported that Sweden had been fighting against prostitution by a legal prohibition introduced three years ago. Men using prostitutes there could now be imprisoned for

[21] Kostiukovskii, 'Treffik bez granits'.
[22] Gennadii Efimov, 'Lolity ponevole, ili kto torguet russkimi devushkami', *Pravda*, 16 October 2003.

up to six months or face a fine. *Pravda* did not explicitly evaluate this but quoted someone from Sweden's crisis centre to the effect that this law did not always deter clients.[23]

In the following month, *Pravda* hammered across its message again with the headline, 'Not One Russian Woman Sells Herself Willingly into Slavery'. The easing of border crossings since the collapse of the USSR was again cited as a key contributory factor to human trafficking. *Pravda* observed that Russian and Ukrainian women were now 'an exotic good' and in demand, toppling women from Latin America, Finland and Thailand from the number one slots. *Pravda* repeated that, whether travelling legally or on false documents, 'the majority of women did not expect sexual exploitation and rape'. *Pravda* underscored that even those who were pre-pared to work as prostitutes did not expect this level of 'manipulation and deceit'. Now the likely destinations were 'Turkey, Greece, Cyprus, Italy, Yugoslavia, Bosnia, Herzegovina, Hungary, the Czech Republic, Khorvatia, Germany, the United Arab Emirates, Syria, China, Holland, Canada and Japan'. Crucially, what or who was to blame, asked *Pravda*. The answer was distinctive 'sex mania' (*seksomaniia*) 'from which practically all the main cities of Europe are suffering'. So, the demand for commercial sex, which in *Pravda*'s prism was synonymous with 'sex mania', called for more work-ers to meet that demand. Moreover, among the most popular destinations were those countries where prostitution was legal, namely Germany and the Netherlands. The message was that these were actually magnets for human trafficking. *Pravda* concluded with the warning that girls as young as sixteen could be in prostitution there which might involve 'specific kinds of sex', including 'sadomasochism and toilet sex'. They might also be drawn into sex shows and into filming for soft and hard pornography.[24] What *Pravda* omitted to note was that there was also a demand for sex inside Russia from Russian men. An implicit image was that of an immoral, corrupt and violent West as 'villain'.[25] *Pravda* also ignored the possibility that some male clients may not wish to purchase sex from a woman who had been trafficked and forced into prostitution against her will.[26]

---

[23] Efimov, 'Lolity ponevole'.

[24] No named author, 'Ni odna Rossiianka ne prodala sebia v rabstvo dobrovol'no', *Pravda*, 11 December 2003.

[25] Other articles in *Pravda* discussed global slavery, how most traffickers go unpunished, slave markets and the trafficking of minors. Examples include: no named author, 'Evropu zakhlestnula detskaia prostitutsiia', *Pravda*, 31 October 2003; no named author, 'Rabstvo v XXI veke: seks, prestupnost', migranty', *Pravda*, 12 May 2005; and no named author, 'Seksual'noe rabstvo – BIch XXI veka', *Pravda*, 6 August 2004.

[26] For discussion of how public awareness campaigns can create heroes and villains, see Erin O'Brien, 'Human trafficking heroes and villains: representing the problem in anti-trafficking awareness campaigns', *Social and Legal Studies*, Vol. 25, No. 2, 2016, pp. 205–224.

Rather more tersely, the newspaper *Trud* (*Labour*) went in for crisp factual exposé, bluntly imparting information. As the years passed, updated statistics were regularly cited of estimates of the number of duped individuals. In 2005 *Trud* cited the OSCE to the effect that the number of those tricked in Russia was 'up to 50,000' and the overall numbers trafficked into Western Europe were as high as 'from 200,000 to 500,000 yearly'. *Trud* quoted Helga Conrad, the OSCE's special representative for fighting human trafficking, to the effect that 60 per cent of these were thought to be women and 40 per cent men. Moreover, the ages were quite varied, ranging upwards from children. Then *Trud* reported a fresh message. Conrad had announced that there was not just trafficking out of countries, but 'new forms of this criminal activity' which involved 'human trafficking within one country'. This was happening not only in the USA and Russia but in smaller states too, such as the Netherlands. In Russia's case, there was also exploitation of the 'labour of illegal immigrants'. As a criminal 'chain' of activities across states, Conrad held that it required all members of the OSCE, which included Russia, to co-operate and monitor. She scolded Russia for its 'far from adequate' action in anti-trafficking. *Trud* highlighted Conrad's argument that human trafficking was based on 'discrimination against women, low levels of education, corruption, the distribution of false advertisements and fear before the authorities', thereby drawing attention to the multivariate factors involved. For addressing the last, Conrad called for the 'necessity' of 'increasing 'the confidence of people towards the organs of law and order'. The concluding message was that 'human trafficking is simultaneously a criminal question and one of defending the rights of the person'.[27]

Young subscribers to the rather gossipy and lightweight *Moskovskii komsomolets* would also have been hard pressed not to pick up something about human trafficking in the early 2000s. Natal'ia Panasenko presented sketches of the fates of 20-year-old Zhanna, 28-year-old Masha and 30-year-old Sveta, who found themselves in slavery in Uzbekistan, the USA and Japan. In Zhanna's case, she had met a man in Omsk who suggested going to Uzbekistan where she could earn more money and live in luxury ('*shikarno*'). Panasenko noted that Zhanna's parents paid little attention to her. The man hid Zhanna in his car and handed her over to Misha in Uzbekistan. At first, Zhanna had to tidy the house and wash up. The work was heavy as there were lots of rooms and guests came most nights. She was not paid and, if Misha found any dust, he would punish her by a beating in the barn with a lash. There were other

---

[27] No named author, 'V RF zhertvami torgovli liud'mi ezhegodno stanoviatsia do 50 tys. chelovek', *Trud*, 31 December 2005.

Russian girls living there too, and Misha's guests raped them. One day Zhanna broke a beautiful vase. In response, Misha beat her badly and sent her off to work on a tomato plantation. Here the workers were given 'only water and flat cakes' (*lepeshki*) except when they managed to eat tomatoes unseen by the forty-year-old man who watched them. One day when he was drunk, Zhanna ran to the road where she asked a lorry driver for a ride to Omsk. He agreed to take her if she paid him in sex since she had no money. She commented, 'there was nothing left for me to do'. The journalist punches across these rather fantastic points in quick succession, building a picture of exploitation, brutality and lack of freedom. The tales of Masha and Sveta are similarly full of lurid detail.[28]

Fresh Reports Keep Coming: 2006–2011

In the early 2000s, hundreds of articles across the press presented a myriad of pictures and commentaries on human trafficking. The above examples illustrate a spectrum from sensible revelations to sensation with some distortions. Six years into the first decade of the century, fresh reports kept coming.[29] An attention-grabbing headline in *Komsomol'skaia pravda* read: 'Man and Wife Sold Twenty Kursk Girls into Sex-Slavery'. Journalist Ol'ga Danilova described how in 2008 Akhmed Guseinov from Azerbaijan had settled in L'govskii district in Kursk oblast and married Tamara. Danilova described it as a place of mud and no work where potential bridegrooms were 'drunken cattle herders'. Prospects were dim, and so it was not difficult for Guseinov, 'in such a backwoods, easily to fool listeners promising riches and a husband-prince'. Danilova pointed out that 'with the "help" of Middle Eastern brothels no fewer than twenty young girls disappeared. Only one of them returned home independently.' The article was punctuated by sensational subheadings: 'Sheikh agrees to marry you!'; 'I'll set you up in work, just give your passport'; 'Little thin ones for $4,000, fuller ones for $7,000'; 'Escape'; and 'I only wished them well.'

Elena lived with her grandmother and had borrowed 30,000 roubles to buy a television. Unemployed, she could not pay it back. She followed

---

[28] Panasenko, 'Piat' devochek kupil – i ty millioner'. The story of Masha here is the same person as Maria in the story above. Panasenko, however, gives more shocking details about her time in New York.

[29] See, for example, Elena Vlasova, 'Devushkam dobavliali vozrast, chtoby prodat' v pritony Dubaia', *Izvestiia*, 10 May 2006; no named author, 'Bor'ba torgovlei liud'mi – delovoego mezhdu narodnogo soobshchestva', *Nezavisimaia gazeta*, 13 February 2008; and no named author, 'V aeroportu Makhachkala predotvratili popytku prodazhi dvukh rossiiannok v Bakhrein', *Nezavisimaia gazeta*, 13 February 2009.

local advice to turn to Guseinov. Apparently, he said 'don't be sad, pretty one. Would you like me to get you a job abroad?' Elena agreed to work as a waitress for payment in dollars. Guseinov promised to arrange necessary documents and a visa. His wife Tamara then accompanied Elena to the UAE and handed her over.[30] The journalist vividly expressed it with, 'the mousetrap slammed shut'. Several other young Russian women were confined in the same apartment. The local *mamka* threateningly said to Elena, 'do you understand where you find yourself? It is a Muslim country! They can tear people like you to bits and shower stones so there is nowhere to run.' From their interview with Elena later, the police in Kursk oblast commented that each girl in that brothel usually had to service two or three clients a day but 'for bad behaviour the norm increased to between ten and fifteen'. According to Elena, the young women had to sit locked up all day, were beaten for breaking rules and could be sold into worse brothels 'for any rabble'. So, they sat quietly. Danilova reported that if they were thin, they fetched less but fuller women, whom the locals preferred, could go for $7,000 into other brothels.

The story revealed that Elena had been 'obstinate'. At first, she had one client a day but was then moved to another flat to service twelve a night. Her new *mamka* had bought her for $4,000. Elena had demanded her passport back and said that she wanted to return to Russia. She was moved into a hotel and told to earn the money that had been paid for her. Here she was meant to entertain thirty to forty men a night. If she did not, she was told that she would be beaten and there were 'special people' to do this. Terrified by what it would be like, she managed with another young woman to run away. Finally, Elena went to the police. They listened, fed her, got her passport and put her on a flight to Turkey. Once there, with no money, Elena cried in the airport. Luckily, a Russian-speaking man went up to her, helped her to telephone her grandmother and arranged for money to be sent to her. Elena was then able to buy a ticket home. The message was that she was fortunate that the stranger was decent and helpful.

Back home, Elena bravely visited Guseinov who clasped his hands and reportedly said 'Lenochka, why didn't you phone me to say it was bad there. I only wished you well!' In interview, Elena in disgust apparently whispered, 'I don't know how I did not take a swing at his mug.' Afterwards she reported Guseinov to the police. Through liaison with the UAE, the police facilitated the rescue of others. The investigator made it known that they had long suspected Guseinov of human trafficking but

---

[30] Ol'ga Danilova, 'Muzh s zhenoi prodali v seks-rabstvo dvadtsat' kurskikh devchonok', *Komsomol'skaia pravda*, 15 December 2008.

had no evidence against him. Elena was the first to give it. Danilova's article was long with minute details of events which brought it shockingly to life through vivid quotations from Guseinov and Elena. Danilova highlighted that Guseinov always offered work as a waitress or as a tour guide for Russian visitors. He then sang the same song: there was lots of money there; they had oil; you'll find a husband; the men are rich. Television soap operas about wonderful lives elsewhere reinforced all this. Elena agreed to be interviewed by Danilova so that others 'did not repeat her mistake'.[31] The article was designed to expose, impart shocking information and deter. It was thus educational in an easily readable and gripping package. It also illustrated how a determined woman fought back and ultimately stood up against her traffickers, and even spoke out publicly by talking to a journalist.

Press articles kept coming after 2010.[32] Sometimes they discussed the fate of trafficked women, and others gave updated statistical snippets. *Argumenty i fakty*, for example, culled data from international sources about the 'slave business' (*rabskii biznes*). Focussing on Israel, it reported estimates in percentages of 'slaves' exported there from Moldova, Ukraine, Russia and Central Asia.[33] Overall, readers of the press cannot have missed news about global human trafficking and Russian 'slaves'. Under the headline, 'They Are Selling Natashas. For Export. Not Expensive', journalist Natal'ia Ostrovskaia even began by exclaiming: 'What? Again, about sex-slaves?' The subtext was that there had already been a barrage of information about trafficked women. On a trip to Khabarovsk krai, Ostrovskaia wondered why again she was looking at 'THIS'. Surely, she posited, these girls were culpable? Quite voluntarily they flew off like butterflies into the fire in distant countries without any guarantees or contracts. Were they not themselves to blame for their plight?[34]

In Komsomol'sk-on-Amur, Ostrovskaia spoke to Dasha, one of these 'guilty' young women, twenty-two years old, whose son urgently needed an expensive operation which was a question of 'life and death'. Dasha

[31] Danilova, 'Muzh s zhenoi prodali v seks-rabstvo'.
[32] For a selection of other stories, see: Marina Korets, 'Deti na prodazhu', *Trud*, 13 January 2006; no named author, 'V Turtsii spasaiut zhenshchin iz seksual'nogo rabstva', *Trud*, 8 February 2006; Rudol'f Kolchanov, 'Futbol seksu ne pomekha', *Trud*, 27 February 2006; no named author, 'V Saranske arestovali bandu torgovtsev liud'mi', *Trud*, 9 March 2006; Elena Vlasova, 'Devushkam dobavliali vozrast'; Nina Doronina, 'Protiv postavshchikov dal'nevostochnykh seks-rabyn' za rubezh', *Rossiiskaia gazeta*, 8 November 2010; Vasilii Voropaev, 'Biznes-plan po torgovle nalozhnitsami', *Rossiiskaia gazeta*, 8 June 2011.
[33] No named author, 'Pochemu v Rossii protsvetaet rabotorgovlia?' *Argumenty i fakty*, 5 May 2008.
[34] Natal'ia Ostrovskaia, 'Prodaiutsia Natashi. Na eksport. Nedorogo', *Komsomol'skaia pravda*, 10 January 2011.

had been persuaded to work in Israel and ended up in a brothel in Tel Aviv. Her refusal to become a prostitute led to her rape and onward sale to Greece. In the boot of a car, she was taken to Athens and left in a basement. Her minder, however, forgot to take his telephone when he left her, and so Dasha called home. The deputy head of the Investigative Department in Komsomol'sk-on-Amur, Iuliia Volkova, commented that she had seen over forty cases similar to Dasha's and that the number 'grows day by day'.[35]

Ostrovskaia asked afresh: who would have thought that from tiny villages and small towns in the east of Russia journeys were beginning to Turkey, Greece, Israel, China, Japan and Korea of 'THOUSANDS of beautiful girls of the most splendid age (17–30 years)'? She portrayed the culprits, such as Rami Sabana in Israel and his business partner Avi Ianai in Moscow, as greedy foreigners. Ostrovskaia named and shamed the traffickers and turned her starting question on its head to highlight where the blame really lay. In this manner, she attempted to question the simplicity of the stereotype of unthinking and stupid girls and women through the complexities of Daria's case. Nonetheless, the reader is left thinking that naïveté is still partly responsible. Ostrovskaia also reported that the MVD now had its own special department for investigating kidnapping, human trafficking and slave labour, headed by Lieutenant-Colonel Andrei Mel'nikov. He had commented that the sale of girls from the Russian Far East was now more profitable than drug trafficking since just one slave could annually bring in between $75,000 and $250,000.[36]

Regarding the huge extent of human trafficking, journalist Vladimir Bogdanov in 2011 regretted in *Rossiiskaia gazeta* that announcements about it had become an almost daily occurrence across the whole of Russia. He cited a statement by the chair of the Investigative Committee, Vladimir Markin, that a 'band of slave-traders' (*band rabotorgovtsev*) from Kostroma oblast had been exposed, leading to the arrest of nine people. A 56-year-old woman was the leader, and her 'shady associates' were inhabitants of Moscow, Vladivostok, Nakhodka, Tambov and Belgorod oblasts. They tricked 'tens' of women into believing that work was available in Spain, Italy and Greece accompanying businessmen to meetings. Instead they were sent to brothels. Investigation indicated that a 'living good' could now earn the criminals €100,000. The group were considered liable for conviction under three articles of the Criminal Code: human trafficking, prostitution and illegal crossing of the state's border.[37]

---

[35] Ostrovskaia, 'Prodaiutsia Natashi'.
[36] Ostrovskaia, 'Prodaiut'sia Natashi'.
[37] Vladimir Bogdanov, 'Zakony nevol'nich'ego rynka', *Rossiiskaia gazeta*, 20 July 2011.

Bogdanov used this case as a springboard for a new discussion about slavery. He observed that 'many lawyers are paying attention to the fact that there is no sharply specified definition of slavery in Russian law'. He argued that the Criminal Code lacked explicit legal norms on slavery even though both the USSR and then Russia had accepted the declarations on slavery made in 1926 by the League of Nations and in 1956 by the United Nations. Bogdanov quoted the head of the State Duma's Security Committee, Vladimir Vasil'ev, who believed that four actions were needed: all countries needed to ban human trafficking and punish it severely; in the worst cases, punishments should correspond to those for other horrific crimes; for any act of human trafficking, the law should be sufficiently strong; and 'serious and tireless' action should be devoted to liquidating it.[38]

It is strange that these ideas were presented as fresh ones. The content of the US State Department's TIP Reports had been calling for global action to end human trafficking since they began in 2001, and they had regularly berated Russia for not proceeding as Vasil'ev suggests. Furthermore, Vasil'ev here is calling for a policy direction reminiscent of the one made by researchers, those in NGOs, women's groups and a tiny number of politicians and law enforcement officers nine years earlier. He falls short, however, of explicitly calling for a full-blown law on human trafficking. If he wants one, he does not say so. What is new is his call for careful reflection on how to define *rabstvo*, or slavery. In the early 2000s it was the definition of 'human trafficking' that was vigorously sought, not slavery itself, although Article 127.2 of the Criminal Code did ban 'slave labour' (*rabskii trud*). Vasil'ev's case rested upon what he perceived as the omission of a neat definition in the Russian Criminal Code as explicit as that in Article 4 in the Convention on Slavery. His points fell on deaf ears.

What became graphically clear by 2010 was the serious need for international collaboration. One reported story described how women from former Soviet republics informed the police that they had been sold into 'sexual slavery' in Italy. The case, however, required the collaboration of the Italians with law enforcement in Israel, Moldova, Belarus, Uzbekistan, Ukraine and Cyprus. Evidence revealed an international criminal business run by eighty-three individuals who took women to Europe and the Middle East. Police found 'underground laboratories' in which the gang prepared false documents for illegal transits. Apparently 2,500 Russian passports had been stolen in thirteen cities.[39]

---

[38] Bogdanov, 'Zakony'.
[39] No named author, 'Po delu o torgovle zhenshchinami ustanovleny 83 podozprevaemykh', *Rossiiskaia gazeta*, 25 April 2011.

Diverse Recent Coverage: 2012–2016

Tales of trafficking out of Russia continued twenty years after the collapse of the USSR. Moral messages about the abuse of authority and betrayal of friends were among the stories along with illustrations of the ways in which traffickers were harnessing the Internet. Blandly and concisely, *Trud* reported the unprofessional behaviour of a school teacher in Rostov oblast. Here the trial was just beginning of six people who were responsible for the human trafficking of girls to Malta. The leader was a fifty-year-old deputy-head school teacher, Natal'ia Boiko, who in Volgodonsk had been approaching former pupils from 'bad families' and offering them highly paid work abroad. After their transit to the island, Natal'ia was paid $1,000 for one 'sex slave' and $2,000 'for an especially beautiful good'. In total the group was paid 'not less than $75,000 for thirteen victims'. *Trud* noted that the leader had eighteen years' teaching experience and had first taught literature before training to work with children with 'deviant behaviour'. She was known for taking an attentive individual approach to the children's difficulties. Without its being explicitly said, it was evident that she had abused her professional position. This exposé added to an earlier trickle of stories on disreputable ties between some police, border guards and officials in children's homes and traffickers and brothel owners. *Trud* also observed with understatement that 'this is not the first case' in Rostov oblast.[40]

Other stories focussed on the arrest of Russian traffickers elsewhere. In 2013 Igor' Subbotin in *Moskovskii komsomolets* reported the arrest in London of six traffickers, four of whom were Russian. Their leader was a Russian woman. The British police had raided thirteen flats in prestigious Chelsea and around the Stamford Bridge football stadium and freed nine girls from Russia, Bulgaria and Latvia. In one apartment shared by two traffickers they found £17,000 in cash. Using the *Daily Mail* as his source, Subbotin described how the traffickers advertised 'the slaves' on their own website. They were renting nine flats in one building and had installed one girl in each. Each woman had been offered work in 'the tourist sphere'. If they refused to be prostitutes, they were told that the traffickers would get even with people close to them at home. Scotland Yard had watched the premises in a secret operation lasting twelve weeks after one of the women had tipped them off. Subbotin claimed that their upmarket prostitution business brought in £20,000 a day.[41]

---

[40] Ekaterina Pogontseva, 'I devochek nashikh vedut v kabinet', *Trud*, 9 August 2012.

[41] Igor' Subbotin, 'V Londone politsiia "nakryla" set' rossiiskikh suternov', *Moskovskii komsomolets*, 15 May 2013. See also no named author, 'Politsiia Londona raskryla set' sutenerov iz Rossii', *Nezavisimaia gazeta*, 15 May 2013.

Several articles gave examples of the increased use of social media in recruitment and sale. Iuliia Grishina reported its role in a different trap. A 21-year-old graduate, Alina, connected with students in Moscow and offered them opportunities to study or work in the UK and a chance to marry an English lord. She invited them to come to a 'casting' which took place on a street where she lined them up and told them that their photographs would be considered by potential bridegrooms. Soon after, she informed them that they had 'pleased' the men and so now they could travel. She had also posted a notice on the Internet advertising the sale of three girls of 18, 19 and 20, for whom she wanted 400,000 roubles. The purchasers who responded, however, were the Russian police. Once she had received payment, Alina was arrested. When the hopeful 'brides' learnt of what their fate might have been, Grishina reported that they 'burst into sobs'.[42] Articles such this could easily fuel the popular notion that the women were indeed short-sighted risk-takers.

Several recent reports focussed on the complexities of collecting evidence against traffickers and how massive the paperwork could become. Natal'ia Kozlova explained in 2014 how the Russian Federation's Federal Security Service (FSB) and the Investigative Committee had worked hard to gather data on a gang of criminals from Moscow, Nakhodka, Vladivostok, Tambov, Kostroma and Belgorod oblasts. Enquiries showed that these traffickers had sent at least fifty women to Spain and Greece. The traffickers were finally found guilty and given prison sentences ranging from three to seven and a half years. The documents for the case filled 157 volumes. Integral to the investigation was the need for technical expertise in analysing a seized computer.[43] As the years passed, more articles referred to the role of computers and to advertisements on the Internet rather than in newspapers.[44] This rendered the business less visible to the regular newspaper reader and more evident to those seeking work on-line.

---

[42] Iuliia Grishina, 'Zaderzhana torgovka seks-rabyniami, predlagavshaia svoim zhertvam braka s angliiskimi lordami', *Moskovskii komsomolets*, 29 May 2014. Throughout this century there have been articles about fake marriage bureaux. Tamara from Petrozavodsk found a Finnish husband through an agency. He was 'predisposed to aggression' and murdered her. See no named author, 'Naidena al'ternativa prostitutsii', *Izvestiia*, 23 January 2002.

[43] Natal'ia Kozlova, 'Uslovnaia rabotorgovlia', *Rossiiskaia gazeta*, 20 June 2014. On huge volumes of paperwork in other cases, see no named author, 'Po delu o torgovle zhenshchinami ustanovleny 83 podozrevaemykh', *Rossiiskaia gazeta*, 25 April 2011. Investigation here resulted in paperwork in 266 volumes.

[44] One article reported that Yahoo and Facebook were being used in the USA for the 'illegal exchange' of twenty-six Russian children. See no named author, 'Vozbuzhdeno ugolovnoe delo po faktu torgovli rossiiskimi det'mi v SShA', *Izvestiia*, 5 December 2013.

Despite claims from a growing number of experts that there were now fewer cases of human trafficking out of Russia, press articles in 2016 nonetheless illustrated its continuation. *Trud*, for instance, reported on a case which had opened in February 2016 under Article 127.1. Two Moscow students of seventeen and eighteen had tried to sell a classmate. In 2015 they had persuaded their 'friend' to go with them to a photo-shoot. On the appointed day, they took her to a restaurant, expecting to hand her over to a purchaser. After they had been paid 700,000 roubles, the police intervened. *Trud* commented that 'the fate of the underage girl' did not concern her attempted traders.[45] Another article in *Trud* covered the arrest of a group attempting to sell Russian women to the UAE. This was a much larger operation in which recruiters worked in Perm krai, Cheliabinsk oblast and Udmurtia. Associates of the recruiters then took the unsuspecting captives abroad. Their latest venture had involved the attempted sale of twelve Russians for 2.4 million roubles, and a case had opened under Article 127.1. During a search, the police had found $75,000 and firearms.[46] The most recent reporting still indicates a variety of ways in which trafficking situations can begin and which may vary in scale from small-time to big-time.

Trafficked Men

Although various different estimates suggested that from 20 to 40 per cent of those trafficked out of Russia were men and boys, their stories have received far less newspaper coverage. Reporting about them was sparse or non-existent in the early 2000s but picked up substantially by the end of the decade, largely due to the trafficking of men within Russia and into it. The available stories about men leaving Russia indicated that they were used on construction sites, in domestic work and in street begging. One case of a man trafficked out in the early 2000s was that of 27-year-old Sergei from Perm, which was profiled on the website of the Angel Coalition. He had seen an advertisement in a local newspaper for work in Spain which paid $1,200 a month, attractively six times his monthly earnings. Sergei was flown to Madrid expecting to have to pay back his travel costs. A man met him at the airport, asked for his passport and took him to Portugal. Here he worked several months without pay on a construction site and was kept behind barbed wire. Sergei managed to

[45] No named author, 'Studentki iz Moskvy pytalis' prodat' podrugu v seksual'noe rabstvo', *Trud*, 21 February 2016.
[46] No named author, 'Zaderzhany chleny OPG, pytavshiesia prodat' 12 rossiianok v seksual'noe rabstve', *Trud*, 3 March 2016.

escape and to reach Germany, begging as he went. From there he was deported. Like many of the women above, Sergei was traumatised and left unable to work for months. No one offered him any counselling.[47]

Another story on the trafficking of male labour out of Russia broke in *Rossiiskaia gazeta*. In 2010 a citizen of Abkhazia set up a 'trans-national criminal group', which investigators described as 'highly organised and strictly hierarchical' in which members had clearly defined roles. They rented an office in the town of Shakhty in Rostov oblast and, in a typical pattern, advertised highly paid work in construction in the local paper. In four months ten men responded. The ones who looked physically strong were selected and offered work in Abkhazia with good earnings, a place to live and free food.[48] Transport was arranged for them, but once in Abkhazia they were passed on to others, and the men were 'stunned' to learn that they had just been 'sold'. As in thousands of other cases, their passports were taken away. The hut in which they had to live lacked 'conditions for a normal life'. The article described how next came beatings, threats and manual labour all daylight hours for just a bowl of soup.[49] In court the judge sentenced the gang members to strict regime colonies for nine, ten and twelve years on the grounds of human trafficking and using slave labour. The newspaper reported that 'all three listened to the verdict silently, not showing any emotions'. The story was followed by a short discussion around the theme of how trafficking was 'not rare', illustrated by other examples.[50] Reporting was informative rather than excitable sensationalism.

Conclusion

This historical overview of articles on human trafficking as they flowed out of the press from 2000 to 2016 shows what sorts of stories were relayed to readers, when, in what manner and from which outlet. As the world changed, so did the content of stories about both human trafficking and kidnapping into unfree labour. Taking all the articles together, it is evident that women and girls were being 'hooked' in a range of ways,

[47] His story can no longer be accessed on the Internet due to removal of the Angel Coalition's website. It is discussed in Mary Buckley, 'Trafficking in people', *World Today*, August/September 2004, pp. 30–31.

[48] In the USSR Abkhazia was an autonomous republic in the north-west of the Soviet republic of Georgia. In the early 1990s Abkhazia wanted to secede from Georgia and in 1999 declared its independence. Russia recognised this status after the war in 2008 between Georgia and Russia. In 2014 Russia signed a 'strategic partnership' with Abkhazia.

[49] Larisa Ionova, 'Zarplata – miska pokhlebki', *Rossiiskaia gazeta*, 19 January 2013.

[50] Ionova, 'Zarplata'.

that there were some variations across the cases and that trafficking operations could be small or huge. Those trapped in forced labour and unfreedom, unless they managed to break out, did not all come from alcoholic and poor families, and their level of education was not necessarily low. Although many indeed fitted these categories which provided strong 'push' factors out of Russia, college graduates were also amongst recruiters and the duped. Whilst most girls and women were young, there were also cases of older women.[51] In all cases the traffickers sought financial gain at low risk.

Whatever the differences across the separate stories, they shared a common outcome: loss of freedom, no personal security and powerlessness, whether temporary or not. The impact on the psyche could be huge, deep and lasting, but psychologists hold that this very much depends upon what the initial expectations were. It is impossible to know the percentage of the trafficked who got away and who built a fresh life compared to the percentage who struggled a little or who were utterly destroyed. It is likely, however, that most in captivity endured some abuse, threats and violence, albeit to different degrees and with different ways of coping. For many women, it was gender politics at its worst. Yet women, too, were among the traffickers and the madams. Unwillingly trapped as well, although less discussed at first, Russian men endured forced labour in other countries too. The relative silence in the press about men may reflect not just their smaller percentage, or possibly their greater reluctance to speak out afterwards, but also the potential for greater sensationalism in stories about girls and women in the sex trade and opportunities for outrage at the abuse of the 'weaker' sex.

Given the content of the articles presented here, a case might be made that it would be extremely odd if Russians by the second decade of the twenty-first century were ignorant of the fact that human trafficking out of their country had been occurring.

---

[51] There was a case of women with higher education and over sixty years old being trafficked from Nizhnii Novgorod to a brothel in Italy where men had a predilection for older women: confidential source, 2007.

Scrutiny of public opinion usefully informs social scientists and historians about how citizens perceive, understand and assess social and political trends. This contributes to knowledge of historical periods and to the grand themes of 'continuity and change' in the social fabric. Specialists on the post-Soviet states have monitored responses to a wide range of issues including system collapse, new state formations, different policies, state capacity and leadership popularity. An accumulating body of public opinion data not only facilitates greater understanding of systems but enables comparative analyses across states and also a mapping of longitudinal trends within states. Undeniably there are always methodological issues to consider concerning the equivalence of the precise meaning of words and concepts across languages or the fact that respondents may hold contradictory beliefs through cognitive dissonance or not answer a question entirely truthfully. The researcher may also have to take into account any attempts by elites to shape public opinion in order to serve their own interests. Despite these complexities, to which one must be sensitive, they do not militate against the utility of conducting surveys.

Given all the reporting across the Russian press in the early 2000s on human trafficking, as well as some coverage on television and in films, the objective here is to examine what, and how much, the population knew about the subject. This chapter explores how the public accounted for it, whom or what they blamed and what policies they advocated. Crucially for system legitimacy, it asks how much confidence they had in the prospect of different institutions tackling human trafficking successfully.

To track social attitudes on human trafficking, opinion polls of 1,600 inhabitants over 18 years of age were conducted in June 2007 and in September 2014 across 45 regions of Russia to investigate views and to generate descriptive statistics. These were run through liaison with the Levada Analytic Center, Russia's independent pollster.[1] Questions were included in the Levada Center's regular monthly Omnibus surveys of stratified random samples which excluded areas in the North and Far East that are difficult to access.[2] The questions were posed in 130 urban settlements and rural districts.[3]

Public Opinion After Amendments in 2003 to the Criminal Code

Examination of responses to similar questions in two polls seven years apart enables not only detailed discussion of the opinions revealed in each survey set in its own socio-political context, but also comparative analysis across the two surveys to see if views have altered and to what extent. Given the significant and rapid changes domestically and internationally in the time frame under consideration, the polls offer a way of looking at consistencies and changes in attitudes.

The first poll in 2007 took place three and a half years after the Criminal Code had incorporated anti-trafficking articles. Results showed that 17.3 per cent of respondents admitted that they did not know how large the outflow of trafficked persons was. Only 13 per cent considered that the problem was 'enormous' at over 20,000 per year, and 18 per cent put it at 'large', meaning 10,000–20,000 annually. The largest cluster, 33 per cent, viewed it as 'growing and serious' and affecting 5,000 to 10,000 people. Almost 12 per cent said it was 'moderate', concerning 2,000 to 5,000, and 6 per cent, most inaccurately, thought that it affected only a few hundred. In fact, many estimates from international organisations and NGOs were considerably higher, and would all have fitted our 'enormous'

---

[1] The Levada Analytical Center (Levada Center) is the core of what was VTsIOM (the All-Union Centre for the Study of Public Opinion), which formed in 1987. In 1992 it was re-named the Russian Centre for the Study of Public Opinion. The full research team of VTsIOM left the company in 2003 over attempts to put government officials on the board. The team founded an independent research company named the Levada Center after the eminent Russian sociologist Yuri Levada, who had been director of VTsIOM from 1991 to 2003 and director of the Levada Center from 2003 to 2006. In 2015 the Levada Center employed 65 staff in its Moscow Office, had more than 80 fieldwork partners and more than 4,000 trained interviewers in Russia and in other post-Soviet states.

[2] Those excluded were Sakhalin and Kamchatka oblasts and the Nenetskii, Iamalo-Nenetskii and Chukotskii Autonomous Okrugs.

[3] The methodology followed in Omnibus surveys can be found at www.levada.ru/omnibusnyi-opros. Face-to-face interviews are conducted in 12 towns of over 1 million inhabitants, 19 towns of 500,000 to 1 million, 29 towns of 100,000 to 500,000, 37 urban settlements of up to 10,000 and in 37 rural districts. Thus, surveys include 135 people in Moscow, 58 in St Petersburg, 9 in Voronezh, 13 in Kazan, 15 in Omsk, 7 in Tiumen and so on.

Table 4.1 'How Large Do You Think the Problem of Trafficking Women, Girls, Men and Boys out of Russia Is?' (2007)

June 2007	Total N = 1600 %	Male N = 725 %	Female N = 875 %
1. Very tiny (affecting just a few hundred each year)	6.0	4.8	7.0
2. A moderate problem (affecting 2,000–5,000 a year)	11.9	11.9	11.8
3. Growing and serious (affecting 5,000–10,000 per year)	33.2	34.9	31.8
4. Large (10,000–20,000 a year)	18.4	18.6	18.2
5. Enormous (over 20,000 a year)	13.2	16.2	10.7
6. Don't know	17.3	13.6	20.4
No reply	0	0	0

category. So, in 2007, only a minority of the population showed awareness of the likely scale, despite newspaper reports. As Table 4.1 illustrates, male and female respondents gave very similar answers. The only slight difference was that 16.2 per cent of men thought that human trafficking was 'enormous' and a lower 10.7 per cent of women. University graduates and those with incomplete higher education were more aware than others that the problem was either 'growing and serious', or 'large'. Sixteen per cent, for example, of those with primary school education or less thought the problem was 'large' in comparison with almost 23 per cent of those with first or second university degrees. Overall, most respondents underestimated the scale of the problem.

Did they then have a better sense of the enormity of the problem seven years later in 2014, after more media coverage? Repeating the same question with an identical sample size did highlight some variations across answers. The starkest difference was that respondents were less likely to name a figure. Table 4.2 shows that, in September 2014, 38.4 per cent, over a third of the sample, admitted that they did not know how many might be trafficked out of Russia, compared to 17.3 per cent in 2007. In fact, this is an honest answer since no one *could* know the precise number due to the hidden nature of trafficking. It is worth bearing in mind also that fewer statistical estimates on outflows were being cited in the Russian press at this time after the initial flurry in the early 2000s. Another clear difference was that the public seemed to think that there were fewer people being trafficked out. By 2014 a negligible 7.5 per cent described trafficking out of Russia as 'enormous' at over 20,000 a year, therefore down from the 2007 figure of 13.2 per cent. Likewise, just over 11 per cent in 2014 thought it was 'large', and 20.9 per cent considered it 'growing and serious'. Both these responses were lower than the 2007

Table 4.2 *'How Large Do You Think the Problem of Trafficking Women, Girls, Men and Boys out of Russia Is?' (2007 and 2014)*

Year	2007	2014
N = 1600 in each year	%	%
1. Very tiny (affecting just a few hundred a year)	6.0	8.6
2. A moderate problem (affecting 2,000–5,000 a year)	11.9	13.4
3. Growing and serious (affecting 5,000–10,000 a year)	33.2	20.9
4. Large (10,000–20,000 a year)	18.4	11.2
5. Enormous (over 20,000 a year)	13.2	7.5
6. Don't know	17.3	38.4
No reply	0	0

figures of 18.4 per cent and 33.2 per cent respectively. The percentages for 'very tiny' and 'moderate problem' were up, but only slightly.

How can one best account for these variations? Firstly, they echoed what some experts in Russia were saying in interviews in 2014 about likely falls in numbers of those trafficked out. The fact that a much larger percentage of respondents admitted that they not know how many were being trafficked elsewhere also resonated with what the experts were saying about a relative silence in 2014 around this topic. Secondly, even though stories about human trafficking of Russians to other countries were still receiving press coverage, reporting on labour migration into Russia had increased and was what troubled citizens most. A convincing case can be made that anxiety about incoming and resident labour migrants from Central Asia, the Caucasus and elsewhere deflected attention away from concerns about Russians being trafficked out.[4] Moreover, migrants were visible on the streets. Frequently articulated Russian nationalist sentiments against labour migrants with dark skins may have heightened focus on them. Respondents may have felt that press coverage on human trafficking was lower than it actually was because they did not 'see' it, or skimmed over it. Chapter 3 shows that articles continued to be published on human trafficking in the intervening years between these two polls, so there was certainly not a total media silence.

The question posed in Table 4.3 was designed to tap into views about why human trafficking was taking place. Respondents could pick more

---

[4] The diverse region of the Caucasus is comprised of the independent states of Azerbaijan, Georgia and Armenia, the self-declared states of Abkhazia, South Ossetia and Nagorno-Karabakh, and the seven Russian republics of Chechnia, Dagestan, Ingushetia, North Ossetia-Alania, Kabardino-Balkaria, Karachai-Cherkessia and Adygea.

Table 4.3 'In Your Opinion, Are Women and Girls Who Find Themselves Trafficked into the Sex Industry Abroad . . .?' (2007)

June 2007	Total N = 1600 %	Male N = 725 %	Female N = 875 %
1. Themselves to blame	40.8	43.3	38.8
2. Duped by criminal gangs	32.8	30.9	34.5
3. Sold into slavery by parents and friends	9.1	10.1	8.3
4. Looking for work abroad because of lack of jobs	37.1	37.4	36.8
5. In the main prostitutes hoping to earn more in other countries	33.4	35.4	31.8
6. Victims of the demand in the West for Slavic prostitutes	13.9	14.4	13.6
7. A manifestation of the breakdown of social order and morality	29.6	27.3	31.5
8. Other	0.3	0.5	0.2
9. Don't know	2.0	2.7	1.4
No reply	0	0	0

than one option due to the many factors involved. Confirming much anecdotal information, findings showed that almost 41 per cent in 2007 blamed the women and girls themselves for being trafficked into the sex trade. Female respondents were slightly less likely to blame them than male, but it cannot be concluded that women were significantly more sympathetic to the plight of their own sex, with only a 4.5 per cent difference. Historically the question of '*kto vinovat?*' or 'who is to blame?' has been posed over the centuries in Russia and has deep roots in political culture. This is why the term 'blame' was included.[5] Yet, although many respondents deemed the trafficked to be at fault, it should be stressed that 59 per cent did *not* blame them. Thus, over half of the sample may have been aware that the trafficked could have been deceived, then trapped. Table 4.4 shows that, by 2014, respondents were only slightly less likely to blame the women for having been trafficked, with a 4 per cent overall drop. This persistent belief that they were culpable had some resilience in the social fabric. In both years, however, female respondents were a little

---

[5] Likewise '*chto delat*'?', or 'what is to be done?', and '*kto kogo*', or 'who whom' (meaning who has done what to whom) have historical resonances with 'what is to be done?', famously posed by Nikolai Chernyshevsky in the nineteenth century and by Vladimir I. Lenin in the twentieth. See Nikolai Chernyshevsky, *What Is to Be Done?*, trans. Michael R. Katz (Ithaca, NY: Cornell University Press, 1989); Vladimir I. Lenin, 'What is to be done?' in *Lenin: Selected Works*, Vol. I (Moscow: Progress, 1970), pp. 121–277.

Table 4.4 *'In Your Opinion, Are Women and Girls Who Find Themselves Trafficked into the Sex Trade Abroad . . .?' (2014)*

September 2014	Total N = 1600 %	Male N = 720 %	Female N = 880 %
1. Themselves to blame	36.7	38.6	35.2
2. Duped by criminal gangs	40.2	38.6	41.5
3. Sold into slavery by parents or friends	10.3	11.3	9.5
4. Looking for work abroad because of lack of jobs	23.6	22.0	24.8
5. In the main prostitutes hoping to earn more in other countries	27.4	27.5	27.3
6. Victims of the demand in the West for Slavic prostitutes	13.5	12.0	14.7
7. A manifestation of the breakdown in social order and morality	21.5	19.9	22.9
8. Other	1.4	0.8	1.8
9. Don't know	4.2	4.0	4.4
No reply	0	0	0

less likely to blame them than men, perhaps reflecting that women could better intuit how the situation could come about.

In 2007, 37.1 per cent overall named lack of jobs at home as a push factor but this figure dropped in 2014 to 23.6 per cent. In 2007 job opportunities were indeed fewer in Russia, and unemployment was a stronger 'push' factor. For example, the closure of textile factories in Ivanovo, known as the 'city of brides' due to a predominance of women in the population, itself due to a segmentation of the labour force and a female concentration in light industry, was catastrophic for those concerned. Unrealistic dreams about high-paying jobs in the West and persistence of the myth about the 'glorious Western present' had fuelled hopes in the era of Mikhail Gorbachev.[6] In 2014, however, as noted, a lower 23 per cent overall cited lack of work at home as an underpinning reason. The altered socio-economic context accounts for these differences. By 2014 Russia had experienced higher growth rates and economic stability under Putin, despite economic crisis in 1998. There were more job opportunities than in the 1990s, lower unemployment and also labour shortages in some sectors. Although sanctions from the USA and EU had just been introduced over Russian involvement in Ukraine, a worsening economic situation was yet to follow at the time the poll was conducted.

[6] For discussion of the roles played by crisis and myth, see Buckley, *Redefining*, pp. 250–253.

Almost a third of the sample in 2007 recognised that criminal gangs played a part in the trafficking process. Nonetheless, neither the factor of lack of jobs nor that of criminal gangs was thought to be so overwhelming in importance that it negated blame cast on the trafficked themselves. By 2014, adherence to the view that criminal gangs had a role was even stronger. This figure now reached over 40 per cent, held by 41.5 per cent of women and 38.6 per cent of men, outperforming the earlier overall figure of 32.8 per cent. It is possible that greater news coverage linking gangs to human trafficking coupled with any local knowledge of criminal groups accounted for this difference. Although in both years women were more likely than men to believe that the trafficked had been duped by criminal gangs, the percentage differences between the genders were again tiny, around 3 percentage points.

In 2007, 35 per cent of men and almost 32 per cent of women labelled the trafficked 'in the main prostitutes hoping to earn more in other countries'. This opinion echoed what some politicians who had opposed adopting anti-trafficking legislation had claimed. In the late 1990s and at the very beginning of the 2000s, there were both denials that human trafficking occurred in the country and dismissals of the trafficked because 'they are just prostitutes anyway'. The implication was that they therefore did not merit concern or effort. These claims coincided with newspaper stories about those who were not prostitutes becoming deceived, many of whom were by implication unsuspecting, innocent and conned. These two contrasting narratives sat rather uneasily side by side. In 2007 respondents were in a context closer in years to the politicians' negative statements than were those in 2014 when, seven years later, support for this option had indeed slipped. As potential recipients of more stories from the press and with distance on the swirling accusations of the early 2000s, now 27 per cent of both men and women thought that the trafficked had already worked as prostitutes. By 2014, respondents were likely to have digested more stories across the media, many of them sensational and grim, about the plight of girls and women being forced against their will into prostitution, serving to adjust the figure. This is not to deny that prostitutes were among those trafficked out in search of higher earnings, but their percentage cannot be known.[7]

The newspaper *Pravda* had criticised 'sex mania' in the West for creating a demand for Slavic women to work in the sex industry, and other

---

[7] The research of psychologists had suggested that only a tiny minority of those seeking work abroad were prepared to go into the sex industry and that many were just clueless about what might be awaiting them there. See Khodyreva and Tsvetkova, 'Rossiianki i iavlenie treffika'.

newspapers had referred to demand for them specifically in the Middle East and also globally. Hence inclusion in the polls of the option 'victims of the demand in the West for Slavic prostitutes'. Respondents, however, did not strongly support this 'market' option as a root cause. A constant of around 13 per cent across these years selected it. Even smaller numbers of respondents in both 2007 and 2014 thought that parents or friends might sell a person into slavery. Just over 9 per cent overall expressed this view in 2007 and 10.3 per cent in 2014. The polls indicated continuity across these years and yet again insignificant differences by gender.

Whereas respondents were not overwhelmingly convinced about a huge role played by 'sex mania' elsewhere or by parents and friends on the make, they did by contrast in 2007 believe that the breakdown in social order and morality had played a part. Almost 30 per cent thought this was a relevant factor compared to 21.5 per cent in 2014. With an official ideology gone after the collapse of the Soviet state, many commentators had remarked on a moral vacuum and growing lawlessness. What stood out in the data for 2007 was that the older the respondent, the more likely they were to name this breakdown as a factor. In the over-65s age band, 34.6 per cent held this, compared with 22.5 per cent among 18- to 24-year-olds. This older generation would have known some Soviet stability under Leonid Brezhnev, having been born in 1942 and earlier and may have coped least well with the upheavals of state collapse and the uncertainties under Boris Yel'tsin. For this option, there were greater variations in reply by generation than according to gender. It is not surprising that this option had more support in 2007 than in 2014, given the former's greater proximity to the unstable early years of the Russian state at a time of 'wild capitalism' and racketeers. Women were consistently only slightly more likely to pick this option than men. In 2007, 31.5 per cent did so in comparison with 27.3 per cent of men and in 2014, with a downward trend, the corresponding figures were 22.9 per cent and 19.9, with only a 3 percentage point gender gap.

There were also only small differences in responses from men and women to the question of which institution could best tackle the problem of human trafficking. Here respondents could select just one answer. These data show a huge pessimism among the public about the likelihood of any institution addressing human trafficking effectively, reflecting little confidence in state capacity. In both 2007 and 2014 there was perceived to be low efficacy in social and political institutions whether at the apex of the system or at the local level. Both the Duma and local authorities in 2007 received low overall percentages at 2.1 per cent and 2.7 per cent respectively, as shown in Table 4.5. At 1.4 per cent, women had the least

Table 4.5 *'Which Institution Is Likely to Be the Most Effective in Tackling the Problem of Human Trafficking?'* (2007)

June 2007	Total N = 1600 %	Male N = 725 %	Female N = 875 %
1. The president	9.5	8.8	10.0
2. The State Duma	2.1	2.9	1.4
3. Regional and local authorities	2.7	2.3	3.1
4. The Foreign Ministry	10.4	9.5	11.0
5. The Ministry of Internal Affairs/militia	11.7	12.9	10.6
6. The judiciary	2.7	3.1	2.3
7. NGOs	8.8	10.9	7.1
8. The Orthodox Church	4.2	3.0	5.2
9. The United Nations	3.0	3.4	2.7
10. Other	0.1	0.2	0
11. No one	23.2	22.7	23.6
12. Don't know	21.7	20.3	22.8
No reply	0	0	0

confidence in the lower house of parliament. The president did fare marginally better at 10.0 per cent among women and 8.8 per cent among men, but again the gender difference is negligible. This figure did not exhibit confidence in what the Russian president could do for this particular policy area. In sum, the capabilities of political arenas were viewed negatively when it came to definitive action against this crime that would guarantee results.

Perhaps not surprisingly, it is the MVD with its militia which fared the best in 2007. Yet, even though it existed for the purpose of tackling crime, the 12.9 per cent of men and 10.6 per cent of women who selected it indicated very weak belief in its likely success rate. These percentages, however, were higher than those given to the judiciary at a mere 2.7 per cent overall. Confidence in the effectiveness of the legal system in convicting and sentencing was thus paltry, although the judicial process depends upon the efficiency of the militia's investigators in getting the relevant information to bring a case to court. Also of relevance are the thorny legal complexities of demonstrating that human trafficking in fact took place. The Ministry of Foreign Affairs at 10.4 per cent received an overall evaluation close to the MVD's at 11.7 per cent, perhaps giving a nod of awareness to the relevance of liaison with other countries.

Some of the most energetic who had called for anti-trafficking legislation were members of NGOs. Their persistence had forced recognition of human trafficking onto agendas, promoted anti-trafficking awareness campaigns and had helped many victims of trafficking who returned, but what they could do to prevent it altogether was limited. Only 7.1 per cent of women and 10.9 per cent of men in 2007 considered them competent in this regard. Likewise, the role of the Russian Orthodox Church was deemed effective in this sphere by only 4.2 per cent of respondents and the United Nations was chosen by just 3.0 per cent.

The response that produced the highest percentage reply was that of 'no one'. A telling 23.2 per cent, with close consensus by gender, pessimistically dismissed the possibility that any institution could do a good job in tackling human trafficking. This suggests a low estimation of institutional problem-solving capabilities when it concerned this particular crime. Perhaps well accustomed to the prevalence of informal practices and patterns of corruption, citizens considered that what Louise Shelley dubs the 'political–criminal nexus' could not easily be overcome.[8] Others declined to give a view, with 'don't know'. Nearly 22 per cent overall fell into this category. Whether it was reluctance to engage with a question on politics, lack of knowledge about human trafficking or genuine puzzlement about which institution could perform well is not known. Taking the responses of 'don't know' and 'no one' together, almost 45 per cent of the sample was unable to name an effective institution. The intractability of the problem and the success of the traffickers, however, have to be taken into account in weighing up these answers. The problem was enormous, not easily detected nor quickly proved.

In 2014, as Table 4.6 illustrates, respondents showed consistency with responses in 2007, indicating a persistence of the low level of confidence in state capacity. Despite Putin's popularity shown in approval ratings sitting at 79 per cent in 2007 and 86 per cent in 2014, a mere 9 per cent in both years was convinced that their president *could* tackle this problem.[9] The option of prime minister was included in the poll of 2014 only, but this generated mention from a dismal 1 per cent. Despite having once been president himself, Prime Minister Dmitrii Medvedev was generally viewed as weak, paling in significance alongside Putin. Similarly, just 2 per cent believed that the parliament could be effective in this regard, with a little more backing for regional authorities in 2014 up from 2.7 in 2007 to 4.8 per cent, but still negligible. The 10 per cent confidence in

[8] Shelley, 'The changing position of women'; and her 'Human trafficking as a form of transnational crime', in Lee, ed., *Human Trafficking*, pp. 116–137.
[9] For these comparative figures, see Levada Analytic Center, 'Vy v tselom odobriaete ili ne odobriaete deiatel'nost' Vladimira Putina na postu Prezidenta Rossii?', www.levada .ru/24-09-2014/sentyabrskie-reitingi-odobreniya-i-doveriya.

Table 4.6 'Which Institution Is Likely to Be the Most Effective in Tackling the Problem of Human Trafficking?' (2007 and 2014)

Years	2007 N = 1600 %	2014 N = 1600 %
1. The president	9.5	9.1
2. The prime minister	–	1.3
3. The State Duma	2.1	2.0
4. Regional and local authorities	2.7	4.8
5. The Foreign Ministry	10.4	7.0
6. The Ministry of Internal Affairs/police	11.7	10.8
7. The judiciary	2.7	4.4
8. NGOs	8.8	4.7
9. The Orthodox Church	4.2	2.2
10. The United Nations	3.0	1.2
11. Other	0.1	1.6
12. No one	23.2	22.7
13. Don't know	21.7	28.2
No reply	0	0

the Foreign Ministry in 2007 had dropped to an even lower 7 per cent by 2014 and the Ministry of Internal Affairs was again assessed as the most likely to be effective, now by 10.8 per cent of respondents, but this is hardly a high level of confidence. Its top ranking amongst the institutional options may have been merely because the police (as the militia had been re-named) were the ones who dealt directly with traffickers when they managed to find them. The low support for the judiciary in 2007 at just 2.7 per cent rose to a minuscule 4.4 per cent by 2014, echoing earlier low expectations.

The option concerning NGOs merits comment. In 2012, a new law was passed in the State Duma which required NGOs to register as 'foreign agents' if they received any funding from the West.[10] This brought much pressure to bear on NGOs and affected their work. This law, together with negative portrayals of NGOs in official political statements, may have affected the drop in the percentage seeing NGOs as effective from 8.8 per cent in 2007 to 4.7 in 2014. In addition, it is relevant that some NGOs that had been active in Russia in the 2000s no longer existed, in particular the Angel Coalition. Shelters for victims of trafficking and

---

[10] Mary McAuley, *Human Rights in Russia* (London: I. B. Tauris, 2015), pp. 296–307.

forced labour had also closed due to lack of funding. Although NGOs had been the main actors in Russia that attempted to work with returnees from trafficking situations, they could never anyway have solved the problem of human trafficking themselves. The extent to which the public knew about their work, however, cannot be inferred from the poll.

The Orthodox Church was not seen as effective either, now down to just 2.2 per cent from 4.2 per cent in 2007. In fact, the direction here is the wrong way around. Although, like NGOs, the Church was unable to tackle the crime of trafficking head on, it was able to offer help and support to victims if its priests chose to do so. In 2007, it was largely not doing this and, according to some in the NGO community, it was highly critical of their work in the press and in person, especially if it also included antiAIDS education.[11] By 2014, however, the picture was rather different. As Juliana Pavlovskaya, Director of the IOM's Information Centre in Moscow, told me, 'there has been a new line from the Church since 2013' and now 'several departments of the Orthodox Church help'. This new involvement had apparently been triggered by initial concern about homelessness. As Pavlovskaya put it, they have 'an understanding of this', and it was the problem of migrant labourers that had drawn their attention to personal difficulties. Pavlovskaya admitted that, 'we did not expect this'. But seeing workers from Vietnam and Tajikistan suffer in Russia had triggered some action by the Church, as had the problem of refugees arriving from eastern Ukraine. Homeless women who may have returned from human trafficking situations or women who had left predicaments of domestic violence could now more easily find support in the Church.[12] Respondents, however, may not have known this. The figures in 2014 for the United Nations and others were also minuscule. The general picture across the seven years was one of low regard for effective action in tackling human trafficking. Around 23 per cent in both years pessimistically replied that 'no one' could tackle the problem and 21.7 and 28.2 per cent respectively did not know who could. Accustomed to numerous narratives over the years about the need to end corruption, respondents may have come to expect human trafficking to remain resilient.

If the Russian authorities were unable to prevent human trafficking, how did respondents think they should treat returnees? Indeed, given that respondents may have blamed the trafficked for finding themselves in the sex trade, did they think that the latter deserved any help at all if they

[11] See, for example, *Pravoslavnyi Iaroslav'*, No. 1, March 1991, p. 1; and 'Seks-raby Russkaia eksotka v tsene', *Iaroslavl': Argumenty i fakty*, No. 17, April 2000, p. 3.
[12] Interview with Juliana Pavlovskaya, Olga Rybakova and Julia Melnichouk in Moscow, September 2014.

Table 4.7 *How Should the Russian Government Treat Women Who Return After Having Been Trafficked into Prostitution in the West?' (2007)*

June 2007	Total N = 1600 %	Male N = 725 %	Female N = 875 %
1. Offer shelter and protection	30.9	29.3	32.2
2. Offer psychological counselling	41.2	38.3	43.6
3. Create new employment opportunities	27.2	25.8	28.4
4. Send them home to their families	36.1	35.9	36.2
5. Leave them to sort out their own lives	14.6	16.7	12.8
6. Send them back to the country they have come from	8.6	8.7	8.5
7. Punish them	3.9	4.4	3.5
8. Other	0.5	0.9	0.1
9. Don't know	4.8	5.0	4.6
No reply	0	0	0

made it back home? They could select more than one option. Table 4.7 shows that in 2007, not quite a third of women and 29.3 per cent of men thought that returnees should indeed be offered shelter and protection. Strongest support, however, was given to the importance of offering psychological counselling. Just under 44 per cent of women and 38.3 per cent of men backed this. In second rank order, 36 per cent of both men and women recommended sending them home to their families. In many instances, in fact, this would not have been feasible. A poor family situation might have been one of the push factors in the first place. Those who had alcoholic parents or who had suffered domestic violence might not see home as a safe haven. Some families also shunned a woman returning from prostitution if they discovered how she had worked. Communities might also stigmatise her rather than welcome her back.

Refusing to back any help for returnees, however, 16.7 per cent of men and 12.8 per cent of women in 2007 decided that they should be left to sort out their own lives. Whether this was because they had little understanding of the possible psychological difficulties faced by returnees, or because they considered them totally at fault and therefore not deserving is not known. Either way, little sympathy for them is shown in this reply. A harsher 8.6 per cent thought they should be packed back to the country in which they had been exploited, and 3.9 per cent even thought that they should be punished. This tiny minority appears not to grasp that those trafficked may have been tricked. More constructively, and connected to the push factor of few jobs at home, an overall 27.2 per thought that the creation of new employment opportunities was needed.

Table 4.8 *'How Should the Russian Authorities Treat Those People Who Have Been Abused Physically and Mentally in Forced Labour After They Have Returned Home?'* (2014)

2014	Total N = 1600 %	Male N = 720 %	Female N = 880 %
1. Offer shelter and protection	21.2	22.6	20.1
2. Offer psychological counselling	28.2	25.1	30.6
3. Create new employment opportunities	15.5	15.7	15.3
4. Send them home to their families	48.6	50.6	46.9
5. Leave them to sort out their own lives	6.1	6.1	6.1
6. If they were working abroad in another country, send them back to that country	17.2	18.4	16.1
7. Punish them	2.2	2.0	2.3
8. Other	1.4	1.8	1.1
9. Don't know	9.9	9.2	10.5
No reply	0	0	0

This ranked in fourth place on the scale of priorities. The 'don't knows' at around 5 per cent were negligible.

The question posed in 2007 focussed entirely on women who came back to Russia, but was re-phrased in 2014 to ask explicitly about how the authorities should treat 'those people' who had managed to get out of 'slave labour' (*ot rabskogo truda*) in which they had suffered 'physical and psychological violence'. This question was much wider by making it applicable to men and women and was stronger by explicitly incorporating mention of physical and mental force, just in case respondents might not otherwise consider these as relevant elements. Consequently, the data in the two years cannot be considered strictly comparable even though the available options were the same.

The replies in 2007 showed greater support for providing shelter and protection to returning women than did those in 2014 for offering the same to men and women who had managed to leave situations of forced labour, as presented in Table 4.8. Advocacy of shelter and protection in 2014 saw slightly stronger backing from men than women at 22.6 and 20.1 per cent respectively, compared with 29.3 and 32.2 per cent in 2007. One wonders if what looks like less kindness in 2014 towards those who have suffered may possibly be because men are included and respondents thought that they would be in less need of protection and more capable of looking after themselves. The level of backing for psychological counselling also surprisingly fell to only 25.1 per cent of male respondents and 30.6 per cent of female, despite physical and mental abuse being highlighted in the question. One would have expected respondents to think that the need for psychological support after being in these explicit circumstances was huge.

The need for more job opportunities was less in 2014 with Russia experiencing labour shortages in some sectors, and so it is less surprising that only 15.5 per cent thought job creation a constructive solution, compared with 27.2 per cent overall in 2007. By 2014, however, the view that those who had suffered should be sent back to their families was much more strongly held, by around 50 per cent of men and 47 per cent of women, representing an overall rise of 13 per cent. There could be different reasons underpinning this view, including whether greater trust was put in the family by 2014. The government had been stressing family values even more strongly than before, as had the Orthodox Church. Increased benefits for mothers also played into the notion of the importance of reproduction at a time of heightened concern about the birth rate and demography. There were visible official narratives about desirable woman's roles.[13] This had generally always been the case, but now it was heightened again, alongside more emphasis on masculinity.[14] So a bolstered and reinforced image of the family as a nurturing place may be relevant here. Returning home, however, was not necessarily a solution, particularly for those who were ashamed to return home or for those without families. This response shows a lack of understanding of the predicament of returnees and of their fears of encountering disapproval either for the nature of the work they had been in or, if they were the male breadwinner, for not bringing back the money expected.

Those thinking that the trafficked should be left to sort out their own lives were more numerous in 2007. Almost 17 per cent of male respondents and 12.8 per cent of females then backed this approach to returning women and girls. It may have reflected the feeling that those who had been prostitutes did not deserve support. The figure dropped down to 6 per cent among the men and women polled in 2014. This may have stemmed from the belief that those who had endured the explicitly named violence in the question could not easily sort out their lives alone without support mechanisms, although this sits curiously alongside lower support for counselling. Certainly, the media had not given much

---

[13] There had been ideological messages along these lines in the USSR too, stronger in some periods than in others. See Mary Buckley, *Women and Ideology in the Soviet Union* (Harmondsworth: Harvester Wheatsheaf, 1989).

[14] See Valerie Sperling, *Sex, Politics and Putin: Political Legitimacy in Russia* (Oxford: Oxford University Press, 2015), pp. 36–79.

coverage to the importance of shelters, the value of counselling for the traumatised or the need for legal and medical advice. Except in specialist publications, there was a large degree of silence around these subjects, which were better understood in Russia's NGO community which dealt with their practicalities.

A possibly harsh 18 per cent of men and 16 per cent of women in 2014 concurred with the slightly reworded option of 'if they were working abroad in another country, send them back to that country'. This was re-phrased for enhanced clarity from the earlier version, since by 2014 it was much more evident that Russians were being trafficked into slave labour inside their own country as well as abroad. The aim was to specify applicability only to those who had gone out of Russia. Sending them back abroad, however, is tantamount to rejecting them as citizens. It compares with just over 8 per cent of both the men and the women in the sample from 2007, who had considered that the women should return to the countries that they had been trafficked to rather than stay at home in Russia. The suggestion that the victims should be punished for their plight was entertained by a tiny minority of just 2.2 per cent in 2014. Those who did not know how they could best be treated doubled in 2014 to 9.9 per cent.

How did the public react to the bigger challenge of addressing and solving the problems of human trafficking? Slightly different questions were posed in the two years. In 2007 respondents were asked how human trafficking could best be solved, whereas in 2014 they had to reflect upon the best way for the authorities to address 'human trafficking into forced labour.' Due to the complexities involved, respondents could pick all the options that they deemed necessary. The data illustrate backing for a cluster of policies. Table 4.9 shows that, although in 2007 a pessimistic 12.6 per cent believed that nothing could stop trafficking in humans and 5.6 per cent did not know how to respond, almost 40 per cent backed better international co-operation across states. The global dimensions of human trafficking had clearly hit home quickly by 2007. In second place came support for better police work in catching the traffickers. Over 34 per cent of women and almost 31 per cent of men advocated this 'law-and-order' variant. A call for convictions from the legal system came with 34.5 per cent backing from men and 29.2 per cent from women. Indeed, given the scale of human trafficking, the number of convictions had been very low, although citizens may, or may not, have been aware of this. Known figures showed that in 2007 the militia had conducted 139 investigations into trafficking cases, of which 104 concerned sexual exploitation and 35 were about forced labour. Accurate figures on prosecution, conviction and sentencing, however, were not compiled by the government, and so there were no official statistics in the public domain.

Table 4.9 *'How Can the Problem of Human Trafficking Best Be Solved?' (2007);*
'How Can the Problem of Human Trafficking into Forced Labour Best Be Solved?' (2014)

Year	2007 N = 1600 %	2014 N = 1600 %
1. Education programmes in schools and in local communities	29.4	15.7
2. Newspaper reports and television programmes	19.0	11.5
3. Better police work at catching criminal gangs	32.8	31.9
4. Convictions in the legal system	31.6	36.5
5. Stricter border controls	31.4	33.6
6. Serious attack on corruption more broadly	26.1	24.6
7. Better international co-operation across states of the world	39.7	25.3
8. Nothing can stop it	12.6	7.3
9. Other	1.4	1.1
10. Don't know	5.6	8.3
No reply	0	0

Media sources drawn upon for the US State Department's annual Trafficking in Persons Reports indicated that there had then been at least 36 prosecutions involving 103 traffickers and that in 2007 at least 46 traffickers were convicted. The annual Report also noted comments from some in the militia that the anti-trafficking legislation was underutilised because national directives on how to apply it had still not been issued.[15] There would, however, have been additional convictions under Articles 240 and 241. Close behind in fourth place was backing from 32.3 per cent of men and 30.7 per cent of women for stricter border controls. This was also a law-and-order issue, and responses illustrated awareness that frontiers had to be carefully monitored.

There was also advocacy in 2007 for education programmes in schools and in local communities from more than 30 per cent of women and 28 per cent of men. Lower backing at 26 per cent was given to a serious attack on corruption more broadly. Once again there were no sharp gender differences in replies. The relevance of newspaper reports and television programmes for addressing the issue was appreciated by 20 per cent of women and almost 18 per cent of men. Overall, answers in 2007 showed more optimism about actions that could potentially be taken than was evident in the low regard indicated in response to the earlier question about the effectiveness of social and political institutions in tackling

[15] US State Department, TIP Report 2008, www.state.gov/j/tip/tiprpt/2008/105388.htm.

human trafficking. One message appeared to be that good policies were theoretically possible but the institutional means and political will to deliver them were not.

Similar support was given in 2007 and 2014 by over 31 per cent of respondents to the 'law-and-order' cluster of better police work at catching criminals, convictions in the legal system and stricter border controls. Five per cent more in 2014 wanted to see convictions. These law enforcement options taken together reflected the belief that apprehending traffickers and convicting them was a positive move, ranking in 2014 as the highest bunch of responses. Given very low rates of imprisonment in comparison with the number of traffickers, arguably these were much needed from a law-and-order perspective. A year before the second poll, the US TIP Report observed in 2013 that prosecutions in Russia 'remained low compared to estimates of Russia's trafficking problems'. Again, relying on media sources, it announced that in 2012 there had been at least twenty-two prosecutions for sex trafficking and ten for forced labour under Articles 127.1 and 127.2. Yet again, the figures underestimated the real number of prosecutions due to the readiness to use Article 241 instead as more straightforward and efficient.[16] The public, however, may not have been familiar with the different articles.

Responses in 2014 to the 'law-and-order' categories knocked 'better international co-operation' out of the top place that it had held in 2007. The context in 2014 was one of worsening relations with the West after critical reactions to the annexation of Crimea and Russian backing for the rebels in eastern Ukraine. Sanctions in 2014 were not popular either and were packaged in daily media reports as attempts to undermine Russia and to revive Cold War thinking. Anti-Americanism in Russia, stoked by official narratives, made international co-operation look less likely. The 14 per cent drop in selecting this option was therefore not surprising. Again, the gender difference was insignificant.

There was surprisingly less support in 2014 for education programmes in schools and local communities, but this may have been because it was felt that they already existed and that young people knew more about human trafficking than they had in the aftermath of the collapse of the USSR. In 2014 only 15.7 per cent saw the need for them, roughly half of the 2007 figure. Likewise, there was a drop in backing for more coverage in newspapers and in television programmes. Then again, by 2014, the media had already imparted many stories of Russians in situations of unfree labour. Quite low percentages of 12.6 in 2007 and 7.3 in 2014

---

[16] US State Department, TIP Report 2013, www.state.gov/j/tip/tiprpt/countries/2013/215551.htm.

Table 4.10 *'If You Had a Daughter Who Returned Home After Having Worked in Prostitution in Germany, Would You . . .?' (2007)*

June 2007	Total N = 1600 %	Male N = 725 %	Female N = 875 %
1. Beat her and exclude her from my life	3.6	4.7	2.7
2. Never speak to her again	5.6	7.5	4.0
3. Speak to her but tell her to live in a different city	5.1	5.2	5.1
4. Speak to her but tell her to live somewhere else in the same city	8.9	10.7	7.4
5. Invite her back home for a short time	10.3	11.8	9.1
6. Welcome her back home	39.4	30.2	47.1
7. Other	1.1	1.2	1.1
8. Don't know	26.0	28.9	23.6
No reply	0	0	0

gave the pessimistic reply that 'nothing can stop it', quietly echoing the earlier very low expectations of state capacity.

What was well known amongst the NGO community was that returnees were often anxious about what their relatives, friends and neighbours might think of them. They were also fearful that, if they returned home, their traffickers would find them again. Anecdotal information indicated that some who had families to return to might either be rejected by them as shameful or be uneasily treated. Accordingly, one question was designed to gauge the degree of possible condemnation by asking respondents the hypothetical question: 'if you had a daughter who returned home after having worked in prostitution in Germany, would you . . .?', followed by eight variants. The aim was to detect the strengths of the willingness either to snub or welcome home and thus to test the validity of the anecdotal evidence. Given high levels of domestic violence in Russia, the option of beating a daughter was incorporated into the possible responses. For this question, respondents could pick only one answer.

One very clear difference in response according to gender jumps out in the figures in Table 4.10. Women were far more likely to welcome a daughter back home from a trafficking situation than men. In 2007, 47 per cent of women declared this in contrast to just 30 per cent of men. Put differently, a high 70 per cent of men in this sample would not receive her warmly back home. Yet just over half of the women fell into this category too. One might consider this reaction very harsh given what a trafficked person in the sex industry was likely to have endured. The 17 point difference between the responses of men and women can probably be explained by two factors: firstly, the greater likelihood that women could empathise more easily with quite how awful the experience might have been; and, secondly, the curious emotion amongst some men that it was something that offended them personally. One Russian male social scientist commented to me 'don't you see, it goes right to the heart of the Russian male'. To emphasise the point, he thumped on his chest. In his eyes, it meant that shame of the worst kind fell on the father himself. This was not about sympathy but about offence, injury, lost pride and shame.

Some were also prepared to take in the daughter but just 'for a short time'. Ten per cent fell into this category. Nearly 11 per cent of men and 7 per cent of women were prepared to talk to her but preferred that she lived somewhere else in the same city. Five per cent would speak to her but wanted her to live in a different city. An unforgiving 7.5 per cent of men and 4 per cent of women chose 'never to speak to her again'. The most unpleasant response of 'beat her and exclude her from my life' was expressed by 4.7 per cent of men and 2.7 per cent of women. The complexity of the situation is suggested by nearly 29 per cent of men and 23.6 per cent of women who did not know how they would react. Suddenly confronted by a pollster with a list of options with no advance warning of the topic may have made it hard to give a considered answer.

In 2014 the question was strengthened, as presented in Table 4.11, to make explicit the fact that the work was non-consensual with the words: 'if you had a daughter who returned home after having been forced into the sex industry in Germany against her will, thinking that she was being sent there for completely different work, would you . . .?' The re-phrasing of the question most likely increased the expression of greater sympathy. Nonetheless, as in 2007, data for 2014 still saw a tiny percentage who were willing to beat a daughter upon return anyway and then snub her even though she had been unwillingly forced. As before, men were more likely to beat her than women with the figures now at 1.8 per cent and 0.2 per cent respectively. Two per cent of men and 1.2 per cent of women said they would never speak to her again, and 3.1 per cent of men and 2.4 per cent of women would tell her to live in a different city although they would speak to her. All these negative answers, however, show lower figures than in 2007, as expected.

At the other end of the spectrum, regarding the most positive response of 'welcome her back home', the gender difference seen in responses given in 2007 repeated in 2014. Now 59.6 per cent of men were prepared to welcome her and a higher 71.4 per cent of women, showing an 11.8 per cent difference between the sexes. Although the gender gap is narrower in 2014 than it was in 2007, at 11.8 per cent rather than 17, predictably the nature of the difference is the same. It merits underscoring, however,

Table 4.11 'If You Had a Daughter Who Returned Home After Having Worked in Prostitution in Germany, Would You . . .?' (2007); 'If You Had a Daughter Who Returned Home After Having Been Forced into the Sex Industry in Germany Against Her Will, Thinking That She Was Being Sent There for Completely Different Work, Would You . . .?' (2014)

N = 1600 in 2007 and in 2014	Total 2007 %	Male N = 725 %	Female N = 875 %	Total 2014 %	Male N = 720 %	Female N = 880 %
1. Beat her and exclude her from my life	3.6	4.7	2.7	0.9	1.8	0.2
2. Never speak to her again	5.6	7.5	4.0	1.6	2.0	1.2
3. Speak to her but tell her to live in a different city	5.1	5.2	5.1	2.7	3.1	2.4
4. Speak to her but tell her to live somewhere else in the same city	8.9	10.7	7.4	2.1	1.9	2.2
5. Invite her back home for a short time	10.3	11.8	9.1	3.8	2.8	4.6
6. Welcome her back home	39.4	30.2	47.1	66.1	59.6	71.4
7. Other	1.1	1.2	1.1	3.7	3.9	3.6
8. Don't know	26.0	28.9	23.6	19.1	24.9	14.5
No reply	0	0	0	0	0	0

that 40 per cent of men and 30 per cent of women still would not welcome her home. This may seem particularly harsh given that the altered question had stressed that the girl had been in prostitution against her will. Evidently, not all respondents would automatically welcome back a daughter 'come what may' and give her shelter. There was still a not insignificant portion of respondents who were unable to stomach the thought of living alongside such a returnee.

Both years had relatively substantial percentages of 'don't knows' but these fell in 2014. What stands out is that 14.5 per cent of women in 2014 still did not know what they would do, compared to 23.6 per cent in 2007. One might have expected that responding to this altered hypothetical situation which included the phrase 'against her will' would have been less emotionally challenging, making the choice of option easier. Also relevant here is the higher percentage of women unreservedly welcoming her back home, who clearly do 'know' what they would do. Closer to the 28.9 per cent in 2007, almost 25 per cent of men seven years later did not know what they would do upon a daughter's return.

General attitudes towards prostitution as a form of work may have shaped responses to this question, so it is important to discover what they were. In 2007, but not repeated in 2014, Russians were asked

Table 4.12 'In Your Opinion, Is Work in Prostitution . . . ?' (2007)

2007	Total N = 1600 %	Male N = 725 %	Female N = 875 %
1. A good way for unemployed women to earn money	2.4	3.9	1.2
2. A good way for women to earn money whether or not they are unemployed	9.0	9.3	8.8
3. Not a good way for women to work	22.3	23.8	21.1
4. A morally unacceptable way for women to work	61.6	59.1	63.7
5. Other	0.1	0.1	0.2
6. Don't know	4.5	3.9	5.0
No reply	0	0	0

for their opinions on it. Their task was to select one of six options. As Table 4.12 shows, almost 4 per cent of men and just over 1 per cent of women thought prostitution was 'a good way for unemployed women to earn money'. A higher 9 per cent overall considered that prostitution was 'a good way for women to earn money whether or not they are unemployed', thereby giving it stronger backing. So a minority did not reject it outright. A distinction between 'unemployed' and 'employed' was specifically drawn because in the Gorbachev era research showed that in hard times a woman might try to supplement her wages with a little prostitution on the side to enable purchase of winter boots or to feed a child.[17]

In disagreement with these opinions, 23.8 per cent of men and 21.1 per cent of women considered it 'not a good way for women to work', and a higher 59.1 per cent of men and 63.7 per cent of women couched their disapproval more strongly by including the words 'morally unacceptable'. The age of the respondent appeared to affect the evaluation of the morality of the work. Just under 50 per cent of the 18–24 age group (N = 233) viewed prostitution as 'morally unacceptable', in contrast to 76.8 per cent of respondents over 65 years (N = 243). Younger generations will have known little of the Soviet state, with 24-year-olds having been born in 1983 during the brief years of Iurii Andropov at the helm, experiencing only as toddlers the short era of Konstantin Chernenko, then leadership under Gorbachev. At eight they would have witnessed the collapse of the Soviet state and in their teens experienced the new values

---

[17] See Anzor A. Gabiani and Maksim A. Manuil'skii, 'Tsena "liubvi"', Sotsiologicheskie issledovaniia, No. 6, 1987, pp. 61–68.

of a wild capitalism Russian style. The Soviet official denial of the existence of prostitution on the territory of the USSR and its condemnation
as a blight of capitalist states was a message that the over-65s had heard
regularly until *glasnost* under Gorbachev permitted a flurry of articles
which admitted that it was a social problem in the Soviet Union too.[18] In
short, Soviet socialist morality officially did not approve of prostitution.

Of all the questions posed, this one might have caused respondents
to feel that they should give an 'acceptably right answer' so as not to be
perceived badly. Respondents could have been uncomfortable expressing an opinion that they worried others might condemn. The issue of
whether or not respondents actually tell the truth is probably most
poignant here. They may feel happier giving one response with a view
to appearing decent, but actually believe another. It is a methodological
problem for all sample surveys. Despite these concerns, it is evident that
not everyone in the sample viewed prostitution negatively. Moreover,
it is a complex issue. More than 20 per cent rejected prostitution as a
sound way of making money but still hesitated to condemn it morally,
perhaps seeing that in some cases it was unavoidable and did not automatically mean that the women's morality was questionable. Financial
necessity might demand it. Furthermore, a long-known historical lesson
is that, in periods of high unemployment, women are more likely to
turn to prostitution, which is not necessarily an occupation freely chosen, apart possibly from amongst those women who advocate 'sex work',
some of whom support its unionisation.

Conclusion

What is the significance of these comparative results? As aggregate
data, they provide representative patterns of social and political attitudes sixteen and twenty-three years into the new Russian Federation.
Respondents in 2007 underestimated the scale of human trafficking out
of Russia set against the estimates of the OSCE, IOM and experts, but
by 2014 they were more confident to admit that they did not know the
numbers involved. What stands out is that more than a third of respondents in both years blamed the women and girls themselves for their plight
with a drop of just 4 per cent in 2014, despite many press articles suggesting that they had often been forced into it. Across most questions
in both years, men and women gave very similar answers, rather than
distinct opinions, except in two instances. Women accorded slightly less

---

[18] See Buckley, *Redefining*, pp. 87–91.

blame to returnees from forced prostitution but offered a significantly warmer welcome to a hypothetical daughter returning home from this ordeal. It seems likely that female empathy and male pride were contributory factors to the gender differences

A key and stark result is the huge continuity in pessimism across these years about the effectiveness of political and social institutions in tackling human trafficking and in delivering results. The appraisal of state capacity to deal with this issue was consistently extremely low. At most, both polls illustrated that what little hope there was in the system went to the MVD and its policing – but at 11.7 per cent and 10.8 percent respectively in 2007 and 2014, confidence in law enforcement to address effectively the seemingly intractable issue of human trafficking was evidently very low. Putin may have become a very popular leader, despite minor fluctuations in his high support levels, but Russians deemed this particular problem too huge and intractable for him to solve. Also, by 2014, greater negativity about the productiveness of international co-operation was clear, reflecting Russian effrontery at global reactions to developments in Ukraine and to sanctions. A 14 per cent fall in the recommendation to work globally most likely reflected changes in international context. Overall, comparative analysis of these descriptive statistics reveals not only changes in attitude to fit and to reflect the wider socio-economic and political context but also some resiliencies and continuities in opinions over time. These surveys lead into questions about how qualitative data from focus groups can illuminate explanations for the trends detected here.

5   How the Public Talks About Human Trafficking

Quantitative data from surveys have shown *what* the public thinks about several aspects of human trafficking. Discussion here turns to look at *how* Russians reflect, argue and explain their thoughts to add texture to the earlier percentages. The objective here is to present how beliefs and opinions were expressed and justified in interactive contexts of focus groups as they unfolded and developed. Qualitative data illustrate the responses and disagreements of members of the Russian public to a series of questions and tasks about the significance of human trafficking in society. Interactions reveal participants' assessments, thought processes, contentions, concerns, feelings, hopes and prejudices, generating 'thick descriptions' of what transpired.

Assumptions and Methodology

I embarked upon arranging focus groups on the assumption that, in two-hour time slots, small groups of Russians would share their views and evaluations and explain why they felt the way that they did. A starting expectation was that probing questions, interactions and discussions would better reveal through qualitative data how participants reasoned than the restricted multiple-choice options of nationwide public opinion polls. The aim was tap into how citizens thought as well as what they believed. This approach was also predicated on the assumption that looking at both quantitative and qualitative data would offer as full a picture as methodologically possible.

In 2007 focus groups were held in Moscow and Vladimir and in 2014 in Moscow and Yaroslavl. One aim here was to see how opinions in the large capital city compared with arguments made in smaller ones. Data from the 2010 census show that Vladimir was then the smallest with a population of 345,373 and Yaroslavl was a little larger with 591,486 inhabitants. Moscow had more than 10 million inhabitants in 2005 and 11.5 million in 2010; this had increased to more than 12 million by

2014.[1] All four groups had an equal number of men and women and a wide age span from those in their late teens or twenties up to their late fifties or mid sixties. Participants came from a diverse range of occupations which they described as: student, teacher, barman, lathe operator, technologist, doctor, lawyer, factory worker, seamstress, professional singer, sound producer, bookkeeper, economist, engineer, electrician, manager, fireman, housewife, post-office worker, technician, specialist in tourism, polyclinic employee, beautician, unemployed and retired. The object was to have representatives from various walks of life with different education levels and experiences.

The plan was not to duplicate exactly the ages and professions across the four groups, nor was the moderator asked to keep to a constrained and rigid pattern of questioning or to impose an identical grid on the running of each group. Although he worked from clusters of questions and prompts written by me, how they might be delivered would vary according to the nature of previous responses. This flexibility enabled spontaneous follow-ups to lines of argument that might develop in different directions. There was space for variation in what the moderator might ask. Inevitably the dynamics varied, which affected how each group unfolded. The atmospheres generated were shaped by the nature of interactions, the points raised and the personalities involved. Each group had its own distinct dynamic, shaped in part by the knowledge of the people participating and by how they gelled and debated. For this reason, data are examined sequentially by year and group rather than thematically.[2] Separate coverage offers the best overview and flavour of how each one developed. Their courses were far from identical even if some overlapping views came out. Participants in 2014 were asked fresh questions about labour migration into Russia, so time devoted to human trafficking out of the country was cut by roughly half. I watched the proceedings in Moscow and Yaroslavl through a one-way window which meant that I could see the group but they could not see me, and in Vladimir I followed it on a television screen in the next room. I had the

[1] Rossiiskaia Federatsiia, Federal'naia Sluzhba Gosudarstvennoi Statistiki, *Itogi Vserossiiskoi Perepisi Naseleniia 2010 goda*, Vol. 1 (Moscow: IITs Statistika Rossii, 2012), pp. 17, 51 and 53. For recent figures see Rosstat's website, www.gks.ru/wps/wcm/connect/rosstat_main/rosstat/en/figures/population.

[2] The results of the groups held in 2007 were analysed thematically in Mary Buckley, 'Public opinion in Russia on the politics of human trafficking', *Europe-Asia Studies*, Vol. 61, No. 2, March 2009, pp. 213–248.

opportunity of sending in a note to the moderator if I wished the discussion to change course.[3]

The first Moscow group included twelve people. Due to the sometimes heated nature of its debates and simultaneous interventions, we reduced all subsequent groups to eight. To settle participants, the moderator assured them of their anonymity and asked for a first name only, or a pseudonym, their age and their type of work. They were informed that the object of the exercise was not to judge them and that there were no 'right' or 'wrong' answers. The purpose was rather to learn what they thought. They were also asked to respect what others in the group said.[4]

One should not assume that the views expressed are necessarily representative of the entire society. They are, at best, barometers of opinions and indicators of prevailing beliefs, notions, thoughts and arguments. If attempts are made, however, to span generations, education levels and professions in bringing men and women together, then the groups that result are as representative as one can make them within the confines of their size. Focus groups can be indispensable sources for charting contemporary thought processes and narratives in another state where historical factors and cultural filters may shape attitudes differently from elsewhere in the world.

There are also inevitable methodological problems that may arise, and their successful management hangs on the abilities of the moderator. If, for example, one view emerges that gains dominance in the group, or if it is put very strongly by someone, this might make it harder for dissenters to say their piece if they feel in an exposed minority. The skill of the moderator, however, usually drew everyone out. A second potential problem is whether the moderator steers the group too far 'off topic' to pursue a line of enquiry that he or she personally finds engaging.

The chosen way into the topics was carefully crafted. In none of the focus groups did the moderator announce that the discussion was going to be about human trafficking, slavery or labour migration. Rather, he began in 2007 with the broad question of what sort of work someone could find quickly if they wanted to make a lot of money. He worked towards this same question in 2014 but first posed a wider contextual

---

[3] It is important that the moderator was Russian, not only for linguistic fluency. Russians are often reluctant to criticise their country to foreigners. Knowing my nationality could have biased results. Moreover, the state of British–Russian relations in 2007 was strained after the death of Aleksandr Litvinenko in London in 2006 and again in 2014 after Russian involvement in Crimea and eastern Ukraine and the introduction of Western sanctions.

[4] All sessions were filmed, and I was provided with Russian texts and video recordings.

one concerning what positive and negative developments group participants expected to see in Russia's future. One aim was to see if anyone
named 'human trafficking', 'forced labour', 'slavery' or any associated
concepts unprompted or, if they did not think conceptually, would they
anyway name migration processes and identify possible negative consequences?[5] A key objective was to discover what people knew, how they
presented and evaluated it, and the extent to which the problems under
discussion mattered to them.

The moderator orchestrated direction but throughout did not know
what responses he might trigger. What resulted was a perpetual motion
that was unpredictable to all participants as they bounced off each other.
In the sharing of points, some members prompted others to think more
carefully about what precisely they were saying, even to reformulate their
positions. In all groups a process of what I call ongoing 'interactive opinion formation' was taking place, albeit with some participants more recep-
tive than others to the influence of what fellow group members argued.[6]

Moscow, 2007

In response to the wide question of how to make money quickly, a
30-year-old teacher and a 32-year-old technician advised against work in
teaching or in a factory. A 63-year-old female economist thought that a
woman could go to an agency and get a job as a nanny which might pay
'very well', and perhaps study later. In response, a 46-year-old professional male singer argued against agencies on the grounds that they could
give bad advice. A young 26-year-old female engineer jokingly added
that 'they might advise you to go into crime' and recommended instead
looking on the Internet. The flow of discussion led into the dangers of
'falling under the influence of bad people' (*pod vliianie durnykh liudei*) or
into the traps of 'swindlers' (*aferisty*). The technician next warned against
'criminal business' and 'criminal finances', and a 28-year-old barman
said, 'if it is a young man, in the first place I would advise him not to
fall in with bad company' and added 'it is a bog that it is practically
impossible to pull yourself out of. Prison. Wooden beds.' The moderator
asked why prison had entered the picture, and he answered, 'if a young
man knows nothing about life and he falls under the influence of bad
company, they will simply use him and at the last minute discard him'.

---

[5] There is no literal equivalent in Russian of the term 'unfree labour'. There is no coinage
in '*bezsvobodnyi trud*'. The nearest equivalents are *prinuditel'nyi trud* (forced labour) and
rabstvo (slavery).
[6] See Buckley, 'Public opinion in Russia'.

A 26-year-old female engineer thought that a young woman could similarly be 'drawn in by bad company' (*sviazat'sia s plokhoi kompananiei*), find herself a street prostitute (*na panel'*) and be made to steal from clients. A 66-year-old aviation consultant who had been a flight engineer shouted 'she's a fool!' The moderator then introduced the topic of risks faced by the young. The female economist suggested that an unlucky marriage could result in a husband requiring his wife to sign a contract, go into prostitution and 'learn a lesson in life from that'. A 25-year-old electrician said he fully understood this sort of situation and narrated how a young women could go to a modelling agency and discover from the clothes given to her that it was really a massage parlour. The barman then interjected, 'in large towns, I saw this notice literally yesterday: "Girls are needed in a sauna. No work experience necessary" – interesting, in principle'. A 24-year-old woman who worked as a bookkeeper in a theatre finally managed to find a space to say something in what had become a series of lively exchanges. Her example was a personal story about an acquaintance:

> I know a young girl, she is very pretty, and she is attached to a modelling agency. Another alleged modelling agency offered her a contract for three months in Italy. Since she was underage, her parents forbade her. She was lucky because she really wanted to go there. Then it turned out that this agency was not so.

The moderator asked the technician what fate would have befallen her had she gone to Italy. He replied: 'charter flight. They meet her, everything is lovely, they take her passport and she starts working as a prostitute.' The barman kept up the pace with 'someone will leave that country using her passport and come to Russia. The girl is formally in Russia, she does not exist any more.' He added 'don't think that I engage in this business. She will never come back.'

'Is this a typical story?' asked the moderator. The technician thought 'there is less of this now', and others quickly agreed. He went on with, 'if it is to go into prostitution, a young woman from the provinces will travel. Of course, she knows where she is going.' A 63-year-old female doctor, by contrast, disagreed that this was typical. She pointed out that people worked in markets, cleaned the streets and could find work if they needed money. Some, in fact, came into Russia and had done so, too, when the USSR existed when there was 'Soviet friendship'. She developed her argument further:

> The mass of people somehow live like this. And there are separate cases when people want a lot of money, they have a sort of mindset. They watch television programmes and pictures of a beautiful life. They very much want it, but have no money. And so, two routes open up: they accidentally disappear, gullible; or they take a risk.

A different danger for the economist was that 'people arrive to earn money, want to get a job and fall into the hands of organised crime'. Here she was not talking about human trafficking out of Russia but what could happen to those who came into the country searching for employment.

Picking up on her cue, the moderator asked if it was indeed the case that individuals were falling into the hands of organised crime. A burst of replies came back: 'it's organised', 'well, of course', 'basically', 'not definitely', 'it could simply be a swindler' and 'it is easy to take a person'. The economist elaborated: 'I don't think that it is one person, but several are involved in this. They have special flats in which they hold people in order later to send them somewhere into slavery. Well, not slavery, but some sort of work. That is how they sell people. I don't know what next.' Her words led the moderator to ask the group how someone like the female economist could know about all this. The male singer said:

> From the media. I would like to say that it started at the beginning of the 1990s in Russia. It was the Chechen war, it was the openness of society, the break up. Then human trafficking appeared and they began to talk about it. Do you remember? It came from Chechnia and went to the West. Prostitution.

A 26-year-old theatre seamstress also dated the changes:

> It seems to me that it came from our practices after the collapse of the Soviet Union when Moscow, Petersburg and the central cities became the only sources of income for those people who lived in the provinces, in towns or who were left outside the boundaries of Russia in the Commonwealth of Independent States. People came to Moscow. They went without money and sought easy routes to make it quickly.

Prostitution, she pointed out, was just one outcome. There were also construction firms that provided work, housed migrant labourers in dormitories and took their passports, whilst the migrants 'simply worked like a *batrak* labourer for a crust of bread'. The seamstress used the verb *batrachat'*, which harked back to the past and had connotations of exploitation. There was already awareness in 2007 of the negative fates that incoming labour migrants from the Caucasus, Central Asia and elsewhere might endure.

In her stride, she went on to argue that there were 'two understandings' of human trafficking. The first was 'figurative'. This referred to when 'they abduct people, kill them and sell their organs'. The second concerned 'the surreptitious conveying [*perepravlenie*] of people abroad so that it was hard to find them later'. It followed, therefore, that 'the fate of the person does not stay in the hands of those who conveyed them [*perepravliaiut*], but in the hands of those who receive them'. Furthermore, 'those who transport them receive money and that is it.

It does not concern them after that.' Her belief was that they ended up 'in prostitution mainly' or in those jobs in which 'the local population does not want to work'. A 30-year-old female sound producer agreed with the seamstress's periodisation and showed awareness that passports were taken away and that a woman could think that she was going to be a dancer but instead be thrown into the sex industry. She then imparted that, if women refused to prostitute themselves, they would be killed and their corpses would end up in the sewers. She summed it up as 'an unknown fate and no one can do anything'. It was 'sale'. The job agency that had set up the purchase simply received money and then after that 'nobody knows anything'.

The blame for all this according to the now angry aviation consultant was the end of the USSR. He launched into an animated historical sketch of slavery and serfdom in the past. Then he praised the USSR for having delivered 'strict, strict order', insisting that 'there was no other path to achieve great advances'. He regretted 'a different revolution' in 1990 that meant 'everything that had been created, everything was sold off for kopecks, everything, human resources, one deficit, then another deficit, and people were destitute'. He perceived destitution as the key to understanding why people fell into human trafficking.

The barman wanted to go further back:

> If you dig deeper, trafficking in persons has existed for many, many years. It was there several centuries ago when human life was cheap. People fought and they sold people as slaves from state to state. Little princes re-sold these people, argued with each other, said I will give you 100 slaves if you leave me alone, don't attack me. So, this was an exchange.

He lamented that today 'human life is worthless' and that developments were reverting to the distant past.

The group struggled to give a clear definition of human trafficking but overall came up with some of its central characteristics. The female teacher chipped in with: 'I don't know how to say it more precisely, it is when a person, irrespective of the means, loses their rights. To the self.' The technician declared that he agreed with what had been said but stressed that human trafficking was more to do with being sold abroad, particularly into prostitution and 'all for the sake of money'. The electrician described it as being about 'using people' and 'possessing' them. A 20-year-old male student in road transport stressed that kidnapping for human trafficking and the sale of a person 'was not rare'. He thought that blackmail (shantazh) could be involved. The female doctor picked up this thread and said that the press showed that it happened in the Caucasus when people were taken and sold on. 'Deceit' (obman) was also integral to the process when young girls were promised 'allegedly beautiful specialisms' before their passports were taken. In these answers, participants started using the concept of 'human trafficking' with some ease even though they had not first volunteered it.

The moderator requested thoughts on how the process of conveying people elsewhere really worked. Was the business purely Russian, did it originate from just one town or were all the connections international? The replies that came back included: 'any variants', 'international', 'both international and between towns' and 'they grow and develop their networks'. Reflecting on international links, the barman said, 'putting it crudely, Russian girls are rated in Italy. The flow goes to Italy. In ten years' time, they will begin to be rated in the United Arab Emirates.' The economist qualified this with, 'they will be taken where tourism is growing most'.

They all thought that between 80 and 90 per cent of those 'sold' abroad up to 2007 were women. The doctor volunteered that, 'I read that two million Russian girls, the most blossoming ones, found themselves abroad in street prostitution.' She believed that these problems were everywhere in small doses, but nowhere else suffered on the scale that Russia did. The seamstress put it down to 'economic and political instability', and the sound producer saw it in terms of 'probably the lack of social protection'. Others, like the bookkeeper, talked about 'cynicism', which prompted the singer to note that 'at the time of the Soviet Union we had an ideology and everyone held onto that. The Soviet Union disintegrated, there is no ideology, there are no directions.' The economist quipped: 'there was no unemployment in the country, there was industry'. The barman thought that the goal in life 'was lost'. From childhood, they had been brought up by their parents to study, get good marks, go to an institute, get a profession, receive good wages and be protected. But why study now, he asked? The economist, as one of the two over-60s in the group, commented that 'our generation is different' and 'educated'.

The moderator asked how human trafficking stemmed from a loss of goals. What was the connection between them? The doctor believed that 'today our society does not value what is moral'. The same went for 'personal dignity. So, a person is alone and left to himself or herself.' She thought 'crime stems from this' and criminal structures 'go unpunished'. Gravely, she went on to say, 'who of us today would say that he or she does not fear going out, is not afraid that they will approach, thrust with a knife?'

The female teacher looked uncomfortable with the notion that human trafficking was 'business'. Instead she asserted that 'it is not business, it is moral crime' (moral'noe prestuplenie). To her this meant 'an insult to people' and a loss of rights. The electrician thought a woman would be 'totally dependent upon the person who took her documents' and he could take her 'to any other place'. The student emphasised that 'a person must be free', and the economist portrayed trafficking as a 'coercive act against an individual' which required criminal punishment. The entire Moscow group agreed.

They also felt that such a woman or girl, although 'deceived', was likely to be 'stupid', 'naïve', 'weak-willed', 'not bright', 'lower than average intelligence', 'who watches Dom-2',[7] 'not educated', 'in rare cases educated', 'secondary school only', 'low cultural level' and 'beautiful'. The barman held that the strong-willed were unlikely to be trafficked, but others disagreed and insisted that they were vulnerable too. In answer to how long a woman might be trapped, the group offered various estimates from five to fifteen years. The technician, however, thought that 'the person adapts. They kill their will. If their will is not crushed, the person will run away.' This account provoked others to demand 'where to?' He persisted with 'someone or other runs away, a stronger one. Someone tries to build good relations with a client and attempts it through him. She leaves with help.' The barman contested the likelihood of this scenario. He rhetorically asked: 'Get out of this profession?' He portrayed a woman physically frayed from her work, suffering a morally crushed psyche and who could easily break down. Her pimp, he went on, 'used her as he wanted, and not always in prostitution. Today, to put it crudely, you service fifteen men and tomorrow at a party you dance for some sheikh or other.' Afterwards the barman believed these women were just tossed onto the street when their pimp had exhausted them. The technician interjected, 'they can kill'.

When asked how many returned home to Russia, people doubted very many. The electrician contributed that 'our embassy does not want them, for the most part'. The barman asked how they could leave another country anyway without a passport. Others suggested that, if they were not killed, they might commit suicide or drink themselves to death. The view emerged that they were 'victims' (*zhertvy*) and 'deceived victims' (*obmanuty zhertvy*). If they did manage to return home, then there were various views including: 'no one would meet them', 'she would soon die', 'they lose their human qualities', 'odd person out' (*izgoi*),[8] 'no, something of her remains', 'her mother would meet her', 'if there are parents, of course' and 'prostitutes are basically from broken families who throw them out'. If she returned to her town, the sound producer graphically suggested,

---

[7] A Russian television programme, 'House-2' is similar to 'Big Brother' in the UK.

[8] *Izgoi* is a term which refers to someone in Kievan Rus with a changed status. It could, for example, be a freed slave or a ruined merchant.

'they would hunt her down' (*ee zatraviat*)[9] due to 'what she had done. Most people would know.' The bookkeeper regretted that 'it seems to me that no one will want this girl. If she has no one, she will simply be lost.' The barman returned to his theme of psychological breakdown and thought that, if she did 'by some miracle' return, she would not be '100 per cent a person'. Then ensued a lively debate about just how broken she might be with the optimistic singer hoping that, through 'strength of will', she might overcome it.

Having all argued that her reception home would be negative, the participants followed with more positive reassessments. The barman hoped that, alongside those who dismissed her as 'an idiot', there would be others who were 'decent people' and who would pity her and help in some way. Others then reflected that it was all much more complicated. There were 'compassionate' people who might feel sorry for her. Her future might also depend upon whether she was in a rural area or a big city. The seamstress immediately expressed a contrary view that those around her would 'cover her in contempt'. The doctor did not like this and stressed that 'girls, little young ones, beautiful ones. What unhappiness that a child fell into such a situation.' Discussion was fast-paced. A 20-year-old student studying road transport wisely asked what information they had upon which to base any of these points.

Debate turned to the fate of young girls trafficked into Russia from Moldova, Ukraine and other countries in Eastern Europe. They, too, had their passports taken away and found themselves in similar predicaments to the Russians trafficked out. The question now was: how did the Moscow police treat them? Some thought that the militia would help the women, but the bookkeeper believed that they 'had their way with them. They use their services for free.' In slang this practice is called a '*subbotnik*'.[10] Others followed on with 'and then they simply release them'. Important for the police is that 'no one investigates afterwards'. The view also emerged that, whether a prostitute in Moscow had been trafficked in or was working this way voluntarily, the police would take advantage of both categories. The bookkeeper added 'the militia are not in the loop whether she has been sold or if she has her own passport. She won't have her passport at work.'

The moderator then asked the group to consider how important the problem of human trafficking was for contemporary Russian society. The economist felt strongly that 'it is the most important, of course.

---

[9] This verb is particularly strong and connotes hunting down an animal.

[10] This harks back to Soviet times when citizens participated in unpaid labour days and would engage in 'socially useful' work such as clearing rubbish from the streets. The work was often done on Saturdays and was called a *subbotnik*.

It's our young people, our brains, our successors.' The moderator probed whether all other problems were therefore ranked lower in importance. The student thought that drug taking was of equal weight but the barman suggested that 'any problem is connected with another'. A loud voice offered that 'drugs and unemployment engender human trafficking', and the doctor added that, 'well, the most important must be that society is healthy'. The moderator was not satisfied and asked for a proper ranking. The bookkeeper believed that 'this is problem number one because drug taking is not connected with human life in the same way'. Others agreed with 'we are losing people', and one reflected that, 'while you are not stagnating in it yourself, you don't ponder it'.

The singer struggled with any ranking and volunteered that 'I would put all problems spinning in a spiral.' He viewed matters as mutually reinforcing. For him, 'we are returning to where we began. The collapse of society.' For him it was time to 'gather bricks' and build. The bookkeeper came in with, 'if we generalise from all of Russia's problems, then human trafficking is connected with crime. And crime in Russia stands in the number one place.' The barman considered that, if both physical and moral problems were included, then morality could also be number one. The aviation consultant, who had been quiet for a while, intervened with 'implementing the state's laws. Isn't that the most important?' Again the moderator pressed them: 'whether you see it as a crime, as breaking a law or as equal to other problems, is it still ranked at the top?' Everyone cried 'yes' and 'that's true'. The doctor added forcefully, 'and it's a direct violation of a person's rights!'

Did these women, then, deserve help and, if so, from whom? Most thought that assistance should come from 'the state' and 'from conversations with a psychologist'. The bookkeeper qualified the discussion with 'not only the state. The state must help in getting psychological and medical help and so forth. But the people who surround her, they must give moral support.' The moderator asked if they should join forces and work together or offer support separately. Someone piped up with a reference back to the Soviet past: 'the *kolkhoz* situation always hinders. Everyone should act according to their own mind.'[11] The bookkeeper disagreed and suggested that social organisations could help, just as the Soldiers' Mothers had done for young men in the armed forces.[12] Others agreed

---

[11] On the *kolkhoz*, or collective farm, there were meetings of all members. The quotation refers to the difficulties of involving a large number of people in decision making and hints at problems of interference.

[12] See Kathryn Pinnick, 'When the fighting is over: the soldiers' mothers and the Afghan madonnas', in Buckley, ed., *Post-Soviet Women*, pp. 143–156.

and supported the idea of some sort of 'society of assistance'. Suggestions followed that someone who had suffered in human trafficking could set up a social organisation or their relatives could.

The next task was to consider how Russia could stop the selling of people. Several recommendations were forthcoming: 'people should be more compassionate', 'state structures should work at the required level and must investigate', maybe create a 'department', 'change economic policy', 'if they found work in their homeland, no one would apply to work abroad', 'above all bring people up properly', 'everything begins in the family', 'stricter laws', 'more social protection', 'create an organ that will control it and not the Migration Service', 'the media can play a very important role' and 'different television channels can show it, explain, thoroughly chew it over and propagandise'. The group was not short of ideas. They doubted that the FMS could do much regarding human trafficking out of the country on the grounds that it would inevitably lose track of those who left.

Their overall conclusions in the summing up exercise focussed on education, the media, the role of the family and strong leadership. Recommendations from group members included: 'wage propaganda', 'yes, among the population' and 'higher education'. The aviation consultant, however, remained disgruntled. He maintained that 'any society is only capable when it is organised, when there is a party. But everything now is messed up.' He sighed and proclaimed 'poor Russia! They take everything away from us – morality and the right to work. There is no Union, no holidays.' He continued, 'why do they plunder Russia? I have flown around half the world, even fought in Africa, but I have never seen anywhere poorer than us.' The younger ones looked on tolerantly at this 66-year-old as he persisted on this track of 'we cannot do anything! The country needs a leader, leaders make history – Alexander the Great or Caesar.' Someone followed his outburst with a point about the need to 'improve social conditions and increase control', but he exploded back with 'and who? Who will do this? You? Me? Who will triumph? Lenin? Stalin? Yel'tsin?' A calm reply answered him with 'whoever is in power'. The economist partly supported him, saying 'there must be very strong power, a strong media which must lead youth into what they should be doing, into how they should think. At the moment it is taking us backwards.' Others stressed that family life and instruction about human trafficking in school were key.

Their final regret was that 'laws are not obeyed' and that law enforcement organs actually 'give these people, either alone or in groups, the possibility of occupying themselves in human trafficking'. The Russian president, however, was let off the hook by the group, with the singer declaring that 'in principle, none of this depends upon the president'. Others chorused 'that's right!' The electrician commented that, 'it depends upon the bureaucracy'. This was reminiscent of statements sometimes heard from prisoners in the 1930s in the Gulag along the lines of 'why doesn't someone tell Stalin?' Those surrounding him were often blamed for the excesses of the purges and not the leader himself.[13] Likewise, under the tsars, it was often the boyars who were blamed for policies, not the tsar.

Vladimir, 2007

How did reflections in the group held in Vladimir compare with the arguments made in Moscow? At the outset, more focus was devoted to the concept of 'risk', which figured prominently. Pessimistically, a man in the fire service aged 35 argued that 'for young people – everything is risky'. A female doctor of 45 agreed. In her view, 'there is risk in the most simple things, not to receive the desired pay because the documents don't exist, or simply to find oneself in a criminal circle' (*v kriminal'noi srede*). A 52-year-old engineer interjected 'don't take any credit' and avoid criminal circles, illegal work and racketeers' (*reketery*). There was agreement that the best way to steer clear of criminality was to have a good education. Those with only secondary schooling were at greater risk, and if they wanted to earn more money they would have to leave Vladimir for Moscow. A 69-year-old former university teacher confirmed that all her young students who could not find work in Vladimir went to Moscow and worked there mainly as bodyguards or janitors. The doctor stressed the importance of getting a job 'through official channels' with a proper company, and she thought that there were opportunities in seasonal agricultural work and in road building. All believed, however, that the level of local criminality had been much higher in the 1990s than it was now, and one remarked 'there are fewer shootings now'. They felt that life was more stable, despite the ongoing criminality that they had just described.

Initially their replies focussed on male labour. When asked subsequently what advice they would give to young women, the topic of human trafficking immediately came up, although the concept itself was not used. The fireman said he would warn a woman 'do not agree to various job recruitments in other countries where they sell them into various dens [*pritony*]. It is an obvious danger for young girls.' The group warned again against 'the black economy' and 'criminal structures'

---

[13] See Evgenia Ginzburg, *Into the Whirlwind*, trans. Paul Stevenson and Manya Harari (London: Harvill Press, 1999).

which could 'use' a woman 'practically as a slave' (*kak raba*) and create 'slave work conditions' (*rabskie usloviia truda*). The doctor thought it was much harder and 'considerably more complicated' for a woman to earn a lot of money, especially 'if she takes an honest route', and 'the risk is huge'. Moreover, 'there is sexual discrimination in pay, although they don't say it openly'. She argued that men had greater opportunities 'to earn big sums of money', but it was harder for women to get jobs. A related problem, she felt, was that Russia had really put off setting up a good search system for labour which could link up people looking for jobs with employers. In its absence, she feared that those with low levels of education in Vladimir would not be sufficiently cautious.

The fireman seemed quite troubled by this topic and said that, 'judging from the newspapers, they print "young girls wanted" offering work as a telephone operator but in fact it is for a massage parlour or strip club'. The housewife agreed and cautioned against taking a job as a nanny in another country which could have negative consequences. The teacher said that some of her students took jobs as waitresses in Vladimir or as shop workers but others felt that being a waitress also carried risks. The fireman thought that low-paid waitresses could be asked to work at night as well in order to earn a better wage and then they 'fall to such levels – terrible!' He admitted that 'I come across this in my work.' He named a particular restaurant which 'everyone knows' and in which this occurred. With disapproval, he went on, 'how many girls stand there! Easy money! . . . How much filth they pile up.' The situation was 'interminable'. The fireman declared that the majority of young women would not choose to work in prostitution willingly. He knew cases, however, of parents pressing their daughters into it. He reminded everyone that, 'there was a period when there was no work at all and the lower classes sank to such a level that it simply wasn't possible to live'. He had in mind 'our small towns' and named the tiny settlement of Orsh where problems stemmed from the end of local farming. A 65-year-old boiler specialist added that his wife worked in a college, and he knew from her that girls went abroad. The youngest group member, a bookkeeper of 18, finally spoke and volunteered that she would advise a young woman to avoid being attracted by 'easy money' and not to accept 'such offers' or go anywhere that she 'did not know'. A 19-year-old lathe operator agreed but was unsure how he could best direct a woman. When the moderator asked how easy it was to find the people responsible for recruiting young women, the housewife replied, 'ask a taxi driver. I know that they know. Some of my acquaintances are taxi drivers.'

When requested how to name this business of recruiting girls, no one immediately came up with 'human trafficking' (*torgovlia liud'mi*).

The replies were 'souteneur' (*sutener*), 'accomplice' (*souchastnik*) and madams (*mamkami*). When they were asked if they had heard of the term 'human trafficking', they immediately described its consequences and referred to 'slavery' (*rabstvo*) and 'sexual slavery' (*seksual'noe rabstvo*) rather than offering its precise definition. It had cropped up, they said, in crime reports on the television but not in their everyday conversations. Instead, they preferred to refer to it euphemistically as a young woman experiencing 'an unpleasant history' or falling into 'an unpleasant situation'. The boiler specialist added that his wife thought that 'they dress in a vulgar way, even in class', and that 'every year it's all worse and worse'.

The doctor then dropped a bombshell on the group. She admitted that:

> It's very complicated for me to talk about this because it was my first specialism. I am a surgeon and gynaecologist. And I worked with the consequences of this. Not just to heal them but to talk to them. I tried somehow to put them on an honest path. It did not always work out. The lower the social and material status, it is more complicated to solve all these problems.

This unexpected revelation led to requests for more details. She narrated how 'these girls are afraid'. They said very little about their lives, and 'usually the boss of the establishment where they work brings them'. She thought their owners (*khoziaeva*) or those who had taken them on (*rabotodateli*) 'have a specific appearance'. The young women 'follow very precise instructions'. They were 'traumatised' and 'hold back'. She characterised women trafficked out of Russia as quite varied: 'one falls into it knowingly, and another is a victim of circumstances. She cautioned against taking one position on 'this mass of people who work in prostitution'. Throughout the two hours together she stressed the complexity of developments and advised against simplistic generalisations. The doctor said 'the flow is two-way. They bring in a female population for that business from countries of the "near abroad", mainly from Ukraine and Moldova. And they take them out to all countries. And if you believe the media, Russian girls even work at Chelsea football team.'

The moderator asked the group to name the people who recruited women. They suggested that they were once tear-aways (*krutye*) who later became bandits (*bandity*), not people (*neliudi*), animals (*zveri*), boss or master (*khoziain*), racketeers (*reketiry*), underground organisations (*podpol'nie organizatsii*), but no one specified 'people traffickers'. When the moderator asked if they had heard the words, most said 'no'. Again, the group preferred to describe the process rather than analytically define it. The boiler specialist thought that people traffickers were 'freaks' (*urody*), and the fireman thought they were 'little people who lived a good and easy life from birth' (*kak za pazukhoi*).[14] He elaborated that 'from birth everything seemed easy and direct, he is tsar and God, and people for him are insects'. The teacher thought they just came from criminal circles, and the housewife considered it was all about the uneducated who might fall into criminal circles when trying to make money. The fireman volunteered that traffickers were various sorts of people. Some had been in prison, some had been evil all their lives, some were 'rich little kids' (*bogaten'kie detishki*), and some were well connected, by which he meant 'former party workers'.

The doctor had a different take on it:

> There are businessmen with exceptionally cold calculations. They first make an estimate of how profitable this business is and they are largely indifferent to what they go into, so long as they earn a lot. Human trafficking is highly profitable and you can put it on the level of trade in cigarettes or spirits. I think businessmen make a cold calculation. There are among them people of a lower position who have a criminal past, and in my opinion there is a particular group of people with peculiarities of the nervous system who have some kind of undiagnosed sexual predisposition which leads them into this business. This is painstakingly covered up. Psychological help is not well developed in our country and no one looks at the psychological health of the population.

The others did not feel qualified to comment upon this.

There followed a lively debate about whether traffickers worked alone or in an organised gang. Most thought organised groups ran human trafficking because 'it is well planned'. Only the man in the fire service thought that maybe one person could be responsible too. Even livelier was the discussion about the nationality of traffickers. The housewife thought that the people who took young women into prostitution in other countries came from those countries. Another said 'no, they are ours, ours are cleverer'. A third chipped in with 'the Americans also work here'. The engineer reasoned, 'probably everybody. Crime knows no borders, no nationalities.'

So how should this activity best be categorised? Was it simply business, morally doubtful business, a moral crime or a purely criminal activity? The group was asked to ponder these four options. Three voices immediately said it was 'criminal'. The doctor preferred to view it as a moral crime, and the fireman reflected that, 'I would like to say that it is criminal, but knowing our legal process, the court will justify putting them on probation, so I shall say that it is immoral business.'

---

[14] There is an expression in Russian of 'zhit' kak u Khrista za pazukhoi', which is literally 'to live as with Christ on the bosom'. Its sense, however, is to live a very good and safe life, and it refers to someone for whom everything is easy.

The moderator then asked what sort of person could actually choose to go willingly with the traffickers. The bookkeeping student thought 'someone naïve and hopeful'. As in Moscow, this group thought her fate would be a tragic one. The teacher believed that if she was already working 'as a slave' then 'that is how she will work'. Unless she managed to run away, she would be stuck if no one would pay to get her out. The housewife regretted that 'there are very often cases of drug addiction and murder'. She thought a young woman could be killed for any recalcitrant behaviour or for trying to get away. The engineer interjected that a television programme showed how sometimes law enforcement finds them and frees them. After going back home, however, and giving birth to a child, they then decide, 'I will go back.' The engineer referred to a well-documented pattern by researchers and psychologists that women sometimes hope that 'it will be different this time'. The doctor from her professional experience dwelt upon what was involved in 'fulfilling a stranger's will'. She saw it as:

> violence against her person, physical and moral. All depends upon the girl's nervous system, how much she can cope with, how much she can resign herself to the situation or will rebel in some way. I think that to predict further is extremely complicated. There are different cases.

The psychological state of the victims (*zhertvy*) – which is how indeed the group saw them – was, according to the doctor, one of 'despair' (*otchainie*) when they came to see her for treatment. She revealed that sometimes 'these slaves' took drugs in order to cope. Her owner might also supply drugs to make her more dependent and passive and then deduct their cost from wages. So then 'she becomes accustomed to narcotics'. For those who did not overdose, the doctor believed that 'over 25 years old this good [*tovar*] won't be interesting to anyone'. Pessimistically, she predicted that what followed was 'moral degradation: nowhere to go, nowhere to live, no money' and 'no future'. The fireman thought, 'they all take drugs to relax in order not to absorb emotional filth into themselves. Once they inject, they forget.' He imagined that they would finish their days in railway stations or basements and 'die', but the housewife, drawing on religious conviction, mused that 'there is someone higher, they will be somewhere later. I don't think they all end up on the street.' The boiler specialist agreed with the housewife that it might be possible for those who had been trafficked to return to 'a normal life'. The teacher believed more strongly that they could return home, get married and 'live wonderfully'. The quiet lathe-operator and bookkeeping student concurred. The teacher added, 'you forget that many go willingly who are not those who were caught and held'. This triggered heated disagreement.

The fireman insisted that no returnee could live a normal life immediately. Even if she were strong, 'it takes time' and 'not one year and not two'. He doubted whether after this 'violent male humiliation' she would have 'a normal psyche' and questioned whether she would ever be able to 'live normally with a husband in a sexual sense'. He concluded that what she needed most was 'warmth, care and time'. The heating engineer then lightened the atmosphere with 'there is an understanding that prostitutes make good wives'. The fireman joined in with 'there is a saying that a wife must be a prostitute in bed and a cook in the kitchen'. The female doctor did not laugh. The heating engineer defended his position with 'she has been through a lot and after misfortune her life will naturally appear differently to her'. He thought that suffering gave perspective.

How would others treat her? The engineer wisely said 'people are different. It depends on the person, circumstances and personality.' Another chipped in with the saying 'you cannot stop people from saying what they want' (*na kazhdyi rotok ne nakinesh' platok*). When the moderator imparted that someone in the Moscow group had said 'they would hunt her down', they agreed that perhaps so in a rural area or small town. The doctor suggested that 'in order to relate adequately to people and to their own past, a person needs to approach a psychologist'. She then told the group about the existence of a centre in Vladimir for 'women who have suffered violence at home in the family'. She described how 'there is a psychologist, a lawyer and a medical worker who can give help'. It was a 'social organisation' on Osipenko street with foreign financial support and some money from the municipal budget. It had been set up voluntarily by a surgeon who gave up her job for two years to find funding. She did this because someone close to her had suffered domestic violence and she wanted the problem tackled. The teacher added that there was also a 'centre for psychological relief' (*tsentr psikhologicheskoi razgruzki*) on Lenin prospect.

When asked how human trafficking could be prevented, the lathe operator and bookkeeping student thought it was vital 'somehow to direct youth after school into the right direction in life'. The engineer argued that law enforcement should be more active. He reflected:

It's a Russia-wide problem. For example, a 'boss' or a 'madam' knows when someone is not working and is living badly. In the Soviet Union, and I am not saying that everything was good, but if a person had not worked for four months, he was put in prison for being a parasite. And now if he does not work, there is everything and anything can happen.

The doctor viewed it differently and argued that the problem was best considered from three angles: problems in the family, in the state and in civil society. Firstly, she recommended that children should learn about 'home economics', as they did 'in the West', and about how to plan a budget. She felt that, if they understood this, they were less likely to be trafficked. Secondly, the state should pursue two main tasks: create economic conditions to end unemployment, especially in small towns, and combat the black economy. Thirdly, social organisations in civil society (*grazhdanskoe obshchestvo*) that are involved in 'explanatory work' were essential. She was the only person out of participants in all four focus groups explicitly to refer to the concept of civil society, defining it as 'social organisations of any kind'.

There was general agreement that the family should not suffer materially. Then the lathe operator's Soviet theme was picked up again by the teacher who reflected that, 'abolishing the Young Pioneers served no purpose. Let them call it something else. Komsomol organisations, after all, united children. I remember how it was when I was a Young Pioneer and a member of the Komsomol. I conducted myself appropriately. We carried our Komsomol card every day.'[15] The fireman interjected, 'there was structure'. The teacher did not like this word and retorted 'why structure?' Enthused, she took off again with 'it was not bad for children because they did not limit them. In schools, we had all possible groups, we were always busy.' Moreover, 'parents knew where we were and where we were going. That does not exist now.' The housewife also underscored the importance of school as a 'support' alongside good rearing in the family. She regretted that today instead there was a 'disconnectedness' (*razobshchennost'*) as children finished school and then merely dispersed. The teacher declared, 'they are abandoned'.

What could group members themselves do about it, the moderator asked? The bookkeeping student thought that they should all talk more about it 'so that other people know about it and do not go'. The housewife concurred about sharing its negative aspects with others. The engineer was doubtful that one person could do very much apart from telephone the militia. The fireman called for human decency. He suggested that, whereas there had been such excellent people 'before', now there were 'all sorts'. He thought Vladimir's radio stations should give human trafficking more coverage because 'now they don't say much about this. There is more about crime, money and murders.' If there was just one reported case in Vladimir, they could 'stir things up'.

---

[15] The All-Union Pioneer Organisation named after Lenin, known as the Young Pioneers, was for youngsters aged from ten to fifteen. The All-Union Leninist Communist Union of Youth, known as the Komsomol, was for those aged fifteen up to twenty-eight or thirty.

The housewife puzzled why she did not know about the social organisations that the doctor had talked about and pondered the lack of information. The boiler specialist considered that coverage was 'poor' on the radio and television. Beyond Vladimir, at the federal level, the group thought that the law should be strengthened, greater responsibility taken and the traffickers more strictly punished. The housewife said that the president should be told that this was 'a very big social problem' and that 'the organs of power should think about this'. The doctor held that the state should commit administrators and money to tackle it, yet stressed that 'such problems need to be addressed in stages. Before you can solve it, you need to recognise it as a problem. Bring it to the attention of people, stop talking quietly about it, reveal it.' After that it was vital to locate people who were 'not indifferent' and who could act 'professionally' and 'like-mindedly'. The doctor showed the best grasp of how politics worked.

The heating engineer blamed the fast pace of change for making many things difficult and considered that 'we were not prepared for democracy'. It happened 'unexpectedly, immediately. We are going through this transition badly.' The doctor thought Russia lacked 'a system of social adaptation', and the man in the fire service wistfully mused that 'someone said that Russians are fools. There are people who, not thinking of the consequences, throw themselves into destruction head first, wanting it all quickly. They simply wreck and steal. That is what I think – simply the human factor.'

The moderator then asked the fireman if he would talk about the topic at work. With some reticence, he replied 'yes and no'. He felt that he could not arrive at work and immediately deliver a lecture about it but, 'if this problem appears' and 'even in a small way', then with his close workmates 'I could have this conversation.' After this the moderator left the room briefly for the group to prepare a summing-up of views. At this point, the man in the fire service had the courage to tell a tale that, so far, he had kept quiet:

> Here is a story from real life. The mother died and the daughter reached seventeen. Then there was a fire in the countryside. Everything burned. All her documents were burnt and she came to Vladimir but she couldn't do anything. She went to the market to work without documents. She worked for a while and then disappeared. Where she is now, I don't know.

He was visibly distressed as he told this.

When the moderator came back, the group volunteered that they had learnt from their time together and that the subject was a 'surprise' to them, one with which they were not all conversant. It was 'interesting' and 'a terrible thing'. The more knowledgeable doctor said she was pleased that others had 'understood the significance of this problem'.

Moscow, 2014

In Moscow seven years later and with greater distance from the wilder 1990s, group members began with an exercise to ponder the future direction of Russia and its problems. During this no one volunteered problems concerning 'human trafficking', 'forced labour' or 'slavery'. After an unproductive thirty minutes in which the group bounced around many problems except these, finally the moderator asked them if they had ever heard the word '*treffiking*'. A chorus of 'no' and 'I have never heard it' came back. The moderator pushed on with 'have you heard anything about the sale of people anywhere?' At this group members showed some recognition. A 19-year-old female student said, 'I think it was on the television', adding 'it isn't written about anywhere'. Another added that the television programme *Wait for Me* (*Zhdi menia*) publicised cases of people who had gone missing. A 55-year-old beautician reflected that during the war in Chechnia 'very many were kidnapped and taken into the hills and there they really worked as slaves'. A 28-year-old female manager in a car showroom chipped in with, 'I haven't heard about it recently.' A male technical worker of 29, however, had picked up something from the media but this was connected with migrant workers coming into Russia rather than with women and men being trafficked out. A 35-year-old manager in telecommunications then drew attention to a film about a young woman trafficked to France by an Albanian gang. A 59-year-old who was currently unemployed also indicated that from 'hearsay' he knew of similar tales either from a neighbour or from the media, but 'in recent times they have been absent'. The general message that emerged was that participants had vague recollections of hearing about this topic but that its visibility in the media had dimmed. Two other topics were dominating news coverage: *gastarbaitery* coming into Russia and events in Ukraine. Reporting, in their estimation, had gone quiet about human trafficking.

One participant was suspicious of this conclusion and believed that people were 'being guided by the mass media'. He questioned the certainty of what they saw and heard and posited that statistics might be covered up. In his view, the situation regarding human trafficking out of Russia had not changed at all. The female manager now agreed. She suggested that those with a 'low cultural level' and little education were more likely to fall victim to trafficking than those with a good salary. She thought that the regions of Russia were most affected. The technician insisted, on the contrary, that it had to be less nowadays and observed that newspaper advertisements of the 1990s calling for dancers had disappeared. Indeed, one of his acquaintances had fallen into being trafficked. Others then disagreed with the view that human trafficking had decreased on the ground that there had been changes in recruitment mechanisms. Fewer job advertisements no longer constituted a reliable indicator. Overall, at the end of exploring three options of 'a decrease', 'an increase' or 'about the same', the group ended up divided with advocates of each position.

Pressed further by the moderator, a 37-year-old polyclinic employee who registered patients recalled how women could end up 'in a brothel'. The moderator asked participants how the trafficked would be received upon return. The female manager volunteered that, if a girl returned at all and 'if they are normal parents, they will rejoice, but if they are not, then they will not take her back and will not believe her'. The polyclinic worker added that 'as a rule in these situations the parents would initiate a search for their children. All the time they would have been looking for her.' She believed that they would go to meet her, overjoyed. Six raised their hands in agreement with this optimistic view. But a word of caution followed with 'oh, I don't know. It would be half and half.' Another view was that not all families were so kind.

More doubt crept in when it came to discussing how friends would react. The polyclinic employee declared that 'as a rule in these situations there are no friends, they will all immediately turn away'. Others thought that 'it is best not to tell friends'. The clinic worker considered that 'a good friend will all the same know what happened to her. At worst, the friend will have been in this story. As a rule, these girls don't go alone.' A 51-year-old who worked as a transport technician thought it was more complicated. He felt that 'it is better not to say but in fact it is then deceit, and she will not be able to get accustomed to living'. Another agreed and went further with, 'if she is young, she won't have her own family'. Again, the clinic worker came in with the view that the family would be opposed to her having children and would say: 'why do you need that?' She posited that the woman would be negatively labelled as 'such a person' (*takaia-rassekaia*).[16]

The moderator probed whether the experience of having been trafficked would have changed her. All agreed with 'undoubtedly', 'of course', 'psychologically damaged' and 'embittered'. An unemployed man of 59 contributed that she would have endured a 'shabby life'.

---

[16] This phrase has negative connotations which go way beyond its literal translation.

He then narrated how his former wife had told him a story about one of her friends who, fifteen years ago, had found herself in exactly this post-trafficking situation. The woman 'had been in a terrible state psychologically'. The more optimistic male manager in telecommunications thought that a woman could get over this but others, particularly the female manager, concluded that it would be with her for the rest of her life. The clinic worker thought a successful outcome required help from a specialist. The technical worker suggested that a man would be able to cope with this sort of situation if he had been in it, especially if he was a positive thinker. The clinic worker concluded that only if a woman went to live in a different town where she was a stranger to everyone, and if she said nothing about herself and effectively 'buried herself', then 'perhaps' she too could cope.

The moderator queried how others such as the police, her doctor and local housing officials might react to a girl or woman who returned to her own town. The male manager said that the police would not know about it, and the clinic worker added that they would only do so if the parents had initiated a search. The transport technician dismissed the police immediately from the equation with 'in fact, no one needs the police. We don't and she doesn't.' If they thought about her at all, it would be just 'a couple of times, then they will forget about her'. The clinic worker admitted that 'the polyclinic in general does not know anyone, the town is big, they retrieve the documents, that's all'. A 29-year-old technical worker thought that people might feel 'sympathy' for her but, coming from a very different position, the beautician mused 'everyone has their fate'. The clinic worker believed that, 'if it is a big city, then no, she will be lost in it. In a small one, on the periphery, naturally there they know everything about you. Maybe, yes, around the town they might feel for you, but others perhaps will judge you.' The male manager qualified this with the view that neighbours might be 'wary'.

The moderator asked them to consider what would happen to a returnee who had been trapped for five years in a brothel in another country. One thought it would be like stepping out of prison. Another believed she would never get married, and a third said 'of course not, who would want her?' Others agreed until the clinic worker re-thought it all with, 'perhaps she will get married, I don't know, depending upon who she is'. The woman from the beauty salon argued that the best thing for her would actually be to go into a nunnery. She believed that 'everything that does not happen in life comes from the Providence of God'. Following on from this cue, the moderator questioned the nature of morality in Russia today. A range of views came forth: 'everyone is for themselves', 'everyone survives as they can', 'basic spiritual values are being lost', 'there is no understanding of honour and dignity' and 'money rules the world'. The transport technician regretted that, unlike for his generation in the Soviet Union, people were now less prepared to die for an idea. The young female manager jumped in with, 'we have a lot of negative propaganda on the television. I won't name anything, you all understand very well – these programmes, these serials.' It turned out that she had in mind a permissiveness according to which it was acceptable to 'get married ten times'. The younger technician tempered the discussion with 'I think it all depends upon upbringing.' The unemployed man, however, was reluctant to judge. As he viewed it, 'evolution happens and things change. I won't say that it is better or worse.'

The moderator probed the group on what sort of morality a returnee might have. The female manager defended a girl with: 'she might be good. Yes, she is simply not well informed, not educated. She is not very knowledgeable and was very trusting. From a simple family. That does not mean that she was bad or loose.' Asked directly if the girl was to blame for what happened to her, the clinic worker thought 'not especially. She was simply gullible.' Whereas the women in the group refused to blame her personally, all the men did. The telecommunications manager who had moved to Moscow in the mid 1990s from Krasnodar stressed that it was her fault. In her defence against the male participants, the clinic worker volunteered that perhaps in the girl's family 'someone was very ill and they promised her golden mountains. Let's say – "work for half a year and you will earn this amount" which the person needs for the operation. Maybe a friend had placed her.' They then debated whether the girl could get out of the situation. Again, the male manager stood out for being the most convinced that she could succeed, but others disputed this, saying it would be possible only if she was 'very smart' and 'very cunning'. In an attempt to convince, the telecommunications manager said, 'in Chechnia, for example, they took our lads into slavery, but all the same they got out'. The cautious in the group qualified this with 'some get out, some do not' and 'some will be afraid'. Pointing out the stark reality of slavery, the transport technician intervened with 'when a girl is locked up in a cellar', then 'of course she cannot. Look, they sit there for five years.'

One of the final tasks was to categorise this overall picture. Most responses did not generate concepts, but rather value judgments or descriptions. The unemployed man declared it to be 'terrible', the older technician said it was not moral but 'theft' and 'simply wild' and others labelled it 'beyond acceptable limits' and 'criminal'. The beautician regretted it was 'reality', the female manager considered it 'not normal, but scandalous', and the quietest in the group, a young female engineering student of nineteen, who had moved to Moscow from Tverskaia oblast, summed it up most concisely and aptly with 'it is slave holding' (*rabovladenie*). She made this sudden intervention after the group had talked about both human trafficking out of Russia and labour migration into it.

Yaroslavl, 2014

How did responses in 2014 in Yaroslavl compare to those in Moscow? Participants more readily came up with the topic of women and girls leaving Russia for work. A 27-year-old male technical worker remembered friends who had worked as a waitress and as a cook leaving for jobs elsewhere. He described an outflow of 'professions with these lower qualifications'. Only 'from media sources', however, had he heard of cases of forced prostitution. An unemployed 56-year-old-male bodyguard quickly interjected with 'yes, and it is going on now'. When asked if he meant within Russia, he came back with 'no, why? They go abroad and for good. There are no documents – no person.' He quickly claimed he had no personal links to this world but had learnt about it 'from the television'.

Others were asked what they knew. A 30-year-old woman in medicine said, 'yes, I probably remember', adding it was all about 'criminality' and 'slavery' (*rabstvo*). Another voice repeated 'slavery', and the bodyguard used the term 'swindling' or 'cheating' (*moshennichestvo*). Another thought that people travelled on their own, but the bodyguard disagreed with 'in so far as I know, they collect groups'. The moderator enquired what those who gathered the groups were called, and a 45-year-old factory worker said, 'tricksters' (*aferisty*) and then a 'psychologist'. The moderator corrected him with 'well probably a psychologist inside, but what is he?' Once more the unemployed bodyguard who seemed conversant with this topic finally said 'a middleman' (*posrednik*). He was the only participant in all four groups to volunteer this word.

As in the group in Moscow, no one readily came up with the term 'trafficker' or the process of 'human trafficking'. Pressed again to think further, the technical worker offered 'banditry, terrorism – whatever'. A 20-year-old female law student suggested 'a foolish gamble' (*lokhotron*).[17] Finally, a 47-year-old female post-office worker was led into saying that there was 'trade' and 'in people'. When the entire group was asked if members had heard the term '*torgovlia liud'mi*' or 'human trafficking', they found it

---

[17] A *lokhotron* is a 'rigged card game'. But the term can also refer to any gamble. A '*lokh*' is a naïve fool who is easy to deceive and who usually loses. *Lokhotron* is therefore a game for fools. I am grateful to Maria Zezina for explaining this to me.

easier, like participants in the other groups, to respond in terms of concrete examples rather than by discussing the concept. The law student knew about the process from the Internet and imparted: 'they collect girls and send them to Europe, for example. They work there. They sell them.' Then, 'either they kill them there, or lock them up somewhere and they don't often return to their homeland'. She went on that they were used 'with force' and made to work in prostitution. The young male technician also said he knew about this 'and not from the television'. When pressed for his source, he said 'from one of my acquaintances'.

The tale that unfolded was an illustration of the trafficking of male labour within Russia. He put it like this:

> They offered a man good work in some sort of construction project in Moscow oblast. He went and was met by armed men who took his passport and took him to a wooded area. It was overgrown there, no one was nearby and they set them all to work. This work was, as I remember, felling trees and there was a whole camp. It was practically impossible to break free. By a miracle he somehow ran successfully. They have unofficial connections [*podviazki*] at all levels, with both the police and all the security forces that are located nearby, who are unofficially involved [*podviazana*].[18] There is such a thing. He ran and there were dogs and it was raining. He had to get out of the forest, practically everything was unreal. And to leave on a train.

The moderator asked if this story was believable and the unemployed bodyguard quickly replied: 'I believe it.' He, too, had heard similar stories 'not directly, but in conversations somewhere or other'.

He refused, however, to recount them or to give details. It seemed that he knew far more about this topic than he was letting on, so the moderator pressed him 'just for the essence'. He replied that 'the essence is the same. They promise high wages, stability and consequently a rich life. The person decides, sells everything here, leaves, but there are no letters, no telegrammes, no phone calls.' In short, he ends up 'in slavery'. The post-office worker, too, had a story to tell. She revealed:

> I know exactly. For example, five years ago, the husband of an acquaintance disappeared, a man from Yaroslavl. My family even took part in the search with his wife. There are lots of cases like this. They still have not found him, neither dead nor alive. There are various rumours, even the police say that anything is possible.

When asked what 'anything' might include, she clarified 'slavery'. When asked where this slavery was taking place, she volunteered 'maybe in Russia, maybe wherever they take them. People frequently do go missing in Yaroslavl, both men and women.' A female pensioner, however,

---

[18] I am grateful to Nikolay Kozhanov for translation of this colloquial usage.

declared she had heard more about this 'for the most part at the beginning of the 2000s'. The female medical worker contributed that she knew nothing about this from her social circle, 'only from the television'. The law student interjected that it was 'not just slavery, but also people's organs'. The group concluded that Russians were trafficked out of the country into slavery and also trafficked within Russia. The bodyguard insisted that it was 'flourishing' in Yaroslavl itself and put forward a novel explanation. He thought that in the 1990s criminals in this sphere had been sent to prison for ten or fifteen years and now they were being released and offending again. Using this as a springboard, the moderator set the task of comparing the situation in the 1990s with that of 2014.

The reflective male technician pointed out that:

> The answer isn't simple. Before there were serious shocks in the next transition period. Amid all the turbulence in this period, I think that it was possible to engage in these things more, it was more secretive. On the other hand, in the Moscow area practically no one knew about this. Only from acquaintances. I suspect that now it can flourish.

The law student contradicted him with 'it's the same. That is – it was, it is and it will be.' The moderator pressed her on the comparative extent. All she could muster was: 'it always was'. A 59-year-old pensioner qualified it with 'at any rate, they talk about it less'. A 45-year-old male factory worker came in with the point that ten years ago there was a higher unemployment rate and so people were more likely then to find themselves trafficked: 'it was an unstable time and everyone went somewhere to work in various regions and towns. In my opinion more could disappear.'

A rather silent 21-year-old who worked in tourism admitted that he did not have much of an idea about it at all. At best, he thought that 'there should probably be fewer because after all they are warned. People must think, must beware.' The medical worker, however, struggled with this and remarked: 'it is complicated to say. But now fewer have left.' The male manager immediately disagreed with, 'I think more.' His reasoning was as follows: 'when it was a critical moment in the 1980s, all this was just beginning. The door was opening and all sorts of things were happening. And now, already, there are some established flows, and therefore it is flourishing more.'

Listening to this, the law student was swayed into thinking, 'it is growing, in effect. They offer them lots of money and they go.' The female pensioner generalised that: 'somewhere they speak less about this, somewhere they say more, somewhere something is exposed, somewhere else less is uncovered'. The bodyguard added that the abduction of young girls into prostitution was less frequent than it had been. He also thought that before 'they tried to be quiet about this – the television and radio. They didn't divulge it. Now they have started to show more and, yes, to say be careful.' They finally concluded that before people did not know about it and now they should. The tourism worker thought that fewer Russians now left. Instead, it was the turn of foreigners who came to Russia from Central Asia who disappeared into slavery.

The group was then given the task of debating the fate of a hypothetical young woman from the town of Ivanovo where there was unemployment. She was offered work in Turkey as a dancer but upon arrival was expected to work in prostitution. She refused and instead was made to recruit other young women into it. The question was: could this person be respected or not? The law student reacted sympathetically: 'she went to earn and she did not know what awaited her. Then she did not do that, but began to live as she could. She earned for herself. I have nothing against her.' The man in tourism declared the opposite. He could only see her 'negatively'. She had earned money on the backs of others. The male manager thought that she should have found different work at home. A debate then ensued about the difficulties of life in Ivanovo and how there may not have been alternative work for her. The manager dug his heels in on this issue and insisted that 'you can always find another way'. The bodyguard was more sympathetic to her and said she had only accepted work as a recruiter because of 'the hopelessness' of her predicament. The pensioner, however, thought there were better solutions. She angrily emphasised that, 'I simply relate negatively to this profession. There is always a possibility of work without prostitution.'

When queried about this, she exploded with: 'There is! My life has been far from easy, and there have been different blips. But I always found the right thing to do. Maybe less money, maybe more. But she wanted lots of money all at once. In my opinion she could do things slowly. There are other ways. You simply need to think.' The post-office worker retorted 'well, if it is Ivanovo oblast, there is such destitution'. She argued that the abject poverty there made life hard, and 'prostitution is prostitution, but everyone does as they can in order to survive, and the girls are young there'. The medical worker contributed sympathetically that she could not judge the young woman negatively either.

They were then asked to ponder how she would be greeted if she managed to return home to Ivanovo. The pensioner who had judged her so critically now volunteered: 'I don't know. If they really missed her, then they might say "come home, my dear".' But on the other hand, she believed that they could also say 'go back where you came from'. The factory worker took a compassionate position of: 'I think parents should always understand and forgive.' The law student hypothesised that 'the first question that they would put is "why did you go there? Why did you go into that?"' The male manager had a different take on it. He said, 'if the parents were alcoholics, that's a supposition, then they would not say anything negative. Of course, at the beginning they could argue, but then take her in as they should.' The bodyguard joined in again with: 'if the parents are normal, then they are obliged to take her into the family'. The law student concurred with 'they will take her back with "thank God you have returned!" And then anything might happen.'

The moderator asked what the neighbours would say. Various options came forth including: 'where have you been all this time?', 'they would use a bad word' and 'how much did you earn?' At the last reply, the group burst out laughing. They figured that the neighbours would find out if she had done well financially or come back with little. They were then asked if she would ever get married. Again, they all laughed as Ivanovo's population had far more women in it than men, having been dominated by textile factories employing women. It was known in the USSR as a 'city of brides'. In the segmented Soviet labour force, women were concentrated in light industry. So 'not there' was the reply. Then other calmer replies were forthcoming, such as: 'if she had earned a lot of money, she might marry'. The bodyguard thought that 'often, as far as I know, if you were engaged in that, you try to leave for another town, change where you live and build a new life'. And had she in some way altered due to the experience? The women in the group immediately responded that it would be with her for the rest of her life.

The group was next given the task of comparing two young women from Ivanovo who went to Turkey. They both ended up in prostitution but the first had been told she would be working as a waitress while the second had agreed in advance to work as a prostitute. The law student pronounced a clear difference as one had been deceived and the other had gone willingly. The young man in tourism also saw the contrast between being forced and doing it freely. The moderator then asked an unexpected question of 'and from the point of view of God?' One view emerged that God would not differentiate between them. The pensioner, however, was struggling with the earlier question. For her, prostitution was morally wrong so, whether a young woman was in it willingly or unwillingly, it was all the same to her. She believed that 'the morality is the same. Whether she wants it or does not want it.' The male manager, however, defended the huge difference between them, making clear that he thought that the pensioner was just not seeing complexities.

In both Moscow and Yaroslavl in 2014, responses showed some differences of opinion according to gender, but not always rigidly so. The sharpest contrast was for women to feel more strongly that the experience of being trafficked into prostitution would afterwards mentally never leave the women and girls. Also, all the female participants except one harsh critic in Yaroslavl were reluctant to judge the trafficked women and call them immoral if they had been duped by traffickers. By contrast, some of the men viewed them very negatively.

Comparisons Across the Years

The groups have been presented separately to highlight four distinct inter-active processes and atmospheres. Each had its own build-ups, disagree-ments, consensuses, light-hearted moments and even distress and anger. No participant, however, came up spontaneously with the concept of '*tor-govlia liud'mi*'. Across the years, this particular term had not easily rooted itself in the consciousness of the wider population even though experts in NGOs and sociologists used it frequently. Common replies from group participants were either 'that is new to me' or a vague nod of recognition that it had been used in a television programme on crime. Only once the moderator had introduced it did a handful in Moscow in 2007 explicitly refer to the term when attempting to define it. Just three in Vladimir said that 'yes' they had recognised it, although they themselves did not ini-tially apply it. Most comfortably of all, the doctor in Vladimir started to incorporate it into her ruminations. Others in Moscow in 2007 revealed that they would speak euphemistically about a woman who had fallen into 'an unpleasant situation' (*v nepriatnoe polozhenie*) or had endured 'an unpleasant history' (*v nepriatniu istoriiu*). In sharp contrast, group mem-bers in 2014 all shied away from adopting *torgovlia liud'mi*. The notions of *treffiking* and *treffiker* were also only vaguely recalled, if at all.

It was the terms *rabstvo* (slavery), *rabynia* (slaves) and *seksual'noe rab-stvo* (sexual slavery) that were readily mentioned in Vladimir. Similarly, *rabstvo* was referred to with confidence in both groups held in 2014. With much more in the news about migrant labourers by the later date, the terms *rabovladenie* (slave holding) and *posrednik* (middleman) also came up, but just once each. Neither had surfaced in the earlier groups. News coverage in the media to some extent determined what group members were aware of and how their opinions were shaped. In both 2007 and 2014 people grasped what human trafficking generally entailed, even if they did not use its concepts.

In 2007 there was more discussion about criminal gangs and 'risks' in society, and also more heated condemnation of the process of human trafficking and some outrage at the fate of the trafficked. In Moscow, the barman, the bookkeeper and the technician were particularly conversant with the process, its central characteristics and its implications. This group strongly criticised the traffickers, the process of deception and organ-ised crime more widely. Trafficking into prostitution was condemned as a 'violation of rights', a 'moral crime' and an affront to human dignity, which involved a loss of rights and the inappropriate 'possession' of people. They concluded it was then Russia's top problem, that perhaps a special department should be created to tackle it and that society should show more compassion to those who managed to return. Likewise, in Vladimir, the doctor and the man in the fire service were particularly troubled by the significance of human trafficking into prostitution both inside Russia and into other countries for reasons of exploitation, criminality, morality and physical and psychological health, and for treating a person as a 'good' or 'commodity' to be sold. They did not explore the concept of 'rights' as had been referred to more than once in Moscow in 2007 but could see what it meant in practice to lose them. The doctor in Vladimir also possessed a level of first-hand and detailed knowledge about the consequences of being trafficked into prostitution that all other participants lacked. She alone was aware of the hazards of generalising across cases. The fullest information others had was from stories from acquaintances or from the disappearance of someone whom they knew. Otherwise details came from the media. There was a hint, however, that the bodyguard in Yaroslavl may have endured a bad experience working in Germany, but he would not be drawn on what had happened there, nor divulge the extent of his knowledge.

There was a huge contrast between the explicit worries and emotions expressed in Vladimir and Moscow in 2007 about the loss to Russia of young women who had disappeared and of what they would have endured, and the rather cool distance from it, almost desensitisation or indifference, of those in Moscow seven years later. It was clear that by 2014 that the topic of male forced labour was on people's minds, whereas that of human trafficking into the sex industry had somewhat receded. There were, nonetheless, some critical appraisals of it in 2014 which included 'terrible', 'theft', 'simply wild', 'beyond acceptable limits', 'criminal' and 'not normal, but scandalous'. One shrugged it off as 'reality'.

Participants in the Moscow group in 2014 also made clear that addressing human trafficking was not a top priority. The remarks 'distant from me, thank God' and 'no one has kidnapped me yet, thank God' conveyed little concern for others. The group was not motivated to do anything about in the way that the citizens of Vladimir had called for a greater promotion of awareness, a letter to the president and a bigger role for civil society. The earlier Moscow group had also advocated setting up state institutions to tackle it, a role for social organisations possibly set up by those who had been trafficked as well as some sort of wider 'society of assistance'. Overall, the level of compassion expressed in 2007 was missing in 2014 in the capital. One should not conclude, however, that replies are necessarily representative of all Muscovites. Nonetheless, the contrast in discourse across the years is stark and may be illustrative of altering trends. By 2014, the earlier condemnations of traffickers seem to have been swapped for hostile feelings towards migrants for reasons of their alleged crimes and their purported stealing of the jobs of Russians, to be examined later.

Can any conclusions be drawn about responses in smaller cities differing from those likely in a huge metropolitan area? Participants in Yaroslavl did express more concern than their compatriots in the capital in the same year. This particularly applied to the case of the man who disappeared from Yaroslavl who had been an acquaintance of the post-office worker and to the tale about the Russian man trafficked into a wood to fell trees. The lives of three in the group had definitely been touched by slavery second-hand, with one appearing to know far more than he was comfortable to reveal, possibly first-hand. They had a strong sense of what was happening in their region, and some showed sympathy for the unemployed women just fifty-seven miles away after the textile industry had collapsed. Another thought that slavery was 'flourishing' in Yaroslavl and believed that human trafficking routes out of the country were well established.

The groups in Vladimir and Yaroslavl shared this stronger identification with what was local. In the former, there was also an insistence that their city was decent and special. One stressed that the people were *kul'turnye* or cultured, a term connoting civilised with proper behaviour. They described 'their' people as particularly 'kind' and calmer than in other regions. For this reason, they felt that fewer young girls would have been trafficked out. They were uncomfortable with the fate that might befall them. Yet the more they talked about it and as examples came forth about the growth of local drug taking and the locations where prostitutes could be found, it was evident that reality may not have matched their ideal picture. No one explicitly acknowledged the tension between the two images that they projected of Vladimir. There was a level of cognitive dissonance. The housewife, however, attempted to resolve it by suggesting that people with low levels of education from surrounding areas were attracted to the wonderful city of Vladimir. Another blamed the local narcotics trade on incomers from Georgia, Azerbaijan and Armenia. Nonetheless, the engineer persisted with an emphasis on Vladimir as being special: 'we have our own path, set apart'.

Conclusion

Any expectation that time would have enhanced general knowledge and understanding about human trafficking out of Russia was not fully borne out given the vague recollections of some group members in 2014. Although some of their lives had been touched by people's disappearances, the burst of sensational headlines in the 2000s about girls trafficked out and their abuse in unfree labour elsewhere was more distant. Participants in 2007 certainly showed a more acute historical perspective on human trafficking and were closer to the unstable 1990s after the collapse of the Soviet state, although a couple in 2014 did make historical references. Older group members in both Moscow and Vladimir in 2007 harked back to the stability of the USSR, its ideological guidance and work opportunities. The push factors out of Russia were keenly felt.

It is important to ask what themes were underplayed or absent from points that arose. In all groups, extremely little was volunteered about the global economy, its impact on Russia and integration into it. Focus instead fell on the 'push' factors of unemployment and state collapse and on the 'pull' of hoping to earn a lot of money quickly rather than on wider globalisation processes. Neither did the market demand for sexual services abroad and at home figure prominently. With regard to casting blame, as shown in the opinion polls, some pointed to the foolishness and naïveté of women and girls for being deceived and for believing the false promises made to them. Only the doctor and the fireman in Vladimir thought that reality was more complex than this stereotype. No one, however, blamed the men for foolishly being tricked into forced labour in other countries. No one apart from the doctor in Vladimir really raised wider structural questions about gender differences. Yet her point about wage discrimination was a fleeting one. No one explored the relevance of international co-operation across states of the world for tackling human trafficking across borders. Likewise, few referred to the relevance of the domestic political system and to the constructive role that social organisations could play, apart from the doctor in Vladimir. Both groups in 2014 steered away from mention of the domestic political system, although they did bring up Russian policy in Ukraine when going off at a tangent. One participant vigorously demonstrated his backing for Putin's policy and also called for 'the final battle' between Russia and the USA, which he declared Russia would win. The others chose not to engage with this. Lastly, even though most observations were about domestic impacts on lives, no one showed knowledge of the anti-trafficking articles in the Criminal Code adopted in 2003. Nor did anyone refer back to the history of political pressures for legislative change or show awareness of the serious deficit of shelters and help in rehabilitation. The reflections of the public contrasted greatly with those of experts.

The preceding chapters have discussed international and domestic political pressures for anti-trafficking legislation, explored key outcomes, looked at how the press has packaged stories about human trafficking out of Russia and scrutinised public opinion. The objective here is to introduce the views, assessments and priorities of experts in the years following the introduction in 2003 of Articles 127.1 and 127.2 into the Criminal Code. Some attention has already been devoted to how some professionals assessed with hindsight the process of mobilising pressure on the state when battling for an anti-trafficking law. The aim now is to present up-to-date expert reflections from those who have daily contact either with problems surrounding human trafficking or with the hazards of labour migration. Interviewees were all well placed within NGO communities, in research circles and in policing to comment on working with the consequences of trafficking into unfree labour. Discussion draws on data gathered in face-to-face interviews in Russia in 2013 and 2014, from correspondence since and from recent articles.[1]

A range of interview questions explored how experts regarded the current state of human trafficking out of Russia, how they evaluated policies to address it and the obstacles to success. They talked about their own work, its achievements and what hampered it most. From their distinct and sometimes overlapping perspectives, they identified trends, named and characterised central problems and suggested what needed to be done. The interviews show which cluster of issues each chose to elaborate upon. Taking each in turn highlights their prioritisations and emphases.

---

[1] All those named have granted me permission to cite them and have approved my translations and quotations. All were given the opportunity to make any alterations. I have respected any requests for anonymity.

Trafficking, Prevention and Law Enforcement

A question that had prompted disagreement in the focus groups was whether or not the public thought that human trafficking out of Russia had reduced in scale. At the Moscow office of the IOM, I met Juliana Pavlovskaya, Director of its Information Centre, Olga Rybakova, Information Resource Centre Co-ordinator of the Migration Assistance Division, and Julia Melnichouk, Head of the Migrant Assistance Division. As spokesperson, Pavlovskaya emphasised that 'human trafficking has not fallen. It still exists and will do so as long as there is crime.' She thought that the issue was less visible in the press because 'it is now done through the Internet. They try to hide more what they do.' Moreover, 'the routes that it takes are connected to what is happening outside the Russian Federation in other countries. They go to Lithuania, Germany and the USA. They reach Turkey, Greece, Cyprus and Italy through Georgia. Egypt and China are more active.'[2]

Pavlovskaya outlined how at the IOM there had been ten preventative projects to date. These began in 2006 with some finance from the EU. Help was given to victims and then research was conducted in 2007 which involved Karelia, Astrakhan and Moscow oblast. From what she said, however, and from other sources, it was clear that funding was generally short-term, and so preventative projects would not endure until the Russian state or its local authorities permanently took them on. Recall that the IOM shelter in Moscow had funding for only three years. She went on to talk about the productive work of another shelter that had opened in St Petersburg under the auspices of the IOM and Red Cross together. When it had been operating, this shelter could take in eight at a time and those who passed through it included people from Ukraine, North Korea and Vietnam. Thirteen had received what Pavlovskaya described as 'complex help'. She described how 'they may stay there several days. It is two weeks on average. One family stayed there a month.' She also revealed that St Petersburg's Investigative Committee had been an active supporter. When I expressed surprise at this, she explained that 'society in Petersburg relates differently to this. There is *tolerant'nost'* [tolerance] in Petersburg and so they can move forward.' We have already seen, however, that this shelter had ceased to help victims of trafficking in order to focus on refugees.

Elena Timofeeva, who had worked at the IOM's Moscow shelter as a psychologist, described how changes that had occurred in Russia over a period of five to ten years had been 'frustrating'. She regretted that

[2] Interview at the IOM in Moscow, September 2014.

'we had no governmental support. We went backwards. It was very sad.'[3] Having been 'hugely disappointed' at the closure of the IOM's rehabilitation centre in 2009, Timofeeva began working in an orphanage, where she discovered that 40 per cent of the orphans had been trafficked into begging rings or labour of some kind. She considered that orphanages had been 'poor at identifying this problem and were at first suspicious of this idea'. Reflecting on child trafficking, she volunteered that 'maybe it is increasing or maybe we identify it better'. She named Mitino as a high-risk area on the outskirts of Moscow and also the streets Tverskaia and the Arbat in central Moscow.

Timofeeva, together with Veronica Antimonik who had also worked at the IOM's rehabilitation centre, next began to implement independent programmes designed to prevent the exploitation of girls through empowerment and education. These included outreach projects designed to teach teenagers how to 'keep safe' and be 'self-sustainable'. Through their registered Safe House Foundation they ran several programmes. One entitled 'Jewel Girls' encouraged teenagers, some younger ones and women up to thirty years old to join sessions in which they made jewellery for sale. Therapy was integral to this group activity. Another on-line programme called 'Charm Alarm' (*Sharm Alarm*) included on-line tests about relationships and job opportunities. One quiz asked 'do you know who your boyfriend is?' It posed a series of questions with opportunities for feedback on the participant's answers. Useful warnings and advice taught young people about how the process of recruitment into trafficking took place on-line, using the very tools employed by the traffickers themselves. Another educational test asked about 'dream jobs' along the lines of 'you dream about being a model', followed by sound pointers and suggested life skills. Thus, anti-trafficking work moved on-line with the goal of deterrence. The Safe House Foundation, which is non-profit, refers victims of trafficking to other organisations and provides training sessions for specialists.[4]

Timofeeva also reflected that 'we used to have well-established relations with the police' and added that 'even though they are not quite as stable now, we still co-operate'. When I asked Pavlovskaya about the activities of the police in fighting human trafficking, she said that 'there is a police criminal investigation department and inside that there is a unit for dealing with human trafficking'. She admitted that 'they do fulfil their duties', but regretted that 'this is limited'. Furthermore, 'there is no real offensive against human trafficking. They are over-cautious.'

[3] Skype interview with Elena Timofeeva, August 2014.
[4] For further details, see safehouse.foundation/en/home.

It amounted, she thought, to '*podvizhka*' which connotes 'ice motion'. She believed, as did many in NGOs, that 'it is hard for the police to get to grips with the relevant articles in the Criminal Code'. This was so 'because there are no mechanisms to spur them on'. She believed the identification and investigation of human trafficking cases 'are in need of a more pro-active approach'.[5]

Other experts concurred with Pavlovskaya about the current deficit in news reporting on human trafficking. A specialist on borders, Sergey Brestovitsky, who is Director of Monitoring and Evaluation at Development Solutions, commented that 'there is no information on the presence of human trafficking'.[6] Moreover, 'there is not a big social resonance'. He considered that 'at the moment the big problem is labour trafficking rather than human trafficking out'. Brestovitsky recognised that 'occasionally there is an announcement about the trafficking of women'. He thought that border guards 'are well informed about human trafficking and can recognise it'. This was because 'there is an intelligence organisation there – and it is well developed'. He thought 'their methodology is OK. Most do recognise it. They are prepared.'[7] When asked if he thought they knew when trafficking routes altered, he responded that 'they do study the changing routes. There are seminars for border guards. They collect data on routes and look at them. There is a practical approach on the borders. They see the risks.' He went on to say 'they recognise different percentages of risk on different borders. Finland is low-risk, but it is a higher risk into Central Asia. They see this within the limits of their expertise.' He did not expand upon what their 'limits' were. Brestovitsky's view was that most problems stemmed from the legal difficulties of dealing with human trafficking.

Somewhat distinct from Pavlovskaya's appraisal at the IOM, Dmitry Poletaev, Director of Migration Research Centre, a regional public organisation, subscribed to the view that 'today fewer girls are trafficked out'. He agreed that 'many went in the 1990s' but the situation had changed. He put the difference down to the fact that 'the economic situation is different now and those young women can today get better wages in other jobs at home'. As a consequence, being trafficked out of the country had been 'much cut back'. Like many focus group participants, Poletaev thought that those women and girls who were still trafficked out were

---

[5] Interview with Pavlovskaya, Rybakova and Melnichouk, September 2014.
[6] Interview with Sergey Brestovitsky in Moscow, September 2014. Details about Development Solutions are available at www.devsolutions.ru.
[7] Part of the official brief of the FSB is the 'protection and defense of the state border' with its border service (Pogranichnaia sluzhba Federal'noi sluzhby bezopasnosti Rossiiskoi Federatsii). See www.fsb.ru.

those 'without experience. No education. From the countryside. Naïve ones with lower skill levels.' Also of relevance was how the overall picture of prostitution had altered as 'there is a big demand inside Russia'. To help meet this, a flow of women from Central Asia were being trafficked into Russia into the sex industry. Given their Muslim backgrounds, he stressed that it was very hard for them if they returned home. He regretted that, 'for victims of human trafficking, returning home carries risk. Society may not accept them, will judge them, make their life extremely difficult and even unbearable.'[8]

Considering press coverage, Poletaev believed that the focus on sex slaves had lasted just five to seven years, but now it had gone. He criticised the police and said 'it is not a priority for them and there is corruption. There is always a bribe and few traffickers are convicted.' He added that 'investigation takes time and there is a feeling that they are not able to do it'. One key problem in investigating trafficking crimes was that 'witness protection does not work'. Although there was a shelter in Petersburg, 'most have nowhere to go to be safe. They cannot go home as there is no protection there. There are no shelters. They are afraid to speak.' No one in the NGO community contested the apt criticism of a serious lack of adequate support for men and women out of unfree labour situations, whether by escape, release or rescue. There is a general consensus that what is needed immediately is psychological support, medical checks, legal help and somewhere to live. Victim protection was crucial but the provision of essential shelters has been both rare and short-lived due to closures. Poletaev did not hold back about what he assessed as inadequate.

Commenting in early 2015, Natalia Khodyreva also believed that 'fewer women are trafficked abroad if we compare with the 1990s'. At her centre in St Petersburg in the 1990s, she had received around 120 women and girls per year who had been trafficked and who were looking for help, but 'now there were none'. In her view, more women were now being trafficked into Russia for prostitution, including from Africa. She was seeing between five and ten women per year from there. She volunteered that 'far more women were being trafficked from provincial Russia and from towns across the CIS'. Looking at Uzbek women who were working in St Petersburg in trade and in households from 2010 to 2014, Khodyreva's research had been unable to identify any as trafficking cases. After the beginning of the economic crisis in 2014 due, in part, to Western sanctions, she believed that fewer were entering from the CIS but yet at the same time all the central streets 'were plastered with

---

[8] Interview with Dmitry Poletaev in Moscow, September 2014. Details about the Migration Research Centre are available at migrocenter.ru. See, too, migrocenter.livejournal.com.

advertisements for sex services'. She assumed that 'the number of prostitutes will increase because of the crisis. Many of them will be brought from other towns – mostly from in Russia and perhaps from eastern Ukraine.'[9] In an update in 2016, Khodyreva remarked that now migrant women from Uzbekistan could be added to this list. She had noticed 'advertisements for prostitutes in Uzbek – that is for Uzbek men – migrants'.[10] It appeared that more nationalities were being drawn into sex work and the client base was possibly widening.

A Moscow-based lawyer, Roman Rybakov, also thought at first that the extent of sex trafficking out in 2014 'looked less', but then qualified this conclusion. Rybakov admitted that this could be because his workload with labour migrants had increased as the migration flow into Russia had grown, and so his main focus was not on sex trafficking simply because labour migration was bigger now. Nonetheless, he was especially clear that 'we need a policy' against human trafficking. He stressed that, firstly, 'more information is needed' rather than silence; secondly, more shelters should be opened; and, thirdly, a 'special legal status' for victims should exist. He observed how in the USA those who had suffered from human trafficking were protected, 'but they are not so in Russia'. He added that the continued existence of the St Petersburg shelter depended upon funding which is not yet permanent. The Ministry of Social Protection did run day centres (*priemniki*) for the homeless but 'there is not enough initiative for shelters'. There was, however, 'money for children' but also 'there are victims of domestic violence on the streets with nowhere to go'.[11] That was another huge problem.

I asked Rybakov about the significance for Russia of the legal case of Rantsev versus Cyprus and Russia that Nikolai Rantsev had taken in 2004 to the European Court of Human Rights (ECtHR).[12] Russia became a member of the Council of Europe in 1996, ratified the 1950 European Convention for the Protection of Human Rights and Fundamental Freedoms in 1998 and formally recognised the ECtHR's jurisdiction and the right of individuals to complain to the tribunal.[13]

---

[9] E-mail communication from Natalia Khodyreva, February 2015.

[10] E-mail communication from Natalia Khodyreva, August 2016. See her 'Rasprostranennost' sluchaev gendernogo nasiliia i seksual'noi ekspluatatsii v otnoshenii zhenshchin-migrantok v Rossii (na primer Sankt Peterburga)', paper delivered at the 9th World Congress of ICCEES, Makuhari, Japan, 3–8 August 2015.

[11] Interview with Roman Rybakov in Moscow, September 2014.

[12] For official details of the case, see www.coe.int/en/web/human-rights-convention/slavery1; and 'Landmark judgment on human trafficking', echrblog.blogspot.co.uk/2010/01/landmark-judgment-on-human-trafficking.html.

[13] For Russia's participation in the Council of Europe, see www.coe.int/en/web/portal/russian-federation. For details of the European Convention of Human Rights, see www.coe.int/en/web/human-rights-convention.

Were there, I wondered, any positive consequences on the ground from the Court's ruling on Rantsev? The case concerned his daughter Oksana who had been trafficked to Cyprus at twenty years old and forced into prostitution. In 2001 she fell to her death from a seventh-floor balcony in Limassol. She had thought she was going to work as a dancer and when signing her work contract had specifically asked for reassurance before leaving Russia that this was not in prostitution.[14] Rantsev argued that the investigation into the circumstances of Oksana's death had been inadequate in Cyprus, that the Cypriot police had not protected her when she was alive and that there was failure to punish those who had exploited her. Rantsev also blamed Russia for not trying to discover how Oksana had been trafficked out of the country. The Court ruled that Cyprus had indeed failed to protect Oksana from trafficking or from being unlawfully detained there. Nor had Cyprus investigated the death fully. The Court concluded that Russia likewise had not sufficiently looked into how Oksana had been trafficked. The ECtHR required the Cyprus government to pay Nikolai Rantsev €40,000 in damages as well as legal costs of €3,150 and the Russian government to pay €2,000. Rybakov replied that the Court's ruling

> did result in activities in the region that she came from – Khabarovsk. So some action came from the MVD there. The police did do something about the criminal group that had been trafficking from Khabarovsk to Cyprus and to Greece. They did get information from those who had suffered.

So, overall, 'it had an immediate impact' but afterwards 'less'. The MVD, Rybakov told me, had at least put the details of the case up on its website.[15] This was some sort of progress.

As the first ruling from the ECtHR concerning human rights and human trafficking into sexual exploitation, it was described by lawyer Kirill Boychenko in 2010 as 'historic' and as a 'turning point' for all states that had signed the European Convention on Human Rights. He hoped that in Russia it would positively influence law enforcement, state structures, anti-trafficking work and the defence of the trafficked.[16]

---

[14] For Oksana Rantseva's story in Cyprus before the ruling, see Mary Buckley, 'Human trafficking in the twenty-first century: implications for Russia, Europe and the world', in Linda Racioppi and Katherine O'Sullivan See, eds., *Gender Politics in Post-Communist Eurasia* (East Lansing: Michigan State University Press, 2009), p. 126. See, too, Karacheva, 'Krasavitsy-rabyni'.

[15] Interview with Rybakov, September 2014.

[16] Kirill A. Boychenko, 'Istoricheskoe reshenie Evropeiskogo suda po pravam cheloveka v otnoshenii Kipra i Rossii, kasaiushcheesia torgovli liud'mi', *Rossiiskii kriminologicheskii vzgliad*, No. 2, 2010, pp. 13–18. Boychenko notes how the number of complaints against Russia coming before the European Court of Human Rights has been increasing in recent years. In 1999 there were 971 and by 2009 as many as 13,666.

Many others, too, saw it as a significant 'landmark' for holding police forces accountable for inadequate investigations. In fact, the ECtHR did not often look at a case in light of Article 4 of the Convention on the prohibition of slavery and forced labour. Before the ruling, Russia had told the Court that it did not have a legal responsibility to investigate.[17] The ruling, however, indicated responsibility in both the state of destination and the state of origin, thus making Russia culpable. Both Cyprus and Russia were seen as violating Article 4, and Cyprus was ruled to have violated Article 2 on the right to life and Article 5 on the right to liberty and security.

The trend has generally been for Russia to pay fines that the ECtHR imposes, but not always to change policy in accordance with a judgment. Until recently, at least, the advantage of the court in Strasbourg for Russians who appealed to it, as Alexei Trochev has observed, is 'nearly complete enforcement of its judgments in terms of compensating those who won their cases'. Moreover, this is 'something that all other Russian courts lack'. Although Russia has reneged on some of its early promises to the Council of Europe, Trochev notes that Russia's judges do also 'draw on the judgments' of the tribunal in Strasbourg as well as 'on the standards of the 1950 Convention to decide cases in their everyday administration of justice in Russia'. Despite this, he views as a key problem the slow trickle down to other Russian courts, mainly because the judiciary is part of public governance and all the pressures that entails in Russia.[18] More recently, however, during Putin's third term as president, the Duma adopted a law in December 2015 enabling referral of a ruling to the Russian Constitutional Court which could declare an order unenforceable if it was deemed to contradict the Constitution, thereby overruling it. The *Moscow Times* observed that this was 'the first time a signatory country to the European Convention on Human Rights has authorised a local court to choose which decisions to enact and which to ignore'.[19] William Pomeranz has characterised Russia's relationship with the ECtHR as 'turbulent'.[20]

---

[17] Boychenko, 'Istoricheskoi reshenie Evropeiskogo suda'.

[18] Alexei Trochev, 'All appeals lead to Strasbourg?' *Demokratizatsiya*, Vol. 17, No. 2, Spring 2009, pp. 145–178; and his *Judging Russia: The Role of the Constitutional Court in Russian Politics, 1990–2006* (New York: Cambridge University Press, 2008).

[19] Peter Hobson, 'Russia to rule on European Court of Human Rights decisions', *Moscow Times*, 10 December 2015. The article noted that, between 2013 and 2015, 45,000 Russians had appealed to the ECtHR. Court rulings which the Russian government did not like included payments to former shareholders in Yukos and criticism of the secret interception of mobile phones as a violation of privacy.

[20] William E. Pomeranz, 'Uneasy partners: Russia and the European Court of Human Rights', *Human Rights Brief*, Vol. 19, No. 3, 2012, pp. 17–21.

For a more 'inside' police perspective, I spoke to one young MVD officer. He told me that when he began his training in 2005 'there was no focus on human trafficking'. He observed that 'it was very rare to come across it in the education system'. There was, however, 'talk about it in Chechnia when soldiers were held there as slaves'. Then came changes. He felt that the situation today was much improved and that there is 'a better understanding of human trafficking'. Those who undergo police training now have special courses on *viktimologiia*, or victimhood. So 'younger police are more up-to-date'. In the past ten years criminology as a subject has been taken more seriously. When asked whether the police receive special instruction in how to treat victims or relate to them face to face, he replied 'no'. Interpersonal sensitivity was not on the university curriculum but discussion of the predicaments in which victims found themselves was. Changes, although happening, were slow to come to fruition. Before the new course on *viktimologiia* was put on the syllabus, he shared that 'it took a prior year and a half of debating it'.[21]

When asked how the police viewed the law, he responded with 'the problem is not the law. It is the way in which they write these laws and how the MVD and the Procuracy interpret them.' He argued that there were so few convictions because 'there is a need for huge resources to get proof. It is a heavy workload. There is a need to ask all around. And it is complicated.' The way the investigative system worked meant 'deadlines' and 'bureaucratic procedures'. Moreover, 'there is a consciousness that it is not such an important problem'. Theft, for example, by contrast, was seen as 'more important'. When I asked him if he would like to see any changes to the article on human trafficking, he immediately replied, 'any more changes to the law on human trafficking would mean more complications. It takes six months from a change in the law to develop an understanding of its practice, that is, how to apply it.'[22]

In reflecting on the relevance of opinion surveys for law enforcement, the officer revealed that 'the MVD never conducted opinion surveys on human trafficking and attitudes towards it. But the MVD does commission surveys on attitudes towards migrant labourers.' He felt that prevention, or *profilaktika*, was really the key to addressing human trafficking. He regretted that 'we only look at preventative measures when a *zakaz* [order], comes from the top'. He believed that 'without *profilaktika* there is no solution to human trafficking because running around never really addresses it'. As he saw it, *profilaktika* was about 'concrete measures'. It could be done 'by apartment buildings'. The aim would be to go to

[21] Confidential source, 2014.
[22] Confidential source, 2014.

people at home and ask questions about problems and crime prevention. Moreover, 'only the MVD can do this'. The problem was that '*profilaktika* is expensive and would involve more resources'. He added that it was something that 'had been effective in the USSR. It had begun under Brezhnev in the 1960s.' He observed that one could read about *profilaktika* in textbooks but it was no longer practised.[23] Another interviewee from inside the Investigative Committee estimated that 'the Belarusans are effective in the fight against human trafficking'. This source believed that 'we do not have enough cases to create a separate unit' to deal specifically with human trafficking but acknowledged that in St Petersburg the Investigative Committee, as Pavlovskaya described above, had 'played a participatory role' in the preparation of a social programme.[24]

Like Khodyreva, the man from the MVD observed that there was a known problem of trafficking into prostitution that took place within the borders of the Russian Federation. In particular, there 'is trafficking from the Far East to cities. There have been warnings there for a long time.' But again came the topic of secrecy and silence. He pointed out that 'now organised crime tries to hide it. They actively and visibly sought people before. Now it is all hidden.' Nikolai Kurdiumov, President of Mezhdunarodnyi Al'ians 'Trudovaia Migratsiia' (MATM), or International Alliance 'Labour Migration', also argued that 'there is a flow from the countryside in Russia into the big cities', but that 'there are no figures on human trafficking'. Echoing others, he was sure that 'leaving Russia over the last ten years is greatly different from in the 1990s'. He believed, however, that 'prostitution may persist for the highly paid ones in Florida or France. But there is not a mass exodus now.' Trafficking into prostitution was inside Russia rather than migrating out of it. As a specialist on labour, he added that 'the flow of qualified workers out of Russia continues', such as specialists on short-term contracts and engineers, or for housework in Greece or gathering in the harvest in Spain.[25] This was the subject he knew most about.

By contrast, some working in NGOs on the ground may be more likely to agree with Pavlovskaya's assessment of human trafficking's scale and trends. As one director of a regional centre put it: 'I cannot say that there is less human trafficking today but there is silence from all spheres. There are no special organisations concerned with human trafficking now – they

---

[23] Confidential source, 2014.
[24] Confidential source, 2014.
[25] Interview with Nikolai Kurdiumov in Moscow, September 2014. For details of MATM, refer to www.ialm.ru. Kurdiumov was also a member of the Social Council of the Federal Migration Service.

have been liquidated.' She went on to illustrate that the local FSB no longer had a department that concentrated on human trafficking. There used to be one in her region, and she had then worked as productively with it as had been possible. If a woman in difficulty rang her, she could pass on information to the FSB and ask for their help. Now, however, she was saddened that, locally, 'when people call me and ask whom they can talk to for help, the answer is "no one"'.[26]

Problems could, however, arise due to constraints in the law. On the one hand, she was pleased that 'I had a good working relationship with the FSB.' But on the other, action was not always successful. She told the story of how one day a frightened woman managed to ring her and said 'they are holding me' (*menia uderzhivaiut*). The director telephoned the FSB, and they encircled the building where the woman had said that she was being detained. The dilemma was that they could not enter without evidence. The director said 'let me speak to her and I will get evidence'. The FSB, however, would not let this happen as those involved were not convinced that she could obtain the required information. The director was certain that she could have done so due to her experience as a qualified psychologist. Co-operation, therefore, could have its limits, not always with positive results. In this case, the most that had been done was that a building had been temporarily surrounded. Because of such difficulties, the director concluded that 'the human trafficking law does not work'.

The centre director was also convinced that human trafficking 'had always existed'. She felt that 'it was not understood as such, but it was there'. As a psychologist, she also openly talked about a dimension of human trafficking that the other experts did not select. She pointed out how there was 'the problem of a syndrome with the person who sells her'. There can be 'a type of psychological relationship between them. She feels drawn to him and will do it again thinking it will be better next time.' There are also 'serious post-traumatic consequences'. She recalled one returnee 'who washed all day'. She was 'a woman in a terrible state'. She described how 'she rented a flat and could not keep still. She had to move all the time. One day she got on a bus and went miles. Those at the centre tried to find her.'

Despite some of the reservations about statistical estimates, evidence that flows of women and girls trafficked out of Russia were persisting was cited at a roundtable held in Moscow in April 2014 which was part of co-operation between Russian and Greek prosecutors. This high-level

[26] Confidential source, 2014.

meeting included Russian prosecutor general Iurii Chaika and his Greek counterpart. Referring to numbers, Deputy Prosecutor General Viktor Grin observed that 'tens of thousands of women are sent every year to Western Europe alone to work as prostitutes'. The problem from the roundtable's 'law-and-order' perspective was that 'young women and sometimes young men are trafficked from one country to another via well-organized channels'. Grin viewed the reasons behind its scale to include 'the openness of borders and an increase in international migration flows, flaws in migration laws, official corruption, not excluding the countries of destination'. Those present wanted to target 'transnational organized criminal groups' whose members sought profits from trafficking in humans, drugs and weapons. As well as calling for information exchanges and joint co-operation with Greece, Grin drew attention to the need for 'concerted preventative efforts' and also 'measures to rehabilitate crime victims'.[27] He appeared aware of the potentially dire consequences of having been trapped in unfree labour and then receiving no help afterwards.

By 2014 support for specialist rehabilitation centres in Russia was still being demanded by the IOM, other NGOs, Interior Minister Kolokol'tsev and Deputy Prosecutor General Grin. What had been an integral part of the draft bill that came out of the Duma's Legislation Committee in February 2003 was still unmet in law and in state provision, yet was stressed as vitally necessary by those who worked in key agencies very familiar with trafficking's impacts and outcomes. Despite differences in emphasis across the experts' answers, all were well disposed to improving anti-trafficking policies and were united in calling for an end to the deficit of rehabilitation provision. At the IOM, for example, Pavlovskaya, Melnichouk and Rybakova concurred that, 'there is a need for a national action plan'. Pavlovskaya underlined that, 'co-operation is needed' and 'we need a person at the top for information exchange'. She commented that developments on this score were 'good' in Uzbekistan.[28]

Although Russia still lacks a national action plan on human trafficking, there have been some formal productive developments within the CIS. Kirill Boychenko has praised the leading role played by the General Procuracy of the Russian Federation as well as Russia's law enforcement organs in working on anti-trafficking legislation with other CIS states. As a consequence, an Agreement on Co-operation in the Fight Against Human Trafficking in Organs and Tissues had been reached in 2005. There followed for the years 2007–2010 a Programme of Co-operation

---

[27] Voice of Russia, 'Russian, Greek prosecutors to cooperate in fighting human trafficking', 9 April 2014, www.sputniknews.com/voiceofrussia/tag_56708601/2014/04/.

[28] Interview with Pavlovskaya, Rybakova and Melnichouk in Moscow, September 2014.

of the States of the CIS in the Fight Against Human Trafficking. This led to a call for states to improve efficiency, collaborate and make their laws consistent with international norms. Improved training for specialists was also on the agenda. Collaboration involved work on model laws 'On countering human trafficking' and 'On providing assistance to victims of human trafficking'. The aim, in Boychenko's words, was to provide a broad foundation of principles which importantly included 'a guarantee of protection by the state of specified rights and legal interests of the victims of human trafficking'. Social adaptation and rehabilitation were integral to goals. The next stage brought 'Recommendations for the unification and harmonisation of states' legislation of the members of the CIS in the fight against human trafficking'.[29]

Despite positive collaboration across the CIS, Boychenko regretted that by 2010 the states, including Russia, lacked co-ordinating mechanisms at national levels between their own institutions involved in anti-trafficking. Furthermore, the need for legal harmonisation across states still remained. There followed another document in September 2010 updating the Programme of Co-operation, now covering the years 2011–2013. This was worked on by the secretariat and scientific-method centre of the Co-ordinating Council of the General Procuracies of the states of the CIS. Again, a key aim was 'to modernise co-operation' with reference to international principles and norms. Boychenko commented that it was vital for this programme to become 'an effective instrument in questions of protecting the rights and freedoms of the citizen' (*zashchity prav i svobod grazhdan*).[30]

At the IOM in Moscow in 2014 there was some enthusiasm for the latest CIS programme for co-operation in preventing human trafficking. This document had been signed in Minsk in October 2013 at a meeting of the CIS Council of the Heads of State after discussion in the Council of the Ministers of Foreign Affairs of the CIS. The main aim of the gatherings of presidents and foreign ministers was to discuss trade expansion, economic co-operation, law enforcement, and cultural and humanitarian links.[31] Under this wide agenda, several agreements and documents were signed, including an updated one on human trafficking spanning the period 2014–2018.[32]

---

[29] Kirill A. Boychenko, 'Pravovye osnovy sotrudnichestva gosudarstv – chlenov Sodruzhestva Nezavisimykh Gosudarstv (SNG) po voprosam predotvrashcheniia torgovli liud'mi', *Iuridicheskii mir*, 2010, pp. 14–17.

[30] Boychenko, 'Pravovye osnovy'.

[31] See 'Meeting of the CIS Council of Heads of State', en.kremlin.ru/events/president/news/19489.

[32] 'Programma sotrudnichestva gosudarstv – uchastnikov Sodruzhestva Nezavisimykh Gosudarstv v bor'be s torgovlei liud'mi na 2014–2018 gody'.

The document echoes some of the aims of earlier CIS materials. It sets out to improve and to standardise legislation and policy across CIS states consistent with international principles and norms as laid down by the UN, CoE and the OSCE. The document's ten sections include commitments to passing laws on help for victims of trafficking and on protection of their rights. It calls for a legally defined status of 'victim of human trafficking' and a working out of priorities for protecting the rights and interests of children. Commitments are expected at national, inter-state and regional levels, facilitated by co-operative inter-state mechanisms. A section on organisation and practical preventative measures requires expert groups to be formed at national levels to work on policy implementation. The programme specifies the need for special sessions inside law enforcement agencies which include women in anti-trafficking work to ensure an input of women's views. Results were to be monitored at the CIS level and information exchanged. Another objective is regularly to analyse the practices followed in the prevention of human trafficking, in assistance to the trafficked and also in ways of combating corruption with a view to learning from each other. A continued aim is to inform the public about the threats awaiting potential victims of trafficking. Yearly meetings of specialists to assess developments are planned along with seminars and exchanges. In addition, more specialist courses and training for those who might have to deal with trafficked persons, including social workers, psychologists and those who answer hotlines, were to be arranged. There are also plans for budgetary scrutiny across the states to monitor funding.[33] If the entire programme were to be successfully implemented and the necessary funds forthcoming, there was hope at the IOM that this would make a significant difference on the ground.[34] On paper, the goals looked good, but – how formal were they? A key question is whether the necessary political will to implement them and to make sufficient funding available is present, especially at a time of economic strain. Time will show how high a priority its implementation is.

At a different level, co-operation was certainly continuing across institutions inside the city of Moscow, and some key referral mechanisms were in place. The IOM announced that from January to April 2015 it had assisted more than sixty victims of human trafficking, 56 per cent of whom were females and 32 per cent were males. Minors were 12 per cent of the total. These people had been trapped in forced labour, in sexual exploitation or in begging. Twenty-three referrals had come from NGOs, fourteen from the Orthodox care organisation Miloserdie (Mercy), eleven

33 'Programma sotrudnichestva gosudarstv'.
34 Interview with Pavlovskaya, Rybakova and Melnichouk, September 2014.

from social centres under the Department of Social Protection in Moscow, eight from other IOM missions, five from foreign diplomatic missions and four from law enforcement. Here were individuals in institutions keen to ensure that the trafficked received help, even if the political system still dragged its feet in working out a national plan and in providing resources.[35] The will and commitment to act were evident in busy NGOs.

Conclusion

Without doubt, there are experts in Russia with different professional skills who are committed to the prevention of human trafficking and to the rehabilitation and protection of those who have been trapped in unfree labour in the sex industry and managed to leave it. The voices quoted above are a selection of important actors within the NGO community and in other relevant organisations. Their efforts matter, and their opinions may be shared with each other and feed into other official institutions. Their estimates of the scale of human trafficking out of Russia may vary, or indeed of how long it has existed, but they all condemn the process and wish to alleviate its consequences and deter more recruits.

Whilst many experts also continue to note the difficulties in investigating trafficking cases due to their complexity, or point to the reluctance of some police to take the initiative in actively pursuing the perpetrators of trafficking, it would be wrong to suggest that there have not been any successful convictions or that all police officers take a relaxed attitude to tackling forced labour. To claim that they are all corrupt is inaccurate, and there are indeed those with motivation to strive to solve individual cases. We have seen how when the police reckon it will be difficult to gather enough evidence for convictions under Articles 127.1 and 127.2, then they may turn to using Articles 240 and 241, which they may anyway prefer or have greater experience of applying.[36]

Experts, however, would like to see a more pro-active police approach to anti-trafficking and an end to the *podvizhka* which deadlines, promotion procedures and attitudes may foster.[37] Many NGOs continue to work co-operatively with the police in instances where that is possible, or at least try to do so. Some experts hoped in 2014 that the latest CIS Programme would productively move anti-trafficking action forward by heralding progress in inter-state collaboration, particularly in the defence of trafficking victims, but they recognised that the tasks for future agendas are still huge.

---

[35] *IOM Moscow Times*, Issue 32, January–April 2015.
[36] McCarthy, *Trafficking Justice*, pp. 182–184.
[37] McCarthy, 'Beyond corruption', pp. 1–12.

7   Labour Migration Flows into Russia and Reports on Forced Labour

Human trafficking out of the country is just one of the labour-migration trends affecting Russia which might lead people into a predicament of unfreedom or into some form of exploitation. Into the 2000s, it became increasingly evident that other nationalities migrating to work inside Russia could also find themselves in a tapestry of positive and negative situations. Even though many *gastarbaitery* settled well into short-term or longer-term jobs, others found themselves in more vulnerable positions along a spectrum which included deceit, recourse to middlemen, confiscation of documents, acquisition of fake documents, demands for bribes, threats, underpayment or non-payment of wages, problems with the bureaucracy, deportation or, at worst, forced labour and unfreedom. The media relayed numerous stories about the plight of migrants, and MVD press releases revealed different instances of forced labour.

As before, exposé prompted criticisms from NGOs, human rights groups and international organisations. Both the range of work situations in which migrant workers found themselves and the impact on their lives of changes in laws on foreign workers sparked discussion among experts, academics, policy makers and politicians. Commentaries, reports and debates examined issues of registration, quotas, work permits, affordable housing and tests for migrants in Russian language, history and law. Findings and arguments appeared in specialist journals, in the press and on the Internet. Conferences and seminars drew academics, those in NGOs, local politicians and policy makers together to consider the significance of developments and to recommend which laws needed to be changed. International organisations concerned with global slavery attempted to estimate its scale inside Russia and to rank it against other countries. The perceived numbers of legal and illegal migrant labourers also triggered anti-immigrant outbursts from some politicians and opposition from right-wing organisations and youth groups, to be discussed in the next chapter. Thus, various narratives about the *gastarbaitery* circulated, and some harassment and violent attacks occurred.

Incoming labour migrants sought jobs in Russia for reasons of lower wages at home, unemployment and poverty, some of the same reasons why Russians had also wanted work elsewhere after the collapse of the Soviet state. These factors meant that Russia became a magnet for many, particularly labourers from Tajikistan, Uzbekistan and Kyrgyzstan and other post-Soviet states such as Moldova. Visa-free regimes with most former Soviet republics made travel for unemployed or low-paid Central Asians alluring. Anticipation in the years 2010 to 2014 of receiving wages three or four times higher than those at home was a strong pull factor. There were, moreover, push factors of the financial dependence of families in the country of origin on earnings made elsewhere and the expectation that someone would go to Russia. When there is economic crisis in Russia, however, as in 1998 and 2008, and subsequently in 2014 and 2015, job opportunities for migrants may shrink and remittances become less predictable. In 2009, for example, after lay-offs and unemployment, Uzbeks were taking jobs in South Korea, Turkey, the Czech Republic and Oman as alternatives to Russia.[1]

Alongside exposé of the plight of labour migrants, other stories started coming to light, initially less prominent, about Russians being confined in forced labour in their own country, be it in forestry, construction, agricultural work, brick kilns or the sex industry. They, too, could be hired into a particular job locally or in a different part of the country and unexpectedly find themselves captive. A minority of Russians have endured threats and violence on Russian soil in new jobs, as had many Russians who were trafficked into other countries a decade or two earlier.

This purpose here is to explore the sorts of predicaments and outcomes for labour migrants that have been uncovered and reported. Discussion looks at variations in how known labour exploitation begins, perpetuates and possibly ends. It presents a selection of stories from NGO reports, Russian newspapers and MVD press releases to illustrate types of forced labour. A methodological problem is that one cannot determine how representative each may be. It is possible to discuss only what the reported data reveal and what distinguishes cases. Available information can indicate patterns and tendencies, but not the probabilities of being recruited in different ways, or the scale. Like human trafficking out of Russia, many problems are hidden.

---

[1] Farangis Najibullah, 'As work dries up, Central Asian migrants return home', RFE/RL, 10 February 2009, www.rferl.org/a/As_Work_Dries_Up_Central_Asian_Migrant_Workers_Return_Home_/1490902.html.

In order to complete the macro-picture of labour flows affecting Russia which sit along a wide spectrum of exploitation, the remaining chapters examine different categories of unfree labour and labour vulnerabilities inside Russia experienced by both Central Asians and Russians, and illustrate views about them amongst experts and the public. Since labour migration played an important part in the Soviet past and in the early years of the Russian Federation, before proceeding it is pertinent to present selected historical points of relevance.

Recent Migration Flows in Context

Even though Soviet citizens had to have a *propiska*, or permit, to live in a particular place, and movement to settle elsewhere was not necessarily easy, automatic or linked to free choice, migrations within that vast landmass did, nonetheless, occur. Stalin's forced industrialisation project needed huge waves of migration from the countryside into towns. In the later Khrushchev and Brezhnev years, workers might receive inducements to work miles away in especially inclement climates on particular work projects and earn higher wages in compensation. The Komsomol, too, was encouraged to mobilise its members on projects such as the Baikal–Amur Mainline, for which more than twenty-five new settlements were needed. Upon graduation, students might also be assigned to work in their specialisms in a particular place where the state needed them and where they may, or may not, have wished to be.

In the 1960s industries in big cities needed more workers, who came from smaller towns and villages. Donald Filtzer has pointed out that, as women left low-paid factory work for the expanding service sector, their places needed to be filled, and simultaneously industry was expanding. To meet the challenge, factories were permitted to hire specified numbers of migrant workers, 'most of whom came from Central Asia'.[2] Recent migrant flows therefore follow an earlier trend from Central Asia and are not new, first-time flows. At the beginning of the 1970s, there were also arrivals of Russians back into the RSFSR from other republics in which an ethnic nationalism was developing. Subsequently, in the 1980s and 1990s, people flows into the Russian republic accelerated due to ethnic conflicts and war in Tajikistan from 1992 to 1997. There was also a 'growing influx

---

[2] Donald Filtzer, *Soviet Workers and the Collapse of Perestroika* (Cambridge: Cambridge University Press, 1994), p. 27. Central Asian workers were allowed limited residence permits and were known as *limitchiki*.

of undocumented immigrants and asylum seekers'.[3] In addition, the termination of highly paid projects in the North, Siberia and the Far East, together with the loss of the extra state benefits which they had paid, led to a 're-orientation of inter-regional flows'.[4] Beginning in July 1992 the FMS began monitoring these. Between then and 2005, 3 million were known to have migrated into Russia, and of these just over 1 million were officially registered as 'forced migrants or refugees'. Of those who were registered, more than 180,000 came from Tajikistan, around 160,000 from Kazakhstan, approximately 140,000 from Uzbekistan and over 70,000 from Kyrgyzstan. In these years, the majority were ethnic Russians.[5] Within the Russian republic itself, there was also movement. In the same period, 117,000 refugees were counted from Chechnia due to the push factors of instability and war. Chechnia endured its first war under President Boris Yel'tsin from December 1994 to August 1996 and its second under Putin from August 1999 to April 2009.

Not only were there huge patterns of urbanisation and out-migration from the countryside during industrialisation and the upheavals of the 1930s, not forgetting the deportations of Crimean Tatars and other smaller nationalities eastwards during the Great Patriotic War, but also subsequent migrations linked to several factors in different contexts. War in Tajikistan triggered both Russian out-migration and a Tajik outflow looking for work. Independence in Kazakhstan after the collapse of the USSR prompted fears in the Russian population of Kazakh nationalism and what it meant for their positions in the workplace, their status and their identity. In 1989 there were 25.3 million Russians living in Soviet republics outside the RSFSR and, when the republics became independent states, not all Russians wished to stay outside the new Russian Federation. Some were anxious about their children or felt vulnerable for reasons of minority status, fears of discrimination and worries about job security, their sense of belonging and possible instabilities or conflict.[6]

---

[3] See Cristiano Codagnone, 'The new migration in Russia in the 1990s', in Khalid Koser and Helma Lutz, eds., *The New Migration in Europe: Social Constructions and Social Realities* (Basingstoke: Macmillan, 1998), pp. 39–59. On emigration, refer to Vera D. Voinova and Igor' G. Ushakov, 'Sovremennye protsessy v Rossii', *Sotsiologicheskie issledovaniia*, No. 1, 1994, pp. 39–49.

[4] Leonid L. Rybakovskii and Nina V. Tarasova, 'Vnutrirossiiskaia migratsiia naseleniia nyneshnaia situatsiia i prognoz', *Sotsiologicheskie issledovaniia*, No. 1, 1994, pp. 31–38.

[5] Hilary Pilkington, *Migration, Displacement and Identity in Post-Soviet Russia* (London: Routledge, 1998), pp. 5–10; and Codagnone, 'The new migration'.

[6] On attitudes, see Pilkington, *Migration*; and Pilkington, '"For the sake of the children": gender and migration in the former Soviet Union', in Buckley, ed., *Post-Soviet Women*, pp. 119–140.

In short, over the twentieth century, migrations and movements into and out of Russia were not rare. A word frequently heard was *priezzhii*, a rather elastic category referring to a newcomer or anyone who had 'arrived' – and someone always had. An ideology of 'the friendship of peoples' (*druzhba narodov*) was part of the glue that was meant to hold different nationalities together in harmony. What increasingly mattered to public opinion, however, was *who* was arriving. Russians were one category, and they were not without their difficulties and hostile receptions in what they may have considered to be 'their' republic. Central Asians and those from the republics of Azerbaijan, Georgia and Armenia in Transcaucasia were another matter, and in Soviet times they were sometimes contrasted in social gossip with the *kul'turnye* peoples of Lithuania, Latvia and Estonia. After the collapse of the Soviet Union, there was one narrative which lamented the loss of the Baltic states to a much greater degree than the states of Central Asia. The contrast was contrary to the spirit of *druzhba narodov*, but one with some coinage.

There are variations in the available statistical breakdowns on the numbers of labour migrants arriving in Russia but general similarities across them. For example, data for 2009 compiled by the Mezhdunarodnyi Al'ians 'Trudovaia Migratsiia', or International Alliance 'Labour Migration', suggested that 30 per cent came from Uzbekistan, 16 per cent from Tajikistan, 12 per cent from China, 9 per cent from Ukraine, 8 per cent from Kyrgyzstan, 6 per cent from 'other countries within the CIS', 4 per cent from Turkey and 10 per cent from 'other countries outside the CIS'.[7] Valerii Tishkov, Director of the Institute of Ethnology and Anthropology, cited data for 2009 which suggested that 40 per cent worked in construction, 30 per cent were in selling and others did housework, repair work and various forms of hired labour.[8] The United Nations recognised in 2010 that the Russian Federation hosted the largest foreign population on its territory among the states of the world, estimated at 12.3 million. Tishkov observed that, although migrants by 2012 made up between 7 and 10 per cent of workers in Russia, in comparative terms this was fewer than in the USA and Switzerland at 15 and 22 per cent respectively.[9] Moreover, many migrant workers from Central Asia were temporary with flows going in both directions. In a meeting with Putin, then prime minister, Konstantin Romodanovskii, head of the FMS, declared that in 2010

[7] Mezhdunarodnyi Al'ians Trudovaia Migratsiia, 'Osnovnye gosudarstva – postavshchiki trudovykh migrantov v RF (2009)', leaflet.
[8] Valerii Tishkov, 'O chem zabyl skazat' kandidat v prezidenty, kogda govoril o migratsii', *Migratsiia XXI Vek*, No. 1 (10), January–February 2012, p. 4.
[9] Tishkov, 'O chem zabyl skazat' kandidat v prezidenty', pp. 4–5.

more than 10 million foreigners had entered Russia. He added, however, that 5 million were employed, but only 1 million of these were working legally. The others had entered the country legally, 'but are working in violation of the law'.[10] In addition, expert estimates in 2012 suggested that around 600,000 in Russia were thought to have been trafficked into slave conditions.[11]

Figures published in 2012 in *Argumenty i fakty*, which had been cited by the FMS, World Bank and other organisations, claimed that around 12 million migrants were in Russia. Of these, 38 per cent came from Uzbekistan, 24 per cent from Tajikistan and 23 per cent from Kyrgyzstan. Workers from these three Central Asian republics together, then, made up the majority at 85 per cent, a higher figure than the previous one of 54 per cent in data for 2009. A further 15 per cent came from a wide cluster of migrants from Moldova, Ukraine, Azerbaijan, Armenia and Turkmenistan. These figures, however, exclude those from China and Vietnam and do not allow for the subsequent rise in Ukrainians in 2014. It was also estimated that, in 2012, 37 per cent of labour migrants worked in construction, 30 per cent in trade, 10 per cent in industry, 7 per cent in agriculture, 5 per cent in transport and 11 per cent in 'other'.[12] Estimates of the number of illegal foreign workers in Russia, however, varied. The FMS then put it at between 3 and 5 million whilst others suggested higher figures.[13]

The picture of migrant flows became more variegated in 2014 and 2015 due to the arrival of refugees from fighting in Ukraine. According to the FMS, by January 2015 more than 2.4 million Ukrainians were living in Russia, or 5.6 per cent of Ukraine's population.[14] In February 2015 Valentina Kazakova, Head of the FMS's Naturalisation Department, revealed that over 260,000 Ukrainian citizens had already been granted asylum or the status of refugee and that, in 2014, 70,000 Ukrainians had applied for Russian citizenship. Furthermore, over 900,000 Ukrainian

---

[10] RIA Novosti, 'Russia reports 4 mln illegal migrant workers', 8 September 2010, sputniknews.com/russia/20100908160519155/.

[11] Khristina Narizhnaya, 'Slave labor on the rise in Russia', 27 May 2012, www.pri.org/stories/2012-05-27/slave-labor-rise-russia.

[12] No named author, 'Migrant – uzhe kak okkupant?' *Argumenty i fakty*, No. 43, 24–30 October 2012, p. 5.

[13] The Organisation for Economic Co-operation and Development (OECD) held that Russia has the largest number of illegal migrants, amounting to almost 7 per cent of the country's working population. For an overview of unemployment statistics, job sectors across regions and migration flows, consult Ol'ga D. Vorob"eva, *Rynok Truda i Migratsiia* (Moscow: MAKS Press, 2011).

[14] Cited in Olga Gulina, 'Re-drawing the map of migration patterns', Open Democracy, 16 February 2015, opendemocracy.net/od-russia/olga-gulina/redrawing-map-of-migration-patterns.

refugees were now in Russia.[15] The UN declared that more than 1 million Ukrainians had been displaced by the conflict, as did some Russian officials. Crucially, the presence of Ukrainians meant that more migrants were looking for work. A narrative began to circulate in society that it would be preferable to hire Ukrainian labourers rather than those from Central Asia. Another discourse backed paying Ukrainians less than Russians until they took citizenship.

In 2015 and 2016 the labour market was also affected by Western economic sanctions that had been adopted in March 2014. Other key factors were falls and fluctuations in the global price of oil and reduction in the value of the rouble. Even though wages in Russia were higher than those in Central Asia, they were now falling in real terms. Some employers chose, in addition, to lower them due to increased costs. Vital for labour migrants, however, was the continued ability to send remittances back home to sustain families. In 2007 remittances sent to Tajikistan had amounted to $1.8 billion, or 36 per cent of Tajikistan's GDP.[16] Other reports suggested more but, whatever the precise percentage, Central Asians' pay abroad was routinely expected within households.[17] By 2013 these transfers to Tajikistan had reached more than $4 billion, then 52 per cent of GDP.[18] Similarly, remittances sent to Kyrgyzstan in 2007 were 27 per cent of GDP, then ranking fourth in the world in terms of the proportion of remittances to GDP.[19] By 2013 remittances to Kyrgyzstan were equivalent to 31 per cent of GDP and to Uzbekistan equivalent to 16 per cent of GDP.[20] Tajikistan has the status of the world's most remittance-dependent economy, and so it relies heavily upon work inside Russia.[21] Consequently, it is seriously affected by downturns in Russia's economy and by the nature of its labour policies. Figures, albeit

---

[15] No named author, 'Russia says almost 300,000 Ukrainians asked for asylum', RFE/RL, 16 February 2015, rferl.org/a/russia-says-almost-300000-ukrainians-asked-for-asylum/26852070.html.

[16] Erica Marat, 'Labor migration in Central Asia: implications of the global economic crisis', Silk Road Paper, May 2009, p. 3. See, too, Marlène Laruelle, 'Central Asian labour migrants in Russia: the "diasporization" of the Central Asian states?' *China and Eurasia Forum Quarterly*, Vol. 5, No. 3, 2007, pp. 101–119.

[17] Marat, 'Labor migration in Central Asia', p. 19, held that 98 per cent of remittances to Tajikistan were spent on consumption which included spending on celebrations such as weddings, birthdays and funerals and that only 2 per cent were invested in small businesses.

[18] David Trilling, 'Tajikistan: migrant remittances now exceed half of GDP', 15 April 2014, eurasianet.org/node/68272; and David Trilling, 'Tajikistan tries to hide embarrassing remittance data', 26 July 2013, eurasianet.org/node/67310.

[19] Marat, 'Labor migration in Central Asia', p. 3.

[20] Trilling, 'Tajikistan: migrant remittances'.

[21] In 2007, almost 12 per cent of the Tajik population were working in other states and 90 per cent of these were in Russia. See Marat, 'Labor migration in Central Asia', pp. 8–9.

fluctuating, indicate that around 40 per cent of Tajiks aged between eighteen and thirty seek work abroad, mainly in Russia. These drop to 20–25 per cent in the eighteen-to-forty age bracket. Taking illegal workers into account, however, would increase the percentages.[22]

By 2015 this picture was changing due to the above factors which contributed to falling real wages, wage reductions and job losses. According to the Russian Central Bank, a comparison of the first three quarters of 2015 with the same period in 2014 showed that remittances sent to Uzbekistan fell by 51 per cent, to Tajikistan by 47 per cent and to Kyrgyzstan by 37 per cent.[23] The number of Uzbek migrant workers in Russia had fallen by 22 per cent and the number of Tajiks by 15.6 per cent. Membership of the EEU seemed to be influencing Kyrgyz workers, whose numbers had increased by 5.4 per cent. One NGO estimated that 33 per cent of Kyrgyz migrants hoped to settle permanently in Russia.[24]

To focus briefly here on economic data for Tajikistan only, the World Bank estimated that in 2015 Tajikistan's economic growth had slowed to 4.2 per cent from 6.7 per cent in 2014, due in part to slowdown in Russia and also to slowing growth among its trading partners in China, Kazakhstan and Turkey. The US dollar value of crucial remittances fell by around 33 per cent in 2015 compared to 2014, mainly due to depreciation in the rouble, and 80 per cent of these remittances came from Russia.[25] The head of the National Bank of Tajikistan in 2016 commented that remittances sent to Tajikistan in 2015 in dollars had fallen by 33 per cent and in roubles had increased slightly by 3 per cent. His figures showed that 95 per cent of all remittances received had come from Russia. The banker commented that reductions had 'seriously hit Tajikistan's economy'. The Tajik somoni had fallen in value from 5 to the dollar to 8, and consequently the purchasing power of Tajiks had fallen. He reckoned in 2015 that remittances from Russia had fallen from 40 per cent of Tajik GDP to just 25 per cent and predicted that the Russian economy would not pick up before 2017, with Tajikistan not feeling the benefits of an upturn until 2018. He remarked that Tajiks would still go to Russia, but that in crisis periods 'they will wait at home', recalling 'that's how it was in 2008–2009' at a time when labour

[22] Dmitrii Popov, 'Trudovaia migratsiia iz Tadzhikistana v tsifrakh', RISI Analytics, 29 May 2015, riss.ru/analitycs/17465.
[23] IWPR, 'Russian crisis continues to bite for labour migrants', 10 March 2016, iwpr.net/global-voices/russian-crisis-continues-bite-labour-migrants.
[24] IWPR, 'Russian crisis continues to bite'.
[25] World Bank, 'Overview on Tajikistan', 7 October 2016, www.worldbank.org/en/country/tajikistan/overview, last accessed 13 December 2016. This site is regularly updated and content changes.

migration to Russia fell by 20–30 per cent, before it grew again.[26] Experts believed that for the next fifteen years at least Russia would continue to attract labour migrants from Central Asia.[27]

In this context, a flurry of press articles warned that migrants were not returning to Russia in the new year of 2015 and that fewer returnees meant deficits of street cleaners and janitors. Citizens in St Petersburg complained that snow was piling up and did not take kindly to the deputy governor's advice to clear it themselves.[28] The FMS, however, continued to note that illegal migrants were still an issue. In February 2015, a representative estimated that there were more than 2 million illegals in Russia 'among whom a considerable number are Tajiks'.[29] Problems for migrants were exacerbated by deportations from Russia and bans on re-entry. The Tajik Ministry of Labour announced that, by May 2015, 276,000 Tajiks had been banned from entering Russia for violating rules of their stay and was concerned that over 400,000 working there were 'a group at risk'.[30] By January 2016, more than 1.6 million foreigners were on Russia's blacklist.[31]

The FMS frequently made light of the numbers of Central Asians not returning. Taking Petersburg, Elena Dunaeva looked at figures for the beginning of 2015 and remarked that, although migrants were down by 10 per cent, the number who were declaring honestly the reason for entry as work, not tourism, was up 49 per cent. She admitted more Uzbeks were leaving than arriving, but noted that more Ukrainians were coming in and that in two months a total of 56,000 foreigners had applied for work permits.[32] The FMS also commented that buoyant numbers from Tajikistan were applying for resettlement in Russia as erstwhile compatriots in the USSR. This involved an insignificant number of Russians, and mainly Tajik families. Since January 2016, 1,200 families had made this request, and they were in a queue which stretched to June for appointments to discuss documents.[33]

---

[26] No named author, 'Perechisleniia migrantov iz Rossii v Tadzhikistan sokratilis' na tret'', *Vzgliad*, 26 January 2016, vz.ru/news/2016/1/26/790731.html.

[27] TV Tsentr, 'Rossii predskazali potok trudovykh migrantov iz Azii do 2030 goda', 11 November 2015, www.tvc.ru/news/show/id/80476.

[28] No named author, 'St Petersburg politician tells residents shoveling snow is good for them', *Moscow Times*, 12 January 2015.

[29] Popov, 'Trudovaia migratsiia'.

[30] Popov, 'Trudovaia migratsiia'.

[31] No named author, 'Migranty-aziaty prodolzhaiut massovo uezzhat' iz Rossii', *Pravda*, 22 January 2016.

[32] Svetlana Gavrilina, 'Migranty prodolzhaiut priezzhat' v Piter i ego okrestnosti', *Nezavisimaia gazeta*, 21 April 2015.

[33] Ekaterina Trifonova, 'Dokhody gastarbaiterov prodolzhaiut sokrashchat'sia', *Nezavisimaia gazeta*, 22 January 2016; and no named author, 'Migranty-aziaty prodolzhaiut massovo uezzhat' iz Rossii'.

The recent history of aggravated push factors may have accounted for the desire to relocate permanently. Looking in detail at the months from November 2015 to March 2016, a project by the World Bank documented falls in average per capita real income in Tajikistan by 24 per cent across its selected subgroups due to declining remittances combined with reduced self-employment and agricultural income over the winter period. The picture is partly seasonal, but reduced remittances remained the pattern. Evidence showed that the share of households able to pay for enough food fell to 53 per cent in January 2016, but rose to 61 per cent in March.[34]

Next, the picture changed again. In mid 2016, Ekaterina Trifonova reported that recent data showed that the migrants were not rushing to leave Russia, but were instead working illegally or just surviving as best they could. Whereas foreign specialists in finance, health and education were indeed leaving, migrants from Uzbekistan and Tajikistan were staying. She quoted expert Vyacheslav Postavnin who reminded Trifonova that 'the crisis affected not only Russia, but also many other countries of the CIS, and the economies of Uzbekistan and Tajikistan badly suffered'. Therefore, he argued, for those workers 'there was no sense in returning home'.[35] Official figures for the beginning of 2016 suggested that 'about 10 million foreign citizens' were in Russia, of whom 'around 4 million' were illegal. A further 900,000 had acquired all the necessary documents when they arrived, but by now should have left again, yet had not. It was thought that some had obtained a Russian passport 'by cunning means', reckoned on average to cost more than 10,000 roubles, and then hired the passport out to others.[36]

Trifonova also indicated that earlier prognoses of migration trends had been inaccurate. The labour mobility of Russians inside the country was up by 15 per cent in the first quarter of 2016 as opportunities narrowed for them too. Russians were readier to pick up work in jobs as janitors, loaders and cleaners usually done by the *gastarbaitery*.[37] In early 2017, Trifonova confirmed that the flow of migrant workers coming into Russia had been steadily increasing again. She cited the MVD's figures

[34] World Bank, 'Listening2Tajikistan: Survey of Wellbeing', 25 April 2016, www.worldbank .org/en/country/tajikistan/brief/listening2tajikistan, accessed 12 May 2016. This has since been updated. See, too, World Bank, 'Tajikistan: a moderate slowdown in economic growth coupled with a sharp decline in household purchasing power', Fall 2015, world bank.org/en/country/tajikistan/publication/economic-update-fall-2015.

[35] Ekaterina Trifonova, 'Rossiiane tesniat gastarbaiterov na rynke truda', *Nezavisimaia gazeta*, 15 July 2016; and Ekaterina Trifonova, 'Migranty iz SNG ne speshat pokidat' Rossiiu,' *Nezavisimaia gazeta*, 20 June 2016.

[36] Trifonova, 'Rossiiane tesniat gastarbaiterov'.

[37] Trifonova, 'Rossiiane tesniat gastarbaiterov'.

which showed that around 15 million had entered in 2016, mainly from states of the CIS, exceeding the number of arrivals in 2015 by several thousand. It was now officially reckoned that there were around 3 million illegal migrants inside Russia, although other experts put the figure at 5 million. Some thought that the cost of purchasing a work permit was driving migrants into the shadows.[38]

Unfree Labour from Central Asia

Evidence from a huge number of cases cited across sources illustrates different patterns of exploitation into which migrants may fall. The story of Farukh from Uzbekistan came to the attention of the Angel Coalition in Moscow.[39] A compatriot had told 27-year-old Farukh that he could find him work in Moscow earning $500 a month. Farukh and other Uzbeks travelled there by bus and began working on a construction site in the suburbs. Upon arrival, their documents were taken away, and they received no pay at the end of the first month. When the Uzbeks asked what was happening, they were told remuneration was 'temporarily delayed'. They continued to work but still, over months, were given no pay. In this predicament, without documents and money, they lacked the means to leave. Assurances continued that they would be paid. They worked a little longer and then managed to escape. Alone and vulnerable in Moscow, they telephoned the Angel Coalition.[40]

The story ended successfully. The Angel Coalition contacted officials in Uzbekistan and relayed all the necessary information for documents to be restored. Farukh and the Uzbek workers were issued with 'certificates of return' to enable them to leave Russia and travel home. While the paperwork was being sorted out, the Angel Coalition helped the men to secure places in a rehabilitation centre, where they were given psychological and medical help. Thus, the NGO sector was the guarantor here of security and of 'restored legal citizenship'. Necessary mechanisms involving the Uzbek state were essential in the restorative process but, without NGO action, the future of the Uzbeks would have been unclear. If, however, they had not escaped in the first place, they could not have accessed the mechanisms of civil society to help them. The key elements in this case included persuasion and entrapment by another Uzbek

---

[38] Ekaterina Trifonova, 'Gastarbaitery edut v rossiiskuiu "ten'"', *Nezavisimaia gazeta*, 6 February 2017.

[39] For discussion of the Angel Coalition, refer to Chapter 2.

[40] The story was told on the Angel Coalition's website at angelcoalition.org, last accessed 19 November 2009.

in the country of origin, successful transit in a group organised by the same man and finally confiscated documents and exploitation with no wages in Moscow. The Uzbek who initially deceived and recruited Farukh had links with the construction industry in Moscow and was the middleman who profited by handing the Uzbeks over. The trafficker both facilitated and benefited from their exploitation.

Siarkhon Tabarov's case followed a similar pattern but with variations. After seeing a television advertisement in Tajikistan, he was tempted by the offer from a local recruitment agency of a good job in the Russian Federation. After signing a document which made it all seem legal, he travelled with more than thirty other Tajiks to Rostov. Their passports were confiscated, and they were driven into a mountainous area. From here the labourers were made to walk to their final remote destination, where they were instructed that they would be quarrying, digging out stones with hand tools. They all immediately refused but were bullied, told that they had to work and that they would be deported if they refused.[41]

The men worked for eighty-five days without pay. They lived in an 'abandoned refrigerator truck containing filthy mattresses and a few cots'. Their diet consisted of macaroni, bread and porridge. Due to an insufficient water supply, they were reduced to drinking whatever water they could find. Any protest at conditions resulted in a denial of food. The reporter of this story does not indicate precisely how Siarkhon 'managed to contact some relatives who alerted an international organisation and the Tajik government to the case' (one assumes by mobile phone), but that is how the men were finally freed.[42] Like the example of Farukh, work was advertised in the home country, this time on television, and group transit to Russia was arranged. Throughout their time in Russia, their rights were denied by the seizure and denial of access to their documents and non-payment of wages. The severity of the labour, however, in a remote location, with threats and appalling living conditions had not been anticipated when responding to what appeared to be a legitimate job advertisement in Tajikistan. Without some initiative on their part to receive outside help, their predicament could have worsened.

Abror's passage into Russia from Uzbekistan was different from Farukh's and Siarkhon Tabarov's, since he travelled independently to Volgograd without being trafficked. He was an unemployed engineer from Urgench in north-west Uzbekistan searching for work in order to send money home to his family and elderly mother. Unable, however,

[41] Jane Buchanan, 'Undefended – Russia's migrant workers', Open Democracy, 18 March 2009, opendemocracy.net/article/email/russia-s-undefended-migrant-workers.
[42] Buchanan, 'Undefended'.

to find any employment matching his engineering skills, he agreed to work for a local farmer. His tasks included weeding vegetables, feeding poultry and cleaning out the hen house. In return he was promised 'a small wage'. The farmer then turned owner. He took Abror's papers and informed him that wages would not be forthcoming since Abror would have 'nowhere to spend' them. For eight months, this situation of unfree labour prevailed.[43]

Abror's exit was possible when another Uzbek visited the farm and threatened the owner that he would tell the police what was happening. Abror could leave thanks to this intervention but he soon discovered that his compatriot and rescuer was, in fact, a trafficker who then 'demanded 300 dollars for services rendered'. Abror was thus left in the situation of feeling pressured to hire himself out again in order to repay this new debt, now caught in the trap of debt-bondage. As he put it: 'once it gets warm, I'll sell myself into slavery again . . . What else can I do? Otherwise, my family of four will be left to live off my sick mother's pension.'[44] Some migrants without advice from reliable sources end up not seeing other options. Whether Abror would receive wages at all would, however, be unpredictable. Like those women and girls trafficked out of Russia in the 1990s and early 2000s, who after a first negative experience were subsequently prepared to try again in the hope that next time it would be 'better' or 'different', Abror retained hope plus a deep sense of there being no alternative.

Other typical cases are reported on the website of the MVD, sometimes briefly, sometimes fully. One such concerned an Uzbek citizen who had promised unsuspecting Uzbeks manual labour in construction with monthly pay. When his recruits arrived in Irkutsk, he took their passports so that they could not easily return home. The MVD commented that there were 'intolerable working conditions' and 'harsh exploitation' as the Uzbeks toiled 'as slaves'. At the time of the report the criminal had been caught and was awaiting extradition.[45] The MVD gave fuller details of a case in forestry in Amursk oblast in the Far East which was especially violent. Here six Uzbek workers with an age range from thirty-six to fifty-four had been promised monthly wages of 18,000 roubles. Immediately, however, their migration cards and passports were taken from them, and they found themselves living in 'wretched conditions

---

[43] IWPR, 'Uzbeks prey to modern slave trade', 9 March 2008, iwpr.net/global-voices/uzbeks-prey-modern-slave-trade.

[44] IWPR, 'Uzbeks prey to modern slave trade'.

[45] Press-sluzhba GU MVD Rossii po Irkutskoi oblasti, 'V Irkutske po podozreniiu v torgovle liud'mi zaderzhan grazhdanin Uzbekistana', 11 February 2013, mvd.ru/news/item/839142.

in a wooden house on the site of the sawmill'. They were made to work twelve hours a day 'practically without days off'. They were also largely cut off from local inhabitants and the outside world. Those workers who could see what was happening to the migrants were later witnesses to the fact that the Uzbeks were 'continually insulted and beaten'. Often they lacked the strength to fulfil their daily work norms. Other 'faults' were also punished. When the owner sent an Uzbek to buy some wine and he did not return with the right label, yet again he was beaten. Medical help was also denied to the migrants. When one Uzbek was seriously hurt at work, others were forbidden to call an ambulance or to take him to a doctor. At one point, locals secretly tended to the Uzbeks and fed them. When the police eventually came, they learnt that each Uzbek had lost more than 10 kg. They were freed because a local worker had telephoned an acquaintance in the local Khabarovsk Uzbek diaspora. He in turn contacted the police. The MVD press release reported that the guilty man would be charged under Articles 127.1 and 127.2 of the Criminal Code, which would likely bring 'long' prison terms.[46] The MVD has also issued reports and statements on individuals who profit from promising to provide migrants with legal papers. Its website tersely imparted that three men from December 2014 had illegally 'registered' 175 foreigners at a false address, estimating that the men made around 2,000 roubles for each 'registered' foreigner. They were given sentences between six months and one year and each fined 50,000 roubles.[47]

Not all reports on unfree labour situations are later followed through to show what happened to the criminals who were caught. One complete story is that of a forty-year-old Tajik who was travelling on an electric train from Moscow to Monino. Three young residents of Moscow oblast in their teens and early twenties threatened him with a gun and took his money and passport. Then the eighteen-year-old amongst them took the Tajik home and forced him at gunpoint to clean out the attic. Evidence collected on the train was sufficient to open a case against the men. All three Russians were convicted under article 162 in the Criminal Code for robbery and the eighteen-year-old for the use of slave labour in accordance with Article 127.2. Two were sentenced to six years in a general

[46] Press-sluzhba GU MVD RF po DFO, 'Sotrudniki Glavnogo upravleniia MVD Rossii po Dal'nevostochnomy federal'nomu okrugu osvobodili iz rabstva gastarbaiterov', 6 September 2010, mvd.ru/news/item/182841.
[47] Ministry of Internal Affairs RF, 'V Permi vynesen prigovor prestupnoi gruppe, osushchestvliavshei nezakonnuiu registratsiiu migrantov', 12 January 2016, mvd.ru/news/item/7030715.

regime prison and one to six and a half years in a hard labour prison.[48] The news item was sparse on detail but illustrates a case that did not begin with trafficking but which was one of abduction when travelling freely on a train followed by coercion into forced domestic work.

Shops are another site of exploitation. Many newspapers discussed the story of twelve citizens from Kazakhstan and Uzbekistan (five women, four men and three children) who were imprisoned for ten years in a shop's basement and made to serve customers during the day and to unload produce. This occurred in the Gol'ianovo district of Moscow in the shop Produkty on Novosibirsk street. In its treatment of the story, *Rossiiskaia gazeta* narrated how a husband and wife from Kazakhstan owned the shop and 'mercilessly exploited' the migrants, who had to sleep on the floor. For vivid reporting, this newspaper quoted what some of the workers said after they were freed. One revealed: 'I did not receive a kopeck for ten years. We worked for sixteen hours, were fed twice a day with skilly [*supom-balandoi*] or sometimes with food past its expiry date.' Another said 'the female owner beat us with her hands, feet, sticks and rolls of foil. The male owner did not beat us, but watched. It was offensive and they did it for nothing at all.' When one asked to go out into the daylight, which was forbidden, the woman 'struck me with the door key and scars have remained. She beat hard, like a maniac.'[49]

Then *Rossiiskaia gazeta* took a novel approach by posing the question of how people can 'submissively [*pokorno*] bear slavery for ten years?' There followed serious discussion about the psychological effects of 'paralysed fear' and 'total lack of rights'. Even if they had run away, it asked, where would they go, with no money or documents, all the time knowing that illegal workers would be taken into a special reception centre and then prohibited from working in Russia for five years? The article pointed out that, since people came into the shop every day and were served by the 'slaves', the latter in fact 'lived among people'.[50] Another article in the same newspaper reported that the workers were, in fact, 'close and distant' relatives of the owners, and a case of human trafficking had been opened.[51]

If we compare narration of this story in *Pravda*, we see different emphases despite overlapping details. More is made of the fact that they were found in October 2012 by a group of volunteers and journalists

[48] No named author, 'Osuzhdeny za obrashchenie v rabstvo grazhdanina Tadzhikistana', 11 December 2009, actualcomment.ru/news/8605.

[49] Lidiia Grafova, 'Rabototorgovlia v magazine "Produkty": nashumevshie fakty eksplu-atatsii rabskogo truda nuzhdaiutsia v proverke', *Rossiiskaia gazeta*, 7 November 2012.

[50] Grafova, 'Rabototorgovlia v magazine "Produkty"'.

[51] Ivan Egorov and Natal'ia Kozlova, 'Sledstvennyi komitet pristupil k proverke: sledim za situatsiei', *Rossiiskaia gazeta*, 7 November 2012.

and freed without police involvement. More is made of the presence of children in the basement who, when the captives finally came out, were quickly whisked away in a car by the owner of the shop. They were off-spring of one of the women workers. Earlier Bakii Kasimovoi had given birth in the basement, and the owner had then allegedly said to her 'what will you do with a child? How will you look after her and feed her when you live in the basement?' The shop owner had taken the child away to her own flat and when the offspring was five years old had declared that she would take her to Kazakhstan. For two years, Kasimovoi had no news of her child. Then one day she was informed 'your daughter died', and there 'was no diagnosis, they told me nothing'.[52] *Pravda* highlighted the heartless dimensions of the story. Whether the child had really been sold on was unclear.

In *Pravda* the story pivoted around the question of 'blame for slavery', just as it had in its reporting a decade earlier on the human trafficking of Russian women and girls into the sex industry elsewhere. Who was respon-sible for forcing these migrants to work from twelve to fourteen hours a day, beginning at 6 a.m., without ever being paid, not being allowed to go out onto the street and denied phone contact? Who stole the child? Blame squarely fell on the shoulders of the shop owners Zhansul Istanbekov and Sakena Muzdybaeva. They had deceitfully 'enticed' the workers with promises of good jobs and decent pay. Instead, the enslaved workers had to serve customers, unload goods, wash the floor and do whatever they were instructed. The women were 'severely beaten' for minor faults.

Initially, the shop owners were taken to the OVD (Otdel Vnutrennykh Del), or Department of Internal Affairs, then referred to the Investigative Committee (Sledstvennyi Komitet), but not detained. The loud message from *Pravda* was that blame fell on the bad shop owners from Kazakhstan and on corrupt police.[53] It was suggested that the only restriction on the owners during the investigation would be denial of permission to leave the country, but not arrest. A lawyer declared that 'the use of slave labour for ten years on their territory went unnoticed by the police. It makes me draw a conclusion about their irresponsibility in doing their duties.' He added: 'another variant is not excluded: it is possible that they had an agreement [*sgovor*] with the shop owners'.[54]

A week later *Pravda* regretted that the Procuracy of Preobrazhenkii raion had closed the case. They had decided that it did not merit

---

punishment under the articles on slave labour or on the illegal denial of freedom. Apparently, the Investigative Committee had already lodged a complaint about this, and the citizen activists who had freed the slaves 'were in shock'. The leader of the movement Al'ternativa, Oleg Mel'nikov, declared that, if this case was not considered suitable for criminal prosecution, then 'anyone can now take slaves'.[55] A year later, the paper reported that the legal system was continually postponing meetings and that the case was stuck in the General Procuracy. Once again *Pravda* insisted on exposing injustice, apportioning blame and discussing the consequences.[56] Having got nowhere in the Russian legal system, in November 2016 lawyers and an expert from the Civic Assistance Committee, Grazhdanskoe Sodeistvie, took the case to the ECtHR, arguing that the workers had been slaves and that their rights were violated under several articles of the European Convention.[57]

Just as Russian women had left the country and ended up in brothels, so too some foreign women arriving in Russia endured that fate. The numbers of women from Central Asia arriving in Russia for work have been increasing over recent years. By 2012 Tajikistan's state migration service estimated that 12 per cent of Tajiks travelling to Russia were female, and the Russian MVD thought that overall 30 per cent of incoming migrant labour was female.[58] Some were being transported in groups, and others travelled independently.[59] These women had begun to tell NGOs about deceptions regarding work and pay and of hoodwinking within their own communities. There were reported cases of Kyrgyz women turning to Kyrgyz men for advice about how to acquire a work permit. The men charged them around $500 for the alleged permit which was, in fact, fake. All the women had really needed to do was obtain a permit from the Russian authorities and not rely on fellow migrants. Lack of knowledge and experience was costly, and fellow countrymen could not always be relied upon. Some women were also forced into prostitution by men in their diaspora and suffered rape and beatings. One hospital in Moscow reported the abandonment of new babies by mothers, and some figures suggested that in 2012 more than 200 babies of illegal Kyrgyz migrants

[55] Frolov, 'Zakryto.'

[56] Anton Frolov, 'V Rossii vse bol'she sluchaev rabovladeniia', *Pravda*, 20 March 2013.

[57] See Iuliia Orlova, '"Gol'ianovo raby" delo dostignuta Strasburg', Grazhdanskoe Sodeistvie, 27 December 2016, www.refugee.ru.

[58] Farangis Najibullah, 'Central Asian women's shattered Russian dreams', RFE/RL, 8 March 2012, rferl.org/a/central_asia_women_shattered_russian_dreams/24509262.html.

[59] Zhanna Zaionchkovskaia, Elena Tiuriukanova and Iuliia Florinskaia, *Trudovaia Migratsiia v Rossiiu: Kak Dvigat'sia Dal'she* (Moscow: MAKS Press, 2012). Chapter 9 discusses gender more fully.

were living in orphanages in Moscow. A Kyrgyz NGO in Moscow revealed desperate solutions to avoid the shame that would be endured in countries of origin where disapproval would run high. These included illegal abortions, infanticide and suicide.[60]

One case in Sverdlovsk that was described on the MVD's website concerned two women who had been brought from Uzbekistan into Russia by an Uzbek with promises of well-paid work. The man then 'sold them into slavery to an acquaintance'. He was being held temporarily in solitary confinement whilst extradition was being arranged. According to Uzbek law, he would be likely to get between eight and twelve years in prison for the crime of deprivation of freedom.[61] The informative website also revealed that a Moldovan who was on an international search list was finally apprehended in Russia in 2014. He had been involved in the trafficking of underage girls and adults and was hiding in Russia on false papers. While there he became active again in a group involved in human trafficking for sexual exploitation, using six Moldovans. When his other gang members were arrested in 2013, he had managed to hide. Finally, the MVD announced, he had been found.[62] An accompanying video showed police forcing entry with a metal bar followed by footage of bedrooms, the floor, a drawer full of passports and three women sitting on a bed looking down or covering their faces. Holding a gun, a policeman questioned a man in a dressing gown and a young woman who had been forced into prostitution.

Such videos sometimes accompany announcements of crimes on the MVD website, usually screening the first moments of police entry into a known site of exploitation followed by pictures of rows of women or men in shoddy conditions guarded by their minders. One such video showed the arrest of a Vietnamese group in 2014 in Moscow oblast which was holding three young women from Vietnam who had been brought into Russia for prostitution after having been promised legal work with high

---

[60] Najibullah, 'Central Asian women's shattered Russian dreams'.

[61] Press-sluzhba GU MVD Rossii po Sverdlovskoi oblasti, 'V Sverdlovskoi oblasti politseiskimi zaderzhan inostrannyi grazhdanin, podozrevaemyi v torgovle liud'mi', 19 March 2013, mvd.ru/news/item/892112. For another case regarding an Uzbek, see Press-sluzhba UMVD Rossii po Tverskoi oblasti, 'V Tverskoi oblasti zaderzhan grazhdanin Uzbekistana, nakhodivshiisia v mezhgosudarstvennom rozyske', 9 December 2014, mvd.ru/news/item/2907434.

[62] Press-gruppa GUUR MVD Rossii, 'V Moskve zaderzhan grazhdanin Moldovy, razyskivaemyi po podozreniiu v organizatsii torgovli liud'mi', 26 March 2014, mvd.ru/news/item/2094329. In an earlier case, six Moldovans trapped in sex work had been under guard in flats and houses in Moscow oblast before the police rescued them. See Press-gruppa GUUR MVD Rossii, 'V Moskve politseiskie osvobodili iz seksual'nogo rabstva shest' inostrannykh grazhdanok', 2 December 2013, mvd.ru/news/item/1377835.

wages.[63] The men had isolated the women in flats, taken their passports and left them under guard. The video showed a Vietnamese man smoking and another being asked his name, how long he had been in Russia, what the aim of his trip there was and what he did with the women in the flat. Three worried-looking women sat on a bed. Footage also showed one of the women being questioned. The police had opened a case under Article 241 of the Criminal Code concerning the organisation of prostitution, but not under Article 127.1 on human trafficking. As we have already seen, such a case is easier to prove.

Most published stories about unfree labour in Russia concern adults, but some refer to children who have been trapped. The MVD press office gave very brief coverage of the freeing of fifteen children from Kyrgyzstan who were being confined and forced to work near Moscow. The children had been under guard around the clock and living in barracks-like accommodation unfit for habitation in Noginsk where there was an illegal sewing factory. These children were made to work at night and, if they did not fulfil the plan that was set for them, they were punished. One youngster of eleven was found 'with many bruises and signs of beating'.[64] Such reports shed light on the existence of a type of crime even if they do not permit categorisation of how it began or its likely scale.

Television news reports have also flagged up the unsafe accommodation that some migrants are required to live in. In February 2016, Channel One's news showed a building that had quickly burnt down. Just its brick walls remained but the wooden roof had gone. Arson was suspected. It appeared that illegal migrants from Central Asia had lived and worked there and that the building was an underground factory for making bedding where synthetic material for filling pillows had helped the fire to spread. A child's shoe and a woman's photograph were found in the rubble. The newsreader told viewers that 'their living conditions compare with detention'. There was only one way out of the building, and it was blocked by a metal bar through which rescuers had to saw. Twelve people died, including a child of five. The message was that risks to migrant workers could be immense.[65] In another example of unsafe

[63] Press-gruppa GUUR MVD Rossii, 'Politseiskimi osvobozhdeny iz seksual'nogo rabstva tri grazhdanki V'etnama', 6 November 2014, mvd.ru/news/item/2787812. For video footage, see 'Politseiskimi osvobozhdeny iz seksual'nogo rabstva tri grazhdanki V'etnama', 7 November 2014, mvd.ru/document/2795199.

[64] No named author, 'Pod Moskvoi naideny deti-raby', 28 December 2009, actualcom ment.ru/pod_moskvoy_naydeny_deti_raby_html.

[65] Relayed on Russia's Channel One television news at www.1tv.ru on 1 February 2016. A terse Interfax statement published in the press reported three child deaths out of the twelve. See no named author, 'Zhertvami pozhara v shveinom tsekhe na ulitse Stromynka v Moskve stali 12 chelovek', *Nezavisimaia gazeta*, 1 February 2016.

working conditions, three Tajiks died in construction work in Petersburg on a fourteen-storey housing project after falling off a ladder. Investigation showed that the site 'did not observe elementary rules of safety', and even hand rails and lighting were absent. *Rossiiskaia gazeta* reported that 'there was no chance of saving them' because the migrants had died immediately. The company was being charged with breaking safety rules.[66] In August 2016, another fire in a printing warehouse in Moscow killed seventeen migrant workers from Kyrgyzstan. Lax standards were again to blame. A faulty lamp near flammable liquids and paper appeared to be the cause. The room where the Kyrgyz died had no easy exit.[67]

Russians in Unfree Labour in Russia

Just as migrants from outside Russia have ended up in cities or in the countryside confined in situations of harsh forced labour which is unpaid, so too have Russian men and women within their own country. Fresh cases to hit the headlines in 2013 and 2014 were of men trapped working in brick kilns in the republic of Dagestan. The newspaper *Kavkazskii uzel* told readers that Sergei Khlivnyi, aged forty-three and from Murmansk, had been confined in slavery for an astonishing eighteen years. He had arrived in Makhachkala in 1996 looking for work. As soon as he got off the bus, a stranger approached and offered to set him up in a brick-works in Petrpavlovsk. Subsequently all Sergei's documents were taken, 'he received only food and old clothes' and 'they kept him locked up'. After several months, he managed to escape but was caught and taken to the village of Talovsk to herd cattle. He was then moved on to Iurkovsk, Kazariut, Kamysh-Kutan and elsewhere. He escaped again and was once more captured. He was finally rescued by the voluntary organisation Al'ternativa which had freed the aforementioned shop workers in Moscow.[68] In fact, whilst Sergei was in Dagestan, his mother and brother had reported him missing to the police, who allegedly did little to help. From Al'ternativa Mel'nikov commented that 'during this time the law enforcement organs did not want to work'. This man from Murmansk was one of many trapped in Dagestan. In 2011 it became known that Andrei Popov from Saratov oblast had been in slavery in a brickworks since 2000. So, too, was Vadim Kucherbaev from Bashkiria, and he was

[66] Vera Chereneva, 'Na peterburgskoi stroike pogibli tri migranta', *Rossiiskaia gazeta*, 15 April 2016.

[67] Sergei Babkin, 'Chislo pogibshikh na pozhare v Moskve vozroslo do 17', *Rossiiskaia gazeta*, 27 August 2016.

[68] No named author, 'Zhitel' Murmanska soobshchil politsii o 18 godakh svoego rabstva v Dagestane', *Kavkazskii uzel*, 28 September 2014, www.kavkaz-uzel.eu/articles/249862.

also freed by Al'ternativa. He explained that he had been in Ekaterinburg when he met a man who offered him work. The man then suggested that they have a beer. However, 'Kucherbaev does not remember what happened after taking the frothy beer.'[69]

Offering work followed by drugging is one pattern of trapping victims and facilitates their kidnapping. A 39-year-old with the pseudonym Dmitrii Shubin travelled to Moscow from Smolensk oblast. He worked on a farm as a tractor driver. After a couple of days in the capital, he returned to the station for his homeward journey. While waiting for the train he was approached by a young man. They got chatting, and the man suggested going to a nearby café. The last thing Shubin remembers is the man coming towards him with a tray with two cups of tea on it. He later explained that 'klofelin was in the tea or some sort of strong sleeping pill'.[70] Thereafter he found himself with eight others in a car and to his surprise was transported to Dagestan. Upon arrival, they were told that they had been 'paid for' and that for the next year they would have to work off this debt. Shubin added that they took away passports, money and mobile phones. A Slavic man, not someone from the Caucasus, showed them the barn where they would sleep and told them they would begin work early. Ten dogs ran around the area. Shubin asked if he could wash, but ran to a nearby village and was helped by some Tajiks who gave him a phone so that he could call his wife. He did not go to the police as the Tajiks warned him that they might return him to the brickworks. Apparently, it may not have been just a financial arrangement between the police and owners of the brickworks but one also connected with 'kinship relations', which complicated policing matters. Once back in Moscow, Shubin was stunned that this had happened to him and was keen to write a complaint about his kidnappers.[71] Al'ternativa freed at least twelve slaves from Dagestan in 2013 and five more by the autumn of 2014.[72] Kidnapping was a common factor across the cases.

A law enforcement officer spoke to Komsomol'skaia pravda on the understanding that his words would be anonymous. He shared that: 'I know definitely that recruiters work in all the capital's stations, not

---

[69] No named author, 'V Dagestane iz rabstva osvobozhdeny tri cheloveka', *Kavkazskii uzel*, 13 September 2013, www.kavkaz-uzel.eu/articles/230055.

[70] *Klofelin*, also called *klodilin*, reduces blood pressure and heart rate and, when mixed with alcohol, is a dangerous hypnotic.

[71] Aleksandr Rogoza, 'Rabstvo v Rossii', *Komsomol'skaia pravda*, 2 January 2013.

[72] One local official said that there had been eighty-six brickworks in Dagestan with large concentrations in Makhachkala and Kaspiisk. Another gave a lower number of twenty-seven in these two cities. There are also ecological and health issues connected with impact on the land and dusty air. See 'Eighteen years a slave in Daghestan', RFE/RL, 30 September 2014, rferl.org/a/caucasus-report-daghestan-slave/26613556.html.

only those who drug but several who press men to work in construction in the south of Russia.' He pointed out that it was not only the homeless who were trapped but also inhabitants from different parts of the country who arrived in Moscow looking for work. The officer repeated the well-known fact that the men were promised good pay then often taken down into autonomous territories where the usual Russian laws had little sway.[73] Mel'nikov imparted that the bosses 'bought' men from the recruiters for around 15,000 to 20,000 roubles. He had also heard that the 'bosses' did not feed their slaves well but did give them spirits to drink every night 'to convince the man to submit'. Two young girls from Nizhnii Novgorod made to work in a local sauna in Dagestan, however, were 'bought' for as much as 150,000 roubles.[74] Females cost more as they would generate quick and lucrative income for their 'owners'.

Another tale of forced labour in Russia is that of 34-year-old Liudmila from Odessa, who may have been Russian or Ukrainian. On the Internet, she found information about a shop in Moscow that wanted to hire sales assistants. She was a divorced hairdresser with two children and found that her earnings were insufficient. She contacted the employers and decided to set herself up in Moscow and bring her children later. Upon arrival, she was met at the Kiev station by a man who said he would take her directly to the shop, but instead they went to a flat in the Liubertsy area of the city where he asked for her documents and told her that she would be living at this address. The next morning Liudmila was made to put on a headscarf, take a walking stick and limp so that 'people on the metro will give more money'.[75] She protested that she had come to work in a shop but was told that, if she refused to go out begging, they would beat her and then hand her over to the police. Since she no longer had her documents and no one knew her in Moscow, she would be in trouble. She cried but went off with other women to ask strangers for money.

Twenty other Slavic women also lived at this address. Half of them were about Liudmila's age but others were seventy or eighty, for whom this was 'the hardest'. They were all taken to the station 'dressed in rags' and made to beg on electric trains and in the metro. Liudmila revealed that, if she did not earn at least 4,000 roubles per day, they would beat her. If she made 5,000 or 6,000, they fed her vodka and sausages. She eventually decided to run away. The first two local police departments would not listen to her and shooed her out 'because I was dressed like a

---

[73] Rogoza, 'Rabstvo'.
[74] Rogoza, 'Rabstvo'.
[75] Rogoza, 'Rabstvo'.

beggar'. The third helped her and put her in touch with the volunteers who freed slaves so that she could receive help.[76]

Some situations of unfree labour are more violent than others. The tale of 52-year-old Viktor Erke was one of long hours and beatings. Journalist Vladimir Demchenko described how Erke was down on his luck and so he accepted an offer of work, money and food. But 'life turned out not to be sweet. Work – ploughing, in pastures from dawn to dusk with no free days and no pay. For a slight fault – either a fist on his teeth or a whip on the spine.'[77] Erke ran away, but was caught and beaten. Erke had been trapped by 61-year-old Aleksandr Komarov from Kurgansk oblast. From having a business making felt boots and a furniture factory, Komarov had decided to move into cattle, horses, sheep and geese. He leased abandoned fields on the edge of the district, which were not always possible to reach by a four-wheel drive.

Several workers were badly treated on Komarov's farm. Svetlana had worked only one week for Komarov before being blamed for selling his goats and was fined 4,000 roubles, a debt which she was required to 'work off'. When several calves died, the debt was 500,000 roubles. Demchenko reported that the debts could reach 'astounding [*umopom-rachitel'nye*] sums'. One worker even owed 1 million roubles, allegedly for the theft of ten horses, and another several million for pilfering grain and for arson. This worker was found dead with his head in a noose. When his widow turned up to ask for his wages, Komarov yelled 'he owes me!' And Galina Makhova, a cook who ran away, was chained to a bed upon her return. Komarov also tried to throw Ivan, a stoker, into the oven for bad work, and his legs were burnt. Ivan became so desperate that he tried to cut off his arm 'in order to escape slavery'.[78]

Why, asked the journalist, did no one complain to the police? In provocative journalism, he suggested that:

> The majority of former slave workers are not people of the highest social status. They like to drink – to put it mildly. Some have nowhere to live. And in engaging to work for Komarov many knew what they were going to. Slave conditions? Yes, all right. They give grub [*kharchi*] – wonderful. And they beat [the workers] – it serves them right, they are to blame themselves.[79]

On making a visit to Galina Makhova to get her story, Demchenko was told by her that 'I have no grudges' (*a ia pretenzii ne imeiu*). When he pressed

[76] Rogoza, 'Rabstvo'.

[77] Vladimir Demchenko, 'Byvshaia rabynia Kurganskogo fermera: "v kolkhoze eshche khuzhe. Ta zhe nevolia, no ni deneg, ni edy ni daiut"', *Komsomol'skaia pravda*, 13 May 2013.

[78] Demchenko, 'Byvshaia rabynia'.

[79] Demchenko, 'Byvshaia rabynia'.

her that she had been chained to the bed and not paid, she responded 'when was that?' She also asked 'where do they pay now? On the kolkhoz? It is even worse there.' Many, like Makhova, were asked to give evidence, but they would not. What is it, asked Demchenko? Non-resistance to evil (*neprotivlenie*)? Or is it internal acceptance to be slaves? Even Erke, who gave evidence against Komarov on video recording, then regretted it. Later he said that after running away he had returned to the farm with pleasure and that all was well there. The guilty Komarov predicatably dismissed any accusations as 'rot' (*chush*'). *Komsomol'skaia pravda* pointed out that, in fact, local investigators had also feared Komarov. One commented that he was a 'big man' in the oblast and that 'he knew all the rural heads'. Apparently, the head of the district administration 'guzzled' his geese. Local leaders would telephone Komarov about matters, not the police. Demchenko speculated that the police anyway may have 'shielded' Komarov. Similarly, doctors at the hospital quietly treated the injured without filling in the usual forms. In sum, Komarov was a corrupt and violent man with important informal connections.[80]

Demchenko regretted that the story of Komarov was not an isolated case. He reported that slaves in such conditions had been found in the Kuban, Altai, Stavropol and Novosibirsk. Where there was unused land in the countryside and lots of people, such events could occur. In Komarov's case he had agreements with the district and municipal authorities, even the police. The victims and also their relatives were failing to report what had been happening. Was it not odd, posed Demchenko, that people were thinking that slavery was normal? Why don't they see it differently? Some don't even ask if this is slavery. In the face of beatings, Demchenko regretted that it was not surprising that silence reigned. Yet another question troubled him. Why did Komarov have to be like this? Why did he beat workers? Demchenko asked the arrested Komarov why he did not employ 'normal, sober workers'. Komarov replied that 'in the countryside today they are not to be found'.[81]

Demchenko summed up by claiming that Komarov was a cunning man. In fact, there were examples of successful farms without slave labour. With some odd sympathy, Demchenko's last words were, 'Komarov probably did not set out to become a despot and tyrant. It happened that way.'[82] What makes his and some other journalists' sensational reporting in *Komsomol'skaia pravda* different from that in papers such as *Izvestiia* and *Rossiiskaia gazeta* is its provocative, often rhetorical questioning, which

[80] Demchenko, 'Byvshaia rabynia'.
[81] Demchenko, 'Byvshaia rabynia'.
[82] Demchenko, 'Byvshaia rabynia'.

tunes in to populist thinking in Russia, then challenges some aspects of it. Such sensational modes of packaging of articles are just one genre and can also be found in papers such as *Moskovskii komsomolets*. Demchenko's intent, however, was graphically to shed light, to shake his readers, to pose troubling questions and to condemn.

Echoing this theme of non-resistance to slave-like conditions, Sergei Nikolaev writing in *Pravda* asked why slavery was possible in Russia. He answered this by arguing that one of the main reasons was 'slave psychology'. Nikolaev felt that the bulk of the Russian population had been 'inculcated' with this 'over hundreds of centuries' and that, in Soviet times, the 'massive use of slave labour' had been accompanied by a corresponding ideology. He urged readers 'to look around' and see examples. He listed several: non-payment of wages on time; sudden cutting of bonuses; making people work with no pay on weekends and outside agreed times. He suggested that people tolerate this as it is important 'not to lose work' and so workers 'are silent'. But this means that 'it is possible to go on further in this spirit. It is profit that is most important.' He observed that, even if someone is not silent, there is huge competition in the labour market and always people who are more 'compliant'. Moreover, these are often *gastarbaitery*.[83] Whilst most Russian journalists do not make this link across the centuries nor suggest that unfree labour in the Russian past is a determining antecedent of unfree labour today, Nikolaev poses this possibility and echoes Daniel Rancour-Laferriere's notion of Russian obedience.

There are many other articles in the press which touch on aspects of human trafficking and forced labour. Examples from *Rossiiskaia gazeta* include: how a corrupt lieutenant-colonel engaged in trafficking;[84] the attempted sale of babies, including by a former head of a children's home in Vladikavkaz;[85] how a gang in the Urals took minors from the streets, forced them into prostitution and killed at least thirteen 'obstinate' ones who refused to comply;[86] the involvement of corrupt police in the trafficking of Siberian women into prostitution in Tiumen by taking a cut in the money the women earned in a hotel;[87] and the MVD's co-operation with the police in other CIS states regarding trafficking.[88]

---

[83] Sergei Nikolaev, 'Rabstvo-XXI vek: Rossiia spolzaet v antichnost'?' *Pravda*, 30 May 2011.

[84] Vladimir Fedosenko, 'Rabyni shli optom', *Rossiiskaia gazeta*, 20 December 2011.

[85] Irina Chechurina, no title, *Rossiiskaia gazeta*, 14 August 2013; and Elena Brezhitskaia, no title, *Rossiiskaia gazeta*, 2 August 2013.

[86] No named author, 'Prodannaia svoboda', *Rossiiskaia gazeta*, 6 September 2007.

[87] Anatolii Men'shikov, 'Prokliatyi rai', *Rossiiskaia gazeta*, 22 October 2008.

[88] Mikhail Falaleev, 'Rabstvo pod prikrytiem', *Rossiiskaia gazeta*, 24 November 2009.

A number cover the abuse of a professional position to profit from the exploitation of others.

One case which led to a cluster of articles of the Criminal Code being applied and which also involved the target's son concerned a woman from Irkutsk. The MVD described how she had been sold in 2012 by her partner for 50,000 roubles 'for sexual exploitation in Moscow oblast'. When she refused to become a prostitute, the criminals kidnapped her young son, threatened her and forced her to comply. She finally managed to run away but they still held her son. Months later the police detained the criminals as they were boarding a train in Moscow at the Kazan station. The boy was returned to his mother. A few days after, two more of this gang's members were apprehended in a forested area of Iushnoe Butovo for arranging sexual services for two guests in the capital. The articles of the Criminal Code applied here were 126 (kidnapping), 127 (illegal deprivation of freedom), 127.1 (human trafficking), 240 (recruiting into prostitution), 241 (organisation of prostitution) and 210 (organisation of a criminal association). Two further group members were arrested much later under Article 241. The MVD also announced 'a range of supplementary investigations' in order to establish 'other episodes of their criminal activity'.[89]

Other MVD reports regarding arrests connected with forced prostitution inside Russia refer to different parts of the vast landmass. In 2011, a report described a case of human trafficking in Nizhnii Novgorod. A female inhabitant of the city in 2006 had set up an organisation which in four years had grown to twenty-four people who worked as pimps, controllers and drivers for a network of thirteen brothels. The money earned by the women and girls was shared out amongst group members, who had now been arrested for human trafficking.[90] An even larger operation was exposed in 2013 in which the activities of 'an inter-regional organised group' ran a racket using a wide network of brothels across Moscow, Saransk, Nizhnii Novgorod, Penza, Voronezh, Rostov-on-Don, Krasnodar and Sochi. The police had evidence of kidnappings in Moscow oblast followed by the transfer of the captured to other regions 'using psychological and physical violence'. Raids across brothels and at an address in the Russian republic of Mordovia established that the gang was Mordovan. More than thirty women were freed. Police searches had also found

[89] Press-sluzhba GUUR MVD Rossii, 'Operativniki osvobodili iz seksual'nogo rabstva 24-letniuiu zhenshchinu i vernuli ei pokhishchennogo 4-letnego syna', 24 May 2012, mvd.ru/news/item/153926.

[90] Press-sluzhba GU MVD po PFO, 'V Nizhnem Novgorode v sud napravleno ugolovnoe delo po faktu torgovli liud'mi', 11 October 2011, mvd.ru/news/item/161717.

firearms, ammunition, a police uniform, telephones, SIM cards and confiscated passports. The gang was to be charged under Article 126 of the Criminal Code on kidnapping, Article 127 on illegal deprivation of freedom, Article 127.1 on human trafficking and Article 210 on criminal organisation.[91]

Quite distinct from most examples, in 2011 a skilled man from Krasnodar krai was forced to make jewellery and metal objects in the republic of Adygea. Among the illegal objects that he was required to produce were knives, swords and sabres. He could not refuse due to the violence used against him. In captivity, he was made to work without rest. A criminal case had opened under all three parts of Article 127.[92] Another case came to the attention of police in Khabarovsk krai of a man being held against his will in a private house in the countryside. He had been promised a job in a sawmill and had arrived expecting that. His captors took his passport and made him sign papers permitting them to privatise and sell his residence. While this process was ongoing, the report noted that the man lived 'as a slave'. His captors made him work hard and 'beat the man unmercifully'. He was freed after the house was surrounded. Investigators found a pistol, a rifle and several knives. Two men were arrested, one of whom had previously been convicted for robbery and grievous bodily harm.[93]

Unfree labourers are sometimes also coerced into acts of theft. A police department in Ul'ianovsk oblast concerned with 'banditry and other crimes of theft' had discovered a group whose members were stealing from a cement works using forced labour. Three men living in Novoul'ianovsk had been threatening drivers from different firms and making them take from 5 to 10 per cent of their lorry-load of cement into a hangar. It was then sold on to 'contacts'. For this underground business to be successful, it needed 'working hands' as drivers and packers. Initially a thirty-year-old was willing to earn some extra money, but the police imparted that 'soon he understood that he had in fact fallen into slavery'. When he tried to stop, he was told, 'don't rock the boat', and that there was no way out for him as he was now 'entangled in criminal business'. He was then locked up in the hangar with bread and water and

---

[91] Press-sluzhba GUUR MVD Rossii, 'V neskol'kikh regionakh Rossii zaderzhany podozrevaemye v torgovle liud'mi s tsel'iu seksual'noi ekspluatatsii' (audio), 14 February 2013, mvd.ru/news/item/842912.

[92] Press-sluzhba MVD po Respublike Adygeia, 'V Adygee fakt ispol'zovaniia v techenie neskol'kikh let rabskogo truda s primeneniem nasiliia', 12 November 2011, mvd.ru/news/item/160715.

[93] Press-sluzhba GU MVD Rossii po DFO, 'Politseiskie Khabarovskogo kraia osvobodili plennika', 16 May 2013, mvd.ru/news/item/995427.

had to sleep on an old sofa in the middle of cement dust. He escaped for a week but was found, badly beaten, and threatened that he could lose his life. Later he tried again to escape, but was captured once more and beaten into a car. This time the police were watching and apprehended the culprits. They were likely to be charged with deprivation of freedom and also slave labour. The police report remarked that, since the amendment to the Criminal Code in 2003, so far there had only been eight criminal cases for slave labour under Article 127.2. This case would be the ninth.[94]

The most recent articles have highlighted the role of the Internet in recruitment into slavery. *Moscow News* in 2014 reported that in Moscow a 28-year-old woman had been detained for trying to sell teenagers of 15 and 17, whom she had befriended on-line, into sexual slavery. Allegedly the potential buyers had reassured the woman that her culpability would not be exposed 'because the girls would be chained in a basement' and there 'exploited for sex'. An undercover police officer posing as a potential buyer then met her. The woman asked for 1.5 million roubles (then worth $37,000) for each of the girls but subsequently agreed to lower the price to 900,000 roubles (or $22,000). She was arrested after the money was paid.[95] The same story was covered in *Argumenty i fakty* as part of a broader piece on child abuse. It began by quoting Pavel Astakhov, the presidential envoy for the rights of the child, saying, 'unfortunately every fifth rape in the country is committed in relations with children. And every third victim is coerced into sexual acts.' The article exposed how lifts, hallways and basements were the 'dangerous territory' used by paedophiles. Official statistics indicated that 50 per cent of rapes of minors occurred at the victim's home or as a guest elsewhere, and 20 per cent of crimes against children were committed by their parents. Data suggested that 30 per cent of parents reared their children with force, the most widespread methods being beating or use of a belt.[96]

Another arrest in early 2015 was of members of a group who had been recruiting on the Internet by targeting women and underage girls for sexual exploitation, but promising well-paid work in the Moscow region. Investigators had received information that the group was going to sell three girls, one of whom was a minor, for more than 1 million roubles.

---

[94] Press-sluzhba UMVD Rossii po Ul'ianovskoi oblasti, 'V Ul'ianovskoi oblasti vpervye vozbuzhdeno ugolovnoe delo za ispol'zovanie rabskogo truda', 22 July 2011, mvd.ru/news/item/164961.

[95] Denis Abramov, 'Woman held by Russian police after trying to sell girls as sex slaves', *Moscow Times*, 20 October 2014.

[96] Galina Tarakanova, 'Iunyi – znachit slabyi? Pochemu prestupniki vybiraiut dlia napadeniia detei?' *Argumenty i fakty*, 3 December 2014.

The criminals were apprehended at the time of payment and turned out to be a 22-year-old inhabitant of Kazakhstan and a 21-year-old woman from Kemerovo. A case opened under Article 127.1, and the MVD reported that it was investigating further to establish whether or not the group was responsible for other recruitments.[97]

Across a variety of sources, it stands out that those who are in forced labour in remoter parts of the Russian Federation are harder to detect. The Uzbeks trapped in Amursk oblast in the Far East were made to live on the site of their workplace, just as Siarkhon Tabarov and his fellow Tajiks in the mountains were out of public view. Reporting by Khristina Narizhnaya has also drawn attention to parts of the Federation, 'particularly in southern regions farther from Moscow' where 'anti-corruption efforts hold the least sway'. She argues that those 'criminal syndicates' who 'illegally import labour' into Russia in these regions 'have tended to operate with relative immunity from government intervention'.[98] Yet, as reports have illustrated, traffickers may not be part of huge syndicates but rather operate just occasionally, or even as an opportunistic once-off. Furthermore, those held captive, even in Moscow, may not necessarily be quickly discovered, as was evident from the case of the shop workers who lived in the basement. Once discovered, there was little in the way of social rehabilitation available to them, a similar deficit which had confronted those returning to Russia after having been trafficked out.

Conclusion

Reports have shown some of the different ways in which both foreigners and Russians have been trapped in unfree labour on Russian territory. Whilst commonalities have been illustrated across cases, in particular regarding deceit, the confiscation of documents and non-payment of wages, examples have indicated some variations in starting points, patterns and outcomes. Beginnings include: crooked recruitment agencies; newspaper and television advertisements; Internet searches; middlemen who arrange a deal; recruiters who befriend over a drink, then drug and kidnap; abduction from the street; sale by relatives or acquaintances; and professionals abusing their status in some way. When hired by a decent boss, foreign migrant workers do not endure the problems described above, although they may be paid less than a Russian would have been.

---

[97] GUUR MVD Rossii, 'Politseiskimi zaderzhany podozrevaimye v organizatsii torgovli liud'mi s tsel'iu seksual'noi ekspluatatsii', 5 February 2015, mvd.ru/news/item/3078668. This includes two videos.
[98] Narizhnaya, 'Slave labor'.

It is at the worse end of the continuum of exploitation that workers endure confinement, restrictions on food and health care, threats and coercion. Ways out have included escape, the ability to contact someone who can help, or rescue by police or volunteers. Although discussion has largely concentrated on Central Asians and Russians here, many other nationalities too have experienced what Russian journalists describe as 'slavery', including those from Vietnam, Moldova, China and the DPRK.

Given the deficit of manual workers in the Russian Federation in the early twenty-first century and the economic need for migrant labourers, it is important ask how policy has developed in recent years, how it might have inadvertently contributed to migrants working in the shadows, and what experts, academics, policy makers and those in NGOs have to say about it.

By 2016 there was still no national anti-trafficking plan despite repeated calls for one inside and outside Russia. The US State Department's TIP Reports every year noted its absence, calling for its formulation and for a body to be responsible for implementation. Since Russian leaders generally perceived US criticisms and recommendations as unwelcome interference in their domestic affairs, admonishments may have backfired rather than helped. In comparison with other issues surrounding migrant labour coming into Russia from Central Asia and with refugees arriving from eastern Ukraine, putting together a national anti-trafficking plan was a considerably lower priority. Even if such a plan were to have existed on paper, there would be huge difficulties in practice in apportioning responsibilities across Russia's labyrinthine bureaucracy for all its aspects and in gaining agreement on budgetary sources. While the notion of setting up a national anti-trafficking plan languished, politicians were able to laud their success in having formulated a programme of co-operation on human trafficking across the CIS, which kept being updated.[1] Even though more had been achieved on paper than on the ground, it was a document that could be cited as progress, and some in NGOs had positive expectations of it.

Of higher priority for politicians and policy makers was labour migration into Russia because there were deficits of workers in some sectors of the economy. Policy makers were, however, concerned about negative reactions in society to the *gastarbaitery*. In addition, media coverage of illegal migrants suggested that 'too many' were arriving and that the system was not robust enough. These were factors which tugged policy makers in different directions. In response to economic needs and socio-political issues, migration policy received increased attention and went through several formulations. Whilst discussions and reporting on human trafficking out of Russia appeared to many to fall quieter than at the start

---

[1] For announcement of the initial draft agreement, see Falaleev, 'Rabstvo pod prikrytiem'.

of the 2000s, media coverage of in-migration increased as debates took place about what the appropriate policies should be. Various narratives developed among policy makers, experts in NGOs and academics, and fresh ideas were put forward. Many of these were not so readily visible to citizens, nor followed by the public in their changing details; nor were the minutiae of legislative amendments on migration law. By contrast, anti-immigrant rhetoric from some politicians and other political actors, protests from citizens and street attacks on migrants were talked about in the press and NGOs as well as around kitchen tables.

This chapter examines the recent history of how policy, laws and regulations developed and discusses the implications for incoming migrants from Central Asia, particularly for those from Uzbekistan and Tajikistan. It also introduces a selection of key incidents in society against incomers with darker skins that made national headlines and which served to put pressure on policy directions.

Policy Changes, Legal Developments and Reactions in Society

Since 2002 there have been various new laws on immigration and amendments to them, followed by amendments to the previous amendments and also further laws, resulting in some inconsistencies. The picture is far more complex and shifting than had been the case in the formulation of policy on human trafficking and the amendment of the Criminal Code in 2003 – itself not an easy or smooth process. Multiple changes and some about-turns in migration policy have led academics, such as Vladimir Malakhov, to characterise it as having gone through stages of 'confusion, indifference, restrictions and liberalisation'.[2] Without going into immense detail, what main points are relevant for the context of our wider discussion?

In 2002, new laws were introduced 'On Russian citizenship' and 'On the legal status of foreign citizens in the Russian Federation'.[3] One consequence of these was that a number of former Soviet citizens who had previously lived legally in Russia were now considered illegal. An attempt was made to correct this by legislation in 2006 in a law 'On the census

[2] Vladimir S. Malakhov, 'Russia as a new immigration country: policy response and public debate', *Europe-Asia Studies*, Vol. 66, No. 7, September 2014, p. 1065.
[3] Key for this discussion is Russian Federation Federal Law No. 115-FZ of 25 July 2002, 'O pravovom polozhenii inostrannykh grazhdan v Rossiiskoi Federatsii' ('On the legal status of foreign citizens in the Russian Federation'), docs.pravo.ru/document/view/1197, and in English at www.legislationonline.org/documents/action/popup/id/4355 with amendments of 2003 and 2004.

of foreign citizens' and by an amendment to the law 'On the legal status of foreigners'.[4] The aim was to facilitate the legalisation of foreign workers with regard to employment. A new restriction, however, was introduced which again provoked criticism. Migrants were now prohibited from working in certain jobs. The ban on work in markets caused the biggest stir. Critics of migration legislation argued that 'the situation of migrants was extremely precarious' and that 'migrants were extremely vulnerable'.[5] By this time it was evident that migrants often found themselves in shades of illegality due to problems of falling into the shadows outside official regulations. Some also ended up as victims of forced labour either due to being trafficked into it or because they arrived legally but were recruited through deception later.

There were positive results as well. Amendments to the law 'On the legal status of foreigners' did simplify applications for work permits and also abolished quotas for those workers who did not require a visa.[6] A vocal strand of public opinion by this time, however, was denouncing an 'invasion' of migrant workers from both republics inside Russia and states outside. In September 2006, violence and rallies against Chechens and others from the Caucasus had been sparked by a fight in a restaurant in Karelia in the small city of Kondopoga. The Chaika restaurant was owned by a Chechen, and the fight between Russians and Chechens

---

[4] Relevant legal changes in 2006 were: Russian Federation Federal Law No. 109-FZ of 18 July 2006, 'O migratsionnom uchete inostrannykh grazhdan i lits bez grazhdanstva v Rossiiskoi Federatsii' ('On registration of foreign citizens and stateless persons in the Russian Federation'), docs.pravo.ru/document/view/1197; Resolution of the Government of the Russian Federation No. 681 of 15 November 2006, 'O poriadke vydachi razreshitel'nykh dokumentov dlia osushchestvleniia inostrannymi grazhdanami vremennoi trudovoi deiatel'nosti v Rossiiskoi Federatsii' ('On issuing temporary employment authorization documents to foreign citizens'), www.77.fms.gov.ru/documents/resolutions/item/2759/, last accessed 12 February 2016; and Resolution of the Government of the Russian Federation No. 783 of 22 December 2006, 'O poriadke opredeleniia ispolnitel'nymi organami gosudarstvennoi vlasti potrebnosti v privlechenii inostrannykh rabotnikov i formirovaniia kvot na osushchestvlenie inostrannymi grazhdanami trudovoi deiatel'nosti v Rossiiskoi Federatsii' ('On assessing the foreign workforce demand and establishing quotas for foreign workers in the Russian Federation by the bodies of executive power'), www.77.fms.gov.ru/documents/resolutions/item/2740, last accessed 12 February 2016. Updates in English on the registration of foreigners are available at www.mid.ru/en/migration-registration.

[5] Joint Report of the Civic Assistance Committee and the International Federation for Human Rights, 'Migrant workers in the Russian Federation: use of forced labour', July 2008, refworld.org/docid/48f4496e2.html.

[6] For further explanation of changes in migration legislation, see Vyacheslav A. Postavnin, Nataliia I. Vlasova and Inna G. Matveeva, *Stsenarii Razvitiia Migratsionnoi Politiki v Rossii* (Moscow: MAKS Press, 2011); and Margarita Petrosyan, 'The system of immigration-related legalisation in the Russian Federation', paper of the CARIM East Consortium for Applied Research on International Migration, carim-east.eu/publications/explanatory-notes/migration-related-legislation.

left two Russians dead. The restaurant was then burnt down, events spiralled with destruction to shops run by incomers, and street demonstrations called for incomers to be expelled.[7] In 2007 there was a new peak in attacks on non-white incomers with five known killings per month.[8] Many migrants were unlikely to report attacks, either reluctant to draw attention to themselves or especially concerned if their papers were not in order. The replacement in 2005 of celebrations to mark the anniversary of the Bolshevik revolution with National Unity Day had already given nationalist groups the chance to express their patriotism alongside other Russians out for holiday celebrations. Slogans such as 'Russia for Russians' and 'Forward Russia' were finding a place in a state-initiated annual demonstration.[9] The events in Karelia, coupled with the expulsion of thousands of Georgians inside Russia due to tensions and fighting in 2008 between Russia and Georgia, were accompanied by loud anti-immigrant rhetoric from nationalists such as Aleksandr Belov and his Movement Against Illegal Migration and later from its next leader Vladimir Yermolaev. Some political leaders in the regions and in Moscow also voiced anti-migrant sentiments which targeted incomers from other regions of Russia, particularly from Chechnia, as well as migrants from CIS states.[10]

Fresh legislation brought in further amendments, effectively amendments to previous amendments, which reintroduced the quota system. At this point, the concept of a 'tolerance threshold' gained some popularity. In accordance with this, in November 2006 Decree Number 683 was adopted, which specified 'acceptable proportions' of foreign workers in retail. It made it illegal for foreigners to sell alcoholic drinks and pharmaceutical products and reduced the percentage in retail on market stalls to below 40 per cent from January 2007 and with a zero quota from April 2007.[11]

---

[7] For details of events in Karelia, see 'Russia: Kondopoga violence continues unabated', RFE/RL, 6 September 2006, rferl.org/a/1071116.html.

[8] Khristina Narizhnaya, 'Russia's xenophobia problem', *Global Post*, 29 April 2012, www.pri.org/stories/2012-04-29/russias-xenophobia-problem.

[9] In 2014 estimates of numbers participating in the annual march fell to between 2,000 and 5,000 from a peak of 10,000. Differences were developing among right-wing groups over events in Ukraine. See no named author, 'Pravyi raskol: pochemu natsionalizm v Rossii teriaet populiarnost'?' *Argumenty i fakty*, 19 November 2014.

[10] Valerii Tishkov, 'O chem zabyl skazat' kandidat v prezidenty, kogda govoril o migratsii', *Migratsiia XXI Vek*, No. 1 (10), January–February 2012, p. 4.

[11] For further details, consult Joint Report, 'Migrant workers in the Russian Federation', p. 2.

Quotas, Registration and *Patenty*

The Russian state developed a policy of quotas so that, in theory at least, the number of incoming workers would match the number needed by employers in all of Russia's regions. Quotas were meant to be tied to economic need. They have, however, varied. For example, in 2007 the work permit quota for foreign workers was set at 6 million in total; it fell to 1.8 million in 2008 but was increased by the end of the year to 3.3 million. Then in 2009 it was 3.9 million, but down to 1.9 million in 2010.[12] From 2011 to 2013 it was stable at 1.7 million and then went down a little in 2014 to 1.6 million.[13] Mayor Sergei Sobianin reduced Moscow's migrant quota of 392,000 in 2009 down to 250,000 in 2010 and was planning a further cut for 2011 to around 200,000, when he announced that he would work with trades unions to 'clamp down on "groundless" employment requests for foreign workers', all the time insisting that 'I have nothing against migrants – the city needs them.'[14] Fluctuations were, in part, affected by economic crisis, hostile public opinion and political considerations. Yet, whatever the legal targets, they never seemed adequate. More workers were invariably needed by employers than official quotas permitted.

One immediate problem stemmed from the fact that if the set quota was actually too low to meet the demand for workers, then right away it triggered more illegal hiring and provided opportunities for corruption too.[15] Moreover, it was difficult to establish precisely what the 'economic need' for migrant workers would be a year in advance, especially since many were working in the shadow economy anyway and were already inside Russia. Resilient informal arrangements for hiring already existed and continued to do so. There were known ways of bypassing the official system, even if they were legally dubious. Then, rather undermining the whole point of setting initial quotas, the Ministry of Social Development and Health Care introduced a quota adjustment mechanism which gave yet more space for corruption.[16]

From 2002, migrant workers entering Russia were legally required to register their presence within three days. This was not always easy or

---

[12] Postavnin et al., *Stsenarii Razvitiia*, p. 8.

[13] Denis Sinyakov, 'Government seeks to abolish migrant worker quotas', 31 March 2014, rt.com/politics/russia-migrant-worker-quotas-313/.

[14] RIA Novosti, 'Moscow Mayor Sobyanin to fight against immigration', 2 December 2010, sputniknews.com/russia/20101202161590733.

[15] For a recent analysis of corruption, see Evgenii P. Tavokin, Zhanna A. Shishova and Olesia V. Shirokova, 'Korruptsiia v organakh Rossiiskoi gosudarstvennoi vlasti', *Sotsiologicheskie issledovaniia*, No. 5, 2014, pp. 80–88.

[16] Postavnin et al., *Stsenarii Razvitiia*, p. 14.

possible, so those who did not do so immediately fell into an 'illegal' category. Once in it, the best route to obtaining work was to develop contacts through the diaspora who might 'help', but not legally. Once they were working in the shadows, fear kept many in a zone of illegality with some apprehension. Also before 2007 migrants could not themselves obtain a work permit as this was done on their behalf by employers. New legislation became effective in 2007, and many specialists viewed this as more liberal and a 'turn' in a more humane direction. Its critics, however, noted that, even though some of the previous impediments had been removed, the state's management mechanisms 'did not drastically change', and so the liberal direction failed 'to find adequate implementation mechanisms'.[17] Laws passed in 2002 and 2006 also resulted in 'a series of gaps and dual interpretations' which complicated practice and also fuelled corruption.[18] There was also not one sole co-ordinating body responsible for administering migration policy.

The new rules for registration from 2007, however, meant that far more migrants legally registered themselves. Consequently, they were in a better position to stay legal than had they not registered. An estimated 20–25 per cent of migrants, however, still did not register. This often occurred when hosts, be they employers or landlords, were reluctant to register a migrant for reasons of their own costs and tax liabilities. It is at this point when the migrant was effectively forced to turn to firms or criminal groups who would provide documents. As experts Vyacheslav Postavnin, Natalia Vlasova and Inna Matveeva have commented, this effectively meant that the notion of a 'hosting party loses its meaning'.[19] A second reason why migrants might experience a worsening illegal status was because they were afraid that they would be punished for not having registered within three days. In this event, they could not legally stay beyond three days and certainly not work legally.

Given that there was visa-free entry into Russia for a ninety-day stay for the Central Asians under scrutiny, the assignment of annual quotas was further challenged as a regulatory mechanism. Uzbeks, Tajiks and Kyrgyz looking for work could enter Russia quite legally and through 'informal' channels attempt to set themselves up in a job. In so doing they made themselves vulnerable to exploitation and abuse from employers. Also, police checks of migrants on the streets could lead to demands for bribes to supplement police salaries. Postavnin, Vlasova and Matveeva summed up the multiple problems surrounding migrants by lamenting

[17] Postavnin et al., *Stsenarii Razvitiia*, p. 3.
[18] Postavnin et al., *Stsenarii Razvitiia*, p. 4.
[19] Postavnin et al., *Stsenarii Razvitiia*, p. 5.

that not only was the migration management mechanism 'a source of corruption' but its 'inefficiency and defective character' actually 'encourage the growth of illegal structures'.[20] The lack of government control over a migration infrastructure meant 'an uncontrolled growth of firms procuring counterfeit authorisation documents for a legal stay and permission to work'.[21]

A further problem was that seven institutions were then involved in developing and administering migration policy. These were: the FMS, the Ministry of Social Development and Health Care, the Ministry of Labour, the MVD, the Ministry of Economic Development, the Ministry of Regional Development and the FSB. Whilst in theory it may be beneficial to have input into migration policy from all of them regarding relevant points from their different spheres, there was in practice no single main governmental institution responsible for migration policy to act as co-ordinator. As it turned out, contradictory decisions concerning migration could be made in different institutions, and there was a further lack of co-ordination with Russia's regions.[22]

Malakhov holds that the picture was further complicated by several institutional re-arrangements. In 1991, for example, a Committee on Migration was set up as part of the Ministry of Labour and Employment. Subsequently this developed into an independent institution, the FMS. In 2000, however, it was closed and its role was taken on by the Ministry of Federation and Nationalities, later re-named the Ministry of Federation, Nationalities and Migration Policy. In the following year, this too was disbanded. Next, migration came under the MVD and then later, in another change, the FMS regained its autonomy.[23] In April 2016, however, Putin dissolved the FMS and transferred its functions back to the MVD.[24]

---

[20] Postavnin et al., *Stsenarii Razvitiia*, p. 13.

[21] Postavnin et al., *Stsenarii Razvitiia*, p. 14.

[22] For the argument that institutions within the bureaucracy pursue their own interests in the migration process using network and patron–client ties 'to signal the acceptable balance of formal and informal mechanisms', see Caress Schenk, 'Controlling immigration manually: lessons from Moscow', *Europe-Asia Studies*, Vol. 65, No. 7, 2013, pp. 1444–1465.

[23] There was also a Governmental Committee on Migration Policy which had been set up in 1998. It continued up to 2001, was reconstituted in 2002, and then was disbanded again in 2004, to re-appear in 2009. See Malakhov, 'Russia as a new immigration country', p. 1066.

[24] For a reference on the Kremlin's site, see 'Podpisan Ukaz o peredache funktsii Gosnarkokontrolia i migratsionnoi sluzhby v sistemu MVD Rossii', 5 April 2016, special.kremlin.ru/events/president/news/51649; and, for a press announcement, refer to no named author, 'Prezident naznachil rukovitelei glavok MVD po migratsii i po bor'be s narkotikami', *Nezavisimaia gazeta*, 14 April 2016.

Analysing anti-migrant sentiments, sociologist Vladimir Mukomel has argued that, while Russians were 'relatively tolerant' towards migrants from Ukraine and Moldova, they felt annoyance and 'negative emotions' about other nationalities, including 'aversion, mistrust and fear'. They perceived an 'influx' and a 'violation of public order'.[25] Greater complexity entered the picture with the arrival of refugees from Ukraine, especially in areas of geographic concentration. By the spring of 2014, for example, 850,000 had arrived in adjacent Rostov oblast, a region of just 4.2 million inhabitants. By summer, numbers kept increasing and daily 750 were being moved out to other regions. The warm welcome that the refugees initially received from Russians, according to Dmitrii Titov, soon changed to one of negative attitudes from locals and a growth of *migrantofobiia*. As the president of a Rostov regional movement that had helped victims from the war in Chechnia, Titov observed that hostility to the Ukrainians had grown faster than that towards the Chechens earlier.[26] Politicians were acutely aware of anti-migrant hostilities in society, and this influenced what they said and had an impact on the changing course of migration policy. In 2010, for example, before his removal as mayor of Moscow, Iurii Luzhkov declared that labour migration was distorting the economy.[27]

Local incidents involving incomers with darker skins continued to fuel enmities. Four years after the aforementioned incidents in Kondopoga, there was violence in December 2010 in central Moscow after a Spartak football supporter had been killed five days earlier during a brawl between fans and a group from the North Caucasus. Rumours spread of a police cover-up, and a rally of an estimated 5,000 in Manezh square resulted in clashes with police, the shouting of racist slogans and fights between Russians and those with darker skins. This was about ethnicity, and a smouldering hostility extending to the *gastarbaitery* from Central Asia was part of this mood. After dispersing, some from the crowd ran in packs in the metro chanting 'white carriage, white carriage'.[28] Intermittently the press reported jail sentences for hate crimes against those of non-Slavic

[25] Vladimir I. Mukomel', *Politika Integratsii* (Moscow: MAKS Press, 2011), p. 5.

[26] Dmitrii Titov, 'Vtoroi dom', *Migratsiia XXI Vek*, No. 6–7 (11–12), November–December 2014, pp. 61–63.

[27] RIA Novosti, 'Labor migrants "distort economy" – Moscow's mayor', 18 September 2010, sputniknews.com/world/20100918160635154.

[28] No named author, 'Rioting erupts near Kremlin walls', *Moscow Times*, 13 December 2010.

appearance.[29] Other demonstrations which made national headlines took place in 2013 in Pugachev in Saratov oblast. After a quarrel which ended with a Chechen killing a Russian with a scalpel, locals demanded the expulsion of all Chechens from the district. Around sixty had settled there over the preceding ten years. At the peak of the protests, citizens blocked the road which linked Saratov to Volgograd and Samara. Rumours spread that provocateurs from the banned National Bolshevik Party were going to arrive too.[30]

Another series of incidents occurred in Moscow's Biriulevo district in October 2013. Violence erupted after a man had been killed, and a migrant worker was blamed. Russia's Channel One television news showed bottles thrown, windows smashed and cars overturned. OMON (Otriad Mobilnyi Osobovo Naznacheniia), or the Detachment of Mobile Special Forces, was called in to restore order. Locals called for vigilante groups in all areas of Moscow to protect citizens from the crimes of migrant workers.[31] The next day Channel One showed the capture and arrest of Orkhan Zeynalov from Azerbaijan. It became clear that a vegetable warehouse in the market had been stormed, and 1,200 people were detained. MVD head, Vladimir Kolokol'tsev, was shown shaking hands of the militia men who found the alleged culprit. The reassuringly constructed message to viewers was that the system was doing something quickly and effectively.[32] Nine months earlier, however, the head of the FMS, Konstantin Romodanovskii, had pointed out that, although in the preceding three years the numbers of foreigners entering Russia had increased by 23 per cent, the number of crimes committed in that community had fallen. Yet at the same time sociologists were showing that anxiety (*ozabochennost'*) amongst the population about immigrants was growing. Romodanovskii announced that, in fact, only 3.4 per cent of known crimes were committed by migrants, and these were mostly about false papers. His message was that 'there is not a wave of crime among foreigners'.[33] Assumptions about migrants among nationalists

[29] No named author, '12 neo-Nazis jailed for 27 hate killings', *Moscow Times*, 12 July 2011; and no named author, 'St Petersburg neo-Nazis sentenced for killing foreigners and homeless people', *Moscow Times*, 24 July 2014. The group NS/WP, or National Socialism/White Power, formed in 2009 with the goal to 'incite racial hatred against natives of the Caucasus, Asia and Africa'.

[30] Sergei Babkin, 'Pugachev murder triggers popular unrest over government's ethnic policies', *Russia Beyond the Headlines*, 11 July 2013, services.rbth.ru/society/2013/07/11/pugachev_murder_triggers_popular_unrest_over_governments ethnic_polic_27981.html.

[31] Russian Channel One television news, 14 October 2013.

[32] Russian Channel One television morning news, 16 October 2013.

[33] No named author, 'Sovsem ne bezopasnaia migratsiia', *Nezavisimaia gazeta*, 22 January 2013.

and beliefs that they did commit crime, however, were turned into 'folk devils' among sections of the Russian public, who showed signs of 'moral panic'. Social unease and heightened patriotic sentiments were evident and much worsened as war in Ukraine continued and Western sanctions increased piecemeal. Narratives about Western states attempting to undermine Russia, twinned with the insistence that Russia was a 'great power' (*velikaia derzhava*), reinforced a 'Russianness' that excluded, and often verbally targeted, non-Russians.

In this wider context of negative reactions in society to labour migrants, many migration experts more positively viewed the introduction in 2010 of the *patent*. This referred not to the English-language meaning of the term but to a licence or permit enabling a foreigner legally to work in Russia when employed by a particular individual. The FMS had announced that around 3 million foreigners were employed by individuals, often as nannies or cleaners, and with a *patent* they could become legal. In the first five months, 120,000 *patenty* were granted out of 150,000 applicants.[34] This process was complicated, however, by the fact that only legally registered migrants could apply for them, so it could not mop up into legality all illegal workers in Russia, despite claims that it did reduce illegality. In 2011, 765,000 *patenty* were granted, 1.08 million in 2012, 1.4 million in 2013 and in the first eight months of 2014 a total of 1.8 million.[35] Ol'ga Vorob"eva and Anatolii Topilin held that, since many were now working 'completely legally', this indicated that 'there was always a desire to live and work legally, but it just was not possible'.[36] Now, in their estimation, it was easier to begin legally.

By 2014 many criticisms of migration policy had been forthcoming, particularly of quotas and corrupt intermediary companies there to 'fix' many of the migrant's dilemmas. The FMS then backed a fresh approach for employing workers with visa-free entry from the 'near abroad', through *patenty* alone, thereby ending the existence of company quotas and widening the applicability of the *patent* so it was no longer restricted to those working for an individual.[37] It could now be acquired by construction workers as well as nannies. The aim was to make policy simpler and easier. The changes meant that a migrant working for a company in need of foreign labour could buy from the local

[34] Postavnin et al., *Stsenarii Razvitiia*, p. 7.
[35] Ol'ga Vorob"eva and Anatolii Topilin, 'Stoit li? Patenty dlia inostrannykh rabotnikov u iuridecheskikh lits', *Migratsiia XXI Vek*, No. 6–7 (26–27), November–December 2014, p. 3.
[36] Vorob"eva and Topilin, 'Stoit li?'
[37] Viktor Komarovskii, 'Immigratsionnye patenty', *Migratsiia XXI Vek*, No. 6–7 (26–27), November–December 2014, pp. 8–10.

authorities a fixed-price *patent*, valid from one to three months. It could subsequently be extended to one year. A minimum price would be set by the federal level but regions could increase it. The aim was for the price to regulate the flow of labour, replacing the quota mechanism. The hope was that illegal migrants could then move into legality and that this would also boost tax coffers. The Ministry of Labour, however, objected on the grounds that labour market tensions would worsen but, despite this criticism, the more widespread use of *patenty* went ahead. Another amendment in November 2014 to the law 'On the legal status of foreign citizens' enabled Russia's regions to set the cost independently. In early 2015, reported fees ranged from 1,568 to 8,000 roubles per month, depending upon the region. Some regions established fixed fees but others raised them. In Moscow, the charge rose from 1,126 to 4,000 roubles per month, but in Chukotka Autonomous Area it reached 8,000 roubles.[38] While it was now meant to be easier for migrants to be legal and to come out of the shadows, the costs for some were deemed prohibitive. The website of Moscow's newly opened multi-function migration centre advertised its costs at 4,200 roubles per month.[39] There were expectations that part of the labour flow from Central Asia would stay in that region and search for jobs in Kazakhstan instead.

Concerns from Russians about job losses, whether accurate or not, also fuelled comments from politicians on how the new *patenty* could function as a regulatory mechanism. At a meeting with leaders of the Moscow Federation of Trades Unions, Mayor Sergei Sobianin reassured them with, 'if in the future we see an increase in the unemployed, we will begin to raise the cost of the *patent* for migrants' and then the inflow of migrants would fall.[40] He claimed that the *patent* equalised the competitiveness of migrants and Russians and also noted that unemployment in Moscow was not more than 0.5 per cent. The Russian state and its regions, however, had a strong interest in the *patent* becoming successful, as it was a revenue raiser. Consequently, its cost to migrants was likely to increase as the years passed. By mid 2015, fifty-two regions were already looking to increase the price by 2 to 6.6 times. In those regions where the number of labour migrants was low, the cost was to stay at 1,216 roubles.[41]

---

[38] Olga Gulina, 'Re-drawing the map of migration patterns', Open Democracy, 16 February 2015, opendemocracy.net/od-russia/olga-gulina/redrawing-map-of-migration-patterns.

[39] For details of up-to-date requirements for the purchase of *patenty* and their renewal, along with warnings about turning to middlemen, see Moscow's test centre at mc.mos.ru.

[40] No named author, 'Patent podorozhaet?' *Migratsiia XXI Vek*, No. 4 (31), July–August 2015, p. 61.

[41] Nataliia Vlasova, 'Skal'pel' ili topor?' *Migratsiia XXI Vek*, No. 4 (31), July–August 2015, p. 24.

The migrant workers who were required to obtain a *patent* were those from states with visa-free entry to Russia and which were not members of the EEU, namely from Uzbekistan, Tajikistan, Azerbaijan, Moldova and Ukraine. Different rules applied to migrant labourers from Kazakhstan, Belarus, Armenia and Kyrgyzstan, who enjoyed visa-free entry too but were within the EEU. They were not required to obtain a *patent* but needed to seek a work contact from an employer.[42] Unlike the Uzbeks and Tajiks, they did not need to acquire international passports for entry into Russia as their national identity cards remained sufficient. When Kyrgyzstan joined the EEU, Aliyasbek Alymkulov, Kyrgyz minister of migration, labour and youth, told journalists that he hoped the new agreement meant that 'everyone will be able to leave for work in Russia, and all the necessary documents will be available even in Kyrgyzstan'. He believed that this would help to reduce illegal migration flows.[43] A draft law which required employers to pay insurance fees for foreign workers from their first day of work rather than six months later should protect the worker but not necessarily provide a profitable reason to employ foreigners over Russians (unless the agreed rate of pay was lower).

Introduction of Tests in Russian Language, History and Law

Further legal amendments to the law of 2002 'On the legal status of foreigners' came into force in January 2015.[44] Migrants could now proceed to purchase a *patent* only if they had first passed not just a Russian language test that had been introduced in 2012 but also tests in Russian history and law.[45] In addition, they had to undergo a medical test to show they were free of infectious diseases and to purchase medical insurance. Success in all tests was a necessary prerequisite for purchasing the vital *patent*. Moreover, migrants were required to apply to the FMS for the work permit within thirty days of arrival. There was thus some pressure

[42] See Maxim Novikov, 'Employment. Attracting foreigners to Russia: options for employers', *Moscow Times*, 16 June 2015. Quotas do apply to foreign workers from states which lack visa-free entry, such as Germany, China and Georgia.

[43] HG Legal Resources, 'Russian migration legislation changes – June 2014 – Part 2', www .hg.org/article.asp?id=32967.

[44] FMS, 'Osobennosti osushchestvleniia trudovoi deiatel'nosti inostrannymi grazhdanami, pribyvshimi v Rossiiskuiu Federatsiiu v poriadke, ne trebuiushchem polucheniia vizy, na osnovanii patenta', fms.gov.ru/foreign_national/trud_migrant/osob_osushch_trud_deyat_inostr_grazhd/, accessed 12 February 2016.

[45] The language test included twenty multiple-choice questions on grammar, a short comprehension, a written 'exercise such as filling in a form or writing a short letter, an audio test and an oral test.

to proceed quickly. The *patent* could be issued for one to twelve months with the possibility of renewal just once for one to twelve months.[46]

Officials and some experts held that the tests would lower the number of illegal migrants, help to curb the activities of middlemen, enable migrants to learn their rights and also reduce corruption and bribery. Experts also hoped that preparation to sit the tests would promote integration and improve daily lives. These were among the narratives that circulated in support of testing. Some migrants, however, found the tests difficult, even though to native speakers they looked easy. Central Asians from rural areas who had left school to earn money did not take readily to aspects of grammar. Practice tests showed that multiple-choice questions included knowledge of the declensions of Russian nouns or asked for a correct preposition after a particular verb. Some experts asked how much Russian did a street sweeper need to know to do his job well, and others queried how well Russians might fare regarding some points of grammar. An article in *Komsomol'skaia pravda* described how Russians who looked at on-line practice tests remarked that they themselves could get wrong answers. One admitted that 'we locals often decline numerals incorrectly'.[47] Another criticism was that the tests were one more opportunity for corruption to flourish through the sale of fake certificates, as there was already a business in payments for licences to work. The case that migrants would benefit in negotiating their daily lives from grasping an expected 950 Russian words, however, was strong.

The rationale behind the history and law tests was that they would encourage migrants to become familiar with Russian culture and traditions. Yet whilst some of the on-line practice examples looked very easy, such as pick out the Russian flag from pictures of three flags, or identify a symbol of the Russian Orthodox Church from three symbols, would a migrant be likely to know when Kuzma Minin and Prince Dmitrii Pozharskii defended Russia? The multiple-choice options might make the guess easier: was it during the Time of Troubles, the war of 1812 or the Great Patriotic War? It was, in fact, during the Time of Troubles when an all-Russian volunteer army expelled forces of the Polish–Lithuanian commonwealth.[48] Would rural Uzbeks be likely to know this? One wonders, too, what percentage of Russians would be sure.

---

[46] For details of these and other legal changes, see Pavel Antonov and Lilia Belobrova, 'Changes in the legislation of the Russian Federation', www.accountor.ru/en/news/2014/changes-legislation-russian-federation.

[47] Regina Pogudina, 'Test dlia migrantov: a mogut ego reshit' russkie', *Komsomol'skaia pravda* (Kirov), 17 February 2015, m.kirov.kp.ru/daily/26344.3/3226169.

[48] For examples of practice tests, see 'Tsentr testirovaniia po russkomu iazyku v Moskovskoi oblasti dlia inostrannykh grazhdan i migrantov', rustester.ru/testing/start.

Early reports on the impact of the tests in 2015 and 2016 have been mixed. By February 2015, 29,500 foreigners were reported to have taken them and the test centre run by the Russian University Druzhba Narodov (Friendship of Peoples), announced a 97 per cent success rate.[49] *Izvestiia* claimed that, by April 2015, 440,000 had sat the tests and 95 per cent had received their certificates.[50] In June, fresh announcements reported that now 700,000 migrants had taken the tests, but the rector of the Pushkin State Russian Language Institute imparted that 15 per cent did not pass the first time. The Russian Federation of Migrant Workers disputed the figures and claimed that 'one in three' was unable to pass the test.[51] By the end of December 2015, 1.7 million had sat the tests, and *Izvestiia* again noted a 90 per cent success rate at the Druzhba Narodov University test centre. Data revealed 44 per cent of those taking the tests were Uzbeks and 23 per cent were Tajiks.[52]

In early 2015, fifty instances came to light of test centres giving out certificates to migrants who had not even appeared in person to take the tests. These occurred in Moscow, Obninsk and Ufa.[53] Consequently, Moscow's Druzhba Narodov University ceased to work with four of the guilty centres. Universities could make agreements with other educational institutions and give them the right to organise tests.[54] An electronic database stores details of those who pass, and the FMS should give out work permits only after checking this. Further evidence showed that the system had not yet entirely prevented abuses of this rule. There were also cases of the illegal purchase of documents. Finger printing, however, should tighten loopholes. In Kostroma, charges were brought under Article 327 of the Criminal Code on 'Knowing use of a forged document'.[55] Another press article described how a woman in Moscow

[49] Svetlana Basharova, Tat'iana Borodina and Natal'ia Korchmarek, 'Stoimost' ekzamena dlia migrantov v regionakh dokhodit do 25,000 rublei', *Izvestiia*, 3 February 2015.

[50] Roksana Avetisian, 'Test dlia migrantov, zhelaiushchikh pereekhat' v Rossiiu, uslozhniat', *Izvestiia*, 6 April 2015.

[51] Alexei Stroganov, 'New language exam creates extra obstacle for migrants in Russia', *Russia Beyond the Headlines*, 25 June 2015, www.rbth.com/society/2015/06/25/new_language_exam_creates_extra_obstacle_for_migrants_in_russia_47243.html.

[52] No named author, 'Samymi gramotnymi migrantami stali ukraintsy i kirgizy', *Izvestiia*, 30 December 2015.

[53] Svetlana Basharova, 'Gosduma proveriaet sluchai nelegal'nogo testirovaniia migrantov', *Izvestiia*, 13 April 2015.

[54] Other institutions answerable for administering the tests were Moscow State University, St Petersburg State University, the State Institute of Russian Language and the Pacific Ocean State University. Test centres were also being set up abroad in Vienna, Egypt and Spain. The cost of the tests in Vienna was €105 in 2015. See Basharova et al., 'Stoimost' ekzamena dlia migrantov'.

[55] Anna Skudaeva, 'Migrantov v Kostrome ulichili v pokupke diplomov', *Rossiiskaia gazeta*, 22 January 2016.

had been paid 1,000 roubles for sitting the test on behalf of someone else.[56] *Izvestiia* reported that there was advice on the Internet and from within diasporas on how to obtain the certificate without taking the tests. This illegal route was said to cost between 7,000 and 30,000 roubles.[57] *Nezavisimaia gazeta* described how some 'commercial structures' took advantage of migrants and were 'often of corrupt character', illustrating 'parallel structures'.[58] The cost of taking tests was reported to vary across test centres too, cited in this article as under 5,000 roubles in a state structure but 6,900 in a private one.[59] A fear expressed early on was that many migrants would opt to avoid costs and 'knowingly' move into an illegal status. Another way for foreigners to ease their legal status was to enter into a fictive marriage with a Russian. In 2016 *Izvestiia* held that this was becoming more widespread. An example from Altai krai showed how such marriages were being arranged for a fee on the social media site V Kontakte (In Contact). Article 322.1 of the Criminal Code on 'Organising illegal migration' was being applied to these cases.[60] *Izvestiia* also reported that, in the first quarter of 2016, the Procuracy revealed more than 10,000 violations of migration laws, of which around 400 were criminal rather than administrative cases.[61]

From the start, Karomat Sharipov of the movement Tajik Labour Migrants made it clear that members were keen for the Russian authorities to reconsider the new rules on tests and *patenty*. He had complained earlier that the authorities had initially told them that work permits acquired in 2014 would still be valid in 2015. Subsequently that changed, so some had to leave Russia and come back again, paying out between 1,500 and 3,500 roubles. He claimed that 'they deceived us'.[62] He also regretted that 'money decides everything' and that some officials were 'taking advantage of migrants' naïveté'. He alleged that in the Liublino district of Moscow, migrants were asked for 36,000 roubles for documents and then 'you come to take the exam, fail and the money is gone'.[63] Another commented that the newly opened test centres did not

---

[56] No named author, 'Protiv gendirektora, pisavshei testy vmesto migrantov, vozbuzhdeno delo', *Rossiiskaia gazeta*, 25 April 2016.

[57] Basharova, 'Gosduma proveriaet'.

[58] Ekaterina Trifonova, 'Migranty meshaiut sudam rabotat", *Nezavisimaia gazeta*, 26 June 2015.

[59] Trifonova, 'Migranty meshaiut sudam rabotat".

[60] No named author, 'V Rossii rastet kolichestvo fiktivnykh brakov migrantov', *Izvestiia*, 20 May 2016.

[61] No named author, 'V Rossii rastet kolichestvo fiktivnykh brakov migrantov'.

[62] Anora Sarkorova, 'Tadzhikskie migranty protiv migratsionnykh pravil Rossii', 15 May 2015, bbc.com/russian/russia/2015/05/150514_tajik_migrants_in_russia.

[63] Stroganov, 'New language exam creates extra obstacle for migrants in Russia'.

necessarily solve problems but instead created a 'bureaucratic chain'.[64] In fact, the number of centres by the end of 2015 had increased to 400, and the authorities were aware of the need to expand capacity.[65]

Overall, migrants' reactions to the tests have varied. While some were ultimately satisfied with outcomes, others were not. Among the latter were those who were particularly unhappy about how much money they had to pay to sit the tests. From an equivalent in 2015 of around $90, in 2016 the tests with medical insurance might reach over $200. While most regions were asking for around 4,900 roubles, *Izvestiia* reported that test centres in some regions wanted 'much more', such as 25,000 roubles in Noril'sk and 7,000 in Magadan, linked to local costs.[66] Moreover, as already noted, in some regions the cost of the *patent* in 2016 rose. Increases have been lower in regions where the demand for migrants outstrips supply. One worker concluded that 'migrants run into unbelievable difficulties'.[67]

Taking just the Tajiks, outlays can be prohibitive since the average monthly wage in Tajikistan at this time was estimated at $180, and anyway not all migrants were necessarily employed at home before entering Russia. Those who acquire credit in advance to pay for their tests and accommodation take a risk. If they sit the tests and fail, or if they pass them but cannot subsequently find employment, they end up in debt. The *patent* enables legal work but does not guarantee that a worker will find a job. In addition, as well as having to pay for their medical check and tests in language, history and law before they can legally acquire a *patent* and only then work legally and get paid, Tajiks and Uzbeks also have to acquire an international passport because identity cards are no longer sufficient for visa-free access. The Tajik passport might cost US$ 100 or US$ 300 for a biometric one.[68] Furthermore, Tajiks have to renew their right of residence in Russia three months at a time. Penalties are as follows: overstaying by three months entails a three-year ban on re-entering Russia; by six months brings a five-year ban; and by nine or more means no re-entry for ten years.[69]

Sharilov has commented that 'a migrant hopes that after all this that he will get work; however, no one guarantees it. He searches for it

[64] Sarkorova, 'Tadzhikskie migranty protiv migratsionnykh pravil Rossii'.
[65] No named author, 'Samymi gramotnymi migrantami stali ukraintsy i kirgizy'.
[66] Basharova et al., 'Stoimost' ekzamena dlia migrantov'.
[67] Sarkorova, 'Tadzhikskie migranty protiv migratsionnykh pravil Rossii'.
[68] Irina Umarova and Jamila Sujud, 'Tajiks face new obstacles to work in Russia', Institute for War and Peace Reporting, 23 January 2015, iwpr.net/global-voices/tajiks-face-new-obstacles-work-russia.
[69] Umarova and Sujud, 'Tajiks face new obstacles'.

independently. Those who wrote the new migration laws knew that it is a rare employer who will arrange a contract with a migrant. It is not advantageous [*nevygodno*]. It does not interest them where the unemployed gets 30,000 roubles from.'[70] In the event of failure, or of a pass but inability to secure legal work, the migrant might be tempted to stay illegally and look for other sources of income. The introduction of tests and the wider applicability of *patenty* have not prevented illegal outcomes entirely.

Eligible foreigners with good enough Russian and no criminal background have the option of joining the Russian army on a five-year contract, made possible by a law of January 2015. With an average wage equivalent to around $460 a month (taking into account the fall in the rouble then) and carrying the potential for Russian citizenship, this was predicted to be attractive to some, and a trickle of Tajiks began to sign up. But generally this route was viewed with some caution.[71] For recruits it could mean service anywhere and was not limited to Russia's 201st base in Tajikistan. Reports have suggested that some Tajiks at this base had in fact been transferred to the Ukrainian border.[72] Putin, however, had signed a decree in 2014 making citizenship possible for Russian speakers who had lived in the USSR, providing they could satisfy a commission set up to vet them.[73] Some Tajik families were seeking to pursue the citizenship option. An even riskier route is presented by ISIS recruiters in Russia, who offer attractive financial inducements. One Tajik told journalists that 'in my village I know lads who went off to Syria to fight'. He described how they had taken credit in the hope of working in Russia but they did not find a job. They had nothing to sell to pay back the loan apart from their homes, so they went with recruiters 'out of despair'.[74] Sharilov blamed debt, bureaucratic issues and unsolved migration problems as the reasons behind migrants ending up as fighters.[75] Expert Edward Lemon reckoned in 2015 that between 100 and 200 Tajiks had

---

[70] Quoted in Sarkorova, 'Tadzhikskie migranty protiv migratsionnykh pravil Rossii'.

[71] For information see no named author, 'What you need to know about joining the Russian army', *Moscow Times*, 12 January 2015; Mark Vinson, 'Russia's failing economy likely to drive migrant laborers into "Foreign Legion"', *Eurasia Daily Monitor*, Vol. 12, Issue 33, 23 February 2015; and Farangis Najibullah, 'Russia's foreign legion of doubt', RFE/RL, 18 January 2015, rferl.org/a/russia-foreigners-military-recruiting/26800177.html.

[72] No named author, 'Russian army attracts Tajikistan's unemployed', 10 March 2015, eurasianet.org/node/72451.

[73] On eligibility for Russian citizenship, see no named author, 'Nositeliam russkogo iazyka uprostili protseduru polucheniia grazhdanstva RF', *Moskovskie novosti*, 21 April 2014, www.mn.ru/politics/president/162846.

[74] Sarkorova, 'Tadzhikskie migranty protiv migratsionnykh pravil Rossii'.

[75] Sarkorova, 'Tadzhikskie migranty protiv migratsionnykh pravil Rossii'.

been lured to fight in Syria and Iraq.[76] Given an increase in the number of deportations of Central Asians for violating the terms of entry or terms of employment, those back home without jobs who feel marginalised are potential recruits for ISIS. Labour migrants are also vulnerable to the approaches from drug traffickers looking for recruits. Tajikistan shares a border with Afghanistan and is on the route for narcotics into Russia. Occasionally the press covers individual cases such as the detention in 2016 of a Central Asian caught in Russia with nearly 500 grammes of heroin who was threatened with ten years in prison.[77] One should not, however, be alarmist about these negative outcomes, as they are rejected by most Tajiks. Nonetheless, tales of radicalisation in Russia and back in Central Asia afterwards receive some coverage. In 2015 it was reported that more than 500 Kyrgyz citizens were fighting in the Middle East, and their numbers were growing.[78]

The options, however, for the growing number of labour migrants who have been deported from Russia are limited. In May 2016, the press reported that since 2012 the FMS had banned more than 1.7 million foreigners from entering Russia and that in 2013 Russian courts had passed more than 513,000 deportation orders.[79] By January 2016, according to Tajikistan's Ministry of Labour, Migration and Employment, 333,000 Tajiks had been deported and told they may not return to Russia for periods of three to five years.[80] Most deportations result either from violations of Article 18.8 of the Administrative Code, which covers the flouting by foreigners of the rules of entry or residence, or from violations of Article 18.10 on illegal working.[81] Migrants' work options are also limited by having to be employed in the job specified on their work permit. A painter could thus not be employed as a docker without first applying to the FMS for an adjustment to the work permit. Non-compliance can result in a fine and possible deportation.[82] For those unable to work in

---

[76] 'Interview: most Tajiks in Syria, Iraq appear to be fighting alongside ISIS', RFE/RL, 27 March 2015, rferl.org/a/isis-central-asia-iraq/26923679.html.

[77] No named author, 'V Moskve zaderzhan migrant s polkilo geroina', *Rossiiskaia gazeta*, 25 April 2016.

[78] Grigorii Mikhailov, 'Molodezh' Kirgizii meniaet Rossiiu na Siriiu', *Nezavisimaia gazeta*, 19 December 2015.

[79] No named author, 'Half a million foreigners deported from Russia in 4 years', *Moscow Times*, 10 May 2016.

[80] IWPR Central Asia, 'Russian crisis continues to bite for labour migrants', 10 March 2016, iwpr.net/global-voices/Russian-crisis-continues-bite-labour-migrants.

[81] *Kodeks Rossiiskoi Federatsii ob Administrativnykh Pravonarusheniakh po Sostoianiiu na 25 Oktiabria 2016g* (Moscow: Prospekt, 2016), pp. 309–313.

[82] No named author, KPMG, 'Russia – several statutory changes and updates to immigration system', 22 April 2016, home.kpmg.com/xx/en/home/insights/2016/04/flash-alert-2016-054.html.

Russia as hoped and also possibly not able to find work at home, their options narrow. They may attempt to enter Russia again, but now illegally. Recent press reports have alerted to arrivals in Russia from those who had been banned. Six such Uzbeks were found hiding on a train on the Belgorod–Novosibirsk line, and there have been other reported instances of those on the blacklist trying to conceal themselves in markets.[83] Deportation is no guarantee that migrants will stay away.

The momentum for fresh regulations in migration policy has not stopped. In 2015 announcements were made about the desirability of making the tests more difficult for those wishing to stay and live in Russia, who would have to know 1,250 Russian words, whereas those practising a circular migration would be kept at 950 words. Differentiated tests were advocated on the grounds that different groups of foreigners had different goals in Russia. More challenging open-ended questions were among the suggestions for those wishing to settle, such as: 'in which year was the first Russian revolution?'; 'which statue is the symbol of the city of St Petersburg?'; and 'what is the name of the document which was adopted in Russia on 12 June 1990?'[84] *Izvestiia* also noted that the Ministry of Education and Science was planning to slap a state duty on the cost of receiving the certificate for tests, thought to be between 600 and 1,000 roubles, beginning in 2017.[85] This was guaranteed to be unpopular with migrants. When pressed in October 2016 on whether the tests would indeed be changed, Vyacheslav Nikonov, Chair of the State Duma's Education and Science Committee, affirmed that plans were being made to alter administrative procedures.[86]

Over time, the system tried better to tackle the problems generated for migrants by the exploitative middlemen and by employers reluctant to give contracts. The rules on where a medical certificate could be obtained were also tightened. Yet into early 2017 the press kept reporting cases of 'forged certificates' for language, history and law tests, this time coming before a district court in Novokuznetsk.[87] Criticisms, however, of the harshness of deportations resulted in calls for an easing of policy. There were reports of plans to soften sanctions for the breaking of migration rules. An initiative was being prepared 'for improving the conditions

[83] Natal'ia Graf, 'Migranty popytalis' v"ekhat' v Omsk pod vidom bagazha', *Rossiiskaia gazeta*, 27 April 2016.
[84] Avetisian, 'Test dlia migrantov, zhelaiushchikh pereekhat' v Rossiiu, uslozhniat'.
[85] No named author, 'S 2017 goda dlia migrantov vvedut dopolnitel'nuiu gosposhlinu', *Izvestiia*, 12 January 2016.
[86] No named author, 'V Rossii izmenitsia protsedura ekzamenov dlia migrantov', *Nezavisimaia gazeta*, 27 October 2016.
[87] Iuliia Potapova, 'Znaniia iz "lipy"', *Rossiiskaia gazeta*, 13 February 2017.

of entry into Russia' for those migrants from Kyrgyzstan, Tajikistan and Moldova who had previously been banned for having flouted migration law. There was talk of introducing a fine for the first violation of the Administrative Code of around 7,000 roubles, followed by deportation at the second one. Tajik authorities indicated that 200,000 of its citizens might then return to Russia for work.[88]

The Impact of Recent Terrorism and Violent Events

Terrorist attacks in other countries have fuelled negative comments about migrants who might be Muslims, as have violent incidents in Russia. After attacks in Paris in November 2015, Igor Lebedev of the Liberal Democratic Party (LDPR), a deputy in the State Duma, was reported as suggesting that entry into Russia from Tajikistan, Turkmenistan and Uzbekistan should be restricted as part of Russia's fight against terrorism. He allegedly likened it to the war against fascism in the Great Patriotic War from 21 June 1941.[89] A fresh incident in Moscow in February 2016 sparked renewed anxiety, when a 38-year-old Uzbek nanny killed a child in her care, set the apartment on fire and then held up the child's severed head on the street and shouted '*Allahu akbar*', threatening to blow herself up.[90] In fact, she was not carrying explosives. Russia's Muslims reacted by stressing that this was not an example of Islam. The authorities deterred major television networks from reporting it, fearing a backlash against migrants. A small group of locals and nationalists gathered to lay flowers, and the Communist Party of the Russian Federation (KPRF) called for an end to illegal migration and talked of 'an acute migrant problem'. Their proposal of anti-migrant measures, including a ban on re-entering Russia for those who had committed a crime, quickly received 19,000 signatures in support. Iaroslav Nilov, Chair of the Duma's Committee for Public and Religious Organisations, however, criticised the KPRF's sketch of a woman in black holding a severed head as serving to manipulate public opinion and as inflammatory. Evidence came out that the nanny had a history of mental illness.[91]

---

[88] Ekaterina Trifonova, 'MVD naschitalo 10 millionov migrantov', *Nezavisimaia gazeta*, 29 March 2017.

[89] Quoted by Catherine Putz, 'Fear of terrorists ripples from Paris to Moscow', *The Diplomat*, 17 November 2015, www.thediplomat.com/2015/11/fear-of-terrorists-ripples-from-paris-to-moscow.

[90] No named author, 'Woman holding child's severed head detained in Moscow', *Moscow Times*, 29 February 2016.

[91] Anna Dolgov and Daniel Armstrong, 'Child murder sparks calls for stricter Russian immigration rules', *Moscow Times*, 3 March 2016.

Further anti-migrant hostility was sparked after events on Saturday, 14 May 2016, in the Khovanskoe cemetery in Moscow. A massive fight took place involving an estimated crowd of 200. Russia's Channel One television news that evening showed footage of skirmishes and fights with spades and other weapons between ethnic groups. It was headline news that Russian citizens arriving to bury their dead had to postpone burials until the next day. Early information revealed that during the morning's violence shots had been fired, three had been killed and twenty-three injured. It was initially portrayed in the Russian media as a battle between different ethnic groupings. Attackers from the North Caucasus appeared to have fought Central Asians who worked in the cemetery as grave diggers and who had responsibilities for the upkeep of graves. OMON eventually stopped the fight when police could not.[92]

As clearer details emerged in the following days, *Novaia gazeta* reported that the ethnic picture already painted was 'unfounded'. In fact, among those arrested were Russian sportsmen, some of whom were involved in combat as members of the club Zdorovaia Natsiia, or Healthy Nation. The fight, which the Central Asians did not start, had been about a turf war for control over work at the cemetery. One Central Asian commented that a group of them had been working there for 'about twenty years. There has never been a complaint about us. We have kept order, cleared rubbish and painted the railings around graves.' He admitted that, while some had all the legal papers required of migrants, others did not. All, however, apparently worked with permission from the on-site office. It also emerged that the attackers had previously visited in April and demanded protection money, which the Central Asians were not prepared to pay as 'tribute', never having had a '*krysha*' or 'roof' over them before. Hence the massive attack that followed. Evidently, corruption was embedded in burial services in the capital.[93] *Rossiiskaia gazeta* drew attention to the fact that the MVD had detained 112 participants, and finger printing showed that some had given false names, 12 lacked documents and 15 had violated migration rules.[94] Television news on

---

[92] Russian Channel One television evening news, 14 May 2016. Early reports included: no named author, 'Chto zdes' proizoshlo? – Eto voina', *Novaia gazeta*, 14 May 2016; no named author, 'V massovoi drake na Khovanskom kladbishche uchastvovali 200 chelovek', *Izvestiia*, 14 May 2016; no named author, 'Mer Moskvy prokommentiroval massovuiu draku so strel'boi', *Izvestiia*, 15 May 2016; RIA Novosti, 'V drake na Khovanskom kladbishche uchastvovali 200 chelovek, 50 iz nikh zaderzhany', 14 May 2016, www.ria.ru/incidents/20160514/1433057344.html.

[93] Irek Murtazin, Ali Feruz and Irina Gordienko, 'Peredel zagrobnogo mira', *Novaia gazeta*, 17 May 2016.

[94] Ol'ga Ignatova, 'Moskovskaia politsiia proverit vse gorodskie kladbishcha', *Rossiiskaia gazeta*, 15 May 2016.

the following day reported that 50 were likely to be deported, and the MVD would be checking all cemeteries. The postponed burials would be free of charge, and those who had controlled the crowd would be rewarded with medals.[95]

Events such as those at Khovanskoe cemetery trigger fresh outcries about *gastarbaitery*, reminiscent of earlier events in Kondopoga, Manezh square, Pugachev and Biriulevo. Often migrant workers are lumped together in popular perceptions with others with dark skins who have settled in Russia. Immediately after the events in the cemetery, Lebedev again indicated that he and some other deputies were in favour of closing access to Russia from Central Asia until investigations into the incident were completed. He also called for a new count of all migrants in Russia and for fresh attention to be paid to the question of how many migrants were really needed. He was reported as declaring that, without this reassessment, the police would be unable to prevent further disturbances and the numbers of arrivals would continue to grow.[96] The Federation Council also debated whether or not to stop visa-free access to Russia from Tajikistan and Uzbekistan. This was advocated by Evgenii Serebrennikov, First Deputy Chair of the Committee for Defence and Security. He emphasised that the security of the state was paramount and that it was timely to reconsider and strengthen migration laws. On the same committee, Frants Klintsevich of the United Russia party backed this, but ruled out applying restrictions to Kazakhstan and Kyrgyzstan, which were both members of the EEU.[97] By contrast, the lawyer Gauhar Juraeva warned of xenophobia and described the migrants as 'the victims'.[98]

Many instances of individual and group hate crimes against migrants do not hit the headlines and go unreported. A recent attack which took place in April 2016 on the Moscow metro was exposed by Grazhdanskoe Sodeistvie. A drunken Russian boarded a train, and when he saw a young Tajik he shouted 'what is this? Where are you from? What are you doing?' He called this nineteen-year-old and his older relative 'black monkeys'. He delivered verbal abuse and asked them to leave the carriage immediately because it was 'for Russians only'. The young Tajik, a recent arrival, moved closer to his relative Sulaimon Saidov, who had lived in Moscow

---

[95] Russian Channel One television news, 15 May 2016.
[96] Radio Ozodi, 'Syn Zhirinovskogo: zakroite migrantam dorogu v Rossiiu', 16 May 2016, rus.ozodi.org/content/article/27736840.html, last accessed 7 December 2016.
[97] Quoted in Radio Ozodi, 'Syn Zhirinovskogo'.
[98] Quoted in Eva Hartog, 'Deadly Moscow cemetery feud raises concern of return to 90s', *Moscow Times*, 18 May 2016. An alternative spelling for this lawyer's name is Gavkhar Dzhurayeva.

for more than thirteen years and worked in construction. Sulaimon got up and tried to calm him with the words, 'he is just drunk, don't look at him, don't pay attention'.[99]

Reportedly, the Russian looked at Sulaimon and said 'in three minutes you won't be here. I will kill you.' When Sulaimon saw a gun in the Russian's hand, he thought it was a toy. Next, shooting began and Sulaimon suffered life-threatening bullets in the eye, skull and stomach. The men ended up on the platform of Kaluzhskaia station fighting; when the police arrived, the gun was in Sulaimon's hand and the metro's video recording made it look like a fight. So the police took Sulaimon and secured his hands behind his back but people around shouted that he was the victim. It turned out that his attacker had been detained before.[100] The human rights organisation that was prepared to defend the Tajik pointed out that Sulaimon had simply come to Russia to work and feed his family. Not only did he need a second operation but during a period of rehabilitation he would not be able to work. Moreover, he needed money for his hospital stay, for medicine, for supplementary medical help, for his rent and for food. A call for donations went out.[101]

After Akbarzhon Jalilov detonated a bomb on the metro in St Petersburg in April 2017 which killed sixteen and injured more than fifty, concerns about terrorist threats to Russia were expressed by Aleksandr Bortnikov, head of the FSB.[102] Jalilov had been born in Kyrgyzstan and had become a Russian citizen. Abror Azimov, also from Kyrgyzstan, was subsequently arrested in Petersburg, named by the FSB as responsible for preparing the suicide bomber. Bortnikov called for 'order in the migration sphere' and a consideration of 'supplementary measures' in border regimes.[103] As well as some anxiety in Russian society about the radicalisation of migrant workers once they were in Russia, there were fears among migrant workers of negative stereotyping of them and of increased police checks. Putin was shown on Channel One's television news saying that people from Central Asia and states of the former USSR could not be

---

[99] Elena Srapian, 'Cherez tri minuty tebia ne budet. Ia tebia ub'iu', Grazhdanskoe Sodeistvie, 12 April 2016, www.refugee.ru.

[100] Srapian, 'Cherez tri minuty tebia ne budet'.

[101] 'My ob'iavliaem sbor pomoshchi Sulaimonu Saidovu', Grazhdanskoe Sodeistvie, 20 April 2016, www.refugee.ru. Grazhdanskoe Sodeistvie also collaborates with the SOVA Centre for Information and Analysis in providing legal help and social assistance to those who have suffered hate crimes. Details of SOVA can be found at www.sova-center.ru.

[102] Oleg Odnokolenko, 'Bortnikov obnarodoval kartu terroristicheskikh ugroz Rossii', Nezavisimaia gazeta, 11 April 2017.

[103] TASS, 'Direktor FSB schitaet neobkhodimym poriadok v migratsionnoi sfere', Nezavisimaia gazeta, 11 April 2017.

excluded from Russia and that in 'today's world' migration could not be stopped. He spoke out against what 'people talking of the need to close borders to this or that country' were saying. Putin's message was that this was not realistic.[104]

Conclusion

This chapter has highlighted the significance of the key dimensions of constantly evolving migration policy. Criticisms of the shortcomings of quotas finally led, through multiple legislative amendments, to their replacement by *patenty* followed by the introduction of tests in Russian language, history and law. Among the stated aims of politicians were to match labour demand with supply, to reduce the number of 'illegals', to reassure Russian workers, to curb the role of middlemen and to raise revenue at the regional level from the purchase of the work permits. The tests for migrants were viewed as halting falling language skills in the migrant community and as helping to promote smoother integration. They were not without their critics.

Laws on incoming migrant workers have thus been subject to regular reformulation over time, and the pressures that shape them have been several. Evidence backs Malakhov's argument that migration policies initially were largely reactive rather than coherently worked out. Leaders were pressured by economic demands for migrant workers, on the one hand, and by hostile reactions to incomers from sections of the Russian population on the other. This made for some instability in the making of migration policy which was itself set in a wider context which generated 'a gap between legal decisions and informal practices'.[105] The future is likely to see further changes and refinements.

The Russian government's position on migration was stated at the 13th Coordination Meeting on International Migration at the UN in February 2015. It officially declared 'migration to be a complicated phenomenon' with a vital role in development, in the global economy and in international relations. Moreover, remittances to states of origin had a value 'bigger than international aid'. Remittances to CIS states from Russia, it argued, have made their economies 'more flexible and resilient' and help 'to overcome hunger and poverty'. To improve adaptation, there were now more than 300 centres at which migrants could learn the Russian language and details of Russian culture and traditions. It announced that 'Russian legislation is constantly being improved', driven

---

[104] Russian Channel One television news, 12 April 2017.
[105] Malakhov, 'Russia as a new immigration country', p. 1067.

by the principles of promoting and protecting the human rights and free-doms of 'both Russians and foreign citizens residing in Russia'. It viewed the introduction of *patenty* as 'a new system' which would 'promote legal migration' for foreign workers eligible for visa-free entry and therefore 'reduce illegal migratory flows' and 'allow many migrants to come out of the tax shadow'.[106]

How, then, have experts in Russia appraised these changing policies and official claims?

---

[106] 'Statement by the representative of the Russian Federation at the 13th Coordination Meeting on International Migration', 12 February 2015, www.russiaun.ru/en/news/ga_intmgr.

Given developments in policy on migration since 2002, what have experts in Russia had to say in interviews and in print about quotas, *patenty* and the requirement for migrants from non-EEU states to pass tests in Russian language, history and law before work permits can be issued? What have been their observations over recent years about the impact of middlemen, bribery, corruption and *migrantofobiia*? This chapter examines their assessments of trends and outcomes and the recommendations that they make.

In September 2014, before the new tests for labour migrants from non-EEU states came in, I met in Moscow some of the key commentators on policy who had agreed to let me interview them. Many of their concerns were about how quotas had been reached and applied, what the middlemen were doing, the role of deceit in diasporas, demands by police for bribes, bureaucratic practices and the circulation of misleading stereotypes of migrants. Although some saw positive developments over time, they described various ways in which migrants may nonetheless continue to find work 'in the shadows', sometimes unwittingly and sometimes as the only way that they perceive is open to them. One firm view, then and since, is that it is often a lack of information that can result in illegal predicaments which could otherwise have been avoided. They all, however, expressed some positive hopes for the future and saw ways forward for policy and its implementation, evident in their recent updates too. Concerns about xenophobia, adaptation and integration, however, as well as the increasing costs for migrants to set themselves up in jobs, are ongoing.

Expert Narratives

Which issues and problems have experts prioritised in their reflections on the recent history of policy? The Director of Programmes at the Mezhdunarodnyi Al'ians 'Trudovaia Migratsiia' (International Alliance 'Labour Migration'), Sergei Boldyrev, was especially concerned about the inadequacies of the former quota system.[1] He explained how every year when quotas were in place there had been a *zaiavka* (request) to firms to file figures by 1 May for the number of foreign workers they needed in the following year. One problem with this, stressed Boldyrev, particularly for small businesses, was that it was hard to know exactly how many migrants would be wanted. Future labour needs were often difficult to predict precisely, and so there could be disproportions in the final results. Indeed, if a businessperson did not say anything in advance about what the firm's needs would be, it would not receive a quota at all. Then again, some in business asked for more workers than they could use and would then sell on part of their quota. Thus, a process of 'selling quotas' to another organisation that needed them, but which were surplus to the needs of the organisation that had first acquired them, developed. So, an unintended outcome of the policy of quotas had been financial gain for those who passed them on.

In Boldyrev's view, migration policy had actually been designed around 'the need for the worker to go home' based on short-term employment due to the lack of jobs in the labour migrant's country of origin and the need to take money back home, so it was a 'circular migration'. Boldyrev noted that the critics of migrant labour often say 'they earn it and they take it away', implying that Russia wrongly loses money. He insisted, 'but it is their right to do that'. Boldyrev believed that most migrants were 'forbearing' (*terpimye*) and that 'they bring more help than problems'. What was needed above all, in his estimation, was an efficient way of 'connecting workers to employers'. Boldyrev believed that 'we need a law to get them together' and 'we need an infrastructure for finding jobs'. This was 'very needed' and special rules on how to go about this (*pravila povedenii*) must be specified and made very clear indeed.[2] He had in mind the setting up of a network of job centres across the country and lists of job vacancies that businesses could compile and migrants could search. Linked to this was the 'need to stop' those *posredniki*, or middlemen, who worked 'in the shadows'. He described how, when migrants arrived from Central Asia, they were often 'self-organised'. There was a *shefstvo* of groups, or patronage system, according to which they helped each other. On the one hand, 'they find their *zemliachki*[3] and it is a form of support. They learn the specifics and do not walk into a vacuum.'

---

[1] Interview with Sergei Boldyrev in Moscow, September 2014.

[2] This same point about the necessity of linking up workers with bosses had been made by the doctor in the focus group in 2007 in Vladimir.

[3] This means their country folk. In this case, it might be someone from the same district back home.

On the other hand, learning the ropes this way can lead them into the shadow economy.

The president of MATM, Nikolai Kurdiumov, who had also commented on human trafficking out of Russia, attacked what he saw as another unfair criticism of migrant labour, namely the stereotype that they are responsible for a large portion of crime.[4] In fact, he emphasised, migrant labour represents 'a small percentage' of it. He described how there were elements of illegality in the migration process itself as a consequence of what the laws can make difficult. He regretted that, 'when migrants come from Central Asia they ask for help from the diaspora, especially when an employer has not provided legal permission for them to work. Immediately they pay money. Many of them.' As a consequence, 'a considerable proportion of workers are not set up in the right way. This has been due to a limited number of quotas.' What happens next is that 'they can stay for ninety days. After that they have to leave or get a *patent*.' So, if they do not leave and do not manage to acquire a *patent*, then 'they try to live where they are not seen'. When asked how the system could get around these problems, Kurdiumov responded with 'we could limit the flow in, say have a quota of 5,000, but they could get around this by arriving as tourists and stay. It is not realistic.' More positively, he added, 'we could make access to registering for work easier. Not have quotas.' He explained how in 2014 at the FMS 'they are working on this idea', which indeed subsequently came to fruition after our interview.[5]

From Kurdiumov's perspective, quotas had really existed to defend Russian workers. It was 'a question of how many were needed so as not to offend Russian workers'. He considered that quotas had been complicated to apply in practice since, at whatever ceiling their number was set, there could still be a higher number of migrant workers. Then again, the *posredniki* were a problem. Their mere existence meant that 'illegal ways of doing things develop' and, 'moreover, we cannot really know our needs'. Kurdiumov reflected that perhaps migrants 'could have three months' work, then it could be extended for one month'. If this was guaranteed, then perhaps 'the illegal share might lower. But then there is the danger that if people desire to come, even more might do so. Then Russians would be unhappy if they have no jobs and also if the pay levels are different.' As a way forward, he called for 'more rational thinking'. Like Boldyrev, he stressed that 'the question is how to match the worker with the employer. Then slavery will not occur.'[6] He added that migrant

---

[4] Interview with Nikolai Kurdiumov in Moscow, September 2014.
[5] Interview with Kurdiumov, 2014.
[6] Interview with Kurdiumov, 2014.

labourers should also have some health-care protection, which indeed from 2015 was required through the purchase of insurance.

Summing up on the history of quotas to 2014, Kurdiumov concluded that, 'from 2007 on, it became clear over time that this mechanism was not working'. For this reason they formulated the notion of a *patent* instead of quotas. He thought, nonetheless, that it was still hard to get a 'universal solution'. The CIS is 'so big' and 'migrants come as though this is their homeland' (*ikh rodina*).[7] Boldyrev had also made this point but he put it differently by indicating that, even though the USSR had collapsed, there persisted 'the problem' that 'mentally we live in one country'. He felt that, a quarter of a century after the end of the Soviet Union, 'this carries on across generations'. Boldyrev believed that 'the younger ones get it from the older ones. It is passed down.'[8]

One of the aims of MATM was to work with employers and to explain the situation to them. Kurdiumov regretted that, 'they do not all understand. We explain the need for them to collaborate with specialists and experts in order to seek advice on how to do things legally.' Really, 'an institute for advice to those who hire is needed. They need help. There should be professional consultants for employers and workers.' Kurdiumov called for job centres, as in the UK, 'to make clear what is available so that workers know and can see and so that employers can find labour'. Neither Kurdiumov nor Boldyrev referred explicitly to the concepts of 'exploitation' or 'abuse' of the work force but, in expressing the need to educate businesspeople into behaving legally, this is effectively what they wanted to end. Kurdiumov was convinced that what he named as '*rabskii trud*', or slave labour, was a small percentage of the entire picture.[9] It was, however, complex since there were 'elements' of it when workers fell into the shadows for not complying with regulations.

Kurdiumov's interest in making employers aware of the predicaments faced by migrants contributed to his views on the conducting of language, history and law tests. He was quoted in 2015 by *Izvestiia* observing that the costs of taking the tests in Russia's regions could be 'very heavy', as already illustrated in Noril'sk and Magadan. So, in order to ease the financial burden for migrants, he was a pragmatic advocate of employers meeting some of the costs. Thus the education centre under the auspices of MATM, which had an arrangement with the Druzhba Narodov University, would fly teachers out to administer the tests in places such as Surgut, Nizhnevartovsk and Urengoi, where there were

---

[7] Interview with Kurdiumov, 2014.
[8] Interview with Boldyrev, 2014.
[9] Interview with Kurdiumov, 2014.

no local education institutions to run them. Instead of making migrants pay towards the costs of the flights, they charged the employers who were searching for workers in the region. The cost of the test to migrants in these instances was kept at 4,900 roubles, not inflated. Kurdiumov was nonetheless concerned that, 'if the cost of running tests is not controlled, the market might steeply and unjustifiably raise it'.[10]

The frequency and complexity of legal amendments can pose challenges for migrants. Roman Rybakov, a lawyer who had previously worked at the ILO and at the Moscow office of the IOM, made the point that 'most legal changes connected to migration are difficult to figure out' (*trudno razobrat'sia*). He observed that, if lawyers have difficulties getting to grips with changes, 'how can the migrants?' From his perspective, 'there have been many changes and fast ones in the migration process but it is hard to see what is needed'. Rybakov did not oppose a quota mechanism and noted that 'it exists in many other countries. The main problem here is to help it to work better.' Like others, he believed that 'we need a faster working of the system'. He drew attention to differences of opinion across institutions, highlighting the fact that the Ministry of Labour and the FMS (before it was liquidated) 'do not always see things in the same way'. Rybakov thought that the *patent* was 'good for psychology and for commercial activity', but that some problems with regulation persisted.[11]

Other experts focussed on the positive direction of change, even if they thought that many problems still needed to be ironed out. Sergey Brestovitsky, who commented earlier on human trafficking, also believed that 'not everything is OK' in the changing legislation, but that overall 'the dynamic is good'.[12] On practicalities, he argued that 'to systematise is most important'. He certainly supported the introduction of the *patent*. Nonetheless, he felt that there was still 'not enough focus' on migrants because 'at the moment everyone is looking at Ukraine and forgetting about migration from Central Asia'. He advocated the legalisation of those already in Russia and a granting of an amnesty on the grounds that 'this would be pragmatic for people who have lived here a long time'. He regretted that 'it is hard for migrants to relate to the police when they are not legal here'. Brestovitsky acknowledged that this was complicated by existing negative views about migrants from three main sources: those in

[10] Kurdiumov is quoted in Basharova et al., 'Stoimost' ekzamena dlia migrantov'.
[11] Interview with Roman Rybakov in Moscow, September 2014.
[12] Interview with Sergey Brestovitsky in Moscow, September 2014. For more on Brestovitsky, see p. 176.

nationalist parties; those from a particular youth culture; and those from areas with high geographic concentrations of migrants.[13]

Brestovitsky called for a 'state project' which would amount to a systematic approach to the improvement of the image of the migrant workers (*uluchenie imidzha trudovogo migranta*). Although he believed that the policy direction was positive, the permanent changes that had been made were hampered again by 'not enough focus'. He volunteered that events in Biriulevo, as discussed in the previous chapter, had certainly 'made a focus'. Brestovitsky also addressed the question of various problems arising across different borders and at sections of borders. Of relevance was his view that the flow into Russia of Chinese workers had 'little said about it' and that 'it is quieter. A hidden part. Maybe it is organised. It is set apart and isolated. They do not integrate with others.' He felt that the responsibilities of the FMS, when it had existed, were huge in having to cope with different types of incoming flows, which included refugees, illegal migrants and legal migrants. As a consequence, 'it is hard for the FMS to deal with this'. He summed up with 'it might be a more independent and effective institution outside the MVD, but it does not have all the necessary functions that are needed'. He meant that it was tricky to deal with illegal workers without a police function, and there was also the complication of some corruption.[14] It was criticism of the inadequacies of the FMS from many experts that contributed in 2016 to the decision to reincorporate it into the MVD.

Some experts believed that many problems stemmed from the way in which key institutions worked. Vyacheslav Postavnin, President of the independent foundation Migratsiia XXI Vek (21st Century Migration), readily and openly criticised the FMS, where he himself had once worked.[15] As he put it, 'we have different attitudes towards migration. We hope to be more humanitarian, to try to help and to stop tensions.' He believed that, 'if a law is bad, we must say so'. He lamented that 'recent laws have been very bad for our migrants. We have state *primitivizm*.' Moreover, 'we have lots of laws and there have been negative results from these laws'. He went on that 'the Federal Migration Service writes

---

[13] Interview with Brestovitsky, 2014.

[14] Interview with Brestovitsky, 2014.

[15] Postavnin has had wide experience of migration issues since 1993. He worked at the Russian Ministry of Foreign Affairs and from 2005 to 2008 was Deputy Director of the FMS. He founded Migratsiia XXI Vek in 2009. From 2010 to June 2013 he was Head of the Secretariat of MIRPAL. This was a project of the World Bank to set up a network of migration experts and to enable money transfers across states of the CIS. Postavnin's analytical journal began in 2010 and acts as a forum for discussion of key issues surrounding migration. For details of *Migratsiia XXI Vek*, see mirpal.org.fond.html.

the laws and they don't understand the issues. The mechanisms have not been worked out', and 'policy is leaving people out'.[16]

Postavnin attacked both *konformizm* and corruption and regretted that 'corruption is everywhere. It has exceeded all levels. Until we deal with this, how can we deal with each other? We need to talk about it.' One vehicle for such open discussions is the Foundation's journal of the same name, which comes out once every two months. Funded by the World Bank, it is generally highly respected among migration specialists. Postavnin proudly observed that 'some people say "I don't read anything else." It is obvious this journal is needed. No one questions it.' He stressed that the journal 'reflects all views' and 'it's pragmatic. It's objective.'[17] When told that his foundation had been described in a Western area studies journal by a Russian academic as 'liberal pragmatic', he went along with that categorisation.[18]

In print, Postavnin also criticised recent laws 'On social and cultural adaptation and integration of foreign citizens in the Russian Federation' and 'On immigration control in the Russian Federation'. Again, he blamed the FMS for 'bad laws' which are 'badly implemented'. Once more he saw 'incompetence and *primitivizm*' as well as unprofessionalism, which would continue to harm migrants and do damage to Russia's image. The trouble with the new law on adaptation and integration was that 'in it there isn't even a hint of any real mechanism for the integration and adaptation of migrants'. He viewed the most important mechanism as being the local population, but they did not get a mention.[19] He told me that he had attempted to bring in the people by giving talks in localities, including schools, through press conferences and seminars. Postavnin described how 'I spoke to the Muslims. There are problems of how to live together with Russians and how to integrate. They cluster together.' He felt that 'we do all that we can'.[20]

In an update in early 2017, after Putin had instructed the government in 2016 to develop fresh legislation on the integration of foreigners, Postavnin criticised new adaptation centres that had already been set up in Tambov, Orenburg and other cities in the Urals, as money makers for regional powers. The centres were offering five-week courses on the history and socio-economic development of their region. They also covered

[16] Interview with Vyacheslav Postavnin and Natalia Vlasova in Moscow, September 2014.
[17] The journal's archive of back issues can be found at mirpal.org/migrjournal.html.
[18] Vladimir S. Malakhov described Postavnin as 'liberal pragmatic' in 'Russia as a new immigration country', p. 1073.
[19] Vyacheslav Postavnin, 'Pora prosypat'sia', *Migratsiia XXI Vek*, No. 3–4 (23–24), May–August 2014, p. 30.
[20] Interview with Postavnin and Vlasova, 2014.

questions of security, labour law and sanitation. The cost and living expenses for migrants to attend, however, amounted to 40,000 roubles. Postavnin declared that he had always been against adaptation centres for migrants since new arrivals needed to integrate 'with the people' at the local level and not with government services interested in the regional budget.[21] In our conversation in 2014 Postavnin had argued that a new ministry of experts was needed, run by people who were 'normal specialists and not the police'. He felt that it was important for politicians in the State Duma to have advice on migration policy from experts who knew what they were talking about.[22] Irina Ivakhniuk has similarly called for a reform of migration policy which pays attention to the data and research findings of academics and experts.[23]

When in 2016 the FMS as an institution was liquidated, Postavnin commented that it had not in practice worked as a migration service but rather like 'a federal passport and visa service'. By this he meant that 'the FMS never concerned itself with the problem of adaptation and integration'. Postavnin also criticised it as being incapable of dealing with refugees, illustrated, he thought, by the treatment of arrivals from Ukraine. Furthermore, he accused the FMS of having 'forgotten' about the refugees from the Chechen war. Given all this, Postavnin felt it was quite natural to move it into the MVD again as, 'apart from corruption, we have seen nothing in recent times from the FMS'.[24] He could not have been more disparaging.

Postavnin's Migratsiia XXI Vek is committed to reducing tensions in local areas and to promoting integration. Vasilii Kravtsov, one of its specialists, has described the programme 'Uslyshat' drug druga – znachit poniat", or 'To listen to each other – means to understand'. Launched in 2013 together with the council in Moscow's Troparevo-Nikulino district, it arranged roundtables to discuss relations between different nationalities and faiths in order to plan how to proceed constructively in localities. One offshoot has been the setting up of an Internet site as an information channel for migrants to consult about work possibilities and 'all migration

[21] Postavnin is quoted in Trifonova, 'Gastarbaitery edut v rossiiskuiu "ten"'.
[22] Interview with Postavnin and Vlasova, 2014. See, too, Postavnin, 'Rol' mestnoi vlasti v adaptatsii i integratsii migrantov', paper presented at the Seminar-soveshchanie 'Initsiativy sub"ektov RF po sotsial'noi adaptatsii i integratsii trudovykh migrantov', 22 September 2014.
[23] Irina V. Ivakhniuk, *Perspektivy Migratsionnoi Politiki Rossii* (Moscow: MAKS Press, 2011).
[24] Postavnin is quoted in no named author, 'Migratsiia v MVD: eksperty o reorganizatsii Federal'noi migratsionnoi sluzhby', 6 April 2016, nazaccent.ru/content/20169-sluzhba-v-mvd.html.

questions'. Kravtsov illustrated its success by the fact that, from its first April to June, 'over 21,500 migrants had connected to it'.[25]

Commenting on other local developments, Natalia Vlasova, Vice-President of Migratsiia XXI Vek, praised two of Moscow city's departments for their co-ordinating work and international conferences on 'Edinstvo v razlichiiakh', or 'Unity in differences', which examined experiences in foreign states. Despite many efforts, however, Vlasova regretted that relations between Muscovites and migrants 'are changing for the better very slowly'. She remarked how these were 'sensitive' and how it was 'complicated' to influence 'the mentality of people of a different faith'. Vlasova contended that 'the most important step' was 'to build a channel of communication'. Liaising with the Moscow Duma and local councils, Migratsiia XXI Vek was working to draw together diaspora leaders, youth, nationalist organisations, representatives of different religions, journalists and migration experts. Convinced that Russia could learn from international experience, links had been forged with Switzerland regarding policies of promoting multi-culturality.[26]

Amid her many suggestions, Vlasova advocated the importance of securing the safety of migrants' children, of tackling atomisation and of changing Muscovites' attitudes towards migrants. She argued for directing work at the very young, beginning with kindergarten. She also reported that successful local projects run by other experts in Voikovskii district around cookery classes, exchanges of traditional foods, drawing competitions and veterans' meetings had made an impact on local relationships. Findings showed that as a result of these projects 'the migrants changed their conduct in relation to local inhabitants and the locals to the migrants'. They are no longer afraid to relate to each other. Another successful effort was the organisation of a roundtable held in November 2014 under the auspices of the Kudrin Foundation and World Bank, which brought together representatives of the Russian Orthodox Church and Muslim leaders.[27]

Regret at the slow pace of migration legislation in addressing problems was echoed across the interviews and repeated in articles. Dmitry Poletaev, Director of the Migration Research Centre, put much down to 'the problem of lack of a conception from the government'. He stressed that 'we need the system to be effective but this process around migration

---

[25] Vasilii Kravtsov, 'Migranty zhdut, no . . . poka ne liubiat', *Migratsiia XXI Vek*, No. 3–4 (23–24), May–August 2014, pp. 56–57.

[26] Nataliia Vlasova, 'Razgovor na ravnykh: mestnaia vlast' sposobna regulirovat' otnosheniia mezhdu korennymi zhiteliami i priezzhami', *Migratsiia XXI Vek*, No. 6–7 (26–27), November–December 2014, pp. 66–72.

[27] Vlasova, 'Razgovor na ravnykh'.

laws and implementation is moving slowly'. Poletaev explained in 2014 that to avoid long and slow queues for acquiring permission to work, new arrivals may pay extra 'in order to go faster and to speed this up'. He described how 'they can wait a week in a queue'. But 'they can also re-sell this'. He viewed *patenty*, however, as 'positive and very important'. He argued that many migrant workers were ready to be legal and should be paid accordingly. Moreover, the state could benefit hugely from the sale of *patenty* as they 'brought in 6 billion roubles in the first months of 2014'.[28] In March 2015 Romodanovskii revealed that for the whole of 2014 *patenty* had raised 18 billion roubles.[29] In 2016 it was announced that in 2015 *patenty* brought in 32 billion roubles, with 12 billion of this in Moscow alone. In the first seven months of 2016, 24 billion had been received across the country, which was twice the amount during the same period the year before.[30] One of Poletaev's concerns in 2014, however, was that *patenty* could simultaneously be 'an instrument for corruption'.[31]

Poletaev saw hope for the system in the younger generation and stressed that 'the old Soviet mentality is over'. He saw 'lots of new young people moving into leadership positions and roles. Step by step, things are moving in a positive direction.' He underscored in 2014, before the FMS's closure, that 'there have been changes in the structure of the FMS' and 'understanding has improved'. There were inter-organisational struggles but even these 'had begun to be more open, so it will change'. Even if things were going to 'go backwards', it would 'only be for a short time. It cannot last.' He then qualified this optimism somewhat by characterising the FMS as 'complicated' due to the fact that 'there are not staff for humanitarian goals' and that it was 'police-like'. He went on: 'they use police techniques, not humanitarian ones'. In fact, 'they do not really understand their functions'. There were some 'bad' specialists there and their level was 'low' because they were the 'old *apparat*'.[32] By contrast, he

---

[28] Interview with Dmitry Poletaev in Moscow, September 2014.

[29] TASS, 'FMS: novye patenty dlia raboty inostrantsev v Rossii prinesli v biudzhet bolee 1.6 mlrd rublei', tass.ru/obschestvo/1836953.

[30] Iurii Kondrat'ev, 'V Rossii stychek s migrantami vse men'she, v otlichie ot ES', *Pravda*, 19 August 2016.

[31] Interview with Poletaev, 2014.

[32] Interview with Poletaev, 2014. A more positive view of the FMS was held in 2011 by Asida Agrba. She maintained that the FMS is 'continuously working to develop and improve the efficiency of its migration rules' and that recent amendments meant that the state was now 'interested and focussed on changing migration policy'. She thought that 'the current mechanism' illustrated the 'liberal nature' of 'regulating immigration'. See Asida Agrba, 'Quota system for hiring foreign labor in Russia', *Moscow Times*, 31 August 2011.

praised those at Migratsiia XXI Vek as 'good people'. Once more he reiterated the much-heard refrain that the big problem surrounding migration was 'endless corruption'. Alongside this was a xenophobia that was 'strong' and also 'much silence surrounding slavery'. He regretted that 'a lot of people still do not know about this. There is a need to inform people and change their attitude as to what slavery actually is.'[33] After the official announcement in 2016 of the transfer of the FMS's functions to the MVD, Poletaev remarked that it was not clear 'how in general the situation will develop. An institution for policing is unlikely to occupy itself with adaptation and integration', something which 'in fact, the FMS had not done'.[34] His conclusion on the FMS was similar to Postavnin's.

For the migrant, there were complications in daily life which were often hard to address. Poletaev highlighted the fact that those who arrived from Central Asia were often 'trustful' or 'unsuspecting', exhibiting *dovershivost'*. The diaspora did not always enlighten them. He underlined that diasporas include those who have been in Russia for a long time as well as recent arrivals and that 'sometimes there is a divide between these two groups'. Zamandash is an example of a diaspora organisation which tries to help labour migrants. It is formed from the trade community of Kyrgyz in Russia.[35] Problems can arise, however, when recent arrivals are somehow ensnared or are led into a trap. He believed that 'they might help newcomers, but not many'. Thus, the diaspora could effectively instruct newcomers into how to cope in the shadows, echoing what Boldyrev and Kurdiumov had regretted.[36]

Regarding the tests introduced in 2015, Poletaev summed them up as 'much more progressive and directed at the elimination of corruption in this system'. Fully aware of the teething problems in implementing them that the FMS and test centres had confronted, Poletaev remarked in mid 2015 that 'the migration authorities simply were not prepared for such a flow of migrants'. He also observed that 'it is important to understand that the middlemen for whom the migrants were a form of income are now actively trying to take root in the system in order to prolong preying on the *gastarbaitery*'. One unexpected result in 2015 was a 'different type of corruption scheme – sale of a place in the queue', so further new centres had to be set up to tackle the challenge of numbers. Poletaev believed that there was no malicious intent on the part of the authorities

[33] Interview with Poletaev, 2014.
[34] E-mail correspondence from Dmitry Poletaev, 19 June 2016.
[35] For details of the Association 'Zamandash', see its website at www.zpress.kg.
[36] For analysis of Muscovites' attitudes towards migrants and of the hardships that migrant workers face in the city, see Dmitrii Poletaev, 'Moskvichi i migrant: prestupnost' i vzaimootnosheniia', *Migratsiia XXI Vek*, No. 3–4, May–August, 2014, pp. 51–55.

for the overcrowding. Evidently it was more a case of inadequate initial capacity to apply the new rules that they themselves had adopted.

Poletaev updated the picture a year later and drew attention to important improvements. He commented in May 2016 that the situation in Moscow was 'considerably better than in other regions'. Here the cost of taking the tests was cheaper than elsewhere, and the test centre was run by the city's administration, where 'there are no middlemen and everything is done very well. The migrants take the tests themselves and there is no falsification.'[37] He underscored that progress had indeed been made. In fact, the selling of places in the queue in Moscow had taken place only at the outset and had not occurred since March 2015. Now 'everything there has been put right and in Moscow it is very easy to get the documents'. Elsewhere the picture might be different. He admitted that 'in other regions the middlemen are still there' and that there were 'complications with overstated prices for services'.[38]

Poletaev nonetheless recognised that it was not always easy for migrants working in Moscow to pay the necessary monthly fee, then of 4,200 roubles, for their *patent*. In addition, from 2016 migrants wishing to extend their licence to work had to secure a contract from an employer, and 'often the employer does not want to grant such contracts'. There were other problems for those migrants on the blacklist. In June 2016, Poletaev reckoned that there were 'around 1.6 million people from countries of the CIS on the blacklist (for 3, 5 or 10 years) and they simply cannot arrive legally and work in Russia. They will not be let in at the border and will not be granted a licence to work even if they somehow cross the border.' Those migrants who made it into Russia were knowingly choosing an existence without documents. He thought, 'it is a weak trend, but it exists'.[39]

There was also positive feedback on the running of tests from the Moscow office of the IOM. A consolidated response in 2016 from Juliana Pavlovskaya, Olga Rybakova and Julia Melnichouk described the system as 'fully functioning'. They observed that, since the test certificates were valid for five years, 'the overall flow of migrants who need to pass the tests has decreased'. This meant 'no more long lines', nor waiting periods to receive certificates. The IOM put the pass rate at 80 per cent and commented that the test centres run by the Ministry of Education usefully offered short half-day courses to help migrants prepare. The IOM also published study books to aid migrants to get ready for all three tests

---

[37] E-mail communication from Poletaev, 8 May 2016.
[38] E-mail communication from Poletaev, 19 June 2016.
[39] E-mail communication from Poletaev, 19 June 2016.

and provided them with on-line practice tests. As for the thorny question of corruption, they had confidence in the Ministry of Education and in those universities in the Testing Consortium for paying 'a lot of attention to monitoring the centres' and for their due diligence 'in implementing quality control measures'. The electronic database for the federal system also enabled checks on the validity of certificates. So-called regional certificates were issued in an alternative system locally and valid only in a particular region. The IOM could not judge the quality of these due to a lack of information.[40]

Despite all the hopes placed in more widespread use of the *patent* for addressing some of the problems generated by the quota system, soon came scrutiny and critical observations. In an early review of its impact, Vlasova observed that the changes had been 'revolutionary' in transferring powers for legalisation to the regions so that 'at last' they had a participatory role to play in regulating labour. She had also anticipated that it would 'enable a reduction in corruption in the MVD and FMS' and 'result in protection of the migrants and reduce the number of illegals'. She was, however, concerned about negative results such as the increased demands that had been placed on migrants and the number of documents they had to acquire. Migrants not only had to produce a certificate showing knowledge of the Russian language, history and law, but also show proof of medical insurance and a lack of infectious diseases. Furthermore, the medical certificate cost money, and it had turned out that initially around 80 per cent of those acquired were fake, without any medical verification. Given all the documents required, migrants had to run around a given town where they wished to work to visit different offices, often in very different locations. It was likely to take them more than the legally permitted period of thirty days in which to do this. On top of this, they had to arrive with enough money to pay for food and housing during this period. Vlasova underscored that this was particularly hard for labour migrants from Uzbekistan, Tajikistan, Azerbaijan, Moldova and Ukraine who were outside the EEU. By contrast, migrants from its member states, namely from Armenia, Belarus, Kazakhstan and Kyrgyzstan, did not have to produce a medical certificate in order to work, just as Russians did not have to do so.[41]

Vlasova had another point. She questioned the sense in making migrants pass a language test, arguing that this requirement was 'superfluous' for

---

[40] Consolidated e-mail from Juliana Pavlovskaya, Olga Rybakova and Julia Melnichouk, 10 May 2016.

[41] Nataliia Vlasova, 'Skal'pel' ili topor?' *Migratsiia XXI Vek*, No. 4 (31), July–August 2015, pp. 24–28.

many jobs. While some Russian language skills were useful in trade, housing and housework, were they necessary she asked for a 'considerable' number of Tajiks and Uzbeks who came from rural areas (estimated to be one-quarter of these nationalities) for whom this would be 'especially difficult'. After all, they made up about half of the migrants coming to Russia. She feared this would mean a further growth in illegal migration and corruption. Vlasova recommended limiting the categories of worker that needed to pass tests to those who in their work would communicate with Russian citizens. She even concluded by suggesting a policy re-think about having rejected quotas. That policy, she reminded readers, had been based on best world practices and gave the federal centre the right to establish quotas, or not, based on regional recommendations. Debate on the relative merits of work permits and quotas was likely to continue.[42]

The conditions in and around the first test centres came under some criticism. Konstantin Troitskii, for example, commented that the test centre at Putilkovo 'looks better on paper than in reality'. He feared that the overcrowding resulted in a lack of respect in the treatment of the waiting migrants. He added that outside the building there was 'filth' because 'they don't clear the rubbish'.[43] Eight months after his remarks and five months after Vlasova's critical comments, there was fanfare on television's Channel One news that an important and huge multi-function migration centre had been opened in New Moscow, just one hour by bus from the nearest metro station. Here the newsreader announced that the 'massive plus' for migrants was that they could arrange all documents under one roof in a maximum of two hours. All a migrant needed to do was come along with a passport and migration card. Here they would be processed to undergo their health check and, if successful, be sent for their computer tests. If they passed the tests, they could proceed to receive a *patent*. The news boasted that the centre worked without a break and also at weekends. With 250 employees, it could process 7,500 migrants in one day. The message was 'everything is quick, everything is organised, everything is wonderful'. Moreover, reporting relayed that increasingly often migants were choosing legal ways of proceeding.[44] Now everything was electronic, thereby addressing one of Vlasova's concerns about fake medical certificates.

[42] Vlasova, 'Skal'pel' ili topor?'

[43] Konstantin Troitskii, 'Dva puti v Putilkovo', 27 April 2015, refugee.ru/news/4523.

[44] Russian Channel One television news report by Aleksandra Cherepnina, 'V Moskve ofitsial'no otkrylsia samyi krupnyi v strane Mnogofunktsional'nyi migratsionnyi tsentr', www.1tv.ru/news/social/300967, broadcast on 29 January 2016.

From another perspective, Vladimir Mukomel at the Institute of Sociology in Moscow warned that new requirements could increase illegal working due to the fact that companies which wished to employ migrant workers would not want to wait for the migrants to acquire all their certificates and paperwork.[45] And Gauhar Juraeva, head of Moscow's Migration and Rights, thought that, since migrants wanted to make as much money as they could, something like medical insurance might be perceived as a luxury and really unnecessary. If ill, she added, migrants would be likely to avoid Russian doctors and try to find a Tajik one, who would be cheaper. As far as all the tests went, she held that 'many migrants cannot afford that kind of money'. She thought that increased costs would 'drive some migrants underground'.[46]

In 2016 the Obshchestvennaia Palata (Social Chamber) held a round-table to consider how the tests were being administered. Members were particularly concerned about the lack of a common standard across regions and also variation in how quickly documents were provided. Elena Sutormina, Chair of the Chamber's Commission For Diplomacy and Support of Compatriots Abroad, gave examples. In Belgorod oblast, work permits were ready on the day that tests were passed but in Chuvashia after two days, and it took up to two weeks in Tambov. Furthermore, the length of time for which the work permits were valid could vary across regions, with some giving no time limit at all.[47] Vladimir Shaposhnikov, Vice-President of the Union of Russian Trades Unions, commented on inadequate controls in the use, storage and sharing of confidential information. He also believed that regions should follow a 'federal stand-ard' for work permits of charging 4,900 roubles a month rather than the current variations in cost. The roundtable paid some attention to Romodanovskii's claim that the number of illegal migrants had now halved from the figure of 3.7 million in 2015. Sutormina thought various factors accounted for this but that tougher migration laws had played a role in the reduction. She estimated that unqualified workers were less likely to be able to pay for a work permit and employers were now less inclined to take on illegals due to tougher administrative punishments. Evgenii Bobrov, Deputy Chair of the President's Council for Human

[45] Quoted in Irina Umarova and Jamila Sujud, 'Tajiks face new obstacles to work in Russia', Institute for War and Peace Reporting, 23 January 2015, iwpr.net/global-voices/tajiks-face.new-obstacles-work-russia.

[46] Quoted in Umarova and Sujud, 'Tajiks face new obstacles'. Some sources spell Juraeva's name as Gavkhar Dzhurayeva, and some translate the name of the organisation as 'Migration and Law'.

[47] Roman Kretsul, 'Sistemu testirovaniia migrantov raskritikovali v Obshchestvennoi palate', *Izvestiia*, 17 March 2016.

Rights and head of the human rights organisation Voskhod, was sceptical of the accuracy of Romodanovskii's figures and believed the reduction in illegal migrants to be around 10–15 per cent. He felt that, whenever the FMS had announced that there were fewer migrants, they were really praising themselves for attaining a result.[48]

Regarding the difficulties faced by those who failed tests and then had to re-sit them before being eligible for a licence to work, Vladimir Shaposhnikov had suggested in 2015 a way of easing their predicament. He advocated a policy which issued a work permit anyway to first-time fails, but with a paper attached to it indicating a fail. This would allow migrants to work yet require a re-sit within three or five months, thereby offering more time to prepare. If migrants failed a second time, then work permits could be declared invalid. He wanted a debate on this in the Obshchestvennaia Palata followed by a recommendation to the Duma, but no change in policy resulted.[49]

Before Vlasova and others had questioned the utility of the new language tests for those in some jobs, there had been strong arguments in favour of them. Sergei Riazantsev had made the point that, from 1993 to 2000, 61 per cent of the flow of immigrants into Russia was of ethnic Russians, but this fell to 33 per cent in 2007. After this, Rosstat did not gather comparable data. Riazantsev held that 'so many of them' had poor Russian and that Russia lacked a sufficiently developed 'infrastructure of integration'. Migrants were often living in crowded and cramped conditions, were isolated from locals and often hesitated to walk far beyond where they lived to protect their security and 'so as not to have problems with the police'.[50] None of this enabled social interaction or conversing in Russian. He argued that Russia as 'a great power' (velikaia derzhava) should embark upon 'ambitious tasks' to ensure migrant flows with language skills. He advocated a migration policy of 'building bridges' (vystroit' mosty) and 'pulling down barriers' (sniat' bar'ery) and believed that language skills would enable Tajiks and other migrants to acquire better jobs. Riazantsev observed that there was also great labour potential to be tapped in China and Vietnam to supplement Russia's labour force. As a supporter of a 'broad' state policy rather than a 'narrow' one, he advocated innovative forms of teaching Russian through study trips (stazhirovki) to Russia, 'mobile groups' of teachers, advertising campaigns such as St Petersburg's project of 'Let's speak like Peterburzhtsy',

---

[48] Kretsul, 'Sistemu testirovaniia migrantov'.
[49] Vladimir Shaposhnikov is quoted in Basharova, 'Gosduma proveriaet'.
[50] Sergei V. Riazantsev, 'O iazykovoi integratsii migrantov kak novom orientire migratsionnoi politiki Rossii', Sotsiologicheskie issledovaniia, No. 9, 2014, pp. 25–26.

electronic textbooks and self-teaching on-line.[51] This would constitute a 'language infrastructure'.[52]

Someone who deals more directly with helping migrants is Svetlana Gannushkina.[53] In 1990 she co-founded Grazhdanskoe Sodeistvie and in 1993 the Memorial Human Rights Centre, where in 1996 she established a network of migration lawyers who could give advice.[54] Her experience at Grazhdanskoe Sodeistvie initially concerned advising internally displaced people and emergency refugee cases. She regretted in interview that 'the main problem' concerning refugees and migrants 'is that the state does not fulfil its duties in receiving refugees and is reluctant to accord the status of refugee'.[55] She informed me at the end of 2014 that just 808 people held this status. Gannushkina thought that this was 'paltry for Russia on whose territory there are thousands of refugees from Afghanistan, Syria, North Korea and the former Soviet republics'. She added that, 'of course, corruption is the second problem in this sphere'. Regrettably, the special services effectively 'took money from them'. She observed that 'we cannot control this problem'. At first 'we had so many refugees to help and we were overwhelmed and overloaded'. Grazhdanskoe Sodeistvie then turned to the labour migrants because 'we understood that they were breaking the law in enormous ways, so therefore began to help them too. We were not the first to begin to assist them, but we started giving them serious legal advice.'[56]

Gannushkina confirmed the issues that the press had reported: 'the first problem for migrants was that they were not paid'. Then there was the issue that 'the state never punishes the employer, but punishes the workers'. In fact, 'the state does not protect the migrant at all'. One dilemma is that, 'if he is working without a contract because the employer will not give him one, then the worker cannot easily fight a legal case because he is unable to prove that he worked there. We recommend that he takes photographs of the workplace and has photos taken of himself in his work clothes and gets witnesses to say that he has worked there.' She went on that, 'sometimes our lawyers phone the employers. As a result a worker sometimes receives half of his pay. And he is grateful for that. But if we have evidence, we can go to court and get an

---

[51] Riazantsev, 'O iazykovoi integratsii migrantov', pp. 27–29.
[52] No named author, 'Putin signs new law, foreigners to prove Russian proficiency', *St Petersburg Times*, 22 April 2014.
[53] Svetlana Gannushkina is a retired mathematics professor who graduated from Moscow University and taught at the Russian State Humanities University.
[54] For details of Grazhdanskoe Sodeistvie, see its website at www.refugee.ru.
[55] Skype interview with Svetlana Gannushkina, September 2014.
[56] Skype interview with Gannushkina, 2014.

investigation.' Grazhdanskoe Sodeistvie had employed one permanent lawyer which then increased to two, and also draws in lawyers from the network 'Migratsiia i Pravo' (Migration and Law), who can offer advice in consultations held at Grazhdanskoe Sodeistvie.[57]

Gannushkina revealed that, if a migrant is particularly badly treated, it is only the very expensive lawyers who defend the bosses concerned. There is a department for fighting slavery but she believed that the legal system is on the side of business and that 'it is rare that they get caught'. She regretted that there was also a lot of hatred toward migrants, and sometimes they were confronted by men in masks. When asked how the migrants knew to come to Grazhdanskoe Sodeistvie for help, Gannushkina replied 'by word of mouth. People know.' Moreover, it was not only the diasporas who recommended them but the FMS also sometimes referred migrants to her for advice. When asked if it was correct to characterise Grazhdanskoe Sodeistvie as having an 'humanitarian approach', as Malakhov had categorised it, she replied 'yes, that is correct but more appropriate is "*gumannyi*"' or humane, 'rather than humanitarian'.[58]

Regarding the introduction of Russian language tests, Gannushkina was quoted in 2014 as saying that they were 'pointless both in legal and in practical terms'. Moreover, she feared that, since the sale of work permits was already 'a booming business', new tests could 'intensify this trend'.[59] Gannushkina has also expressed concern that, from 2013 to 2015 inclusive, district judges in Moscow made 154,494 decisions on deportation, and 99 per cent of these were based on Articles 18.8 and 18.10 of the Administrative Code.[60] She observed that the application of these articles 'can change the life of a person forever. Many are left without the means of existence.' Families might also be separated. She called for careful observance of the procedures around these two articles and of the problems of 'group courts' which break rules. She pointed out that, according to international law, a court cannot consider ten people at once. Nor should a migrant be asked to sign a document that he or she cannot understand that is written in a language that is not their own. Nor should procedural rules for the defence of migrants be broken. When this happens, it

---

[57] Skype interview with Gannushkina, 2014. Some articles on this organisation translate its name as 'Migration and Rights'.

[58] Malakhov, 'Russia as a new immigration country', p. 1071.

[59] Gannushkina is quoted in Farangis Najibullah and Umid Bobomatov, 'Russia to test migrant workers on country's history', RFE/RL, 13 June 2014, rferl.org/a/russia-migrants-history-tests/25420832.html.

[60] Article 18.8 of the Code of Administrative Offences of the Russian Federation addresses violations of the rules of entry or residence in Russia. Article 18.10 concerns unlawful labour activities without a work permit or in violation of its terms.

amounts in Gannushkina's view to 'not a court but a profanation of the court's work'. She highlighted Article 8 of the European Convention on the protection of the rights of the individual and the family and Article 13 on the right to effective means of legal defence.[61]

Like Gannushkina, Konstantin Troitskii of Grazhdanskoe Sodeistvie has looked closely at legal practices and concluded that there have been instances when courts broke procedural norms, not clarified the rights and responsibilities of the detained, nor granted an interpreter or a lawyer. A migrant might be swiftly dealt with in two to three minutes, and sometimes a judge will consider a batch of cases grouped together.[62] Troitskii analysed data from the Legal Department of the Russian Federation and discovered that Moscow courts had been deporting migrants more often than those in St Petersburg. In 2014, Moscow's district courts looked at 68,200 cases involving the above violations and 'for these, 65,817 migrants were punished, amounting to 96 per cent'. Of the punished, 59,216 were deported. In the same year, Petersburg's courts considered 13,898 cases and punished 9,618, or 69 per cent, and deported a lower 6,380. Deportations may involve being put on a 'blacklist' which means being banned from Russia for a period of three, five or ten years.[63]

Why the difference between court practices in Moscow and Petersburg? Troitskii sees it as multi-factoral. Lower figures in Petersburg may reflect less-burdened courts, with more time to look carefully at individual cases and to weigh up circumstances 'for' and 'against'. It could also indicate different relationships between the courts and official organs such as the FMS in the past and the MVD. These different patterns, suggests Troitskii, also reflect 'greater independence' of the courts in Petersburg and a different 'legal culture'. So, if a foreign citizen is detained in St Petersburg, the probability of being deported is lower than in Moscow. Moreover, courts in Petersburg are not afraid to stop a case or to give a migrant a full legal defence, regardless of citizenship.[64]

Other experts voiced concern about the expulsions of *gastarbaitery*. In his capacity as head of the FMS, Romodanovskii criticised judges for deporting 'even for an initial infringement of the law'. He thought a 'softening' was in order.[65] Likewise, Evgenii Bobrov from the Presidential

[61] Gannushkina is quoted in Konstantin Troitskii and Elena Srapian, 'Otvechai po-russki. Shapku snimi', Grazhdanskoe Sodeistvie, 15 March 2016, www.refugee.ru.
[62] Troitskii and Srapian, 'Otvechai po-russki'.
[63] Konstantin Troitskii and Elena Srapian, 'Moskva slezam ne verit', Grazhdanskoe Sodeistvie, 7 December 2015, www.refugee.ru.
[64] Troitskii and Srapian, 'Moskva slezam ne verit'.
[65] Ekaterina Trifonova, 'Migranty ukhodiat v seruiu zonu', Nezavisimaia gazeta, 7 December 2015.

Human Rights Council lamented mass deportations 'for an insignificant offence' when, in fact, a fine would suit better. He regretted that many migrants ran into 'bureaucracy and commercialisation' and, despite wanting to register properly, could not.[66] Ekaterina Trifonova observed how it was being confirmed that judges 'ignore any arguments in the defence of migrants'. She quoted Postavnin to the effect that legal procedures were not being followed and that a complaint should be lodged with the Constitutional Court. Postavnin pointed out that the Supreme Court had ordered that decisions should take into account 'family circumstances and the gravity of the crime'. Others thought that officials just did not know how to handle migrants at a time of terrorist threats.[67]

A completely different issue that experts who work closely with migrants see is the shame that the latter may feel. This book has already discussed how women and girls who return from trafficked situations in the sex industry may feel ashamed and suffer stigma and rejection. A very different shame is experienced by those migrant workers who do not manage to earn any, or enough, money in Russia and who return home empty-handed. Julia Melnichouk, Head of the Labour Migration Unit at the IOM office in Moscow, described how 'they cannot tell anyone when they return that they did not earn anything. They feel an internal responsibility.'[68] She added that 'there have been suicides because they felt that they could not return with nothing. They feel ashamed not to have any money. It is expected of them.' Whether money is needed for the family's budget or for a celebration such as a wedding, expectations are high. Melnichouk described how from a young age 'some kids are brought up with the idea that they must go and earn money in Russia'. Then there are the middlemen, or recruiters, who may also feel shame for a different reason. She went on: 'if their deal goes wrong and they are let down inside Russia, then they too have a problem of shame for failure'. Then there are those Central Asian women who go to Russia to work, whether freely or trafficked, but who end up in prostitution. They suffer the same fate as Russian women when they return home from having been trafficked, or worse. Melnichouk underscored that, 'if she returns pregnant, her child will not be accepted'.[69] There was evidently a differential gender pattern in the origin and nature of shame.

[66] Ekaterina Trifonova, 'Migrantam dadut uroki ideologii', *Nezavisimaia gazeta*, 7 April 2016.

[67] Ekaterina Trifonova, 'Pravozashchitniki gotovy sudit'sia za migrantov', *Nezavisimaia gazeta*, 13 May 2016.

[68] Interview with Julia Melnichouk in Moscow, September 2014.

[69] Interview with Melnichouk, 2014.

One scholar who throughout her career consistently argued for awareness of gender dimensions in migration patterns was Elena Tiuriukanova. She, together with Zhanna Zaionchkovskaia and Iuliia Florinskaia, underscored that women migrating into Russia were often 'unseen workers' as they were employed in households and the informal sector. They cited estimates that at the end of the first decade of the twenty-first century, 8–10 per cent of all migrants from Tajikistan were women, 30–35 per cent from Kyrgyzstan and more than 50 per cent of flows from Ukraine and Belarus. Overall, women then constituted 25–30 per cent of incoming migrants. Moreover, the number of women who travelled independently, without a husband, was increasing and by 2010 was reckoned to be around 50 per cent of incoming women. The researchers stressed that, for these women, migration was therefore actively chosen as a 'life strategy'. Surveys also indicated that 80 per cent of married women came with their husbands, and themselves worked as well. They may be perceived as being in traditional roles but, in fact, they too were 'active labour migrants'. Migration thus opened up 'new opportunities for women in terms of material security, education, career growth, independence and confidence in their possibilities'. They, too, send money back home.[70] Recent in-depth interviews by Poletaev with Central Asian migrant women confirmed how some indeed undergo 'a specific transformation in their status', and in Russia their gender roles 'strikingly change'. Kyrgyz women talked of gaining fresh outlooks, freedom, education and no desire to return home to live.[71]

Zaionchkovskaia, Tiuriukanova and Florinskaia made a strong case for a gender-sensitive migration policy (*genderno chuvstvitel'naia politika*), by which they meant 'widening legal and safe migration and employment channels for men and women' with principles of non-discrimination, equal opportunities and equal access to resources. Based on guidelines from the OECD, other points included: the protection of rights and fair treatment; the right to access gynaecological and obstetric care; the right to protection from sexual violence; and an overcoming of sexual stereotypes. They argued that Russian migration policy was 'practically devoid of gender-sensitive elements' and was instead either gender-neutral or gender-blind. The former referred to making an identical impact on men and women, and the latter amounted to ignoring significant differences between them. Their hope, however, was that finally a gender-sensitive

---

[70] Zaionchkovskaia et al., *Trudovaia Migratsiia v Rossiiu*, pp. 41–42.

[71] Dmitrii Poletaev, 'Izmenenie praktik povedeniia trudovykh migrantov iz Srednei Azii v Rossii', in Sergei Panarin, ed., *Vostok na Vostoke, v Rossii i na Zapade* (St Petersburg: Nestor-Istoriia, 2016), pp. 177–193.

policy was in 'a stage of conception'. They wished to see a study of the implications of new laws for female and male labour and scrutiny of whether one gender was disproportionately affected. Women, for example, had been badly affected in 2007 when foreign workers were no longer permitted to work in wholesale and retail trade in markets and kiosks.[72]

Wider attention has been paid by experts to problems of *migrantofobiia* and *etnofobiia*. Vladimir Mukomel has used these terms in connection with the 'marker' of the duality of '*svoi–chuzhoi*' which draws the distinction between 'one's own' and 'strange' or 'alien'. Both *migrantofobiia* and *etnofobiia*, he observed, were linked to a surface superficiality and applied to those seen as 'other'.[73] Mukomel argues that the adaptation and integration of ethnically foreign (*inoetnichny*) migrants is essential since immigration is needed for economic development. He holds that 'xenophobia pervades all layers of Russian society' and that this 'increases the frequency of racist attacks'. He cited research which suggested that 'about 400–600 individuals fall victim to racist and xenophobic violence each year and about 40–120 die'.[74] A key problem for Mukomel is the housing market, which might specify 'Russian family only' and 'Slavic nationals only'. All these factors foster isolationist tendencies amongst migrants and reinforce their social exclusion. What is therefore needed are 'effective and efficient social, economic and cultural institutions' to work to prevent this. Otherwise, he believes Russia would be faced with social segmentation according to ethnicity, the formation of 'sub-cultural migrant enclaves' and expanding ethnic discrimination. Mukomel adds that politics was geared to short-term tasks, not long-term planning, and this, together with what he dubs 'the new imperialistic thinking', seriously affects integration policy. What had been wrong with Russia's 'ideology of migration policy', in his view, was that it had ignored 'the question of the labour migrant's future' and had overlooked the 'adaptation and integration problems of migrants'. The 'weakness of civil society', 'poorly developed civil self-consciousness', 'the expanding culture of cynicism' and 'the absence of traditions of social dialogue' did not help.[75] His picture was a bleak one.

In a similar vein, Valerii Tishkov, Director of the Institute of Ethnology and Anthropology, has traced the growth of anti-migrant attitudes to the first decade of the twenty-first century, when the number of labour

[72] Zaionchkovskaia et al., *Trudovaia Migratsiia v Rossiiu*, pp. 43–44.
[73] Vladimir I. Mukomel', 'Grani intolerantnosti (migrantofobii, etnofobii)', *Sotsiologicheskie issledovaniia*, No. 2, 2005, pp. 56–66.
[74] Mukomel', *Politika Integratsii*, pp. 4–5.
[75] Mukomel', *Politika Integratsii*, pp. 8–11.

migrants noticeably increased from the states of Central Asia, and 'they became objects of special exploitation' and had to endure *migrantofobiia* in daily life and in politics. He described how an army of '*proraby*' developed who gathered up migrants in stations and airports, on roadsides and in markets and 'set them up' in work 'without any agreements, without paying tax and, of course, very cheaply' (*za bestsenok*): in sum 'recruited them into slavery'.[76] The majority of arrivals, he believed, came from rural areas with poor levels of Russian language. They were doing the least prestigious and lowest-paid work in the labour market. Tishkov reflected that migration had noticeably changed the ethnic composition of the population, particularly in areas of high concentration. In the 1990s it was noticeable in Krasnodarsk krai and Stavropol krai and also in Rostov oblast where many Armenians had arrived as well as tens of thousands of Russians leaving the North Caucasus. In the more central oblasts of Vladimir, Yaroslavl and Nizhegorod, Armenians and Azerbaijanis came and stayed, as did Chechens, Ingush and Dagestanis. This was 'palpable' and was received 'painfully' (*boleznenno*) by locals.[77]

In this context, some politicians had started talking about 'cleansing from filth' (*chistit' ot gryazi*). Even though the percentage of Russians had increased in the population of Moscow in the run-up to the 2010 census, Tishkov held that immigration was increasingly seen as a 'negative factor' and 'as a threat to the existing culture and national security of Russia', referring to crime and terrorism.[78] An image of the migrant was constructed that suggested that he or she was a 'potential criminal' and 'unwelcome competitor' in the job market and 'parasite' (*nakhlebnik*). A cluster of negative images frightened migrants and also served the mercenary interests of many employers, who exploited their labour and failed to take any responsibility for their living conditions and health. He argued that the 2000s saw *migrantofobiia* 'reach a heightened level', which included violence against migrants and cruel murders, perpetrated particularly by groups of young nationalists, but 'inspired by quite famous politicians and journalists'. Tishkov considered that these results amounted to 'a moral problem for the whole Russian society'.[79]

Some regional governors, Tishkov lamented, were among the harsh critics of migrants. They dismissed migrants as 'an underground army of strangers', who 'don't want to live according to our laws and customs' and who 'establish their criminal ways'. He regretted that even

---

[76] Tishkov, 'O chem zabyl skazat' kandidat', p. 4.
[77] Tishkov, 'O chem zabyl skazat' kandidat', p. 5.
[78] Tishkov, 'O chem zabyl skazat' kandidat', p. 5.
[79] Tishkov, 'O chem zabyl skazat' kandidat', p. 5.

the former deputy chair of the Duma's committee for relations with the Commonwealth of Independent States, Andrei Savel'ev, saw migration as 'erosion of our ethno-demographic portrait'. He talked about a 'migration deluge' of 'an army of barbarians', 'closed groups', 'aggressive potential', 'aggression of the alien South' and 'aggression against the White person'. Others, too, flagged up 'threats to inter-ethnic balance' which 'provoke inter-ethnic conflicts'.[80] Tishkov contended that this amounted to 'anti-migrant rhetoric' which overall 'serves the pivotal idea of cultural racism'. He suggested that this was accompanied by the notion of unchanging 'cultural codes' and the inevitability of a conflict of cultures and of 'ruinous immigration'. The picture, moreover, was even more complicated due to members of settled diasporas inside Russia who were highly critical of their former states in Central Asia and were also against their incoming compatriots who were looking for work. So further tensions developed within diasporas between 'old' settlers and 'new' arrivals.[81]

Tishkov's thesis is that, overall, *migrantofobiia* had been 'steadily increasing' since the beginning of the century. It was stoked by several myths: migrants steal jobs from the indigenous population; put a brake on wage increases; create 'ethnic enclaves'; put an excessive burden on social services; bring illnesses; are responsible for a significant portion of crime; and do not wish to integrate. Tishkov regrets the growth in Russia of 'a whole anti-migration political philosophy' characterised by 'racist–ethnic arguments and examples', amounting to 'a political philosophy of new racism' and xenophobia. He gloomily reflected that Russia does not have the state competence and strength to tackle this and also lacks the necessary tolerance in civil society.[82]

When, in early 2017, it became clear that over the previous year migrants had been returning in their pre-crisis numbers, even exceeding them, Postavnin spoke out again. He held that, on top of the official MVD figures of legal migrants, there were also tens or hundreds of thousands who 'could simply vanish into "the grey zone"'. He pointed out that their numbers could provoke 'xenophobic conflicts' stemming from a 'clash of cultures'. He recognised that 'our citizens are not prepared to live with people who master the language badly' and who frequently follow 'their own customs'. Postavnin argued that the only way to avert hostilities (*stolknoveniia*) was 'through the integration of new arrivals into

---

[80] Tishkov, 'O chem zabyl skazat' kandidat', p. 5. For Andrei Savel'ev's arguments, see his website at www.savelev.ru.
[81] Tishkov, 'O chem zabyl skazat' kandidat', pp. 5–6.
[82] Tishkov, 'O chem zabyl skazat' kandidat', p. 7.

Russian reality'. But he could see no steps forward happening. Instead, 'those in power are too preoccupied with criticising the West', but not noticing that they themselves could be contributing to similar scenarios. Furthermore, he warned that, as well as hostility from the public towards migrants, Russia might see migrants beginning to protest too, 'insisting on their rights'. These incomers, Postavnin reminded, were largely 'the young' and so long as the government 'keeps them in a semi-forgotten place, arranging total checks with a mass of rights violations', then suddenly they could take to the streets. 'Disturbances', he feared, could happen 'suddenly from two sides'.[83]

Conclusion

Experts' views do feed into the policy process, even if more slowly than their advocates would like and even if they still think that policy does not go far enough. Frank interviews with them on the history of migration policy and their writings show a committed community working hard to analyse and tackle the problems that labour migrants coming to Russia face. The points that they stress are varied, and they each prioritise different aspects of labour problems, simultaneously overlapping in their concerns. Many experts believed that the introduction of *patenty* and tests in Russian, history and law would improve conditions but, once they were in place, a minority began to see some drawbacks. They were all mindful of the importance of linking the foreign labour supply to demand and not exceeding it, yet sensitive to the sometimes misplaced worries of Russian workers about incoming labour 'taking' their jobs. In fact, the jobs were often ones which Russians did not wish to perform. This is much like the fears of British workers in the UK who criticise incoming workers for being too numerous and stealing jobs. These migrant labourers, for example, do vital agricultural work in East Anglia and sweep streets across the country in jobs many Britons do not wish to perform. This is a global issue. Consequently, experts worldwide wish to make clear where labour deficits do indeed exist.

Specialists in Russia are keen to see productive policy solutions and are united in wanting faster legal changes that reduce corruption, end demands for bribes and stop the profiteering middlemen. They want the reluctance of employers to give migrants work contracts to cease and wish to see wages paid that are commensurate with work done. Their shared goal is to help migrants adapt to working in Russia, to

---

[83] Postavnin is quoted by Ekaterina Trifonova in 'Gastarbaitery vozrashchaiutsia v Rossiiu', *Nezavisimaia gazeta*, 10 January 2017.

ease integration and to facilitate their protection. This requires kinder attitudes towards them from the public, employers and some politicians and judges. Experts regret the hostility of nationalist groups and the anti-migrant behaviour of youth groups which constitute thorns in the side of serious efforts to promote harmony and secure livelihoods. There is also a view that Russians need to be made aware of what 'slavery', as they call it, actually is and that slave labour conditions should end. Attempts to address the dangers of *migrantofobiia* are evident in the initiatives of councils and organisations, such as Migratsiia XXI Vek, working at the local level in attempts to tackle the isolation and ghettoisation of migrants. Experts are also aware of the impact of deportations on migrants' lives back home. Lawyers at Grazhdanskoe Sodeistvie are active in exposing what they perceive as the maltreatment of migrants in the legal system and are ready to defend those who suffer hate crimes in society. Their general call is for more integrated local communities and mutual understanding across ethnic groups. Some experts make explicit their optimism about the younger generation of officials, who are less shaped by Soviet norms and practices. How, then, do the attitudes of the public compare?

Previous chapters have contextualised the push and pull factors that encourage Central Asians to seek work in Russia, given selected examples of the vulnerability of migrants to exploitation, explored changes in Russian policy and legislation relevant to the *gastarbaitery* and examined the reactions, views and arguments of experts. Scrutiny now turns to how the Russian population has reacted to labour migrants. My commissioned poll of September 2014 incorporated two questions on attitudes to migrant workers, and fresh focus groups in Moscow and in Yaroslavl tapped into opinions, thought processes and arguments about the impact of Central Asian workers on society and more specifically on these cities. The objectives here are: firstly, to discuss the quantitative results and to look at data from other relevant surveys; secondly, to consider the qualitative data; and, thirdly, to introduce selected quotations from migrants about their positive and negative experiences in Russia.

Opinion Polls

Results from the poll confirmed unhappiness about labour migrants coming Russia. Table 10.1 shows that only 1.7 per cent of respondents felt that migrants from Central Asia should be welcomed. Gender made little difference here with just 1.6 per cent of men and 1.9 per cent of women feeling welcoming. The percentage was not much higher in response to 'Should Russia welcome workers from other parts of the former Soviet Union more than those from Central Asia?' Here, backing came from 5.2 per cent of respondents. So, if ethnicity were the underpinning reason for excluding Central Asians, it appears to apply to others as well, thereby implying that being 'non-Russian' was the disliked category. The even more unfriendly message of 'send migrants back home' was supported by 19.4 per cent in the sample, with men and women sharing this view. Around one-third of those with some university education, but unfinished, advocated this, as did 33.9 percent of those with just

Table 10.1 *'Should Russia . . . ?' (2014)*

September 2014	Total N = 1600 %	Male N = 720 %	Female N = 880 %
1. Welcome workers from Central Asia	1.7	1.6	1.9
2. Welcome workers from other parts of the former Soviet Union more than those from Central Asia	5.2	6.1	4.5
3. Give jobs in Russia to Russians only	48.2	47.6	48.7
4. Give jobs in Russia to Russians first and to migrant workers afterwards if Russians cannot be recruited	14.6	14.8	14.4
5. Send migrants back home	19.4	19.6	19.2
6. Hard to say	1.5	1.0	1.9
7. Don't know	9.4	9.3	9.5
No reply	0	0	0

primary education and a lower 17.7 per cent did so with undergraduate and post-graduate degrees.

Powerful reasons behind this reluctance to welcome Central Asians include concern about Russians losing jobs to incomers and adherence to nationalist sentiments. A strong 47.6 per cent of men and 48.7 per cent of women backed the proposition of 'give jobs in Russia to Russians only'. This was felt most firmly in the 55–64 age bracket, by 54.7 per cent, compared with a lower 42.0 per cent in the 25–34 age band. It seems unlikely that the over-55s felt that they had the most to lose since many jobs performed by migrants were in manual labour and that age group of Russians was less likely to take those on. Also, the official pension age for women in Russia in 2014 was still 55, although many continue to work after that. Such a view is more likely held for a combination of ideological views about Russia first and concern for the job opportunities of younger family members. Attitudes in different regions of Russia varied a little on this question but the sample shows that in all parts of the country more than 45 per cent were keen for jobs to be given only to Russians. This conviction was most strongly held in the Urals region, by 54.9 per cent. Also across the country, looking at population size, towns of around 100,000 inhabitants and more voiced this sentiment most strongly at 57.3 per cent. Within Moscow, however, with a population of more than 10 million, we see a lower figure of 31.2 per cent. Such responses may reflect patterns of job losses in smaller towns such as Ivanovo, and also be explained by greater job opportunities in a vibrant metropolis like Moscow.

Given that in the recent past Russia had experienced job shortages and the government was openly declaring that the economy needed migrant labour, how did respondents view what one might expect them to see as a pragmatic policy of 'give jobs in Russia to Russians first and to migrant workers afterwards if Russians cannot be recruited'? Once again, there was a low level of support for migrant workers on Russian territory. Just 14.6 per cent backed this approach to employment. Even those who had completed higher education showed a low 14.0 per cent support for it, and those with only primary school education gave an even lower 7.4 per cent. Similarly, only 7.3 per cent of respondents with vocational school training favoured this option. The strongest backing, of 17.2 per cent, was from respondents with just secondary school education. Education does not appear always to indicate tolerance or to explain variance. Indecision was expressed by 1.5 per cent who found it 'hard to say' and 9.4 per cent did not know.

These results show similar negative reactions to those found in earlier surveys. Using different questions, a huge study was conducted in 2008 by the Academy of Science's Institute of Sociology and the Centre of Ethnopolitical and Regional Research which reached 11,800 respondents. In this, 15.4 per cent felt that 'our country only needs those migrants who want to stay here for good'. A not much higher 16.0 per cent expressed the country's need for 'those migrants that come here to earn money and do not want to stay here for good'. Just 14.4 per cent considered that 'our country needs both categories of migrants'. A much more hostile 37.5 per cent thought that 'our country does not need either category of migrant'. Those who were unsure and who could not answer made up 16.7 per cent. In reporting these results, Vladimir Mukomel concluded that the bulk of Russians 'don't think that Russia needs migrants'.[1]

The issue of whether or not migrants were needed has also been tapped into by a question that has been asked regularly across the years in polls by the Levada Center. In reactions to 'What policy should the government of Russia adhere to in relation to arrivals [*v otnoshenii priezzhikh*]?', respondents were permitted to choose from three options. Table 10.2 shows overwhelming support for curbing the inflow by backing 'try to limit the inflow of arrivals'. This sentiment has increased over the years from 45 per cent of respondents in 2002, climbing to 54 per cent in 2004, reaching 60 per cent in 2010, peaking at 78 per cent in 2013 and lowering only a little to 76 per cent in 2014. Those opting for a policy of not putting administrative barriers in the path of inflows showed a trend

---

[1] Mukomel', *Politika Integratsiia*, p. 6.

Table 10.2 *'What Policy Should the Government of Russia Adhere to in Relation to Arrivals?'* (2014)

N = 1600	2002	2004	2006	2008	2010	2012	2013	2014
Try to limit the inflow of arrivals	45%	54%	52%	52%	60%	70%	78%	76%
Do not put administrative barriers in the path of the inflow and use for the good of Russia	44	38	39	35	27	20	14	16
Difficult to say	11	7	9	13	13	10	8	8

Source: 'Kakoi politiki dolzhno priderzhivat'sia pravitel'stvo Rossii v otnoshenii priezzhikh?' in *Sbornik 'Obshchestvennoe Mnenie'*, 2014, p. 143, at www.levada.ru.

in the opposite direction. The fall in support for this plummeted from 44 per cent in 2002 down to 16 per cent in 2014. Migrants were steadily less welcome over the years, and so administrative barriers were not contested in this cluster. Smaller percentages above and below 10 per cent found this question difficult to answer.

Table 10.3 *'What Should Be Done About Illegal Workers from the States of the "Near Abroad"?'* (2006 to 2014)

N = 1600	2006	2008	2010	2012	2013	2014
Legalise them and help them to find work and assimilate in Russia	31%	25%	27%	20%	15%	19%
Expel them from Russia	53	54	52	64	73	64
Difficult to answer	16	21	21	15	13	17

Source: 'Chto sleduet delat' s nelegal'nymi immigrantami iz stran "blizhnego zarubezh'ia"?' in *Sbornik 'Obshchestvennoe Mnenie'*, 2014, p. 143, at www.levada.ru.

This very strong preference for limiting the flow of arrivals into Russia was matched in another Levada survey dating back yearly to 2006 in which consistently over half of respondents advocated expulsion from Russia. This question, however, referred specifically to illegal rather than to legal workers who were from the states of the 'near abroad', which included Central Asia. Table 10.3 shows an increase in favour of the expulsion of illegals from 53 per cent in 2006 to 73 per cent in 2013, and falling a little to 64 per cent in 2014. Contrariwise, there was evidence of diminishing support for granting illegals amnesty and helping them into work falling from 31 per cent in 2006, down to 19 per cent in 2014. Quite significant percentages in all years, however, ranging from 13 to 21 per cent found

Table 10.4 'Which Feelings Do You Experience in Relation to Arrivals from the North Caucasus, Central Asia and Other Southern Countries Living in Your Town or District?' (2005 to 2014)

N = 1600	2005	2007	2008	2010	2011	2012	2013	2014
Respect	2%	3%	4%	5%	1%	3%	3%	4%
Liking for	3	3	4	4	4	5	3	6
Irritation	20	19	14	14	15	21	25	20
Hostility	21	23	14	15	20	21	30	21
Fear	2	3	2	6	3	3	6	7
No special feelings	50	52	61	57	57	46	39	42
Difficult to answer	2	2	2	4	1	3	2	4

Source: 'Kakie chuvstva Vy lichno ispytyvaete po otnosheniiu k priezzhim s Severnogo Kavkaza, iz Srednei Asii i drugikh iuzhnykh stran, prozhivaioushchim v Vashem gorode, raione?' in Sbornik 'Obshchstvennoe Mnenie', 2014, p. 143, at www.levada.ru.

this question hard to answer, perhaps indicating awareness of the complexities involved. The simplistic dualism of the clear-cut choice between either 'expel' or 'assimilate' overlooked many nuances. The first option had packed rather a lot into a large bundle of legalise, give work and assimilate. Respondents might have supported one of these, but not necessarily be strongly in favour of all three. Nonetheless, in presenting sharply contrasting options, it enabled easy distinction regarding upon which side of the fence respondents sat.

Another relevant survey question regularly posed by the Levada Center has traced emotions about arrivals from the North Caucasus, Central Asia and other countries to the south, clumped together. Respondents were asked to categorise which emotion they would feel in response to these arrivals if they were living in the respondent's town or district. The options before them ranged from 'respect' to 'fear' along a continuum from positive emotions to negative ones. These results have altered less over time than the above polls on policy preferences and what to do about illegal migrants. Table 10.4 shows a narrow fluctuating band from a low of 14 per cent to a high of 30 per cent experiencing hostility or enmity (nepriazn') towards these groups. A band shifting between 14 per cent and 25 per cent felt irritation or annoyance (razdrazhenie). Taking these negative emotions together, we see 41 per cent in both 2005 and 2014 opting for these responses. Thus, more than one-third of respondents exhibited some sort of anger. 'Fear' was selected by 2 per cent in 2005 and 7 per cent in 2014, but never higher than by the latter figure in intervening years. The percentages admitting to 'respect' for the incomers were low, ranging between 1 and 5 per cent and similarly a liking for arrivals never exceeded 6 per cent. What stands out, above all, is that those respondents who picked 'no special feelings' were in the majority cluster. There was a slight fall in this response down from 50 per cent in 2005 to 42 per cent in 2014, but also with highs of 61 per cent in 2008 and 57 per cent in 2010 and 2011. These respondents claimed to feel none of the animosity recorded by the others. One cannot know if this should be interpreted as tolerance, indifference or reluctance publicly to show any hostile feelings that might indeed be held. If taken at face value, it suggests a lack of aggression towards the incoming labour migrants.[2] The overall picture is thus one of variegated and shifting responses within the Russian social fabric along a continuum.

Evidence also indicates that, among all the nationalities coming into Russia for work, it is those from the Caucasus and Central Asia that respondents would most like to see restricted in number. A Levada poll designed to tap into xenophobia posed the question, 'Should people of the following nationalities living on Russian territory be restricted?' Eight groups were then listed in this way: Vietnamese, Jews,[3] those from the Caucasus, Chinese, 'arrivals from the former Central Asian republics of the USSR', Ukrainians, gypsies and 'all nationalities, except Russians'. The alternative 'no' option was for those not believing that restrictions should be placed on any nationality. In July 2014, 21 per cent were opposed to restrictions on grounds of nationality, and 10 per cent found it a difficult question to answer. Those, however, in favour of curbs most strongly backed restricting those from the Caucasus and Central Asia. Thirty-eight per cent wanted to limit the former and 33 per cent advocated restricting the latter. In rank order after these top choices were supporters of limiting the Chinese (29 per cent), Vietnamese (27 per cent), gypsies (23 per cent) and all non-Russians (14 per cent); in joint seventh place were Jews and Ukrainians (8 per cent).[4]

Across these polls which tap into different dimensions of attitudes towards arrivals there is overwhelming evidence of anxiety and some hostility in the social fabric. Data indicate quite strong support for restrictions to be placed upon entry, and there is also backing for expulsions. Those in favour of granting amnesty to the illegal migrants or of extending a

---

[2] For wider discussion of public attitudes towards migrants, see Irina Popova and Valentina Osipova, 'Otnoshenie prinimaiushchei storony k migrantam', *Vestnik obshchestvennogo mneniia. Dannye. Analiz. Diskussii*, 1 (114), January–March 2013, pp. 81–88.

[3] 'Jew' in Soviet times was officially deemed to be both a religion and a nationality, and so could be entered on passports as the bearer's nationality. Many preferred to put 'Russian', feeling that was safer.

[4] 'Sleduet li ogranichit' prozhivanie na territorii Rossii liudei sleduiushchikh natsional'-nostei?', in *Sbornik "Obshchestvennoe Mnenie"*, 2014, p. 141, at www.levada.ru.

Table 10.5 *'Why, in Your Opinion, Do Men from Central Asia and Other Regions of the Former Soviet Union Find Themselves in Russia in Slave Labour in Manual Work?' (2014)*

September 2014	Total N = 1600 %	Male N = 720 %	Female N = 880 %
1. Themselves to blame	19.1	19.8	18.5
2. Duped by criminal gangs	19.1	19.0	19.1
3. Looking for work in Russia because of lack of jobs	49.5	50.6	48.5
4. Hoping to make more money in Russia	46.2	47.4	45.2
5. A manifestation of the breakdown in social order and morality	9.3	8.2	10.3
6. Mistreated because of their nationality	8.7	7.5	9.6
7. Other	2.2	1.3	2.9
8. Don't know	3.3	2.9	3.7
No reply	0	0	0

warm-hearted welcome to job seekers from elsewhere are in the minority. There is also a notional hierarchy of who is most desirable on Russian soil and who would be best excluded. Had Belarusans been included on the list, one would have expected them, as fellow Slavs, to be among the most welcome ones.

Also within this flow of incomers are those who end up in forced labour on Russian territory. Who, or what, do respondents see as responsible for this outcome? Given the centrality of the question *'kto vinovat?'* or 'who is to blame?' in Russian political culture, the options listed in Table 10.5 from my poll in 2014 attempted to tap into who or what was perceived to be at fault.[5] Responses showed that overall 19.1 per cent blamed the male migrants themselves for getting into this predicament, a view subscribed to by 19.8 per cent of the men in the sample and 18.5 per cent of the women, once more showing little difference in opinion according to gender. Of note, however, from a comparative standpoint, is that overall a higher 36.7 per cent in 2014 and 40.8 per cent in 2007 had blamed the women and girls who were trafficked out.

This prompts the question of why respondents perceived women as more blameworthy than men. How can this different approach *to* gender – indeed *by* both genders – best be explained? Is it evidence of the double standard? Might greater blame be accorded to trafficked

[5] For earlier discussion of the place of blame in Russian political culture, refer to Chapter 4.

women due to the prevalence of the stereotype of 'silly, naïve girls'? Or is it because the women were deemed either to be 'prostitutes anyway' or because prostitution itself is seen as unacceptable work and morally shameful? One could hypothesise that, by contrast, men coming for employment in manual labour may be perceived as altogether more acceptable, even if both types of work might end up in forced labour.

Another question is whether there is a tendency to forgive men more readily than women. The infantilisation of men is one cultural thread within the fabric of Russian society in which wives are deemed to be educators of their otherwise errant men who are in need of guidance and correction. Women have for a long time been socially constructed as the responsible ones, as epitomised in the *obshchestvennitsa*, or wife-activist of the 1930s, and men as rather more helpless and in need of her direction.[6] Following on from this pattern, women are therefore not expected to make moral mistakes, and men are characterised as more likely to do so, and consequently women deserve proportionally more blame when they do get it wrong and fall off their perfect pedestal of the 'good woman'.[7] Several hypotheses could be applied here and the disparity in respondents' assessments could be due to a combination of these factors. The results, however, could also be influenced by the terms used in the polls. The wording of the two questions in Russian was not identical, and different concepts were put to respondents, which may have affected responses. The question about men refers to those 'who find themselves in slave labour', or *'zaniaty v Rossii "rabskim" trudom'*. There is no use of the term *'rabstvo'* in the question about women and girls who get caught in prostitution abroad. So, in addition to the factors suggested above, the explicit mention of 'slave labour' may have prompted greater sympathy and correspondingly accorded less culpability.

Moving away from personal blame, there was recognition of economic need in Central Asian states. Around half of respondents saw that a lack of jobs drove workers northwards. Similarly, respondents understood that remuneration was higher in Russia. Overall, 46.2 per cent of the sample believed that migrants wished to earn more money in Russia. Despite the strong preferences for migrants not to come to Russia at all, and notwithstanding the fact that the media carried stories of their maltreatment, only very low numbers thought that migrants might be 'mistreated

---

[6] Mary Buckley, 'The untold story of *obshchestvennitsa* in the 1930s', *Europe-Asia Studies*, Vol. 48, No. 4, July 1996, pp. 559–576; and Buckley, 'The Soviet "wife-activist" down on the farm', *Social History*, Vol. 26, No. 3, October 2001, pp. 282–298.

[7] For discussion of the 'terrible perfection' of women in Russian literature, see Barbara Heldt, *Terrible Perfection: Women and Russian Literature* (Bloomington: Indiana University Press, 1987).

because of their nationality'. Just 7.5 per cent of men and 9.6 per cent of women claimed that this was the case. This sits oddly alongside other results which indicated anti-foreign sentiments. Cognitive dissonance is often evident in thought patterns, as very early American research into public opinion showed.[8]

There was also a contrast in perceptions regarding the role of criminal gangs behind human trafficking out of Russia and its role in bringing in Central Asian labourers. Whereas 40.2 per cent of respondents in 2014 considered that gangs were responsible for the fate of women sold into the sex industry abroad, a lower 19.1 per cent said that they were to blame for the forced labour situations of Central Asian males. This, however, has some foundation. Since citizens of Uzbekistan, Kyrgyzstan, Tajikistan and Kazakhstan have visa-free entry into the Russian Federation, as do those from Ukraine, Armenia, Azerbaijan, Moldova, Abkhazia and South Ossetia, they can enter freely.[9] They may, nonetheless, become trapped in forced labour once there, and some also are indeed trafficked in, but the picture is generally a different mosaic from women being trafficked out, despite common elements. There are also differences, but smaller ones, in according blame for forced labour to 'the breakdown in social order and morality'. Whereas 21.5 per cent in 2014 saw this as one factor in the trafficking of girls and women into the sex trade, a lower 8.2 per cent of men and 10.3 per cent of women included it as relevant to the Central Asian migrants. Yet again this may be due to the nature of the work under discussion and reflect a moral disapproval of the sex trade itself.

Reactions in Focus Groups

Interactions in the two focus groups held in September 2014 illustrate a tapestry of thoughts, beliefs and arguments that developed in different cities. In both, participants engaged in lively discussions, and a minority made emotionally heated outbursts.

Moscow, 2014

In the group in Moscow there was a great deal of preoccupation with the numbers arriving from Central Asia. A 37-year-old polyclinic employee sighed 'there are so many of them. Dreadfully many.' She claimed that when they come into the polyclinic 'they are impudent, they don't want

---

[8] A classic in the field is Robert E. Lane, *Political Ideology: Why the American Common Man Believes What He Does* (New York: Free Press, 1962).

[9] Citizens of Belarus can enter Russia visa-free for an unlimited period.

an insurance policy and they make demands'. There followed a flurry of points from participants, some thinking that the migrants came voluntarily to Russia, others suggesting that they were kidnapped or forced. A technical worker of 29 was convinced that they arrived in Moscow oblast willingly. When asked if he thought that once there they were given what they had been promised, he responded 'that, no'. Immediate disagreement came from a 51-year-old who worked in a transport technical centre. He insisted that 'they receive quite a lot. I have a friend in business and I know that the Uzbeks work and they receive free housing.' A 28-year-old female manager jumped in and said, 'I heard stories too that they deceive them and don't pay them.' Others in the group concurred. She went on, 'I also heard, an acquaintance told me, that they even hold them in slavery, take away their documents, don't pay them.' These Muscovites were generally aware of the exploitation that migrants might face.

An opposing view was also voiced by a 55-year-old beautician. She insisted 'they came willingly, agreed to this life. They send the money back to their relatives. Furthermore, thanks to this money, they are rich when they return home. It is paradoxical, but it's a fact. They live ten or twelve in a one-room flat here in terrible conditions.' The man from the technical transport centre interjected that 'it's fairy tales that they live in twelves'. He elaborated that 'very many do not live badly and they rent flats in families'. Quite how well migrants lived in Russia turned out to be a contested issue. Taking the Moscow group's responses together, the variegated picture generated was that some migrants may do well and others might be badly exploited.

The female manager then posed a challenging question for the critics of labour migrants. She began with: 'perhaps this is a rhetorical question'. She announced that she did not understand 'why we want to be accepted abroad, but we do not want to accept anyone' here in Russia. She dismissed it as some sort of 'raving'. She pointed out starkly that, 'we don't like new arrivals, we are categorically against them all. But at the beginning of our discussion we debated how we leave for a better life, how we as young specialists will earn money there. But they are not waiting for us there.'

Participants immediately sidestepped this valid point, and the man from the transport technical centre digressed with, 'I simply heard a conversation how one went up to someone and said: "Soon we will live in your homes."' He warned that 'extremism is already blossoming amongst them, extremism'. The beautician added 'we will pay for that'. To this fear of extremism was added the fear of crime. The transport technician, still in his stride, went on 'look, recently a Tajik shoved me with his arm.

I fell and he gripped a bag.' Another quickly agreed with, 'they also steal from me in that way'.

The beautician then nipped the men's diversion in the bud and drew the group back to the female manager's key point about the double standard of Russians wanting to be accepted abroad yet being reluctant to welcome incomers to Russia. She insisted that the two were actually not comparable. She believed that Russians leaving for the West in the years of perestroika was a completely 'different question'. She acknowledged that 'there was a time' when this had happened but what was distinct about it was that in the West 'there are very rich countries and cultured countries. They do not allow poverty and homelessness – that's not there.' The beautician seemed to adhere to the myth of a golden life in the West, where there were no problems at all, which indeed had enjoyed popular coinage during the years of perestroika under Gorbachev and also into the 1990s.[10] The beautician ultimately expressed agreement with others that Central Asians were not welcome. Throughout this discussion the contributions from the man from the transport centre very much echoed the descriptions of *migrantofobiia* outlined earlier by Valerii Tishkov. Even when the moderator intervened and put it to them that Central Asians might be paid 'just *groshi*',[11] which would not be enough to feed their families, the man went on with 'they even have their own businesses. Tajiks are already well-off', and dismissed the suggestion that they were poor as 'far-fetched'. He regularly butted in with comments such as 'I want Russians to be in Moscow.' By now the female manager's comparative point was totally ignored.

When asked who should work in Russia's factories, most in the group favoured Russian workers from the regions. When asked whether Muscovites or Central Asians should be employed in them, a chorus responded against Central Asians. When asked who should work on building sites, even the most seemingly liberal in the group, the female manager, immediately responded 'Muscovites' and added 'with decent pay'. When asked who should be cleaning up rubbish on the streets of Moscow, the chorus repeated 'also Muscovites', with the polyclinic worker adding 'well, just as it always was – ours, of course'. They felt the same about who should work on landfill sites. '*Nashi*' or 'ours' were the favourites for all jobs as distinct from those who were '*chuzhie*', literally 'alien' or 'foreign'. There was no advocacy here of diversity.

---

[10] Buckley, *Redefining*, pp. 250–253. By 1990, anxieties about 'crisis' in the final years of the USSR were nurtured by myths of the 'great Soviet past' and the 'glorious Western present'.

[11] This refers to the old half-kopeck coin and connotes 'hardly anything'.

When confronted with the question of why some bosses preferred to hire Tajik labour over Russian workers, a flurry of evasive answers was forthcoming which included: 'of course, I know why', 'so do I', 'it is not connected to the pay' and 'there are many reasons'. At first, no one seemed able to come out with the fact that often taxes were not paid or that there were payment differentials. A 35-year-old manager with responsibility for corporate clients in a telecommunications company finally said, 'well, simply everyone understands, their labour is cheaper'. A young technical worker of 29 viewed this issue in a more nuanced way. He volunteered that for employers 'there are two factors – prestige and gain'. There was some prestige for a boss who hired Russians, 'but profit' if his workers came from Central Asia.

When pressed about what they would do if they learnt that someone was in captivity against their will, the female manager responded that she would sympathise with that person. As already quoted in Chapter 5, a young female student who had not yet said much suddenly declared, 'I think it is slave holding' (rabovladenie). Her contribution was direct. Its punch was diminished with more light-hearted observations that followed. One remarked 'it's bad luck', and another concurred, 'that is closer to the truth'. A certain flippant heartlessness underpinned some of the Muscovites' responses, true to black humour and a seemingly complacent acceptance of unfree labour. No one advocated action against it.

When probed further as to whether there was a difference between a Russian woman falling into slavery in an Eastern country and a Tajik woman being sold into slavery to work in Russia, the telecommunications manager stressed 'yes'. When asked how this could be so, a 59-year-old unemployed man volunteered 'cultural differences'. Bringing back a more sensible perspective, the female manager was adamant that 'there is no difference. What is key is slavery. That is the key word.' The 51-year-old transport technician simply dismissed this observation and stressed that for him there was a difference. The fullest explanation he could muster was that, 'they have a different mentality. And above all, I am interested in my country, my people. I am an egoist in this respect.' The polyclinic worker respected him for this reply and commented approvingly: 'that is honest'. Evidently, the transport technician did not worry about workers in slave labour unless they were Russians.

Switching direction to look at whether Russia should help Slavs like themselves, thousands of whom who were arriving as refugees from hostilities in eastern Ukraine, the female manager immediately said 'yes' and others agreed. The transport technician, however, added that if they were from western Ukraine, then no, they should not receive support. That should be restricted to those from eastern Ukraine. He added that people from 'western regions are surging here in order to get Russian citizenship'. Others agreed that this was happening 'on the quiet'. Furthermore, the transport technician believed that, once in Russia, Ukrainians from the west left again to go and do battle against the fighters in eastern Ukraine. He claimed that they first worked in Russian factories to earn money which they then sent to the war machine, and 'then they go away to fight against us'. When pressed for details of how they could have done this already, he insisted 'yes, they have succeeded, they came here before. Look there is a whole region of them even – Mytishchinskii district.'

When the moderator corrected him with 'but I am talking about refugees', the polyclinic employee chipped in with 'but they all come under that label'. The transport technician then changed his tune: 'refugees are blessed, we must help them. Unquestionably.' The moderator pressed further by asking if they should pay Ukrainian refugees once they were in work the same as migrants from Central Asia or the same as Ukrainian workers who had already been in Russia for some time. The telecommunications manager quickly said, 'while they do not have citizenship, let's pay them less'. When asked if they should be paid the same as Russians, he responded decisively with 'less'. Another added 'I think less.' The younger technical worker reacted with, 'why, if they work well?' He was then pressed to say how much they should be paid, and he calmly replied, 'in accordance with the work contract'. He saw a need for legality and equal pay for equal work. The transport technical worker, however, now less excitable, concluded that 'the market will decide'. It is telling that this man, who was so exercised about Central Asians and Ukrainians from the west of Ukraine who were in Russia, was now quite relaxed about Slavic brothers from the east of Ukraine. It was the telecommunications manager now who was worked up. He repeated yet again: 'while they do not have citizenship, let them receive less because in these jobs which we are sending them to, let's say giving them, a Muscovite could be working or a Russian. He must receive less.'

The moderator had to remind them that Russia was suffering from labour shortages and so needed workers from elsewhere. He asked them if they were in favour of Ukrainians remaining in Russia to fill this deficit rather than returning to Ukraine when everything quietened down there. The transport technician was straight back in with, 'I think they should stay, otherwise those from Central Asian republics will fill the deficit.' Others replied with 'I agree', including the female manager. The beautician, however, found this hard to answer, and the young technical worker shrugged, 'it's all the same to me'. The unemployed man who said very little throughout, and always concisely, came in pensively and regretfully with 'soon Moscow will not be Russian, not Slavic'.

When pressed to indicate where the problem of slave labour ranked for them as a priority in comparison with other problems such as inflation, the telecommunications manager said it was 'low', and the younger of the two technicians volunteered that 'so far it has not affected me'. The older transport technical worker felt that 'physical slavery is distant for me', and even the female manager decided it was for her too, perhaps swayed by the group dynamic. Once more the unemployed man was thoughtful and observed that 'this problem has been shelved'. The polyclinic worker added that, 'it is distant from me too, thank God'. No one seemed to consider that serious action against slavery was needed. It did not directly touch their lives, nor move them to want to act on behalf of others. At best, one woman had felt 'sympathy', and a younger one had condemned it as 'slave holding'.

Yaroslavl, 2014

Were citizens of the smaller city of Yaroslavl more public-minded and worried about forced labour in their land, just as those in Vladimir had been troubled about the girls and women trafficked out of Russia into prostitution? When asked if many workers from outside Russia came to Yaroslavl, the response was similar to that in Moscow. A group chorus replied 'many' and 'there are lots on building sites'. Asked if they knew any statistics, a bodyguard of 56 who described himself as 'temporarily unemployed' retorted, 'we ought to count them. How many are registered, perhaps just 20 per cent?' A female post-office worker of 47 said, 'if we take Tajiks, they are already everywhere on every street corner'. A male builder of 45 added, 'I was working in construction. A twelve-storey building burnt down and a hundred were working on it. Of those, probably 80 per cent were foreign.' When the moderator asked if others should have worked there instead, the reply came back: 'Russians'. A 27-year-old who said he was a technician but was aspiring to be an entrepreneur affirmed, 'Russians – in order to increase the value' and 'then it would be done well. I know how to do that and know how these *gastarbaitery* work. Afterwards you have to re-do it and the money has already been spent.' The builder thought the same. He argued 'it means hire a specialist. There are few good specialists there because I have seen them work badly.' The general view was that Central Asians and other Asians including Vietnamese and Chinese were hired because they were available, did poorer work and so could be paid less.

When asked if Russia could do without migrant workers, group members chorused 'of course', and 'we have a lot of people who are unemployed'. Later in the discussion the builder went on to say that Russians and locals in

Yaroslavl were losing work places to Central Asians. Moreover, 'one comes and behind him follow along another hundred'. The post-office worker added 'they work here and buy a house at home, so it's very good for them here'. The builder believed that 'they work for a month in Moscow, then they relax the whole year at home'. As in Moscow, the group held onto several stereotypes and images of migrant life. No one said that they knew any Central Asians personally, although it was likely that the builder had experience of them connected to his work.

When asked about the number of Ukrainian refugees arriving in Russia, again a chorus echoed 'many'. A 20-year-old female law student thought that this was not good for Russia because 'we are losing free education and all the places are for them'. A 30-year-old female medical worker was also exercised because, as she saw it, everyone was subsidising the Ukrainians. The law student reverted to her theme: 'the schools are full, overcrowded and again there will be problems with kindergarten'. A 59-year-old female pensioner who used to work as a typist reflected, 'if they send the refugees where labour is needed, in agriculture', that would be 'a positive move', but she opposed giving them 'our places' in education. Then on a different tack she added, 'I have already repeatedly heard that they don't want to work in the jobs we offer them.' The medical worker then challenged what the retired woman was saying by pointing out that qualified people would not want to do just anything: 'if they ran a department there, they won't want to be a cleaner here'. The pensioner declared, 'not everyone there was a head bookkeeper, right? No one wants them to be shot at.' The post-office worker joined in with, 'they come here and say "we won't work. What for?" They are subsidised and get help.' The builder added that support for them for 'three to four months won't be enough'. The welcome for Ukrainian refugees was becoming tepid, as Dmitrii Titov had observed in Rostov oblast.

When it came to equal pay for equal work for specialists, however, opinions immediately changed. The factory worker thought that, if there were job vacancies, then everyone taken on should be paid 'the same'. Moreover, 'if the person is responsible, even more than a local, why not pay him more?' When pressed for clarification, he now held that an outsider could be paid more than a local if he worked to a higher standard. The unemployed man contributed that, 'we have definite pay rates in each factory. Everyone according to the rate.' When pressed to see if he believed that it therefore did not matter where the worker came from, he affirmed: 'no, there is a pay rate for the category, isn't there?' Another repeated with conviction that 'he gets according to the rate'. The moderator made the task even more explicit by asking if it mattered if the worker was Ukrainian, Russian, a Tajik or a Tatar. A chorus of voices came back with 'no difference'. When then asked if a female nursing sister should be paid according to her origin, another chorus came back in favour of equal pay irrespective of country of origin. This group was less discriminatory than the one in Moscow when it came to equal pay for equal work for everyone.

A lively debate followed. The group was asked to consider a hypothetical situation in which a farmer in Tambov oblast every year had apples to be picked. Around 250 migrants from Uzbekistan and Tajikistan usually came to help bring in the harvest. The farmer said he would have preferred to give work to Russians but 'we cannot work with Russians'. He had hired them three times from his own region and the neighbouring one. The difference was that 'Muslims do not drink' and 'they come to earn money, they work, they don't need weekends'. The group was asked to evaluate this situation. The unemployed man observed that the Koran forbade alcohol. The retired woman, however, took serious objection to this scenario and did not like the idea that Russians were now ruled out by the farmer. Firstly, she insisted that the farmer did not really want to find Russians. Secondly, she underlined that other people drank too; and, thirdly, she believed that he ought to find those Russians who could work. Now shouting, she advocated that students could be hired because 'they want money, they won't drink'. The female medical worker, in response, took the pensioner on and quietly said that 'from the point of view of business, he did the right thing. Why should he have these problems?' He had 'tried three times' with Russians. She went on that 'the most important for him is to earn money'. The retiree exploded with 'there are also those who want to work who were not there. It means, he should find them.' In her view, Russian workers should be actively sought until found.

Calmly, the unemployed man came in with 'no, look. He tried but he lost the money he had paid out, the harvest was spoilt, so he decided not to experiment again.' Not persuaded, the woman again blurted, 'the discussion is precisely about Russians' and 'there is no need to say Russians drink'. At this point a 27-year-old technical worker gave his take on the matter. He acknowledged the farmer's dilemma. If he hired those who drank, then he was going nowhere. He then posed a question: 'what was good in this situation for a Russian? If he sees that there are *gastarbaitery* working again and that some of them are not simply *gastarbaitery* but those who are already studying in universities, doing sport, do not smoke, do not drink – they provide a proper example.' He then added that statistics showed that Russians over the past four years were drinking less and that Germans and North Americans drank a lot too. The moderator, however, came back to him to clarify what exactly he was trying to say. The technician said 'there is nothing good or bad in it. It's a process.' Perhaps inevitably, the retiree repeated her dislike of this scenario.

When discussion came to focus on men in forced labour, the moderator asked if there was any slavery in Yaroslavl. The unemployed man said: 'in Yaroslavl it's flourishing . . . mainly new arrivals, largely from Uzbekistan'. Now a shy 21-year-old who worked in the tourist industry added, 'workers come from different countries, they take their passport away and make them work'. The post-office worker picked up the thread and narrated the story covered in Chapter 5 about the disappearance of an acquaintance's husband and how her family had joined in the search for him. She believed that there were many cases like his, affecting both men and women, which might end in what she named as 'slavery'. The retired woman later returned to incoming migrants, insisting that 'in the best event, they deport them when they find them. But again, we know this from the television.' In most that she said, the retiree showed no sympathy for Central Asians whatever their predicament. When the moderator asked how they could best be helped if their passport had been taken away and money kept from them, she reaffirmed that it would be good to deport them 'and never see them again'.

Others, however, were less hard-hearted. Faced with the exercise of having to react to a situation in which they learnt from a journalist that fifteen Tajiks on a local construction site had had their passports taken away, were unpaid and were being 'held like cattle', the builder immediately came in with 'inform the police' and 'you mustn't abandon people. After all, they are people.' When the retired woman was called upon, she recommended telling 'the competent organs, but nothing more'. The young man in tourism volunteered the option of taking photographs or making a recording to gather evidence. When given the additional task of thinking about what to do if they learnt of a railway station where Russians were being kidnapped, the young law student said she would 'naturally go to the police and write a statement'. The young aspiring entrepreneur, however, warned that 'I think that they might often be the middlemen, or so I have heard.' The builder added: 'I have heard that there are these *oborotni v pogonakh*. For money, they agree to anything.' Here he was referring to corrupt police who work with criminals or who take bribes. The Russian phrase had earned widespread coinage after a Soviet television series about gangsters who wore police uniforms. Thereafter it was used to refer to disreputable law enforcers.[12] No one in the group followed up on this line of argument which terminated as fast as it had entered the discussion.

---

[12] The series was popular and entitled *Rozhdennaia revoliutsiei*. It was in its eighth episode, called 'Oborotni', that gangsters wore police uniforms.

When pressed to explain the existence of slave labour conditions in Russia, the medical worker looked to economics and replied: 'because the economic situation in these countries is worse for them now, perhaps just as it correspondingly was for us going to Europe before, when it was less stable. So, they all drift here and Russia has become a soil for slavery.' The builder also took an economic line with, 'the higher the unemployment, the more people fall into it. When it is an unstable time, everyone goes away somewhere to work to different regions and towns. In my view, it is possible that it will get worse.' The young worker in tourism added that the incomers had permission to work but the employers 'deceive' them and, as a consequence, 'they have nothing'.

When asked to characterise what it meant to be driven away somewhere in a lorry and have a passport and telephone taken away, group members declared it was 'kidnap', 'infringement of human rights' and 'displacement'. The group, struggled, however to answer coherently whether they would feel more sympathy or pity for a Russian in forced labour in forestry or for a Central Asian who was trapped in slavery in construction. The post-office worker laughed, immediately favouring 'Russian men'. The construction worker did not grasp the question and launched into a defence of migrant labourers with 'I, for example, have been in construction for fifteen or sixteen years. I am not sorry that they are working – let them work. They already earn more than we do, more than Russians. They have their brigades, they work well.' He said this despite the earlier remarks on substandard work. The moderator had to point out that the builder had lost the thread and that he was asking not about those who were doing well but about those having a hard time 'in slavery', be they Central Asian or Russian. Again, he asked if their reaction to slavery was the same, irrespective of nationality.

Following this new thread, the post-officer worker revised her earlier remark and declared similar regret for all the slave workers. The law student was uneasy with this and volunteered: 'I feel sorry for the Russians. As far as slaves from other countries go – I always see them there, on construction sites.' The moderator yet again explained the question as the law student's answer seemed to misunderstand or sidestep it. She came back with 'you can say it's like their calling. They especially come here, they work, they know that they will take their passports.' She appeared to suggest that the Central Asians knew that forced labour might await them, whereas Russians did not expect it. Yet she was unable explicitly to say so. At this point the post-office worker defended the Central Asians even more strongly: 'No, it is one thing when they work according to their own initiative and when they earn well, but another affair in slavery when they don't feed them.' The group discussion developed momentum as the participants bounced thoughts off each other, some off-beam from the question posed, some more focussed. Finally, the law student reaffirmed that for her the nationality was important when it came to feeling pity for someone.

The technical worker tried to put it differently by making a connection between feeling pity for those in forced labour who were of 'native blood' (*rodnaia krov'*) as opposed to those who were not, such as the Chinese, as though this distinction was safer and somehow conceptually more acceptable. He began his pitch with 'let's take China. China has overpopulation, everyone knows this.' He believed that slavery was widespread there and that the Chinese were also herded into slavery in Russia and 'simply there are more of them here, that's all'. So, he felt pity for Russians in slavery due to common blood. This position, however, was based on a conclusion that was a non-sequitur. The moderator pressed him to be more explicit. The best he could volunteer was: 'I have Russians in mind.'

The unemployed man at this point was unable to contribute and could say only, 'I don't know what to say. I am struggling.' The moderator made a rare value judgment of 'it's good that you are struggling'. In self-defence, the man went on: 'because look, on every construction site, in every enterprise', it is as though 'we are done for' and that 'we don't live in Russia, but, let's admit it, Uzbekistan, Vietnam'. He vented frustration and dismay 'now there are very many Vietnamese, seemingly wishing to live in Russia, earn money. Literally recently, I saw so many of them, busloads and busloads, all well-dressed.' Once more, the moderator intervened, underlining that the topic was not about the well-dressed. The unemployed man still skirted the issue by protesting first that they did not really know if the foreigners arrived willingly or not and, secondly, that 'I don't know what to say.' The frustration of participants about incomers yet again distracted them from answering directly the questions put to them as they digressed back to the number of foreigners in Russia, be they Central Asians, Chinese or Vietnamese. The young lawyer, the unemployed man and the technical worker aspiring to be an entrepreneur generated a picture of discomfort at the thought of any harm to Russians. By contrast, the others felt that no one in forced labour should be ignored and abandoned. The group was divided on this issue.

Migrants' Views on Attitudes Towards Them in Russia

My research funding did not stretch to include a project interviewing migrants but evidence is available from journalists and anthropologists who have done so. In 2013, *Moskovskie novosti* ran an article based on conversations with workers from Uzbekistan, Tajikistan and Kyrgyzstan.

Journalist Andrei Vyrkovskii did not present these labour migrants with formal questions but asked them to offer 'monologues' of their experiences of how they had been received by Russians. Acknowledging the limitations of his methodology, Vrykovskii maintained that nonetheless he had gathered illustrative portraits of Central Asian migrants' lives through both negative and positive stories.[13]

One critical migrant expressed the feeling that while Belarusans, Ukrainians and Moldovans were perceived in Russia as 'second' category people after Russians as 'first', Uzbeks and Tajiks were of a lower 'third' grouping. He had found 'little warmth' in the locals who gave him 'sullen glances'. He experienced 'rudeness' in his first encounters and had gained the impression that citizens hated each other. He reflected that 'perhaps it's the weather'. A completely different view, however, was presented by another who told how his boss treated him like one of the family. When the *gastarbaiter*'s mother had died, the boss paid for his return air ticket, gave money for the funeral and drove him to the airport. This work situation was appreciated as a very positive one. It contrasted with the negative experience of the first man who had once worked for ten days with someone he described as a 'rich man'. He and other migrant workers were told by this boss to throw away the cups from which they had drunk. He asked, 'are we worse than dogs?' He felt that, even if they had been lepers, as guests they should have been respected.[14]

A third thought that all arrivals were first viewed 'with suspicion' and that 'you must earn trust'. He described how in Central Asia it was the opposite and that any new guest had to be accorded 'due respect'. However, he believed that, once trust develops in Russia, relations alter 'sharply' for the better. He said that he greeted everyone around him and that he had helped them all. He felt that the surrounding atmosphere was good and he felt comfortable wearing his *tiubeteika*, or embroidered cap. He added 'I have the keys of several homes. Everyone treats me with respect and they do not think me a person of a lower sort, which I did struggle with when I worked in Moscow.' He thought most Russians were 'soft by nature and sentimental', but that Muscovites were less friendly. Yet another migrant drew a distinction between those who were real Muscovites, born there, and those Russians who had arrived in the capital. He had a 'high' opinion of the former, but not the latter. One thought that 80 per cent of people in Moscow were 'rude' but also recognised that

[13] Andrei Vyrkovskii, 'Migranty i mestnye: svoi sredi svoikh, chuzhoi sredi chuzhikh', *Moskovskie novosti*, 18 April 2013.
[14] Vyrkovskii, 'Migranty i mestnye'.

lots were not Muscovites and thought that this was anyway characteristic of metropolitan capitals.[15]

Another migrant reflected how awful it could be to fall ill in Moscow. He described how at registration in hospital they might say 'another slit-eyed person'. He asked, 'how much evil can there be?' He added, nonetheless, that he fully understood how those arriving in Moscow may not be 'the best representatives of our people. You could say they are the lowest and hopeless cases. Probably from them they judge all the Uzbeks, Tajiks and Kyrgyz.' He regretted, however, that when migrants spoke in their own language they provoked 'dissatisfaction and irritation' among the locals. Morever, 'they don't even hide their hostility'. Another admitted that he did not like the behaviour of some young Russians. He thought that, 'when we walk around the town, the young think it is their duty to pick on migrants and to say bad things'. He thought they knew that migrants would not try to rebuff them and so they would spit at them and cry, 'Look, a dark skin.' He described how such an incident against one of his acquaintances was caused even by a minor. Another view was that Russians did not have respect for the elderly.[16] Reporting in *Moskovskie novosti* thus conveyed different perceptions of prejudice faced by migrants, their feelings about them and also what they saw as positive about working in Russia.

Looking specifically at a small group of just six Uzbeks who were unregistered migrants in Volgograd working with their hands to demolish old buildings for 300 roubles a day (then $10), a report by Khristina Narizhnaya quoted their fears about going out in daylight. They told her that 'they feared that on the streets their dark skin could attract police attention and requests for identification and residency documents which they did not have'. In order to relax, one said that they felt able to go out only at night 'keeping to the unlit river bank'. If stopped in town, their anxiety was that 'no one will investigate what really happened, they'll just deport us'. There was, indeed, a story worth investigating, and these migrants had not intended to be illegal workers. Like many others, they had been offered 'lucrative agricultural jobs' by a man calling himself Shukhrat Amonov, whom they had met a year earlier when doing temporary jobs in construction, working legally. When returning to Russia for these new agricultural jobs, they organised their documents in Uzbekistan and paid Amonov to arrange work permits and registrations. Amonov took them to a cattle farm outside Nal'chik in the Caucasus, where they worked for three months for fourteen hours a day. They were not paid

[15] Vyrkovskii, 'Migranty i mestnye'.
[16] Vyrkovskii, 'Migranty i mestnye'.

but were told that they needed to work off the cost of their transport. They were also regularly beaten. They appealed to Amonov about their situation, and he moved them to Volgograd. They were then paid a sum of 60,000 roubles but Amonov asked for money back in order to arrange new registrations, taking their passports. Their new boss was an Armenian who inspected their registration documents and told them that they were fake. One of the migrants responded with, 'what was our crime? We came with a company, paid for a work permit.' The migrants had believed that they were legal workers and ended up puzzled at being labelled criminals. Narizhnaya quoted Yulduz Atanyazova, a project co-ordinator in an NGO, who said that there were no official statistics on which industries used slave labour but that it was known that the 'farms, cattle ranches and fruit orchards across Russia, especially in the south' were the ones which 'exploit such labourers the most'.[17]

In my interview with Vyacheslav Postavnin he had commented upon how some police supplement their income by taking bribes from migrants, whether or not their papers were legal.[18] A report by *Novosti* in 2010 quoted an Uzbek who swept floors in Moscow's Kazan station. He confirmed that 'it happens all the time'. He elaborated that 'the police will stop you, ask for your papers. If you don't have them, they'll ask you for 200 roubles. If you do, they'll still demand 200 roubles.'[19] A Tajik narrated a similar story. He was working in what the journalist described as a 'wasteland' of Chelobitevo, twenty kilometres outside Moscow, where around 300 Uzbeks and Tajiks lived. As he put it: 'Every night the police come and harass us, demanding money. Even if we have the right paperwork, they still ask us for 200 roubles. It is no life.' His view of Russians in Moscow was that 'they have a certain attitude, and they show that they just don't want you in their country'. Another migrant who had been in Chelobitevo for a year at the time of reporting revealed that, 'we never leave Chelobitevo'. He admitted that, 'I have only been to Moscow once and I remember not knowing how to use the metro. I asked a local and he yelled at me and walked away. Why do I need that?'[20] These experiences, however, contrast with the positive ones cited in *Moskovskie novosti*.

When journalists underscore a multitude of negative experiences endured by migrants in unfree labour, they create a picture of serious victimhood. Migrants' beliefs that Russians hold certain negative attitudes

[17] Narizhnaya, 'Slave labor'.
[18] Interview with Vyacheslav Postavnin in Moscow, September 2014.
[19] Diana Markosian, 'Living in the shadows: a migrant's life in Russia', 6 August 2010. This was first available on RIA Novosti's website and then transferred after Sputnik replaced Novosti in 2014. See sputniknews.com/art_living/20100806/160095214.html.
[20] Markosian, 'Living in the shadows'.

about them and that they also have a hierarchical preference for Slavs over those with dark skins are borne out by the statements that some Russians made in the focus groups. These experiences, however, contrast with positive tales. It would certainly be inaccurate to suggest that all labour migrants endure hardship or do not develop strategies to deal with difficulties and overcome them with successful results. Newspaper reports generally rely for their data on information provided by small groups of migrants to illustrate patterns of exploitation and migrant responses to them. They are not, however, random-sample surveys of a large and statistically significant number of migrants, so give a partial picture that should not necessarily be taken as representative of all migrant experiences. Nonetheless, they shed vivid light on certain trends. Larger sample sizes would offer a clearer picture of the prevalence of different categories of migrant experiences.

The detailed ethnographic work of anthropologists can get closer to more differentiated accounts of migrants' lives and turn a spotlight on how they attempt to negotiate various situations that confront them, including informal negotiations with the police. In her fieldwork with Kyrgyz, Madeleine Reeves learnt about the benefits for migrants of acquiring skills for 'mobilising social relations' and 'knowing whom and knowing how' in order best to acquire what they wanted.[21] Migrants with initiative may strive to find mechanisms for achieving the outcomes that they want, if those outcomes are possible. Small sample sizes, however, make it methodologically tricky to gauge how representative patterns are. If complemented by systematically gathered data from public opinion polls of migrants, a fuller picture of general trends might result.

Conclusion

The results in 2014 of both my nationwide public opinion poll and focus groups showed low tolerance for the presence of non-Russian workers inside the Russian Federation, as had been indicated in earlier surveys by others. Participants in both Moscow and Yaroslavl thought it was appropriate and important to hire Russian workers over Central Asians. Some in the focus groups voiced a preference for employing Ukrainian workers over Central Asians in order to fill gaps in the labour force, with one participant distinguishing between desirable Slavs from eastern Ukraine and undesirable ones from the west.

---

[21] See Reeves, 'Clean fake'. She deems her differentiated account of 'migrant illegalities' to be more useful than adopting the binary 'legal' versus 'illegal'.

Group interactions led to a suggestion that Ukrainians could usefully be sent to work where Russia needed them most, even if the Ukrainians did not really wish to be in that part of the country or in the jobs assigned. There was both anxiety and anger about the numbers of incoming migrant workers from Central Asia and a tepid welcome for Ukrainians escaping violence. There were worries that cheaper labour meant jobs taken away from Russians, even when this was not necessarily the case, and concern that numbers brought pressures on the education system and kindergarten places. Focus tended to fall on how Russians might lose out. Another view was that they were subsidising Ukrainians and that perhaps this was going on for too long. The harshest critics of migrants showed little acknowledgement of labour shortages in certain sectors of the economy which needed filling or of the fact that migrants often took on jobs that Russians did not wish to perform. There was a tendency to hold on to fixed stereotypes about migrants and also of a rosy life in the West. Those in Yaroslavl were, however, more willing to allow equal pay for equal work, irrespective of nationality, whereas in Moscow there was a lobby for lower pay for Ukrainians before they obtained Russian citizenship. Shades of nationalism were expressed, held most fervently in Moscow by the 51-year-old transport technician, the 35-year-old telecommunications manager and the 37-year-old polyclinic employee and in Yaroslavl by the 45-year-old transport technician and the 59-year-old female retiree. Younger group participants aged 19, 28 and 29 in Moscow made calmer and more level-headed points, but their counterparts aged 20, 21, 27 and 30 in Yaroslavl exhibited a mix of rational remarks, fears and contradictory statements. A possible threat of extremism from migrants was raised by only the transport technician in Moscow. There was, however, no general advocacy in these two focus groups of concerted action to terminate unfree labour in the way that there had been in 2007 in the groups in Moscow and Vladimir which wanted to stop human trafficking of women and girls out of Russia.

Conclusion

The ancient and early modern worlds enjoyed trade links across vast distances, had credit networks to facilitate business and possessed patterns of slavery. Today's unfree labour, however, is situated in a faster-paced world than witnessed in the times of Thucydides, Aristotle and Plato and, more recently, even Hobbes and Locke.[1] New technologies mean that 'known' worlds have hugely expanded because news, film and photographs can be relayed across continents in nano-seconds. Traffickers and middlemen can communicate instantly by mobile phone, and money can be transferred electronically from one country to another. Fast travel, speedy Internet connections and global financial markets enhance the potential for profit seekers to recruit and transport adults and children and put them to work.

Although there has been lively debate about quite how 'new' globalisation is due to its evident economic roots in the past, 21st-century worlds are nonetheless faster with high degrees of mobility and interconnectedness and are also worlds in which immense disparities obtain between rich and poor across states and regions, and within them across social classes.[2] Unemployment and poverty mean a ready availability of vulnerable people as potential targets, as do wars and catastrophes. Migration within and across borders facilitates positive opportunities for the vulnerable to improve their lives but also exposes them to the risk of being exploited at a time when global markets can bring high profits in modern patterns distinct from those of Muscovy in the Middle Ages and before, but similarly ending in unfree labour. We have seen how Norse raiders, Pechenegs, and Tatar and Turkic nomads seized and traded slaves and have also noted the complexity in Muscovy of slave

---

[1] Peter Frankopan, *The Silk Roads: A New History of the World* (London: Bloomsbury, 2015); and Monahan, *The Merchants of Siberia*.

[2] For different perspectives on globalisation, see David Held and Anthony McGrew, eds., *The Global Transformation Reader*, 2nd edn (Cambridge: Polity, 2005); and Frank J. Lechner and John Boli, eds., *The Globalization Reader*, 5th edn (Chichester: Wiley Blackwell, 2015).

classifications. Historical contexts shape the origins, contours and forms of unfree labour.

Today there are anti-slavery conventions and protocols in place and anti-trafficking articles in the Russian Criminal Code, absent in Muscovy. According to Articles 127.1 and 127.2 of the Criminal Code, human trafficking and slavery are crimes to be punished. International conventions and national legislation, however, do not necessarily guarantee action against illegalities, nor people's protection, although they are necessary prerequisites for addressing them. By 2016, twenty-one countries were still not yet parties to the Palermo Protocols. These included Bangladesh, Bhutan, Fiji, Iran, Japan, North Korea, Pakistan, Somalia, Uganda and Yemen.[3]

The concept of 'security' is central to the discipline of political science, and for a long time it was a state-centred notion about national interest embedded in a realist perspective on international politics.[4] More inclusive definitions have broadened its scope to include individuals, their personal safety and their right not to be violated against their will.[5] Trafficking through deception and restrictions foisted on labour migrants trapped in unfree work situations deny them their rights and may threaten physical and mental health. Personal security is thereby undermined, and a secure livelihood becomes out of reach. In a Hobbesian sense, those Russians enduring forced prostitution in other states of the world, or Tajiks confined on building sites in Russia without a living wage, endure an existence without rights that is nasty, sometimes brutish and of unknown duration without any social contract.[6] Other migrants who enjoy successful outcomes without deceit and with contracts have very different stories to tell.

If citizens are hidden from view in forced labour situations, their rights cannot be defended by the state unless they are discovered. In this eventuality, the political obligations of the state to its citizens and to visitors on its territory are not fulfilled. If workers happen to be confined in their own country, such as Sergei in a brickworks in Dagestan or underage girls trafficked from Voronezh into prostitution in Moscow, the paradox of their situation is that they are citizens at home without *de facto* citizenship rights since they lack an 'enabled citizenship'. Citizens may consider that

---

[3] The full list is available at www.state.gov/j/tip/rls/tiprpt/2016/258690.htm.

[4] A classic text is Hans J. Morgenthau, *Politics Among Nations: The Struggle for Power and Peace* (New York: Alfred A. Knopf, 1961).

[5] See Terry Terriff, Stuart Croft, Lucy James and Patrick M. Morgan, *Security Studies Today* (Cambridge: Polity, 2003); and Nigel Dower and John Williams, eds., *Global Citizenship: A Critical Reader* (Edinburgh: Edinburgh University Press, 2002).

[6] Thomas Hobbes, *Leviathan* (Harmondsworth: Penguin, 1968).

the state has a duty to them to obliterate its worst Hobbesian pockets but they first have to be detected. Moreover, there must also be the political will to do so and a commitment to provide the necessary resources. This is the challenge for all the world's states, and there are countries where the domestic situation is far worse than in Russia. This is seen vividly by the estimates of the Walk Free Foundations's Global Slavery Index and its rankings of those in slavery, which is measured as a percentage of the total population on each state's territory. In 2014 this index ranked Russia in 32nd place with an estimated 1,049,700 in slavery at home, or an estimated 0.73 per cent of its overall population. Those states in the top rankings were Mauritania (at 4.0 per cent of overall population), Uzbekistan (3.9 per cent), Haiti (2.3 per cent), Qatar (1.3 per cent) and India with 14 million enslaved at 1.4 per cent of its population. In the updated index of 2016, Russia took 16th place, but still at 0.73 per cent of its population size with an estimated 1,048,500 in slave labour. The revised picture of those in the top five was as follows: the DPRK (4.3 per cent), Uzbekistan (3.9 per cent), Cambodia (1.6 per cent), India (1.4 per cent) and Qatar (1.3 per cent). The highest gross figure of those enslaved remained India at an increased estimate of 18,354,700.[7] The likely margins of error in estimates may be debated, and even somewhat controversial, but the prevalence of unfree labour cannot be denied, nor its undesirable extent.

The big challenge for Russia is not just to find the enslaved at home and apprehend their traffickers and exploiters, and the MVD's press releases indicate that it has some successes in so doing, but at the very outset to deter human trafficking out of Russia and within it, as well as to identify outgoing and incoming cases at borders. Prevention is indeed a wide-ranging task, perhaps more elusive in poorer regions. The rule of law is also crucial for effective results, not distorted by bribes and corruption. And, as in all states, professionals in the know call for far more effort to be devoted to the rehabilitation of returnees who have either escaped, been freed or been deported back home. Evidence shows that rehabilitation remains an exceedingly low governmental priority despite broad awareness of the deficit of specialist shelters with care packages geared to protection, legal advice, medical care and counselling. The efforts of the IOM and of NGOs and women's groups have been laudable, but their enduringly thorny problem has been one of insufficient long-term funding and the predominance of short-term grants. Many governments

---

[7] Global Slavery Indexes for 2013, 2014 and 2016 are at www.walkfreefoundation.org/resources.

globally also struggle to devote substantial amounts to rehabilitation due to budgetary pressures to fund other priorities.

For those Russian citizens trapped in forced labour on their own soil, in theory the Russian Constitution of 1993 should uphold their rights. Chapter 2 of the Constitution covers rights and freedoms. Its Article 17.2 declares that rights and freedoms are 'inalienable', and according to Article 17.3 people's rights and freedoms 'must not violate the rights and freedoms of others'. Since traffickers daily do indeed violate the rights and freedoms of others, in so doing they violate the Constitution as well as the anti-trafficking Articles 127.1 and 127.2 of the Criminal Code. In Hobbesian language, there is an underground 'state of nature' either invisible to law enforcement organs or alternatively facilitated by corrupt officials and insufficiently challenged by legitimate structures. Similarly, those in unfree predicaments do not enjoy the provisions of Article 21.1 according to which 'the dignity of the individual is protected by the state'. And those in the worst predicaments do not have the guarantee of Article 21.2 that 'no one must be subjected to torture, violence or other brutal or humiliating treatment or punishment'.[8]

Those in situations of unfree labour lack the 'right to freedom and inviolability of the person' enshrined in Article 22.1 and cannot enjoy the 'right of association' expressed in Article 30.1 when they are confined to a given space against their will. Since Article 37.1 declares 'labour is free', it means individuals enjoy the free right to use their abilities in work or a profession chosen by themselves. Article 37.2 specifically declares that 'forced labour is prohibited', and 37.3 specifies the right to work in safe and hygienic conditions, without discrimination and not receiving an unacceptably low wage. 'The right to leisure' is enshrined in Article 37.5 and 'the right to health care and medical assistance' in Article 41.1. Those bosses who deny workers days off, or access to a doctor when ill, flout the Constitution. One example illustrated how employers in forestry in Amursk oblast of the Russian Far East denied an Uzbek captive an ambulance or a doctor when injured. The Uzbek did not formally come under the Russian Constitution but his labour rights and human rights were flouted. Abducted and trafficked teenagers and minors are also prevented from enjoying 'the right to education' expressed in Article 43.1. Although Article 45.1 proclaims that 'state protection' of rights and freedoms in the Russian Federation 'is guaranteed', in practice this is very hard to deliver when the violations are covert. It is the 'hidden' nature

[8] *Konstitutsiia Rossiiskoi Federatsii* (Moscow: MARTIN, 2016).

of abuse that renders constitutional protection difficult and, in effect, formal rather than tangible and real.

The sheer impossibility of *being allowed to be a citizen*, even when *de jure* one is, renders the Constitution distant for those individuals affected. The 'enabled citizen' should be free to seek opportunities in economy, polity and society and to expect the protection of these rights, in so far as they do not harm others. There were reports at the beginning of this century of women returning to Russia either after their own successful escape or after being released from prostitution due to their exhaustion and breakdown, even occasionally being bought a plane ticket to go home by their 'owner', being stopped at the border or at a Russian airport and refused entry due to the lack of a passport. One Russian television programme broadcast in June 2007 told the story of fourteen-year-old Nina who had been trafficked to Dubai and forced to work in prostitution. She managed to escape her captors and met an airline worker who arranged passage back to Russia. Upon arrival in her homeland, she was put on a plane back to Dubai due to a lack of documents.[9] So in this instance the Russian state refused to let its citizen in without documentary proof, and thus she was not permitted *de facto* to *be* a citizen, even though *de jure* she was. This might be dubbed a 'hollow citizenship'. Although today the Russian authorities are far more aware of the problem facing those whose documents have been confiscated, the example does illustrate how hard it can be in vulnerable situations to prove citizenship and to be believed. Without this proof and sufficient credibility in the eyes of whoever happens to be the official assessor, or gatekeeper, associated rights cannot begin to be claimed or exercised.

The cases of Farukh and Siarkhon who arrived in Russia from Central Asia involved persons who were not in a position to declare that they were Russian citizens. Their forced labour situations, however, flouted articles in Russia's Criminal Code since they were performed under duress on Russian territory. Both Uzbekistan and Tajikistan have anti-trafficking legislation, and there are agreements in place across the region to facilitate co-operation. Had these cases come to the knowledge of law enforcement, justice could have meant the release of the captives and punishment for the offenders.[10] Those Russians, like Elena who was trafficked to the UAE from Kursk oblast, or the thousands who ended up in prostitution across Europe, are all outside the remit of their own

---

[9] The programme entitled 'Nalozhnitsy' (Concubines) was shown on Russia's NTV on 24 June 2007.

[10] In 2008, Uzbekistan amended its Criminal Code to prohibit forced labour. Tajikistan has had relevant legislation since July 2004. A serious problem is that of non-implementation.

constitution when in another state. But legally their situations are likely to violate the anti-trafficking laws of the recipient state as well as those of regional and international conventions. Common to Elena, Farukh, Siarkhon and Sergei were processes of subordination and abuse. Their 'repertoires', as Lewis Siegelbaum and Leslie Page Moch would dub the practices, relationships and networks within each particular 'migration regime', may be distinct, yet they share core commonalities of having to deal with deceit, entrapment, loss of passports and a denial of rights enshrined in law.[11] The repertoires that they develop to handle their predicaments are those of Kevin Bales's 'disposable people'.

Russia is far from alone in needing political will to face head on with increased commitment the many challenges that unfree labour situations present and to take anti-trafficking and anti-slavery work more seriously through increased action. Even states categorised in Tier 1 of the US State Department's TIP Reports, whose governments are meant 'fully to meet the Trafficking Victims Protections Act's minimum standards', still have considerably more work to do, which requires additional resources. In 2016, the Walk Free Foundation estimated that there were 308,200 people in modern slavery in Colombia, 11,700 in the UK, 12,000 in France, 14,500 in Germany, 57,700 in the USA, 129,600 in Italy, 8,400 in Spain, 6,500 in Canada, 4,300 in Australia and 1,500 in Switzerland. These states are all among those categorised in Tier 1. In July 2016, the British press reported that Kevin Hyland, the UK's Independent Anti-Slavery Commissioner, regretted that 'slave masters are acting with impunity because many police officers as well as the public do not take their crimes seriously enough'. Hyland described a complacency about the scale of trafficking as an 'accepted feature of everyday life in car washes, nail bars, building sites and farmers' fields across the country'. Workers from other countries were lured to the UK and put into jobs bringing low wages, even in dangerous work. They would be likely to live in poor accommodation and find their passports confiscated. Hyland lamented that he had 'encountered a refusal to recognise the problem across society'.[12] This was precisely what committed advocates of an anti-trafficking law in Russia, such as Elena Tiuriukanova, had been observing in Moscow at the very beginning of this century. Although in 2006 the UK ratified the UN Convention on Transnational Crime and

---

[11] See Lewis H. Siegelbaum and Leslie Page Moch, *Broad Is My Native Land: Repertoires and Regimes of Migration in Russia's Twentieth Century* (Ithaca, NY: Cornell University Press, 2014).

[12] Sean O'Neill, 'Slavery thriving as police accused of failing to act', *The Times*, 30 July 2016, p. 20.

its Palermo Protocols and in 2015 passed the Modern Slavery Act, which strengthened already existing laws and established the Independent Anti-Slavery Commissioner, this legal machinery, nonetheless, sits alongside a curious societal 'normalisation' of unfree labour and even, from what the commissioner indicated, an acceptance of it as part of life today.[13] The country may pride itself on this act's introduction, including its requirement that corporations operating in the UK publish information on eradicating trafficking from their supply chains, but concrete results remain lower than expectations. In early 2017 as this book was going to press, the media reported that 'pop-up' brothels of East European women who had been trafficked to the UK for prostitution had been appearing in short-term lets in Newquay and Swindon and then quickly moving on.[14] Wiltshire police revealed that up to thirty such brothels could arrive in Swindon in one week.[15] The press also covered a different case of Vietnamese teenagers who had been trafficked to work on a cannabis farm. They had no English and were 'fearful' when the police arrived. Their conditions were described as 'slave-like' and 'grim'.[16] Unfree labour mechanisms show a versatility to adapt to local possibilities, and traffickers seize opportunities that fit localities all over the world. Policing, too, has to adapt to unfolding situations, and banks are currently looking at customer accounts using algorithms in an effort to spot payments by human traffickers to airlines, restaurants and pharmacies. This is termed 'profile-building and proactive transaction-data interrogation'.[17]

What, then, should be done locally, nationally, regionally and globally? Worldwide detection needs to improve and action against exploitation needs to be taken more seriously to counter the complacent acceptance and lack of understanding that Commissioner Hyland has observed. In challenging the acceptance of the sex trade, Kat Banyard has addressed the 'toxic myths' which help to sustain it through prostitution's portrayal as a 'harmless consumer transaction'.[18] Her advocacy is to criminalise its purchase, something viewed as controversial by those critics ready to resist.[19] Another essential link in the chain is the protection and rehabilitation of the trafficked – tasks which appear nationally

---

[13] Details of the Modern Slavery Act are at www.legislation.gov.uk/ukpga/2015/30/contents/enacted.

[14] *The Times*, 5 January 2017, p. 17; *The Times*, 7 January 2017, p. 21.

[15] BBC News, 5 February 2017.

[16] Amelia Gentleman, 'Three on slavery charges after police find four Vietnamese teenagers in cannabis farm', *Guardian*, 25 February 2017, p. 11.

[17] Fiona Hamilton, 'Banks become digital sleuths in fight against sex slave gangs', *The Times*, 17 March 2017, p. 2.

[18] Banyard, *Pimp State*, p. 6.

[19] Banyard, *Pimp State*, p. 6.

and globally under-resourced. The USA initiated the global championing of anti-trafficking policies and gave financial incentives. In the US State Department's TIP Report of 2005, Secretary of State Condoleezza Rice said that the USA had spent more than $82 million in anti-trafficking assistance to foreign governments and NGOs in the previous year.[20] In 2014 it was announced that 'more than $216 million' had been given by the USA 'in foreign assistance funding since 2002'. This had supported 835 projects to combat human trafficking around the world.[21] Critics, however, have argued that little of this ever reaches the victims themselves.[22]

On the question of the global migration of refugees and workers, Zhanna Zaionchkovskaia and Vyacheslav Postavnin have called for Russia and the West to work together on 'the humanisation of migration policies'. Of relevance to the hate crimes against incomers that have arisen across the world, they stress the importance of changing attitudes towards the migrant, not automatically perceiving him or her as a potential terrorist 'but as a person who has faced a difficult situation'.[23] The importance of recognising the suffering of others and empathising with it is just as necessary towards a woman from Vladivostok who finds herself in a brothel in Germany as it is for an Uzbek in Russia, a Syrian in France or a Vietnamese in the UK. The attitudes of the youth in Croydon in the UK who set upon a peaceful teenage Kurdish-Iranian asylum seeker and caused him serious fractures and a brain haemorrhage have something in common with the Russian who shot and seriously injured Sulaimon Saidov, a Tajik, in a carriage on the Moscow metro.[24] Attempts to curb hate crimes face particularly heightened challenges after terrorist incidents which may inflame xenophobia.

We have seen historically how a *modus operandi* can be challenged by critics and thereby moral conceptual schemes can change. Russian history is rich in condemnations of past forms of subordination and

---

[20] Condoleezza Rice's remarks can be found at www.state.gov/documents/organization/47255.pdf.

[21] US State Department, Office to Monitor and Combat Trafficking in Persons, 'Fact Sheet', 20 June 2014.

[22] In 2014, the Global Alliance Against Traffic in Women (GAATW) argued that governments, the UN and foundations have spent millions of dollars in anti-trafficking work but that very little reaches the trafficked. See Mike Dottridge, 'How is the money to combat human trafficking spent?' *Anti-Trafficking Review*, No. 3, 2014, pp. 3–14, www.antitraffickingreview.org/index.php/atrjournal/article/view/62.

[23] Ksenia Zubacheva, 'Why migration represents a new existential threat for Europe', *Russia Direct*, 27 September 2016.

[24] Saeed Kamali Dehghan, '"Hate crime" leaves community in shock', *Guardian*, 4 April 2017, pp. 1, 10.

exploitation that had been legal and morally robust for a long time. Those in the nineteenth century who found serfdom abhorrent and advocated its demise included Radishchev, Pushkin, the Decembrists, Herzen, Chernyshevsky, other radical intellectuals and indeed the serfs themselves, who considered the land to be theirs by right. Radishchev had also observed how some landowners sexually abused women and girls on their estates. He saw an uprising of some kind as inevitable in his words: 'Tremble, cruelhearted landlord! On the brow of each of your peasants I see your condemnation written.'[25] In the nineteenth and twentieth centuries, too, there were harsh criticisms of the prison system and forced labour in penal servitude. Both Chekhov and Dostoyevsky condemned *katorga* and conditions in prison, and Solzhenitsyn and Ginzburg wrote eloquently about their own journeys through the Gulag. Extending Radishchev's expectation of revolt *en masse* to those in today's isolated situations of forced labour, however, is untenable, as they generally lack communal cementing bonds or the potential to mobilise together.

As 'pop-up' brothels and cannabis farms were appearing on police agendas in the UK, in Russia debates were ignited again about the role of forced labour (*prinuditel'nyi trud*) in the penal system. The *Moscow Times* carried the headline 'Russian justice system to reintroduce forced labour in 2017'.[26] The official position was that, despite being labelled '*prinuditel'nyi*', this punishment was deemed to have a more 'social character' than it actually connoted and would be building on the 'best aspects of Soviet experience'. The aim was not to isolate prisoners from society but rather to characterise them as similar to 'shift workers', who would live 'far from home in shared accommodation'. With permission, inmates would be able to leave, then return, and not be subject to the same security measures as in other prisons. They would not, however, have the 'right to choose, switch or refuse the jobs assigned to them', but they would receive a salary to be taxed at 5–10 per cent as well as eighteen days' annual leave after six months. Some argued that this would help to combat overcrowding in prisons, would be 'more comfortable', lower violence levels, humanise the system and reduce the probability of re-offending. Critics pointed out that, since inmates could be employed by the state or private companies, they might end up as cheap labour for both.[27]

---

[25] Radishchev, *A Journey from St Petersburg*, pp. 48 and 134.

[26] No named author, 'Russian justice system to reintroduce forced labor in 2017', *Moscow Times*, 16 February 2016.

[27] Aleksandra Dymchishina, 'V Obshchestvennoi palate obsudili novyi vid nakazaniia – prinuditel'nye raboty', Gazeta.ru, 10 February 2017, www.gazeta.ru/social/2017/02/09/10517639.shtml.

To those who despair that current levels of unfree labour have become 'normalised' and that unaroused majorities refuse to recognise the problem across society, it may be useful to recall that 2007 saw the championing of the 200th anniversary of the end of the British slave trade – itself a system which in its time was considered 'normal' by interested parties. Britain, like Portugal and Spain, had thrived on slavery and, at its peak, a large percentage of the country's foreign income came from it. There was thus considerable self-interest in perpetuating the slave trade for financial reasons. The first anti-slave trade petition was presented to the British Parliament in 1783 by the Quakers, or Society of Friends. The British politician and philanthropist William Wilberforce and others subsequently led a long campaign against the British slave trade which resulted in the passage of the Slave Trade Act of 1807 and later in the Slavery Abolition Act of 1833, which was designed to stop the practice in most of the British Empire. Millions of Africans had sailed in barbaric conditions into slavery.

On the other side of the Atlantic in North America, American Quakers had called for slavery's abolition as early as 1688, and subsequently the Pennsylvania Society for the Abolition of Slavery was a key activist. Some of the earliest calls for the abolition of slavery had come from Thomas Jefferson and Benjamin Franklin, themselves slave owners. Different northern states passed their own separate state laws ending slavery, sometimes gradually. But it was not until the aftermath of the American Civil War that finally in 1865 slavery was abolished there. In 1863 President Abraham Lincoln, through an Emancipation Proclamation, freed slaves in the Confederate states of the south. Coming into effect in 1865, the 13th Amendment to the US Constitution read: 'Neither slavery nor involuntary servitude, except as punishment for crime whereof the party shall have been duly convicted, shall exist within the United States, or any place subject to their jurisdiction.'[28] The tale was recently popularised in Steven Spielberg's film *Lincoln* and the brutalities of slavery in the American south were portrayed by Steve McQueen's movie *Twelve Years a Slave*.

What can be learnt? Recall the Russian barman in the focus group held in Moscow in 2007, who referred back several centuries to a time when he considered that life was 'cheap' and people were sold as slaves. He saw parallels between the past and the present. I leave readers with the question: what more should be done globally to make life less cheap today?

---

[28] The 13th Amendment to the US Constitution can be accessed at www.loc.gov/rr/program/bib/ourdocs/13thamendment.html.

Unfree labour is generally no longer officially state sponsored, nor legal (with some notable exceptions such as in the DPRK). Campaigns of the past calling for the liquidation of a morally questionable legal slave trade are not the solution, since today human trafficking and forced labour have already been declared illegal. Indeed, the celebration of the anniversary of the end of the slave trade felt very ironic given that unfree labour situations were simultaneously evident all over the world. It is not a public clamour against a law that is needed but effective action to stop traffickers and gangmasters from doing what they do and to stop the vulnerable from falling into their hands. What, apart from the availability of other jobs with decent enough wages to sustain livelihoods, and beyond effective action to implement the anti-trafficking and anti-slavery laws that are already in place, should morally be done to end complacency and to make a difference?

Advocates of global social justice proceed from notions of global citizenship, and philosophers in the field of ethics pose the question of what our moral obligations to strangers should be. This has generally been asked about famine and poverty and pivots around the issue of what the wealthy or better-off should do to help those considerably poorer. Peter Singer has argued that 'the whole way we look at moral issues – our moral conceptual scheme – needs to be altered'. From this he proceeds to advocate the following: 'if it is in our power to prevent something bad from happening, without thereby sacrificing anything of comparable moral importance, we ought, morally, to do it'.[29] Singer asked this in 1971 at a time of humanitarian crisis in what was then East Pakistan when 9 million people fled to India to avoid military repression and were struggling in refugee camps. More recently, Kwame Anthony Appiah has broadened this to call for 'truly cosmopolitan conversations' which require 'intelligence and curiosity as well as engagement'. He suggests re-phrasing what he calls the 'Singer principle' to read, 'if you are the person in the best position to prevent something really awful, and it won't cost you much to do so, do it.'[30]

Neither of these eminent philosophers has applied this principle directly to human trafficking or to labour exploitation and slavery, indeed a complicated task. The hidden nature of these processes makes financial donations less easily directly applicable, and it is unclear anyway how they would help to deter the global traffickers. Job creation at

---

[29] Peter Singer, *Famine, Affluence and Morality* (Oxford: Oxford University Press, 2016), pp. 4–6.

[30] Kwame Anthony Appiah, *Cosmopolitanism: Ethics in a World of Strangers* (London: Penguin, 2006), pp. 158–174.

times of unemployment, however, might occupy those who would otherwise succumb to the false promises of traffickers. More education campaigns in the worst-affected areas might further deter the vulnerable, and donations for shelters and psychological counselling might productively encourage the rehabilitation of the traumatised returnees, if they make it home. But these suggestions are not new, nor hitherto have they stopped human trafficking from taking place. Stronger and more consistent enforcement of existing legal protection with possible additional mechanisms for international scrutiny might have some impact, but probably would not deter the traffickers and the employers who exploit and reap huge benefits at low risk, especially if they are situated within organised crime structures which deter them from stopping through peer pressure. A moral cleansing of markets and reduced drive for avarice may be needed – tricky aims in a consumption-driven world where some covet expensive lifestyles and are content to violate others to get them.

At the individual level many, like those in the focus groups in Moscow, Vladimir and Yaroslavl, may not consider themselves to be in the best position to do very much beyond reporting suspicions of human trafficking and forced labour to the police or in discussing them with colleagues and friends. At best, it seems that ways need to be found to spread heightened moral concern from the margins to substantial majorities in order to press for global exploitation and unfree labour to be more effectively addressed. Global conversations need to be stepped up and the underbelly of global markets cleaned up. Corporate responsibility is essential, and there is a serious need for examination of supply chains down to the very last links. A timely question is how to turn the entrepreneurial skills of the traffickers and brothel owners into a force for something good and constructive rather than exploitative or, at a minimum, simply to make them begin to question what they are doing. As long as banks make loans to pornography companies, and while states in which the commercial sex trade is legal reap taxes from it, governments may be reluctant to explore too rigorously the full picture of unwanted exploitation. Simultaneously, while the notion is peddled that the 'oldest profession' can never cease, the global sex trade is thereby sustained and normalised. A further question is what sort of education programmes could effectively be developed in prisons to redirect the moral maps of those who have been sentenced for human trafficking. Could their moral conceptual schemes, one wonders, be successfully challenged and rechannelled, or are the profits that they are able to reap too compelling and their lack of empathy too resilient?

Glossary

apparat	state political machinery or institutions
apparatchik	state operative
barshchina	a serf's labour obligations
bedniak	poor peasant
BNP	British National Party
chinovniki	officials or functionaries
chto delat'?	What is to be done?
chuzhoi	foreign or alien
chuzhie	foreigners
CIS	Sodruzhestvo Nezavisimykh Gosudarstv, or Commonwealth of Independent States
CoE	Council of Europe
DPRK	Democratic People's Republic of Korea
druzhba narodov	friendship of peoples
dvor	household
dvorovye liudi	household people
dvoriane	gentry
ECtHR	European Court of Human Rights
EEU	Eurasian Economic Union
etnofobiia	dislike of other ethnic groups
FMS	Federal'naia Migratsionnaia Sluzhba, or Federal Migration Service
FSB	Federal'naia Sluzhba Bezopasnosti, or Federal Security Service
gastarbaiter	guest worker
gastarbaitery	guest workers

Grazhdanskoe Sodeistvie	Civic Assistance
Gulag	Glavnoe Upravlenie Lagerei, or Main Camp Administration
HRW	Human Rights Watch
ILO	International Labour Organization
IOM	International Organization for Migration
ISIS	Islamic State of Iraq and Syria
IWPR	Institute of War and Peace Reporting
katorga	penal servitude
katorzhnye	convict workers
katorzhane	convict workers
KGB	Komitet Gosudarstvennoi Bezopasnosti, or State Security Committee
kholopstvo	slavery
kholopy	slaves
krai	territory
krepostnye	serfs
krysha	roof, or protection
kolkhoz	collective farm
Komsomol	Communist Youth League
konformizm	conformity
kto vinovat'?	Who is to blame?
kulak	rich peasant
MATM	Mezhdunarodnyi Al'ians 'Trudovaia Migratsiia', or International Alliance 'Labour Migration'
migrantofobiia	dislike of migrants
MVD	Ministerstvo Vnutrennykh Del, or Ministry of Internal Affairs
nashi	ours, or shorthand for our nationality
NGO	non-governmental organisation
oblast	region
obrok	payment in cash
Obshchestvennaia Palata	Social Chamber

OECD	Organisation for Economic Co-operation and Development
OMON	Otriad Mobilnyi Osobovo Naznacheniia, or special forces
Oprichnina	special administrative elite established by Ivan IV
OSCE	Organization for Security and Co-operation in Europe
OVD	Otdel Vnutrennykh Del (Department of Internal Affairs)
otkat	corruption
patent	licence to work, or work permit
patenty	licences to work, or work permits
podvizhka	'ice motion'
pomeshchik	landholder
pomest'e	conditional service landholding
posrednik	middleman
priezzhii	new arrival
propiska	permit (to live in a particular location)
POW	prisoner of war
profilaktika	prevention
PRC	People's Republic of China
rabotorgovlia	trade in people
rabotorgovtsy	traders in people
rabovladenie	slave holding
rabskii trud	slave labour
rabstvo	slavery
raion	district
RFE/RL	Radio Free Europe/Radio Liberty
RSFSR	Russian Soviet Federated Socialist Republic
sgovor	an agreement
seks-rabstvo	sexual slavery
SIDA	Swedish International Development Agency

Sledstvennyi Komitet	Investigative Committee
Sudebnik	Law Code
tiazhest'	gravity or seriousness of a law
TIP	trafficking in persons
torgovlia liud'mi	human trafficking (literally, 'trade in persons')
treffiking	trafficking
UAE	United Arab Emirates
UKIP	United Kingdom Independence Party
UNICEF	United Nations International Children's Emergency Fund
USSR	Union of Soviet Socialist Republics
zaiavka	request

Select Bibliography

Books and Articles in Russian

Avetisian, Roksana, 'Test dlia migrantov, zhelaiushchikh pereekhat' v Rossiiu, uslozhniat', *Izvestiia*, 6 April 2015.

Basharova, Svetlana, 'Gosduma proveriaet sluchai nelegal'nogo testirovaniia migrantov', *Izvestiia*, 13 April 2015.

Basharova, Svetlana, Borodina, Tat'iana and Korchmarek, Natal'ia, 'Stoimost' ekzamena dlia migrantov v regionakh dokhodit do 25,000 rublei', *Izvestiia*, 3 February 2015.

Boychenko, Kirill A., 'Istoricheskoe reshenie Evropeiskogo suda po pravam cheloveka v otnoshenii Kipra i Rossii, kasaiushcheesia torgovli liud'mi', *Rossiiskii kriminologicheskii vzgliad*, No. 2, 2010, pp. 13–18.

'Pravovye osnovy sotrudnichestva gosudarstv – chlenov Sodruzhestva Nezavisimykh Gosudarstv (SNG) po voprosam predotvrashcheniia torgovli liud'mi', *Iuridicheskii mir*, 2010, pp. 14–17.

Danilkin, Aleksandr, 'Zhenu otdai diade . . .', *Trud*, 21 March 2006.

Danilova, Ol'ga, 'Muzh s zhenoi prodali v seks-rabstvo dvadtsat' kurskikh devchonok', *Komsomol'skaia pravda*, 15 December 2008.

Demchenko, Vladimir, 'Byvshaia rabynia Kurganskogo fermera: "v kolkhoze eshche khuzhe. Ta zhe nevolia, no ni deneg, ni edy ni daiut"', *Komsomol'skaia pravda*, 13 May 2013.

Erokhina, Liudmila D. and Buriak, Mariia Iu., *Torgovlia Zhenshchinami i Det'mi v Tseliakh Seksual'noi Ekspluatatsii v Sotsial'noi i Kriminologicheskoi Perspektive* (Moscow: Profobrazovanie, 2003).

Falaleev, Mikhail, 'Rabstvo pod prikrytiem', *Rossiiskaia gazeta*, 24 November 2009.

Frolov, Anton, 'V Rossii vse bol'she sluchaev rabovladeniia', *Pravda*, 20 March 2013.

Gavrilina, Svetlana, 'Migranty prodolzhaiut priezzhat' v Piter i ego okrestnosti', *Nezavisimaia gazeta*, 21 April 2015.

Ionova, Larisa, 'Zarplata – miska pokhlebki', *Rossiiskaia gazeta*, 19 January 2013.

Ivakhniuk, Irina V., *Perspektivy Migratsionnoi Politiki Rossii* (Moscow: MAKS Press, 2011).

Ivnitskii, Nikolai A., *Repressivnaia Politika Sovetskoi Vlasti v Derevne, 1928–1933g* (Moscow: Institut Rossiiskoi Istorii RAN, 2000).

Sud'ba Raskulachennykh v SSSR (Moscow: Sobranie, 2004).

Karacheva, Ekaterina, 'Krasavitsy-rabyni', *Argumenty i fakty*, 5 January 2004.

Khodyreva, Natalia V., *Sovremennye Debaty o Prostitutsii* (St Petersburg: Aleteiia, 2006).

Khodyreva, Natalia V. and Tsvetkova, Mariia G. 'Rossiianki i iavlenie treffika', *Sotsiologicheskie issledovaniia*, No. 11, 2000, pp. 141–144.

Kodeks Rossiiskoi Federatsii ob Administrativnykh Pravonarusheniakh po Sostoianiiu na 25 Oktiabria 2016g (Moscow: Prospekt, 2016).

Konstitutsiia Rossiiskoi Federatsii (Moscow: MARTIN, 2016).

Kostiukovskii, Artem, 'Treffik bez granits', *Argumenty i fakty*, 28 April 2004.

Kozlova, Natal'ia, 'Otrublennaia golova pod krasnym fonarem', *Rossiiskaia gazeta*, 31 January 2003.

'Uslovnaia rabotorgovlia', *Rossiiskaia gazeta*, 20 June 2014.

Kravtsov, Vasilii, 'Migranty zhdut, no . . . poka ne liubiat', *Migratsiia XXI Vek*, No. 3–4 (23–24), May–August 2014, pp. 56–57.

Kretsul, Roman, 'Sistemu testirovanie migrantov raskritovali v Obshchestvennom palate', *Izvestiia*, 17 March 2016.

Lamstov, Mikhail, 'Seks-rabyni v Karlovykh Varakh', *Argumenty i fakty*, 14 August 2001.

Malakhov, Vladimir, *Kul'turnye Razlichiia i Politicheskie Granitsy v Epokhu Global'nykh Migratsii* (Moscow: Novoe Literaturnoe Obozrenie, 2014).

Mizulina, Elena B., *Torgovlia Liud'mi i Rabstvo v Rossii: Mezhdunarodno-Pravovoi Aspekt* (Moscow: Iurist', 2006).

Mukomel', Vladimir I., 'Grani intolerantnosti (migrantofobii, etnofobii)', *Sotsiologicheskie issledovaniia*, No. 2, 2005, pp. 56–66.

Politika Integratsii (Moscow: MAKS Press, 2011).

Murtazin, Irek, Feruz, Ali and Gordienko, Irina, 'Peredel zagrobnogo mira', *Novaia gazeta*, 17 May 2016.

Naryshkina, Anastasiia and Vinogradova, Ilona, 'Kazhdaia Rossiiskaia "devochka" prinosit khoziaevam pritonov po $200', *Izvestiia*, 16 April 2004.

Nikolaev, Sergei, 'Rabstvo-XXI vek: Rossiia spolzaet v antichnost'?' *Pravda*, 30 May 2011.

Olimpiev, Anatolii Iu., *Protivodeistvie Torgovle Liud'mi* (Moscow: Zakon i Pravo, 2013).

Orlova, Ol'ga A., *Protivodeistvie Torgovle Liud'mi: Trenerskii Portfel'* (Moscow: Sestry, 2004).

Ostrovskaia, Natal'ia, 'Prodaiutsia Natashi. Na eksport. Nedorogo', *Komsomol'skaia pravda*, 10 January 2011.

Pogontseva, Ekaterina, 'I devochek nashikh vedut v kabinet', *Trud*, 9 August 2012.

Pogudina, Regina, 'Test dlia migrantov: a mogut ego reshit' russkie', *Komsomol'skaia pravda (Kirov)*, 17 February 2015.

Poletaev, Dmitrii, 'Izmenenie praktik povedeniia trudovykh migrantov iz Srednei Azii v Rossii', in Sergei Panarin, ed., *Vostok na Vostoke, v Rossii i na Zapade* (St Petersburg: Nestor-Istoriia, 2016), pp. 177–193.

Postavnin, Vyacheslav, 'Pora prosypat'sia', *Migratsiia XXI Vek*, No. 3–4 (23–24), May–August 2014, p. 30.

Postavnin, Vyacheslav A., Vlasova, Nataliia I. and Matveeva, Inna G., *Stsenarii Razvitiia Migratsionnoi Politiki v Rossii* (Moscow: MAKS Press, 2011).

Prokhorova, Anna and Gutierres, Khuan, 'Trudovaia migratsiia v Rossii: vygod vse men'she, raskhodov vse bol'she, migranty uezzhaiut', *Migratsiia XXI Vek*, No. 4 (31), July–August 2015, pp. 29–34.

Riazantsev, Sergei V., 'O iazykovoi integratsii migrantov kak novom orientire migratsionnoi politiki Rossii', *Sotsiologicheskie issledovaniia*, No. 9, 2014, pp. 25–29.

Rogoza, Aleksandr, 'Rabstvo v Rossii', *Komsomol'skaia pravda*, 2 January 2013.

Rybakovskii, Leonid L. and Tarasova, Nina V., 'Vnutrirossiiskaia migratsiia naseleniia nyneshnaia situatsiia i prognoz', *Sotsiologicheskie issledovaniia*, No. 1, 1994, pp. 31–38.

Salik, Anzhelika, 'Ratifitsirovana konventsiia protiv torgovli liud'mi', *Izvestiia*, 15 April 2004.

Samarina, Aleksandra, 'Pauell i Poltavchenko pokonchat s rabotorgovlei', *Nezavisimaia gazeta*, 28 January 2004.

Sharov, Andrei, 'Rabotorgovtsy XXI veka: v Moskve obsudili problemy iuridicheskoi pomoshchi zhertvam torgovli liud'mi', *Rossiiskaia gazeta*, 29 October 2010.

Skudaeva, Anna, 'Migrantov v Kostrome ulichili v pokupke diplomov', *Rossiiskaia gazeta*, 22 January 2016.

Svad'bina, Tat'iana, Nemova, Ol'ga and Pakina, Tat'iana, 'Sovremennyi trafik rabototorgovli: prichiny, posledstviia, profilaktika', *Sotsiologicheskie issledovaniia*, No. 2, 2014, pp. 43–48.

Tarakanova, Galina, 'Iunyi – znachit slabyi? Pochemu prestupniki vybiraiut dlia napadeniia detei?' *Argumenty i fakty*, 3 December 2014.

Tatarchenkov, Oleg, 'Novyi zakonoproekt dolzhen zastavit' ikh govorit', *Rossiiskaia gazeta*, 6 August 2003.

Tishkov, Valerii, 'O chem zabyl skazat' kandidat v prezidenty, kogda govoril o migratsii', *Migratsiia XXI Vek*, No. 1 (10), January–February 2012, pp. 4–7.

Titov, Dmitrii, 'Vtoroi dom', *Migratsiia XXI Vek*, No. 6–7 (11–12), November–December 2014, pp. 61–63.

Tiuriukanova, Elena V., 'Gendernye aspekty migratsionnoi statistiki', in Marina E. Baskakova, ed., *Gendernoe Neravenstvo v Sovremennoi Rossii Skvoz' Prizmu Statistiki* (Moscow: Izdatel'stvo Nauchnoi i Uchebnoi Literatury, 2004), pp. 252–278.

Tiuriukanova, Elena V., Anishina, Vera, Poletaev, Dmitrii and Shamkov, Stanislav, *Prinuditel'nyi Trud v Sovremennoi Rossii* (Moscow: IOM, 2004).

Tiuriukanova, Elena V. and Erokhina, Ludmila D., *Torgovlia Liud'mi* (Moscow: Izdatel'stvo Academia, 2002).

Trifonova, Ekaterina, 'Dokhody gastarbaiterov prodolzhaiut sokrashchat'sia', *Nezavisimaia gazeta*, 22 January 2016.

'Pravozashchitniki gotovy sudit'sia za migrantov', *Nezavisimaia gazeta*, 13 May 2016.

'Migranty iz SNG ne speshat pokidat' Rossiiu', *Nezavisimaia gazeta*, 20 June 2016.

'Rossiiane tesniat gastarbaiterov na rynke truda', *Nezavisimaia gazeta*, 15 July 2016.

'Gastarbaitery edut v Rossiiskuiu "ten"'', *Nezavisimaia gazeta*, 6 February 2017.

Troitskii, Konstantin and Srapian, Elena, 'Otvechai po-russki. Shapku snimi', *Grazhdanskoe Sodeistvie*, 15 March 2016, www.refugee.ru.

Ugolovnyi Kodeks Rossiiskoi Federatsii po Sostoyaniyu na 1 Oktiabria 2014g (Moscow: Prospekt, KnoRus, 2014).

Ukolov, Roman, 'Stanet li drevneishaia professiia legal'noi', *Nezavisimaia gazeta*, 28 August 2002.

Vasil'eva, Vasilina, 'Schet seks-rabyn' iz stran SNG idet na milliony: rost torgovli zhivym tovarom stimuliruetsia otsutstviem dolzhnykh zakonov', *Nezavisimaia gazeta*, 18 February 2002.

Viola, Lynne, Macdonald, Tracey, Zhuralev, Sergei V. and Mel'nik, Andrei, *Riazanskaia Derevnia v 1929–1930: Dokumenty i Materialy* (Moscow and Toronto: Rosspen, 1998).

Vlasova, Nataliia, 'Razgovor na ravnykh: mestnaia vlast' sposobna regulirovat' otnosheniia mezhdu korennymi zhiteliami i priezzhimi', *Migratsiia XXI Vek*, No. 6–7 (26–27), November–December 2014, pp. 66–72.

'Skal'pel' ili topor?', *Migratsiia XXI Vek*, No. 4 (31), July–August 2015, pp. 24–28.

Vorob''eva, Ol'ga D., *Rynok Truda i Migratsiia* (Moscow: MAKS Press, 2011).

'Tol'ko za vziatku', *Migratsiia XXIVek*, No. 3 (30), May–June 2015, pp. 23–24.

Vorob''eva, Ol'ga and Topilin, Anatolii, 'Stoit li? Patenty dlia inostrannykh rabotnikov u iuridicheskikh lits', *Migratsiia XXI Vek*, No. 6–7 (26–27), November–December 2014, pp. 3–7.

Vyrkovskii, Andrei, 'Migranty i mestnye: svoi sredi svoikh, chuzhoi sredi chuzhikh', *Moskovskie novosti*, 18 April 2013.

Zaionchkovskaia, Zhanna, Tiuriukanova, Elena and Florinskaia, Iuliia, *Trudovaia Migratsiia v Rossiiu: Kak Dvigat'sia Dal'she* (Moscow: MAKS Press, 2012).

Zimin, Aleksandr A., *Kholopy na Rusi: S Drevneishikh Vremen do Kontsa XVv* (Moscow: Nauka, 1973).

Books and Articles (Non-Russian)

Appiah, Kwame Anthony, *Cosmopolitanism: Ethics in a World of Strangers* (Penguin: London, 2006).

Bales, Kevin, *Disposable People: New Slavery in a Global Age* (Berkeley: University of California Press, 2004).

Understanding Global Slavery: A Reader (Berkeley: University of California Press, 2005).

Banyard, Kat, *Pimp State: Sex, Money and the Future of Equality* (London: Faber, 2016).

Barnes, Steven A., *Death and Redemption: The Gulag and the Shaping of Soviet Society* (Princeton, NJ: Princeton University Press, 2011).

Blum, Jerome, *Lord and Peasant in Russia from the Ninth to the Nineteenth Century* (Princeton, NJ: Princeton University Press, 1961).

Buchanan, Jane, 'Undefended – Russia's migrant workers', *Open Democracy*, 18 March 2009, www.opendemocracy.net/article/email/russia-s-undefended-migrant-workers.

Buckley, Mary, *Redefining Russian Society and Polity* (Boulder, CO: Westview Press, 1993).

ed., *Post-Soviet Women: From the Baltic to Central Asia* (Cambridge: Cambridge University Press, 1997).

'Menschenhandel als Politikum: Gesetzgebung und Problembewusstsein in Russland', *Osteuropa*, Vol. 56, No. 6, 2006, pp. 195–212.

'Press images of human trafficking from Russia: myths and interpretations', in Rebecca Kay, ed., *Gender, Equality and Difference During and After State Socialism* (London: Macmillan, 2007), pp. 211–229.

'Human trafficking in the twenty-first century: implications for Russia, Europe and the world', in Linda Racioppi and Katherine O'Sullivan See, eds., *Gender Politics in Post-Communist Eurasia* (East Lansing: Michigan State University Press, 2009, pp. 119–145.

'Public opinion in Russia on the politics of human trafficking', *Europe-Asia Studies*, Vol. 61, No. 2, March 2009, pp. 213–248.

'Recent Russian press coverage of unfree labour', in Melanie Ilic, ed., *The Palgrave Handbook on Women and Gender in Twentieth-Century Russia and the Soviet Union* (London: Palgrave, 2018).

Chernyshevsky, Nikolai, *What Is to Be Done?*, trans. Michael R. Katz (Ithaca, NY: Cornell University Press, 1989).

Dolgov, Anna and Armstrong, Daniel, 'Child murder sparks calls for stricter Russian immigration rules', *Moscow Times*, 3 March 2016.

Dower, Nigel and Williams, John, eds., *Global Citizenship: A Critical Reader* (Edinburgh: Edinburgh University Press, 2002).

Fayzullaeva, Eleonora, 'Labor migration in Central Asia: gender challenges', in Linda Racioppi and Katherine O'Sullivan See, eds., *Gender Politics in Post-Communist Eurasia* (East Lansing: Michigan State University Press, 2009), pp. 237–265.

Fitzpatrick, Sheila, *Stalin's Peasants: Resistance and Survival in the Russian Village After Collectivization* (Oxford: Oxford University Press, 1994).

Frankopan, Peter, *The Silk Roads: A New History of the World* (London: Bloomsbury, 2015).

Geertz, Clifford, *The Interpretation of Cultures: Selected Essays* (New York: Basic Books, 1973).

Gentes, Andrew A., *Exile to Siberia, 1590–1822* (London: Palgrave Macmillan, 2008).

Hellie, Richard, *Enserfment and Military Change in Muscovy* (Chicago: University of Chicago Press, 1971).

Slavery in Russia 1450–1725 (Chicago: University of Chicago Press, 1982).

Hughes, Donna M., 'The "Natasha" trade – the transnational shadow market of trafficking in women', *Journal of International Affairs*, Vol. 53, No. 2, Spring 2000, pp. 455–481.

Ivakhnyuk, Irina and Iontsev, Vladimir, *Human Trafficking: Russia* (CARIM East – Consortium for Applied Research on International Migration: Explanatory Note 13/55), May 2013.

Johnson, Janet Elise, *Gender Violence in Russia* (Bloomington: Indiana University Press, 2009).

Kolchin, Peter, *Unfree Labor: American Slavery and Russian Serfdom* (Cambridge, MA: Belknap Press of Harvard University Press, 1987).

Lee, Maggy, ed., *Human Trafficking* (Cullompton, UK: Willan Publishing, 2007).

McCarthy, Lauren A., 'Beyond corruption: an assessment of Russian law enforcement's fight against human trafficking', *Demokratizatsiia*, Vol. 18, No. 1, Winter 2010, pp. 1–17.

Trafficking Justice: How Russian Police Enforce New Laws, from Crime to Courtroom (Ithaca, NY: Cornell University Press, 2015).

Malakhov, Vladimir S., 'Russia as a new immigration country: policy response and public debate', *Europe-Asia Studies*, Vol. 66, No. 7, September 2014, pp. 1062–1079.

Monahan, Erika, *The Merchants of Siberia: Trade in Early Modern Eurasia* (Ithaca, NY: Cornell University Press, 2016).

Narizhnaya, Khristina, 'Slave labor on the rise in Russia', 27 May 2012, www .pri.org/stories/2012-05-27/slave-labor-rise-russia.

Pilkington, Hilary, *Migration, Displacement and Identity in Post-Soviet Russia* (London: Routledge, 1998).

Radishchev, Aleksandr N., *A Journey from St Petersburg to Moscow*, trans. Leo Wiener (Cambridge, MA: Harvard University Press, 1958).

Rancour-Laferriere, Daniel, *The Slave Soul of Russia: Moral Masochism and the Cult of Suffering* (New York: New York University Press, 1995).

Reeves, Madeleine, 'Clean fake: authenticating documents and persons in migrant Moscow', *American Ethnologist*, Vol. 40, No. 3, 2013, pp. 508–524.

Schenk, Caress, 'Controlling immigration manually: lessons from Moscow', *Europe-Asia Studies*, Vol. 65, No. 7, 2013, pp. 1444–1465.

Shelley, Louise I., 'The rise of human trafficking and the role of organized crime', *Demokratizatsiia*, Vol. 8, No. 1, Winter 2000, pp. 129–144.

'The changing position of women: trafficking, crime and corruption', in David Lane, ed., *The Legacy of State Socialism and the Future of Transformation* (Lanham, MD: Rowman & Littlefield, 2002), pp. 207–222.

Shelley, Louise I. and Orttung, Robert W., 'Russia's efforts to combat human trafficking: efficient crime groups versus irresolute societies and uncoordinated states', in William Alex Pridemore, ed., *Ruling Russia: Law, Crime and Justice in a Changing Society* (Lanham, MD: Rowman & Littlefield, 2005), pp. 167–182.

Siegelbaum, Lewis H. and Moch, Leslie Page, *Broad Is My Native Land: Repertoires and Regimes of Migration in Russia's Twentieth Century* (Ithaca, NY: Cornell University Press, 2014).

Singer, Peter, *Famine, Affluence and Morality* (Oxford: Oxford University Press, 2016).

Stoecker, Sally and Shelley, Louise I., eds., *Human Traffic and Transnational Crime: Eurasian and American Perspectives* (Lanham, MD: Rowman & Littlefield, 2005).

Szamuely, Tibor, *The Russian Tradition* (London: Fontana, 1988).

United States State Department, Trafficking in Persons (TIP) Reports, 2001–2016, www.state.gov/j/tip/rls/tiprpt.

Walk Free Foundation, Global Slavery Index, www.globalslaveryindex.org/findings.

Williams, Phil, 'Trafficking in women: the role of transnational organised crime', in Sally Cameron and Edward Newman, eds., *Trafficking in Humans: Social, Cultural and Political Dimensions* (New York: United Nations University Press, 2008), pp. 126–157.

Wood, Alan, ed., *The History of Siberia: From Russian Conquest to Revolution* (London: Routledge, 1991).

Websites for Key Newspapers and Journals

Argumenty i fakty	www.aif.ru
Izvestiia	www.izvestia.ru
Kavkazskii uzel	www.kavkaz-uzel.eu
Kommersant	www.kommersant.ru
Komsomol'skaia pravda	www.kp.ru
Migratsiia XXI Vek	mirpal.org/migrjounal.html
Moscow Times	themoscowtimes.com
Moskovskie novosti	www.mn.ru
Moskovskii komsomolets	www.mk.ru
Nezavisimaia gazeta	www.ng.ru
Pravda	www.pravda.ru
Rossiiskaia gazeta	rg.ru
St Petersburg Times	www.sptimes.ru
Trud	www.trud.ru

Websites for Relevant Organisations

Development Solutions	www.devsolutions.ru
Global Alliance Against Traffic in Women	www.gaatw.org
Grazhdanskoe Sodeistvie (Civic Assistance)	www.refugee.ru
International Alliance 'Labour Migration'	www.ialm.ru
International Labor Organization (ILO)	www.ilo.org
International Organisation for Migration	www.iom.int
International Organisation for Migration, Moscow	http://moscow.iom.int
Kremlin	www.kremlin.ru
Levada Analytic Center	www.levada.ru
Migration 21st Century	www.mirpal.org
Migration Research Centre	http://migrocenter.ru
Organization for Security and Co-operation in Europe (OSCE)	www.osce.org
Russian Ministry of Foreign Affairs	www.mid.ru
Russian Ministry of Internal Affairs	www.mvd.ru
SOVA Centre for Information and Analysis	www.sova-center.ru

Index